An Epicure in the Terrible

THE HIPPOCAMPUS PRESS LIBRARY OF H. P. LOVECRAFT:

COLLECTED ESSAYS

Volume 1: Amateur Journalism (2004)
Volume 2: Literary Criticism (2004)
Volume 3: Science (2005)
Volume 4: Travel (2005)
Volume 5: Philosophy; Autobiography and Miscellany (2006)

LETTERS

Letters to Alfred Galpin
Letters to Rheinhart Kleiner
Essential Solitude: The Letters of H. P. Lovecraft and August Derleth
A Means to Freedom: The Letters of H. P. Lovecraft and Robert E. Howard

CRITICISM

Primal Sources: Essays on H. P. Lovecraft, S. T. Joshi
An H. P. Lovecraft Encyclopedia, S. T. Joshi and David E. Schultz
The Monster in the Mirror: Looking for H. P. Lovecraft, Robert H. Waugh
The Unknown Lovecraft, Kenneth W. Faig, Jr.

AN EPICURE IN THE TERRIBLE

A Centennial Anthology of Essays in Honor of H. P. Lovecraft

edited by

David E. Schultz and S. T. Joshi

Hippocampus Press

New York

Published by Hippocampus Press
P.O. Box 641, New York, NY 10156.
http://www.hippocampuspress.com

Originally published by Associated University Presses, Inc.
Revised and expanded version copyright © 2011 by
David E. Schultz and S. T. Joshi.

Cover art by Virgil Finlay, used xby permission of Lail Finlay.
Cover design by Barbara Briggs Silbert. Hippocampus Press logo
designed by Anastasia Damianakos.

1 3 5 7 9 8 6 4 2

ISBN 978-0-9846386-1-1

It is with great admiration and respect
that this collection of essays
is dedicated to
Fritz Leiber,
who blazed the trail.

Contents

Abbreviations

Abbreviations for Lovecraft's works and the editions employed (those currently most reliable) are as follows:

AT   *The Ancient Track: Complete Poetical Works* (Night Shade Books, 2001)

CE   *Collected Essays,* Vols. 1–5 (Hippocampus Press, 2004–06)

D   *Dagon and Other Macabre Tales* (Arkham House, 1986)

DH   *The Dunwich Horror and Others* (Arkham House, 1984)

HM   *The Horror in the Museum* (Arkham House, 1989)

LR   *Lovecraft Remembered,* ed. Peter Cannon (Arkham House, 1998)

MM   *At the Mountains of Madness and Other Novels* (Arkham House, 1985)

MW   *Miscellaneous Writings* (Arkham House, 1995)

SL   *Selected Letters: 1911–1937,* Vols. 1–5 (Arkham House, 1965–76)

Other frequently used abbreviations are:

CoC   *Crypt of Cthulhu* (whole numbers cited)

FDOC   S. T. Joshi, ed. *H. P. Lovecraft: Four Decades of Criticism* (1980)

HPL   H. P. Lovecraft

JHL   Lovecraft Collection, John Hay Library, Brown University, Providence, Rhode Island

LS   *Lovecraft Studies* (whole numbers cited)

SHSW   August Derleth Collection, State Historical Society of Wisconsin, Madison

Full bibliographic citations are provided in the Bibliography.

Preface

In 1945, W. Paul Cook lamented the series of events that had occurred in the years following the death of his friend H. P. Lovecraft eight years before. He complained to a correspondent, in that time of the first Lovecraft boom, that the portrait of Lovecraft he saw emerging was "a fake," and in his subsequent editorial in his magazine *The Ghost* he wrote: "Irreparable harm is being done to Lovecraft by indiscriminate and even unintelligent praise, by lack of unbiased and intelligent criticism, and by a warped sense of what is due him in the way of publication of his works." Yet Cook's "Plea for Lovecraft," published in an amateur publication whose circulation was far removed from the growing circle of rabid Lovecraft fans, went unheeded.

Cook died in 1948, and so was spared the indiscriminate, if well-intentioned, abuses that occurred in Lovecraft's name. Eventually clearer heads prevailed, but only beginning in the mid-1970s with the advent of new research done by a new generation of Lovecraft scholars. Lovecraft criticism became less biased and more intelligent, and the caricature of Lovecraft that Cook so despised is in the process of being expunged as a new portrait is being painted. Although Lovecraft has now been dead for more than fifty years, readers in the 1990s will perhaps be privileged to see a truer representation of the man and his work than has been seen in the past half-century.

This collection of essays in honor of H. P. Lovecraft is an outgrowth of the early work of such pioneering Lovecraft scholars as Fritz Leiber, Dirk W. Mosig, Matthew H. Onderdonk, and George T. Wetzel. Many of the contributors to this volume have been at the forefront of Lovecraft research in the last decade. Their labors, both here and elsewhere, have brought us close to discovering the man whom W. Paul Cook was afraid would be lost to future generations. Quite likely, as they were writing their essays, none of the critics represented in this book had any intention of satisfying Cook's unspoken desire to see the "fake" portrait of Lovecraft destroyed and replaced; and yet each of them has succeeded in contributing to that end.

The essays in this centennial anthology cover a number of critical disciplines: biography, thematic studies, and comparative or genre studies. The authors completed their tasks not knowing what themes their colleagues were pursuing. Yet even though each contributor worked essentially in a vacuum, their individual pieces complement each other to a degree that was unexpected and highly gratifying. Much new ground has been broken, and it is fitting that, on the one hundredth anniversary of Lovecraft's birth, a new era of research is opening.

Note: Ellipses that originally occurred in quoted material are indicated without spaces. Ellipses introduced by the authors are indicated in the conventional manner. Other errors in quoted texts have been silently corrected.

DAVID E. SCHULTZ

POSTSCRIPT (2011)

In this new edition, citations to Lovecraft's work have been updated to reflect newer and more accurate editions that have appeared since 1991, and some of the essays have been slightly revised in other particulars.

—D. E. S./S. T. J.

Introduction

S. T. Joshi

Why study H. P. Lovecraft? In the minds of some critics and scholars this question still evidently requires an answer, and will perhaps always require an answer so long as standard criticism maintains its inexplicable prejudice against the tale of horror, fantasy, and the supernatural. In the space I have, I cannot hope to present a general defense of the weird tale; but I can at least suggest that Edmund Wilson's condemnation of Lovecraft's work as "bad taste and bad art" (*FDOC,* 47) may, at the very least, have been a little myopic. Wilson wrote his offhand review in 1945, and the vicissitudes of Lovecraft's recognition—his adulation in the science fiction and fantasy fan magazines of the forties; the stony silence of the fifties; Colin Wilson's vicious attack on Lovecraft as a neurotic in the sixties; and the systematic clearing away of misconceptions about the man and his work by his many supporters in the seventies and eighties—would make an interesting study in itself.

The ancillary question "Why read H. P. Lovecraft?" seems to have been definitively answered, if the millions of hardcover and paperback copies of his work in this country and the translations of his stories into twenty-five or more languages around the world are any testimony. Lovecraft has always had a divided readership—on the one hand youthful enthusiasts of fantasy, on the other hand a small band of writers and critics (from T. O. Mabbott to Jorge Luis Borges) who can see beyond the tentacled monsters that adorn the covers of his books to the philosophical and literary substance of the work itself. It is perhaps this first group of readers that makes the critical establishment so dubious: how can a writer so popular be of literary worth? This is a very real inquiry, not an attenuated relic of literary elitism: although we are flooded today with volumes of supposed scholarship on Stephen King, there is still little reason to believe that his work merits much attention.

What we must do, then, is to see what there is about Lovecraft that is worth studying, and why, one hundred years after his birth, he commands so large a popular and a scholarly following. Here are some hints: (1) Lovecraft's life, although outwardly uneventful, is of consuming interest—thanks to the existence of tens of thousands of his letters, he is one of the most self-documented individuals in human history; (2) his life, work, and thought form a philosophical and aesthetic unity found in few other writers; and (3) the whole of his work—fiction, essays, poetry, letters—is worth study. The essays in this volume will treat a number of these points far more detailedly than I can do here; but I will offer some suggestions.

I

Howard Phillips Lovecraft was born on 20 August 1890 in his native home at 454 (then 194) Angell Street in Providence, Rhode Island. He came from distinguished ancestry: his maternal line, the Phillipses, could trace its lineage almost to the *Mayflower*, and when Lovecraft later visited some erstwhile ancestral estates in western Rhode Island the name of Phillips was remembered with fondness and respect (see *SL* 2.81f.); his paternal line was of English origin, and he felt he could trace the Lovecraft or Lovecroft name well into the fifteenth century, although many of his assumptions regarding this line are now in question. At the time of his birth Lovecraft's family was quite well-to-do, most of the wealth derived from the extensive business interests of Lovecraft's maternal grandfather, Whipple Van Buren Phillips. That prosperity, however, was not to last. The death of Whipple Phillips in 1904 had two calamitous effects: it robbed Lovecraft of one of his major early influences (for with the death of Lovecraft's father in 1898 of paresis, the raising of the lad had been entrusted to his mother, his two aunts, and especially his grandfather); moreover, because of the mismanagement of affairs by Phillips's business associates, Phillips's fortune was squandered and the Lovecrafts were forced to move out of their palatial mansion. Lovecraft never recovered from the loss of his birthplace: in the short run it drove him almost to suicide, as he took long bicycle rides and gazed wistfully at the watery depths of the Barrington River; in the long run it led to a sense of loss and displacement that his early readings only augmented.

Those readings—done at random in the capacious family library—can be classified into three broad areas: antiquarianism; fantasy and horror; and science. The first may at this point have been most important. Lovecraft gravitated to the eighteenth century, developing a curious affinity for books with the "long s." He read all the standard poets and prose writers (especially the essayists; he was less keen on the early novelists), and through the great translations of the Greek and Latin classics of that age (Garth's Ovid, Pope's *Iliad* and *Odyssey*) he arrived at the ancients themselves. He learned Latin well enough to translate the first eighty-eight lines of Ovid's *Metamorphoses* into heroic couplets at about the age of ten; by the age of twelve he was writing poems heavily saturated in the classicism of Virgil, Horace, Ovid, and Juvenal. In the fantasy line Lovecraft early imbibed both Grimm's *Fairy Tales* and the *Arabian Nights* (the latter impelled him to adopt a playful Mohammedanism until it gave way to the groves of Hellas); at age eight he discovered Poe, and this gave his writing the greatest impetus it ever received. But about that time Lovecraft also discovered the world of science—first chemistry, then astronomy. Lovecraft later believed that Hellenism and astronomy were the two central influences of his early years, the latter especially because it led directly to his "cosmic" philosophy wherein mankind and the world are but a flyspeck amidst the vortices of infinite space. Lovecraft long maintained this duality of science and pure literature in his own writing: on the one hand we have his many juvenile treatises on chemistry and astronomy, as well as his amateur periodicals, the *Scientific Gazette* (1899–1909) and the *Rhode Island Journal of Astronomy* (1903–09); on the other hand his youthful stories, poems, and translations. He would harmonize the diverse strains only in his later "scientific" fiction, especially *At the Mountains of Madness* and "The Shadow out of Time."

The prodigious fecundity of Lovecraft's early writing indicates not only precocity but considerable leisure; indeed, Lovecraft's formal schooling—first at Slater Avenue School, then at Hope Street High School—was always sporadic, and did not in the end lead to a diploma. Poor health was purportedly the cause of his frequent absences, but the nature of his malady is not now easy to discern. Lovecraft claimed to have suffered frequent nervous breakdowns in youth, including a serious one in 1908 that led to his withdrawal not only from high school but also from the world at large. He destroyed much of his early writing, and for the next five years retreated into a hermitry from which little could stir him: we know that on his twenty-first birthday in 1911 he rode the trolleys all day,[1] but aside from this the period is largely blank.

Lovecraft was freed from this sequestration in a curious way. Having fallen into the habit of reading the popular magazines of the day, especially some of the early Munsey pulps (the *Argosy*, the *All-Story*, etc.), Lovecraft became so irked at the contributions of a romance writer, Fred Jackson, that he wrote a letter to the editor in protest; shortly thereafter, following the lead of another writer who had written a brief poem rebutting Lovecraft, the latter responded with a lengthy verse epistle of his own, resurrecting the eighteenth-century mode of verse satire that in many ways remained his natural form of poetic expression. There followed a series of attacks back and forth between Lovecraft and those who defended Jackson, and this battle was observed by Edward F.

Daas of the United Amateur Press Association (UAPA); he urged the leading participants of the fray to join the order, and Lovecraft promptly did so.

The UAPA (and its rival, the National Amateur Press Association, which Lovecraft later joined) was a group of amateur writers who wrote and published their own journals—some of them very crude, others quite distinguished. Lovecraft joined the organization in early 1914, and for the next decade produced an astonishing amount of amateur writing: he edited thirteen issues of his own paper, the *Conservative*; he contributed essays, poems, and editorials to scores of other journals; he edited the official organ of the UAPA, the *United Amateur*, and served as President and as Chairman of the Department of Public Criticism. It was as if a lifeline had been extended to a drowning man: Lovecraft, of frail health, ashamed of his inability to attend Brown University and gain a college degree, buried in a world of his own making that was increasingly remote from reality, was finally rescued by a band of amateur writers with aspirations like his own—so he fancied—but with viewpoints often differing significantly from his. Lovecraft's formidable intellect and literary skill raised him quickly to prominence in the field (a prominence he still holds as one of the pillars of the amateur movement), but Lovecraft knew that he had received as much from amateurdom as he gave it:

> In 1914, when the kindly hand of amateurdom was first extended to me, I was as close to the state of vegetation as any animal well can be. . . . With the advent of the United I obtained a renewed will to live; a renewed sense of existence as other than a superfluous weight; and found a sphere in which I could feel that my efforts were not wholly futile. For the first time I could imagine that my clumsy gropings at art were a little more than faint cries lost in the unlistening void.[2]

It is in the amateur world that Lovecraft recommenced the writing of fiction. His associates—notably W. Paul Cook—praised the juvenile tales that he allowed to be printed—"The Beast in the Cave" (1905), "The Alchemist" (1908)—and urged him to write more. Lovecraft did so, producing "The Tomb" and "Dagon" in quick succession in the summer of 1917; from then on he maintained a steady if sparse flow of fiction until his death. But until at least 1922 Lovecraft regarded himself more as a poet and essayist than as a fiction writer; in sheer volume his collected verse and nonfiction dwarf his fiction threefold.

Even the professional sale of his work was generated through the amateur world. First, some of his poems were reprinted from amateur journals by the professional *National Magazine* of Boston; then, in 1921, Lovecraft received an offer to write a series of six "Grewsome Tales" for a professional magazine, *Home Brew,* launched by an amateur colleague, George Julian Houtain. Lovecraft was paid $5 for each segment of the serial, which we know as "Herbert West—Reanimator," generally conceded to be among his poorer efforts, although it succeeds after a fashion as a self-parody. The next year he wrote another serial for *Home Brew* (which was, in fact, largely a humor magazine, and which Lovecraft aptly termed a "vile rag" [*SL* 4.170]), the much better tale "The Lurking Fear." In 1923 the founding of *Weird Tales* seemed to promise a ready market for his work, but Lovecraft was initially reluctant to submit his stories there; when he did so (remarking in his cover letter that some of the tales had been rejected by *Black Mask*) and when the tales were accepted, he felt it too bothersome to retype the stories in double-spacing. But he finally made the effort, and from then on his work began to appear there regularly. Lovecraft never wrote (or, rather, sold) enough fiction to be a professional writer; instead, his income was provided by an ever-dwindling family inheritance and by the dreary task of literary revision and ghost-writing. This work ran the gamut from textbooks to poetry to novels to articles; but on occasion Lovecraft attracted revision clients who wished to write horror tales, and his "revisions" of the works of such tyros as Hazel Heald, Zealia Bishop, Adolphe de Castro, and others are often tantamount to original composition.

In 1921, however, Lovecraft's domestic life was powerfully affected by the death of his mother after a long illness. Mrs. Lovecraft, her frail constitution destroyed by the death of her husband under peculiar circumstances (it is likely that he, a traveling salesman, died from some form of syphilis, although the evidence now seems conclusive that Lovecraft himself was not congenitally syphilitic) and pathologically overprotective of her only child, died in a sanitarium; the immediate cause of death, however, was a gall bladder operation from which she was unable to recover. Lovecraft, stunned by the blow, felt himself again on the brink of suicide, but the sentiment did not last long: a month after his mother's death he attended an amateur journalism convention in Boston, where he met the woman who was to become his wife. Sonia Haft Greene was a Russian Jew seven years older than Lovecraft, but he was captivated by her devotion to amateur letters and what on the surface appeared to be a similar view of the world. Their courtship cut short a budding romance (of which we know very little) between Lovecraft and the amateur poet Winifred Virginia Jackson, but it took three years for Lovecraft and Sonia to decide on marriage. When they did so Lovecraft told his aunts by letter after the ceremony had taken place at St. Paul's Cathedral in New York; perhaps he feared that Sonia's racial heritage, and the fact that she was a successful executive at a Fifth Avenue department store, would not have met with the approval of two elderly ladies of old New England stock.

Was Lovecraft's marriage doomed to failure? It is easy to say such a thing after the fact, but there is no reason to believe it. Who knows what might have happened had a series of disasters not hit the couple almost immediately upon their marriage?—Sonia's resignation (or firing) from the department store and the subsequent collapse of an independent hat shop she had attempted to establish; the inability of Lovecraft to find a job in New York; Sonia's ill health, which forced her to leave the household and seek recuperation in various rest homes; and, perhaps most important, Lovecraft's growing horror of New York—its oppressive size, the hordes of "aliens" at every corner, its emphasis on speed, money, and commercialism. The many friends Lovecraft had in the city—Samuel Loveman, Rheinhart Kleiner, Arthur Leeds, and especially the young poet and fantaisiste Frank Belknap Long, Jr.—were not enough to ward off depression and neurosis. On 1 January 1925, after only ten months of cohabitation with Sonia, Lovecraft moved into a single room in a squalid area of Brooklyn, as his wife left to seek employment in the Midwest; she thereafter returned only intermittently to New York.

Lovecraft's fiction turned from the nostalgic—"The Shunned House" (1924), set in Providence—to the bitter: "He" and "The Horror at Red Hook" (1925) laid bare his feelings about New York, and the ending of the former tale encapsulates his yearning to return to the tranquil and familiar world of New England. But that return only took place in April 1926, after a complicated series of arrangements worked out by Lovecraft, his wife, Frank Long, and his aunts: Lovecraft returned ecstatically to Providence, settling at 10 Barnes Street north of Brown University. Where did Sonia fit into these plans? No one seemed to know, least of all Lovecraft: he continued to profess his love for her, but refused to return to New York; and when she proposed to set up shop in Providence, there was equal resistance, this time from Lovecraft's aunts. Sonia tells it laconically: "At the time the aunts gently but firmly informed me that neither they nor Howard could afford to have Howard's wife work for a living in Providence. That was that. I now knew where we all stood. Pride preferred to suffer in silence; both theirs and mine."[3] The family's social standing (in spite of their poverty) was too precious to be tainted by a tradeswoman wife; the marriage was essentially over, and a divorce in 1929 was inevitable.

Lovecraft settled down to the reposeful existence he had known before

Sonia and New York; but it was not the same Lovecraft who saw only the eighteenth century or classical antiquity and ignored the modern world; nor was it a Lovecraft who buried himself away as in the 1908–13 period. Instead, after a flurry of literary activity such as he never experienced before or after— in six months he wrote "The Call of Cthulhu," "The Silver Key," *The Dream-Quest of Unknown Kadath, The Case of Charles Dexter Ward,* "The Colour out of Space," and several other works, as well as completing the treatise "Supernatural Horror in Literature" begun in late 1925 in New York—he became, in the last ten years of his life, the man who most comes to mind when we hear the name Lovecraft: the author of tales of cosmic horror; the center of a vast and ever-increasing web of epistolary ties with literary figures in the field (August Derleth, Donald Wandrei, Vincent Starrett, Clark Ashton Smith, Robert E. Howard, E. Hoffmann Price, Henry S. Whitehead, and others); the seeker of antiquarian sites all along the eastern part of the continent—Quebec, New England, Philadelphia, Washington, D.C., Richmond, Charleston, St. Augustine, New Orleans, Key West; the elder statesman of fantasy who, in the thirties, served as the fountainhead and mentor for many young fans and writers (Robert Bloch, J. Vernon Shea, R. H. Barlow, Charles D. Hornig, Julius Schwartz, Donald A. Wollheim, Duane W. Rimel, C. L. Moore, Fritz Leiber, Henry Kuttner, James Blish, and many others).

By 1930 Lovecraft had published many tales in *Weird Tales* and "The Colour out of Space" in Hugo Gernsback's *Amazing Stories*; but when would a book bearing his name appear? There had been a half-dozen pamphlets issued by amateur publishers, and W. Paul Cook's stillborn edition of *The Shunned House* (sheets printed in 1928) held Lovecraft in anticipation to his death. In the late 1920s Farnsworth Wright of *Weird Tales* had toyed with the idea of a collection of Lovecraft's tales (to be called—prophetically enough—*The Outsider and Other Stories*), but the plan had come to nothing. Then, in 1931, G. P. Putnam's Sons asked to look at some of Lovecraft's stories; their eventual rejection, coinciding with the rejection by Wright of *At the Mountains of Madness* (regarded by its author as his most ambitious work), gave Lovecraft a severe setback. Always sensitive to criticism, he later admitted that this double rejection "did more than anything else to end my effective fictional career" (*SL* 5.224). Later inquiries by Vanguard, Knopf, Loring & Mussey, and William Morrow to issue a collection of tales or a novel also came to nothing, and Lovecraft's later work is increasingly tinged with self-doubt: "The Shadow over Innsmouth" (1931) went through two, perhaps three drafts; "The Dreams in the Witch House" (1932), one of his poorest later efforts, was written frenetically in pencil, as was "The

Thing on the Doorstep" (1933); "The Shadow out of Time" (1934–35) went through at least two drafts. In 1936 Lovecraft made what to us seems the astonishing assertion that "I'm farther from doing what I want to do than I was 20 years ago" (*SL* 5.224). He may have gained some pleasure at finally moving into a historic house at 66 College Street in 1933 (the house dates to c. 1825) and at his increasing glorification by the early fantasy fandom movement; but one wonders whether the sense of frustration pervading his later work had anything to do with his failure to seek medical help for the cancer of the intestine that ultimately killed him, and whose symptoms had begun to be evident at least two years before his death. Or did he fear a repetition of the operation that had robbed him of his mother? In any case, when Lovecraft entered Jane Brown Memorial Hospital on 10 March 1937, all that could be done was to give him morphine to ease the pain. He died five days later and was buried in the Phillips family plot in Swan Point Cemetery. A separate marker has now been erected on his grave, the funds contributed by many of his posthumous admirers; the stone reads: "I am Providence."

II

What did Lovecraft mean when he wrote:

> I should describe mine own nature as tripartite, my interests consisting of three parallel and dissociated groups—(a) Love of the strange and the fantastic. (b) Love of the abstract truth and of scientific logick. (c) Love of the ancient and the permanent. Sundry combinations of these strains will probably account for all my odd tastes and eccentricities. (*SL* 1.110)

Whether these are really to be "dissociated," and whether they make up the totality of Lovecraft's thought and personality (he wrote this in 1920), is to be wondered. Later he confessed, acutely, that his very love of the past fostered the principal strain in his aesthetic of the weird—the defeat or confounding of *time*. In any case, the traditional image of Lovecraft—the one we think of when we see Virgil Finlay's exquisite portrait of him as a periwigged gentleman—as the eighteenth-century fossil completely ignorant of and hostile to the twentieth century has, since the publication of his letters, been shown conclusively to be false. Anyone who reads of Lovecraft's careful dissection of the political scene prior to the 1936 election—he was a pronounced New Dealer—will know that he was no "stranger in this century," as the "Outsider" says of himself. Even his fiction, if read carefully, can be seen to be more than the escapist dreams of a doting antiquarian: superficially we have things like the discovery of Pluto cited in "The Whisperer in Darkness" (1930) or the then still controversial continental drift theory in *At the Mountains of Madness* (1931); more profoundly we have Einstein, Planck, and Heisenberg recurring in significant fashion in the later fiction, or the transparent metaphors for humanity's future aesthetic, political, and economic development in the alien civilizations in "The Mound" (1929–30), *At the Mountains of Madness,* and "The Shadow out of Time."

This does not mean that Lovecraft abandoned his love of the past; it is simply that he justified it more rationally. Lovecraft's prose style, for example, always bore traces of his early absorption of the Augustans; but in later years he could defend eighteenth-century prose (quite rightly) precisely because it was more natural and direct than either the floridity of Carlyle or the "machine-gun fire" of Hemingway:

> I refuse to be taken in by the goddam bunk of this aera just as totally as I refused to fall for the pompous, polite bull of Victorianism—and one of the chief fallacies of the present is that smoothness, even when involving no sacrifice of directness, is a defect. The best prose is vigorous, direct, unadorn'd, and closely related (as is the best verse) to the language of actual discourse; but it has its natural rhythms and smoothness just as good oral speech has. There has never been any prose as good as that of the early eighteenth century, and anyone who thinks he can improve upon Swift, Steele, and Addison is a blockhead. (*SL* 4.32–33)

What we see, therefore, in the course of Lovecraft's work as well as his life and thought is a gradual coming to terms with the modern world, but at the same time a belief that that world offered fewer aesthetic riches than certain prior ages of Western civilization. From a naive antiquarian Lovecraft evolved into an informed antiquarian.

His "love of the abstract truth and of scientific logick" compelled him to pursue a wide range of academic interests—literature, philosophy, chemistry, astronomy, astrophysics, anthropology, psychology, art and architecture—and, more important, to fashion a coherent philosophy that served as the fountainhead for his entire literary work. This is hardly the place for a full exposition of that philosophy; but some aspects of its relation to his literary work can be sketched here.

Lovecraft's early studies in the natural sciences, as well as his absorption of the atomism of Democritus, Epicurus, and Lucretius, led to his espousal of mechanistic materialism. The trump card that ensured the truth of this stance, Lovecraft felt, was the landmark work of nineteenth-century science: the nebular hypothesis of Laplace sufficiently explained the evolution of the universe; the Darwin theory abolished the myth of the "soul" and the argument from design; and—perhaps most important for the atheist Lovecraft—the work of anthropologists like E. B. Tylor and J. G. Frazer accounted with overwhelming completeness for the natural origin of mankind's belief in the supernatural. For the rest of his life Lovecraft worked tirelessly to accommodate the potentially disturbing findings of twentieth-century science with nineteenth-century positivism. Einstein showed the fundamental equivalence of matter and energy: well, one could still be more or less of a materialist (as, indeed, Lovecraft's most revered modern thinkers, Bertrand Russell and George Santayana, were), even though the *word* "materialist" would now be used only in a historical sense:

> The truth is, that the discovery of matter's identity with energy—and of its consequent lack of vital intrinsic difference from empty space—is *an absolute coup de grace to the primitive and irresponsible myth of "spirit". For matter, it appears, really is exactly what "spirit" was always supposed to be.* Thus it is proved *that wandering energy always has a detectable form*—that if it doesn't take the form of waves or electron-streams, *it becomes matter itself;* and that the absence of any other detectable energy-form indicates *not the presence of spirit, but the absence of anything whatever.* (*SL* 2.266–67)

Then Planck comes along with the quantum theory; this proves to be a little more troublesome, but ultimately Lovecraft takes it in stride:

> What most physicists take the quantum theory, at present, to mean, is *not that any cosmic uncertainty exists* as to which of several courses a given reaction will take; but that in certain instances *no conceivable channel of information can ever tell human beings which course will be taken,* or by what exact course a certain observed result came about. (*SL* 3.228)

This is in fact false, even though it was endorsed by Einstein ("God does not play dice with the cosmos") and other leading thinkers of the day. As for Heisenberg, he is actually mentioned in "The Dreams in the Witch House," but I do not know how well Lovecraft really came to terms with indeterminacy. The point is, however, that he continued to wrestle with these questions with a tenacity few non-philosophers have exhibited. More important, Lovecraft came to believe that any viable literary work—even fiction and poetry—must derive from a sound and accurate view of the universe. While being entirely opposed to literary didacticism, he sensed that his own work at least was the unconscious embodiment of his metaphysical and ethical thought.

Lovecraft's hostility to religion—for the principal reason that it made false assertions as to the nature of entity ("The Judaeo-Christian mythology is NOT TRUE" [*SL* 1.60])—seems to have increased with the years, to the point that he expressed contempt that orthodox religionists would continue to brainwash the young into religious belief in the face of such massive scientific evidence to the contrary. And yet, the findings of modern science did not lead Lovecraft to waver on the issue, as when he spoke of

> . . . the new mysticism or neo-metaphysics bred of the advertised uncertainties of recent science—Einstein, the quantum theory, and the resolution of matter into force. Although these new turns of science don't mean a thing in relation to the myth of cosmic consciousness and teleology, a new brood of despairing and horrified moderns is seizing on the doubt of all positive knowledge which they imply; and is deducing therefrom that, *since nothing is true*, therefore *anything can be true* . . . . . whence one may invent or revive any sort of mythology that fancy or nostalgia or desperation may dictate, and defy anyone to prove that it isn't *emotionally* true—whatever that means. This sickly, decadent neo-mysticism—a protest not only against machine materialism but against pure science with its destruction of the mystery and dignity of human emotion and experience—will be the dominant creed of middle twentieth century aesthetes, as the Eliot and Huxley penumbra well prognosticate. (*SL* 3.53)

Lovecraft's ultimate position (derived, as much of the above quotation was, from Joseph Wood Krutch's *The Modern Temper*) was one of resigned acceptance of the truths of science—the truth that the world and the human race occupy an infinitesimal and unimportant place in the cosmic scheme of things; the truth that one lives and dies and that's the end of it. When Lovecraft sought freedom from the constraining bonds of reality, it was not the fact-repudiating freedom of religious belief but the imaginative freedom of weird fiction. It was precisely *because* Lovecraft felt the universe to be an unswerving mechanism with rigid natural laws that he required the escape of the imagination:

> The general revolt of the sensitive mind against the tyranny of corporeal enclosure, restricted sense-equipment, & the laws of force, space, & causation, is a far keener & bitterer & better-founded one than any of the silly revolts of long-haired poseurs against isolated & specific instances of cosmic inevitability. But of course it does not take the form of personal petulance, because there is no convenient scape-goat to saddle the impersonal ill upon. Rather does it crop out as a pervasive sadness & unplaceable impatience, manifested in a love of strange dreams & an amusing eagerness to be galled by the quack cosmic pre-

tensions of the various religious circuses. Well—in our day the quack circuses are wearing pretty thin despite the premature senilities of fat Chesterbellocs & affected Waste Land Shantih-dwellers, & the nostalgic & unmotivated "over-beliefs" of elderly & childhood-crippled physicists. The time has come when the normal revolt against time, space, & matter must assume a form not overtly incompatible with what is known of reality—when it must be gratified by im-ages forming *supplements* rather than *contradictions* of the visible & mensurable universe. And what, if not a form of *non-supernatural cosmic art,* is to pacify this sense of revolt—as well as gratify the cognate sense of curiosity? (*SL* 3.295–96)

But if Lovecraft's "love of the truth" led him to embrace scientific facts (as he saw them), however unpalatable and destructive of human self-importance they were, his "love of the ancient and the permanent" allowed him to evolve an ethic that placed *tradition* at its center.

In a cosmos without absolute values we have to rely on the relative values affect-ing our daily sense of comfort, pleasure, & emotional satisfaction. What gives us relative painlessness & contentment we may arbitrarily call "good", & vice versa. This local nomenclature is necessary to give us that benign illusion of placement, direction, & stable background on which the still more important illusions of "worthwhileness", dramatic significance in events, & interest in life depend. Now what gives one person or race or age relative painlessness & contentment often disagrees sharply on the psychological side from what gives these same boons to another person or race or age. Therefore "good" is a relative & variable quality, depending on ancestry, chronology, geography, nationality, & individual tem-perament. Amidst this variability there is *only one anchor of fixity* which we can seize upon as the working pseudo-standard of "values" which we need in order to feel settled & contented—& that anchor is *tradition,* the potent emotional legacy be-queathed to us by the massed experience of our ancestors, individual or national, biological or cultural. Tradition means nothing cosmically, but it means every-thing locally & pragmatically because we have nothing else to shield us from a devastating sense of "lostness" in endless time & space. (*SL* 2.356–57)

This seems a little self-serving—there is no reason why everyone should feel the sense of tradition so strongly that its absence would breed a feeling of "lost-ness"—but it accounts both for Lovecraft's gentlemanly deportment and for many of his political views. His politics became radically altered in the course of his life—he began as a naive monarchist who lamented the American Revolu-tion and the split with England and ended as a confirmed socialist who wished FDR to proceed even more rapidly with reform—but there are points of con-tact all along the way. Lovecraft's aristocratic upbringing never left him, and his suspicion of democracy actually became more pronounced as events following the depression compelled him to adopt socialism. At the heart of Lovecraft's entire political philosophy was the notion of *culture*—the massed traditions of each race, society, and region. "All I care about is *the civilisation*—the state of development and organisation which is capable of gratifying the complex mental-emotional-aesthetic needs of highly evolved and acutely sensitive men" (*SL* 2.290)—men, one supposes, like Lovecraft. What this means is that anything that stands in the way of the flowering of a rich and harmonious culture—for Lovecraft it was principally democracy and capitalism—must go. The conjoining of these two forces in the early nineteenth century actually led to the shattering of that high level of culture maintained by the aristocracies of the past:

> Bourgeois capitalism gave artistic excellence & sincerity a death-blow by enthroning cheap *amusement-value* at the expense of that *intrinsic excellence* which only cultivated, non-acquisitive persons of assured position can enjoy. The determinant market for written, pictorial, musical, dramatic, decorative, architectural, & other heretofore aesthetic material ceased to be a small circle of truly educated persons, but became a substantially larger (even with a vast proportion of society starved & crushed into a sodden, inarticulate helplessness through commercial & commercial-satellitic greed & callousness) circle of mixed origin numerically dominated by crude, half-educated clods whose systematically perverted ideals (worship of low cunning, material acquisition, cheap comfort & smoothness, worldly success, ostentation, speed, intrinsic magnitude, surface glitter, &c.) prevented them from ever achieving the tastes and perspectives of the gentlefolk whose dress & speech & external manners they so assiduously mimicked. This herd of acquisitive boors brought up from the shop & the counting-house a complete set of artificial attitudes, oversimplifications, & mawkish sentimentalities which no sincere art or literature could gratify—& they so outnumbered the remaining educated gentlefolk that most of the purveying agencies became at once reoriented to them. Literature & art lost most of their market; & writing, painting, drama, &c. became engulfed more & more in the domain of *amusement enterprises*. (*SL* 5.397–98)

The answer was not some rearguard resurrection of the aristocratic principle—Lovecraft was realist enough to understand that this was not possible in the America of the 1930s—but socialism. Aristocracy and socialism were really mirror images of the same thing:

> . . . what I used to respect was *not really aristocracy, but a set of personal qualities which aristocracy then developed better than any other system . . . a set of qualities, however, whose*

merits lay only in a psychology of non-calculative, non-competitive disinterestedness, truthfulness, courage, & generosity fostered by good education, minimum economic stress, and assumed position, & JUST AS ACHIEVABLE THROUGH SOCIALISM AS THROUGH ARISTOCRACY. (SL 5.321)

Socialism would mean such basic economic rights as old-age pensions, unemployment insurance, and—a vital issue for many economists and lawmakers of the 1930s, but one ultimately rejected by Roosevelt and subsequent administrations—shorter working hours so that all who were able to work could have a chance to do so. Lovecraft came to this position because he felt that the dominance of the machine in his day had made it possible for all needed work to be done by a very small number of people; working hours would therefore have to be arbitrarily reduced to spread what little work there was to the populace at large. For Lovecraft this would have an added benefit: the increased leisure time accruing to all individuals could then be used for increased educational and aesthetic purposes, with a resulting rise in the tone of general culture. Lovecraft seemed genuinely convinced toward the end of his life that such a utopia was within reach, and that FDR was the man to bring it about—"The recent election gratified me extremely" (*SL* 5.390), he wrote in February 1937—but it now strikes me as somewhat naive for Lovecraft to have expected that socialism would come so readily to this country or that the average citizen, if given more leisure, would use it to uplift himself in a suitably edifying way. As it is, eight years previous he expressed a sentiment that not only was more in keeping with his distrust of the mob and his hatred of mechanization, but is a sadly accurate prediction of our present state of culture:

> Granted that the machine-victim has leisure. What is he going to do with it? What memories and experiences has he to form a background to give significance to anything he can do? What can he see or do that will mean anything to him? . . . What has heretofore made life tolerable for the majority is the fact that their *natural workaday routine and milieu* have never been *quite* devoid of the excitement, nature-contact, uncertainty, non-repetition, and free and easy irregularity which build up a background of associations calculated to foster the illusion of significance and make possible the real enjoyment of art and leisure. Without this help from their environment, the majority could never manage to keep contented. Now that it is fading, they are in a bad plight indeed; for they cannot hope to breast the tide of ennui as the stronger-minded minority can. There will be, of course, high-sounding and flabbily idealistic attempts to help the poor devils. We shall hear of all sorts of futile reforms and reformers— standardised culture-outlines, synthetic sports and spectacles, professional play-

leaders and study-guides, and kindred examples of machine-made uplift and brotherly spirit. And it will amount to just about as much as most reforms do! Meanwhile the tension of boredom and unsatisfied imagination will increase—breaking out with increasing frequency in crimes of morbid perversity and explosive violence. (*SL* 2.308–9)

Perhaps it is just as well that Lovecraft did not survive into his seventies or eighties.

The final component of Lovecraft's political philosophy is racialism. We are past the point of trying (as August Derleth did) to brush this under the rug, but we are, I trust, also moving beyond L. Sprague de Camp's schoolmasterly chiding of Lovecraft for his beliefs without an awareness of their origin and purpose. Indeed, the point at which Lovecraft should rightly be criticized has been misunderstood by many. It is not the mere fact that he expressed obnoxious opinions about blacks, Jews, and just about every other "non-Aryan" race; it is the fact that in this one area of his thought Lovecraft failed to exercise that flexibility of mind that made him come to grips with Einstein and Planck, Eliot and Joyce, FDR and Norman Thomas. In all aspects of his philosophy except this one, Lovecraft was constantly expanding, clarifying, and revising his views to suit the facts of the world; in race alone his attitude remained monolithic. Certainly, his later views are expressed somewhat more rationally (although his comments to J. Vernon Shea in 1933 about the "Jew-York papers" [*SL* 4.247] do not inspire confidence); but they remained not merely essentially unchanged but—more seriously—impervious to evidence to the contrary. The work of anthropologist Franz Boas and his students had, in the first three decades of the twentieth century, shattered the myth of the "superiority" or "inferiority" of the various human races; but Lovecraft paid no attention. To the end of his life he regarded blacks and Australian aborigines as biologically inferior to all other human races and insisted on an impassable color-line. In regard to other races Lovecraft, while attributing to them no inferiority, simply felt that their intermingling would produce a cultural heterogeneity, with deleterious effects on world culture:

No settled & homogeneous nation ought (a) to admit enough of a decidedly alien race-stock to bring about an actual alteration in the dominant ethnic composition, or (b) tolerate the dilution of the culture-stream with emotional & intellectual elements alien to the original cultural impulse. Both of these perils lead to the most undesirable results—i.e., the metamorphosis of the population away from the original institutions, & the twisting of the institutions away from the original people . . . . . all these things being aspects of one underlying & disastrous condition—the destruction of cultural stability, & the creation of a hopeless disparity between a social group & the institutions under which it lives. (*SL* 4.249)

It is as if Lovecraft wished to freeze culture at a certain stage—the stage at which he knew it and in which he felt comfortable.

All this has been gone into at such length not merely because the subject still appears to embarrass Lovecraft's apologists—who fail to realize that his attitude was not especially unusual in his time, and at least eventually came into harmony with his general philosophy—but also because it enters into his fiction in a pervasive way. There can hardly be a doubt that the monsters in "The Lurking Fear" (1922), "The Horror at Red Hook" (1925), and "The Shadow over Innsmouth" (1931) are thinly veiled projections of his racialist fears of an alien overthrow of Nordic culture through excessive immigration and miscegenation. Indeed, when the narrator of the last tale overhears some Innsmouth denizens "exchang[ing] some faint guttural words . . . in a language I could have sworn was not English" (*DH* 341), we are evidently to feel not merely a mild disturbance but a sense of cosmic alienage. Certainly Lovecraft's two years in the slums of New York did not help to reform him; nor, apparently, did his marriage to a Jew.

Lovecraft's aristocratic sentiments also led to the central tenet of his aesthetic theory—that of non-commercial self-expression. We are, of course, meant to smile when Lovecraft writes: "A gentleman shouldn't write all his images down for a plebeian rabble to stare at. If he writes at all, it shou'd be in private letters to other gentlemen of sensitiveness and discrimination" (*SL* 1.243). But the core notion was one Lovecraft acknowledged from the beginning to the end of his career. Once the act of creation—the act of capturing those moods, images, and conceptions that clamor within the artist for expression—is complete, the task of writing is done. Even publication of the work is of no importance—or, rather, it is an entirely separate process that has nothing to do with writing. We can call this "art for art's sake" if we wish; but—although Lovecraft certainly drew upon Poe, Wilde, and Pater for this attitude, as well as for his general hostility to overt didacticism—it was really more than that. "Writing after all is the essence of whatever is left in my life, & if the ability or opportunity for that goes, I have no further reason for—or mind to endure—the joke of existence."[4] To E. Hoffmann Price, the prototypical pulp hack, Lovecraft explained at length why he could not cater to the pulp magazines:

Art is not what one resolves to say, but what insists on saying itself through one. It has nothing to do with commerce, editorial demand, or popular approval. The only elements concerned are the artist and the emotions working within him. Of course, there is a business of magazine-purveying which is perfectly honest in itself, and a worthy field for those with a knack for it. I wish I had the knack. But this isn't the thing I'm interested in. If I had the knack, it would be something performed entirely apart from my serious work—just as my present revisory activities are. However, I haven't the knack, and the field is so repugnant to me that it's about the last way I'd ever choose to gain shelter and clothing and nourishment. Any other kind of a legitimate job would be preferable to my especial tastes. I dislike this trade because it bears a mocking external resemblance to the real literary composition which is the only thing (apart from ancestral traditions) I take seriously in life. (*SL* 5.19–20)

This whole attitude accounts for a number of things—Lovecraft's initial reluctance to submit to *Weird Tales*; his subsequent reluctance to diversify his markets even when *Weird Tales* rejected some of his best work; his diffidence in approaching book publishers with a novel or story collection. To us it seems like near-criminal folly for Lovecraft never to have even attempted to prepare *The Case of Charles Dexter Ward* (1927) for publication, at a time when several publishers would have been more receptive to a novel than to a collection of tales; but it was Lovecraft's prerogative to feel that that novel was not a success and should not see print. His final years were dogged by increasing poverty—in 1936 the providential sale of two stories (arranged by friends acting as agents) to *Astounding* for $630 essentially saved him from the bread line—but even at that time Lovecraft failed to buckle down to hackwork. It need hardly be said that Lovecraft has been vindicated: no one is writing a doctoral dissertation on the work of E. Hoffmann Price or Seabury Quinn.

III

In the short term, Lovecraft's reputation will certainly rest upon his sixty or so short stories, novelettes, and short novels, and it is right that the bulk of the articles in this volume focus upon them. I myself can only touch upon the broadest features of his fiction here, and then dwell briefly on other bodies of his work.

A useful starting point for the study of the philosophy of Lovecraft's fiction is his own epochal statement of 1927:

Now all my tales are based on the fundamental premise that common human laws and interests and emotions have no validity or significance in the vast cosmos-at-large. To me there is nothing but puerility in a tale in which the human form—and the local human passions and conditions and standards—are depicted as native to other worlds or other universes. To achieve the essence of real externality, whether of time or space or dimension, one must forget that such things as organic life, good and evil, love and hate, and all such local attributes of a negligible and temporary race called mankind, have any existence at all. Only the human scenes and characters must have human qualities. *These* must be handled with unsparing *realism,* (*not* catch-penny *romanticism*) but when we cross the line to the boundless and hideous unknown—the shadow-haunted *Outside*—we must remember to leave our humanity and terrestrialism at the threshold. (*SL* 2.150)

This statement—emphasizing the fundamental amorality of his fictional cosmos—was made in conjunction with the resubmittal of "The Call of Cthulhu" (1926) to *Weird Tales*; and there can hardly be a doubt that that tale marks a watershed in Lovecraft's work, although perhaps not exactly in the way many think. To be sure, it marks the debut of Lovecraft's convoluted pseudomythology, dubbed by August Derleth the "Cthulhu Mythos"; but in truth it reveals that Lovecraft has taken not merely the world but the cosmos for his backdrop. The cosmicism that became so distinctive a feature of his later fiction was observable only tangentially in his work prior to 1926, even though it had been an aesthetic goal from the beginning; as early as 1921 Lovecraft had written:

I could not write about "ordinary people" because I am not in the least interested in them. Without interest there can be no art. Man's relations to man do not captivate my fancy. It is man's relations to the cosmos—to the unknown—which alone arouses in me the spark of creative imagination. The humanocentric pose is impossible to me, for I cannot acquire the primitive myopia which magnifies the earth and ignores the background. (*In Defence of Dagon; CE* 5.53)

This is all well and good, but where do we find it in the early tales? The second story of Lovecraft's maturity, "Dagon" (1917), suggests it dimly in its brief glimpse of a vast "Polyphemus-like" (*D* 18) sea-creature; but that is about all. What is even more curious is that the many tales of the 1919–21 period inspired by Lord Dunsany—of whom Lovecraft claimed flamboyantly in "Supernatural Horror in Literature" that "His point of view is the most truly cosmic of any held in the literature of any period" (*D* 429)—are themselves singularly uncosmic, seeking instead to imitate the homely, folktalelike quality that is a feature of some of Dunsany's work.

But all this changes with "The Call of Cthulhu." At this point I will not enter into the vexed question of how useful it is to bracket off those of Love-craft's tales which employ his imaginary pantheon (Azathoth, Nyarlathotep, Yog-Sothoth, etc.) or imaginary New England topography (Arkham, Kings-port, Dunwich, Innsmouth, etc.) or other appurtenances, such as the mythical books of occult lore like the *Necronomicon* or *De Vermis Mysteriis*. After Love-craft's death (or even before, as Will Murray has argued) all this became a sort of "parlor game" (in Maurice Lévy's apt phrase) as second-rate writers imitated the outward form of the "Cthulhu Mythos" but not its inner philosophical substance. Even more so than the countless epigoni of Sherlock Holmes, these imitations have cast a dubious light on Lovecraft himself, and it is understand-able that critics like David E. Schultz would wish to discard the whole frame-work of the mythos as more of a hindrance than a help to the understanding of Lovecraft. But the fact is that Lovecraft *did* use his pseudomythology more concentratedly in some tales than in others, and because of this they really do gain a cumulative power they would not have as independent units.

What we derive from Lovecraft's later fiction is a brutal sense of mankind's hopelessly infinitesimal place in the cosmic scheme of things. In Lovecraft's fictional cosmos, successive waves of alien races (they are always whole cul-tures or civilizations, not isolated individuals) came to the earth millions of years ago, erected vast cities, held sway over enormous empires, and finally vanished long before the advent of humanity. Each of these races is incalcula-bly superior to us—physically, intellectually, and most telling of all, aestheti-cally. The Great Race in "The Shadow out of Time" has a vast archive full of documents about all the species in the cosmos; the record for mankind is housed on the "lowest or vertebrate section" (*DH* 397). Worse, the Old Ones of *At the Mountains of Madness,* who came from the stars and established them-selves in Antarctica, are "supposed to have created all earth-life as jest or mis-take" (*MM* 22). We are merely the inconsequential and accidental byproduct of another race.

The passage quoted earlier citing Lovecraft's desideratum of a "non-supernatural cosmic art" (*SL* 3.296) is also of vital importance in understanding both his fictional goals and his place in the history of weird fiction. The events and entities in Lovecraft's later tales are "non-supernatural" in not overtly con-tradicting reality as we know it; rather, they embody those "natural laws" not yet known to us. When, in "Notes on Writing Weird Fiction," Lovecraft speaks of "one of my strongest and most persistent wishes being to achieve, momen-tarily, the illusion of some strange suspension or violation of the galling limita-tions of time, space, and natural law which forever imprison us and frustrate our curiosity about the infinite cosmic spaces beyond the radius of our sight and analysis" (*CE* 2.177), he is careful to specify "the illusion" of a violation. This notion is clarified in a letter:

> The crux of a *weird* tale is something which *could not possibly happen*. If any unexpected advance of physics, chemistry, or biology were to indicate the *possibility* of any phenomena related by the weird tale, that particular set of phenomena would cease to be *weird* in the ultimate sense because it would become surrounded by a different set of emotions. It would no longer represent imaginative liberation, because it would no longer indicate a suspension or violation of the natural laws against whose universal dominance our fancies rebel. (*SL* 3.434)

This notion that the events in a weird tale must form "*supplements* rather than *contradictions* of the visible & mensurable universe" (*SL* 3.295–96) is what gives Lovecraft his unique place as an unclassifiable amalgam of fantasy and science fiction; it is not surprising that he has considerably influenced the subsequent development of both genres.

If Lovecraft is capable of suggesting the awesome gulfs of the cosmos as well as any writer in literature, he can also in his tales depict the reality of the mundane landscape—the Vermont backwoods in "The Whisperer in Darkness"; the frozen Antarctic in *At the Mountains of Madness*; the insidious decay of a once-thriving seaport in "The Shadow over Innsmouth." There is no paradox in this, and in "Notes on Writing Weird Fiction" he defends both his topographical realism and his diminution of human characters as part of a single aesthetic aim.

> In writing a weird story I always try very carefully to achieve the right mood and atmosphere, and place the emphasis where it belongs. One cannot, except in immature pulp charlatan-fiction, present an account of impossible, improbable, or inconceivable phenomena as a commonplace narrative of objective acts and conventional emotions. Inconceivable events and conditions have a special handicap to overcome, and this can be accomplished only through the maintenance of a careful realism in every phase of the story *except* that touching on the one given marvel. This marvel must be treated very impressively and deliberately—with a careful emotional "build-up"—else it will seem flat and unconvincing. Being the principal thing in the story, its mere existence should overshadow the characters and events. But the characters and events must be consistent and natural except where they touch the single marvel. (*CE* 2.177)

Realism, then, is not a goal but a function in Lovecraft; it facilitates the perception that "something which could not possibly happen" is actually happening. So too with Lovecraft's style. A dense, richly textured style tends to aid in the creation of that "mood and atmosphere" toward which Lovecraft bent all his efforts. His style, of course, has been much criticized, and there is no question but that his early work is "overwritten" in a way he himself later deprecated; but the later Lovecraft prose is as precise, musical, and evocative as anything out of Dunsany or Machen, his stylistic paragons. One is of course at liberty, with Edmund Wilson or Jacques Barzun, not to like the style; but to condemn an Asianic style merely for being Asianic (and that, frankly, is all I can derive from the majority of such criticisms) does not strike me as especially sound methodology. One should merely wallow sensuously in a passage like this:

> The Thing cannot be described—there is no language for such abysms of shrieking and immemorial lunacy, such eldritch contradictions of all matter, force, and cosmic order. A mountain walked or stumbled. God! What wonder that across the earth a great architect went mad, and poor Wilcox raved with fever in that telepathic instant? The Thing of the idols, the green, sticky spawn of the stars, had awaked to claim his own. The stars were right again, and what an age-old cult had failed to do by design, a band of innocent sailors had done by accident. After vigintillions of years great Cthulhu was loose again, and ravening for delight. (*DH* 152)

And we must remember that nearly thirty pages of clinical, meticulous prose have supplied that "careful emotional 'build-up'" for this climactic moment.

The majority of Lovecraft's essays were written during his intensive amateur phase—roughly 1914–22. They are stiff, formal, and dogmatic; Lovecraft certainly showed that he could write like a twentieth-century Addison, but also showed the rigidity of mind that came from bookishness, sequestration, and simple ignorance of the world. But this did not last long. Lovecraft well knew how important was his involvement in the world of amateur letters: his dogmatism began to be chipped away as he encountered opinions very different from his, whether it be the *fin-de-siècle* Hellenism of Samuel Loveman, the orthodox religiosity of Maurice W. Moe, the light-hearted eroticism of Rheinhart Kleiner, or the evangelical atheism of James F. Morton. Lovecraft never completely relinquished his cherished predilections—love of the weird; championing of classicism over romanticism; an earnest but not fanatical or ethically irresponsible atheism—but they were modified and honed through his amateur contacts. In this sense his early essays—along with his staggeringly voluminous correspondence—were formative influences of the most important sort.

The essays of his last decade or so—no longer written spontaneously but only for specific occasions—reflect the change. As early as 1924, in spite of his lifelong opposition to the extremist trends of modern literature—stream-of-consciousness, imagism, plodding realism—he could declare that Joyce's *Ulysses* and Cabell's *Jurgen* were "significant contributions to contemporary art";[5] "Cats and Dogs" (1926) playfully but acutely sees the cat as a symbol for many of Lovecraft's favored human traits—aristocracy, aloofness, dignity, grace; "Some Notes on a Nonentity" (1933) is a moving and eloquent autobiographical summary; and, perhaps most impressive of all, "Some Repetitions on the Times" (1933) is an earnest and almost harried plea to remedy the crushing economic woes of the time through modified socialism. All these essays display a flexibility, crispness of style, and intellectual rigor found in few of their predecessors, save perhaps the superb *In Defence of Dagon* essays (1921), where Lovecraft defends his aesthetics and metaphysics with a scintillating rhetoric found perhaps nowhere else in his work except in some of his argumentative letters.

Lovecraft's essays on amateur affairs remain the bulkiest of his nonfictional work, and testify to the mutual benefit he both derived from and gave to the amateur cause. Even if he eventually became somewhat disenchanted with the movement—even if he found that many of its members were hapless and egotistical tyros rather than disinterested pursuers of self-expression—he never dissociated himself from it. We must read the countless installments of Lovecraft's "Department of Public Criticism"—where with unfailing patience he points out the grammatical and aesthetic blunders of each and every contribution to the UAPA for that season—or his voluminous "News Notes," where he reports on the comings and goings of various amateurs (including himself), to perceive the depth of his attachment to amateurdom. Many nowadays see Lovecraft merely as the most prominent of the pulp writers; but in fact he was never a pulp writer at all (he published in the pulps from necessity, not inclination), and his amateur phase can be seen to be far more significant than his involvement with pulp fiction.

Lovecraft's travel essays form a unique body of his work. True, few of us have the patience to wade through the eighteenth-century diction of *A Description of the Town of Quebeck* (1930–31)—his single longest work, and a self-conscious flaunting of his utterly non-commercial stance—but such pieces as "Vermont—A First Impression" (1927) or "Travels in the Provinces of America" (1929) speak poignantly of his constant need to be aesthetically revivified by actual contact with the relics of the past.

As a general literary critic Lovecraft will never gain much acclaim; but it is arguable that he is still the acutest critic of weird fiction, and this not merely on the strength of "Supernatural Horror in Literature" (1925–27) but also on other essays like "Notes on Writing Weird Fiction" (1933) and especially the masses of incidental comment in his letters. All this body of work shows that Lovecraft's principles of weird writing were clearly formed at a fairly early stage in his career and continued to be elaborated as he read new work or discussed the matter with his many colleagues in the field. As an ancillary to this material one ought to mention his invaluable *Commonplace Book*, a storehouse of plots and images gleaned form his wide readings, dreams, and other experiences. David E. Schultz's critical edition allows us to see how intimately a part of his writing process were the seeming random and disjointed entries in this little notebook.

Lovecraft saw his deficiencies as a poet fairly early on; he knew that his real purpose in such things as "Old Christmas" (1917) or "Myrrha and Strephon" (1919) was not aesthetic expression but undiluted antiquarianism:

> In my metrical novitiate I was, alas, a chronic & inveterate mimic; allowing my antiquarian tendencies to get the better of my abstract poetic feeling. As a result, the whole purpose of my writing soon became distorted—till at length I wrote only as a means of re-creating around me the atmosphere of my 18th century favourites. Self-expression as such sank out of sight, & my sole test of excellence was the degree with which I approached the style of Mr. Pope, Dr. Young, Mr. Thomson, Mr. Addison, Mr. Tickell, Mr. Parnell, Dr. Goldsmith, Dr. Johnson, & so on. (*SL* 2.314–15)

Lovecraft remained faithful to the eighteenth-century poets, although he came to regard as the true giants of English poetry such Romantics as Keats and Shelley and such of his predecessors and contemporaries as the early Swinburne and Yeats. And yet, given his belief that poetry should be "simple, direct, non-intellectual, clothed in symbols & images rather than ideas and statements"[6]—a definition he used to denigrate the Metaphysicals just then reviving in critical esteem—he seemed to realize amazingly early that there may have been something lacking in his beloved Dryden and Pope: "I am aware that my favourite Georgians lacked much in the spirit of poesy—but I do admire their *verse*, as verse."[7] This was written in 1918; and although it is not quite an echo of Matthew Arnold's claim that Dryden and Pope were really masters of English *prose*, it at least acknowledges that the Georgians' principal virtue was not poetic instinct but metrical dexterity. In any case, the unfortunate result of Lovecraft's early adoption of the verse forms of the early eighteenth century is a mass of perfectly competent (from a metrical standpoint) but entirely lifeless and contentless poetry up to about 1925, with only intermittent points of interest: a number of pungent satires, from "Ad Criticos" (1913–14) to "Medusa: A

Portrait" (1921);[8] the flawless Georgianism of "Sunset" (1917); the exquisite self-parodies "On the Death of a Rhyming Critic" (1917) and "The Dead Bookworm" (1919). The horrific verse—from "The Poe-et's Nightmare" (1916), with its potent blank-verse distillation of his cosmic philosophy, to the brooding "A Cycle of Verse" (1919)—retains a little more life, although we could do without such mechanical Poe pastiches as "The House" (1919) or "The Nightmare Lake" (1919).

Curiously enough, however, Lovecraft got away from all this. From 1922 to 1928 he wrote almost no poetry: clearly his creative energies had shifted to fiction. Even some of this poetry reveals an incipient shaking off of eighteenth-century models: "My Favourite Character" and "A Year Off" (both 1925) have something of the flavor of Locker-Lampson and the *vers de société* of the later nineteenth century, and could well have been influenced by Rheinhart Kleiner, an unknown master of this light form. But then—suddenly—we come upon the sonnet "Recapture" (November 1929; later incorporated into *Fungi from Yuggoth*), which is so unlike anything Lovecraft had written before that both Winfield Townley Scott and Edmund Wilson were led to suspect (groundlessly, as it happens) that in it, as well as in the rest of *Fungi from Yuggoth* (1929–30), Lovecraft was influenced by Edwin Arlington Robinson. But if we study Lovecraft's aesthetic thought of this time we may learn that the change was perhaps not so sudden. By 1928 he was already railing against the use of the archaisms, inversions, and "poetic language" that had cluttered his earlier verse. He had begun to realize that living poetry cannot wear the garments of a prior day, and saw that his own previous poetry had merely been a vast psychological game he had played with himself—an attempt to retreat into the eighteenth century as feeble and pathetic as his longing for a periwig and knee-breeches. But when he sent "Recapture" to a correspondent, he added the note: "Speaking of my stuff—I enclose another recent specimen illustrative of my efforts to practice what I preach regarding direct and unaffected diction—a sort of irregular semi-sonnet, based on an actual dream."[9]

What had triggered this radical shift? There must have been a number of factors. Principally it was simply his awareness that the twentieth century was not a nightmare from which one could simply wake up and walk away but an age whose uniqueness demanded expression in art and literature; secondly, Lovecraft may have been struck by the brilliant poetry of his friend Clark Ashton Smith, who could have shown Lovecraft how to harmonize a selective use of archaism with a generally modern and vigorous approach; most directly, there was Lovecraft's work on a never-published poetic handbook, *Doorways to*

Poetry, for his friend Maurice W. Moe, and his reading of Donald Wandrei's *Sonnets of the Midnight Hours* (1927), probably the direct model for *Fungi from Yuggoth*. In any case, his sonnet-cycle, while by no means radical, can take its place with the work of other conservative poets of the day—Rupert Brooke, Ralph Hodgson, Robert Hillyer, John Masefield, Walter de la Mare, and others. Lovecraft may never be known for his poetry; but at its best it offers the same elements of cosmic horror, purity of diction, and philosophic resonance that characterize his prose.

Of Lovecraft's letters it is difficult to speak in short compass. In sheer quantity they dwarf the rest of his oeuvre to complete insignificance. Although at the moment they are known only to the inner circle of Lovecraft scholars, they are without question some of the most remarkable literary documents of their century, and it is even conceivable that in the distant future his reputation will rest more on them than on his fiction. It is to the letters that we go for information on Lovecraft's life, for details about his literary work, for the particulars of his philosophical thought; but more than mere utilitarian adjuncts to scholarship, they are some of the most beautiful things of their kind. Lovecraft had no compunction writing letters of fifty, sixty, or even seventy pages; and it is in these heroic epistles—longer than most of his stories—that he reveals his true greatness and diversity as an artist. From technical philosophizing to farcical and self-parodic humor; from playful archaism to blunt colloquialism; from poignant reflections on the cosmic insignificance of mankind to heated discussions of political and economic regeneration, the letters run the gamut of subject, tone, and mood. I cannot resist quoting at length Lovecraft's chiding of Frank Long for his equation of science and technology:

> Listen, young man. Forget all about your books & machine-made current associations. Kick the present dying parody on civilisation out the back door of consciousness. Shelve the popular second-hand dishings-up of Marxian economic determinism—a genuine force within certain limits, but without the widest ramifications ascribed to it by the fashionable *New Republic* & *Nation* clique. For once in your life, live up to your non-contemporary ideal & do some thinking without the 1930–31 publishers' sausage-grist at your elbow! Get back to the Ionian coast, shovel away some 2500 years, & tell Grandpa who it is you find in a villa at Miletus studying the properties of loadstone & amber, predicting eclipses, explaining the moon's phases, & applying to physics & astronomy the principles of research he learned in Egypt. Thales—quite a boy in his day. Ever hear of him before? He wanted to *know* things. Odd taste, wasn't it? And to think, he never tried to manufacture rayon or form a joint-stock company or

pipe oil from Mesopotamia or extract gold from sea-water! Funny old guy—
wanted to know things, yet never thought of a collectivist state . . . . leaving this
last for the unctuous windbag Plato, upon whom the moustacheletted little
Chestertons of a later aera were to dote. Bless me, but *do* you suppose he actually had the normal human instinct of *curiosity* & simply wanted knowledge to
satisfy that elemental urge? Perish such an un-modern & un-Marxian thought
. . . . . yet one has dim suspicions . . . . And then this bozo Pythagoras.
What did he want to bother with that old "what is anything" question for? And
Heraclitus & Anaxagoras & Anaximander & Democritus & Leucippus &
Empedocles? Well—if you take the word of your precious old satyr-faced
pragmatist Socrates, these ginks merely wanted to know things for the sake of
knowing! According to this beloved super-Babbitt of yours, who brought down
philosophy from the clouds to serve among men—serve useful ends in a civi-
cally acceptable fashion—the old naturalists & sophists were a sorry lot. Your
dear Plato agreed. They were not social-minded or collectivistic. Tut, tut—they
were actually selfish individualists who gratified the personal human instinct of
cosmic curiosity for its own sake. Ugh! take them away! Moustacheletted young
Platonists want nothing to do with such outlawed & unregimented pleasure-
seekers. They simply *couldn't* have been real "scientists", since they didn't serve
big business or have altruistic or bolshevistic motivations. Practically & Marx-
ianly speaking, there simply weren't any such people. How could there be?
"Science" is (they print it in books) the servant of the machine age. Since ancient Ionia had no machine age, how could there be "Science"? (*SL* 3.298–99)

But it is in letters of less intrinsic interest that Lovecraft displays his full humanity. For eight years he corresponded regularly with Elizabeth Toldridge, a
would-be poet who was disabled and could not leave her apartment in Washington, D.C.; and although we can tell, from Lovecraft's side of the correspondence, that she was hopelessly conventional and Victorian in her outlook,
Lovecraft never failed to answer every point made in her letters and acknowledge the books and newspaper clippings she sent him. Lovecraft was neither
condescending nor dishonest with her—he made no bones about not ascribing
to her benign theism, her admiration of tame late Victorian poetry, or her political and economic conservatism. Only his death curtailed this correspondence.
The tireless help and encouragement Lovecraft gave, even on his deathbed, to
all his correspondents young and old makes one understand the admiration and
even reverence that all his colleagues extended to him during his lifetime and
after his death. The publication of Lovecraft's collected correspondence—in
perhaps two dozen volumes—is, at long last, an undertaking that has now
commenced, even though it is still in its earliest stages; but when it is completed,

it may come close to revealing the full stature of Lovecraft the man and writer.

IV

There is now little need to rehearse the details of Lovecraft's posthumous resurrection: the attempts by August Derleth and Donald Wandrei to find a publisher for an omnibus of his tales; their founding of Arkham House when they failed in that enterprise; the emergence of a youthful band of enthusiasts in the growing fantasy fandom movement (blasted by Edmund Wilson as "on even a more infantile level than the Baker Street Irregulars and the cult of Sherlock Holmes" [*FDOC* 49]—a point on which he was probably correct); the gradual dissemination of Lovecraft's stories in paperback, including an Armed Services edition; the periodic publication by Arkham House of volumes of tales, poems, essays, and miscellany from the forties to the sixties; the translation of Lovecraft into French and Spanish in the fifties, German, Italian, and Dutch in the sixties, and Japanese and the Scandinavian languages in the seventies; the stupendous popularity of the Beagle/Ballantine paperbacks in the seventies; the reprinting of minor works by the fan or specialty press in the seventies and eighties; and the republication of his collected fiction in textually correct editions from Arkham House under my editorship. In recent years Lovecraft's work has achieved the pinnacle of literary greatness, justifying what seemed initially to be the exaggerated plaudits of his advocates: first, three editions in Penguin Classics (1999–2004), followed by his canonization in the Library of America (2005). His letters have been published by academic presses, and his poetry and essays are now available in collected and annotated editions.

The fostering of scholarship on Lovecraft has been no less remarkable. Prior to 1971 (the death of August Derleth), the number of academicians or mainstream critics who even discussed Lovecraft could be counted on the fingers of one hand: we have mentioned Edmund Wilson, Colin Wilson, and T. O. Mabbott, and mention should be made of Peter Penzoldt, the Swiss scholar who in *The Supernatural in Fiction* (1952) devoted what are still some of the most illuminating pages on Lovecraft's style and theory of weird fiction. But his is an isolated instance of a non-condescending treatment. In this early stage the foundations of Lovecraft criticism were ably laid by George T. Wetzel, Matthew H. Onderdonk, and especially Fritz Leiber, whose "A Literary Copernicus" (1949) may still be the single best general article ever written on Lovecraft. Little was done in the 1950s (the special Lovecraft issue of the University of Detroit literary magazine, *Fresco* [Spring 1958], is quite ephemeral and insubstantial) or the 1960s; and it seemed to require the death of August Derleth—and, perhaps, the publication of the *Selected Letters* beginning in 1965—to spur renewed scholarly interest in Lovecraft. The dismantling of Derleth's many erroneous conceptions of Lovecraft the man and writer began with Richard L. Tierney and Dirk W. Mosig; L. Sprague de Camp wrote a controversial biography after he saw that Derleth had failed to finish his; the establishment of *Lovecraft Studies* in 1979 provided a focus for informed discussion of Lovecraft, although inevitably that discussion was and is still conducted predominantly by non-academicians. The culmination of the scholarly ferment that had begun in the 1970s was reached with the H. P. Lovecraft Centennial Conference at Brown University in 1990, around which time a spate of penetrating books—by Peter Cannon, Donald R. Burleson, and others—appeared. S. T. Joshi's exhaustive *H. P. Lovecraft: A Life* (1996) attracted wide attention, although less so than de Camp's biography because it was not published by a major commercial press. Since that time, curiously enough, there has been a bit of a slowdown in scholarship, partially because of the demise of the two leading journals in the field, *Lovecraft Studies* and *Crypt of Cthulhu*, and partially because a certain plateau of understanding has apparently been achieved. But such scholars as Timo Airaksinen, Timothy Evans, T. R. Livesey, J.-M. Rajala, and others have done outstanding work, and the new *Lovecraft Annual* (2007f.) bids fair to provide a fresh venue for scholarly work.

Notes

1. HPL to Duane W. Rimel, 1 April 1936 (ms., JHL).

2. "What Amateurdom and I Have Done for Each Other" (1921); rpt. *CE* 1.273.

3. *The Private Life of H. P. Lovecraft* (1992 ed.), 15.

4. HPL to Lillian D. Clark, 17 November 1924 (ms., JHL).

5. "The Omnipresent Philistine" (1924); rpt. *CE* 2.77.

6. HPL to Lee McBride White, Jr., 10 February 1936; *Lovecraft Annual* No. 1 (2007): 55.

7. HPL to Alfred Galpin, 27 May [1918]; *Letters to Alfred Galpin* (2005), 21.

8. HPL's best satire, "Waste Paper" (1923), a vicious but telling parody of *The Waste Land*, of course owes nothing to the eighteenth century.

9. HPL to Elizabeth Toldridge, 26 November 1929 (ms., JHL).

An Epicure in the Terrible

I
Biographical

The Parents of
Howard Phillips Lovecraft

Kenneth W. Faig, Jr.

Dedicated to
Duane Weldon Rimel
Correspondent and Friend of H. P. Lovecraft
Benefactor of Lovecraftian Studies
Upon the Occasion of His Seventy-fifth Birthday
21 February 1990

Howard Phillips Lovecraft was born about nine o'clock in the morning on 20 August 1890 at the home of his maternal grandparents, Whipple Van Buren Phillips (1833–1904) and Robie Alzada Place Phillips (1827–1896), at 454 Angell Street (then numbered 194), Providence, Rhode Island.

His mother was Sarah Susan Phillips Lovecraft, the second of five children, born 17 October 1857 at the Stephen Place, Jr., homestead in Foster, Rhode Island (*SL* 2.85). Susie married Winfield Scott Lovecraft at St. Paul's Episcopal Church on Tremont Street in Boston, Massachusetts, on 12 June 1889. She was admitted to Butler Hospital, an institution for those suffering from mental and nervous illnesses, on 13 March 1919 and died there on 24 May 1921 following an operation for the removal of her gall bladder. She is buried in the Phillips lot in Swan Point Cemetery in Providence.

His father was Winfield Scott Lovecraft, the second of three surviving children of George Lovecraft (1815–1895) and his wife Helen Allgood (1821–1881), born 26 October 1853, in Rochester, New York. He was admitted to Butler Hospital on 25 April 1893 and died there on 19 July 1898 of general paresis. Providence attorney Albert A. Baker (1862–1959) was appointed as his legal guardian on 6 June 1893. Winfield Lovecraft is also buried in the Phillips lot in Swan Point Cemetery. He left an estate of approximately $10,000 to his widow and child (*SL* 3.366–67).

The purpose of this essay is to try to provide a fuller picture of Lovecraft's parents and how they influenced his life. Because so little is known of his parents, particularly of his father, the task is not an easy one. The standard portrait of Lovecraft's parents was already drawn as early as 1944 by Providence literary editor and poet Winfield Townley Scott (1910–1968) in his essay "His Own Most Fantastic Creation: Howard Phillips Lovecraft," which appeared in the Arkham House collection *Marginalia*. The essay represented an expansion of Scott's pioneering article on Lovecraft in the *Providence Sunday Journal* of 26 December 1943; it has since been reprinted, removing some of August Derleth's copyediting, in Scott's collection of essays *Exiles and Fabrications* (1961) and in Peter Cannon's *Lovecraft Remembered* (1998). This seminal essay is of enormous importance to the study of Lovecraft the man and the author.

I. Winfield Scott Lovecraft

The whereabouts of Winfield Lovecraft between his birth in Rochester, New York, in 1853 and his marriage in Boston in 1889 are not well known. Although his marriage certificate states that he was a resident of New York City at the time of his marriage, searches in city directories for New York City, Boston, and Providence have not yet uncovered his name. City directories of Rochester for 1872 and 1873 show Winfield Lovecraft working as a blacksmith in that city. In 1880, he was recorded in the home of his parents George and Helen (Allgood) Lovecraft in East Chester, Westchester County NY; he was then working as a clerk in a tap wines business.[1] (The federal census of 1890, the last in which Winfield Lovecraft would have appeared, perished by fire in the 1920s.) While Lovecraft states that his father was educated at a military academy, it is not probable that he actually served in the military or his son would doubtless have proudly recalled the fact.

The marriage and death certificates of Winfield Lovecraft confirm that he was employed as a traveling salesman, or "commercial traveler" as he himself would probably have preferred to be called. Although H. P. Lovecraft never emphasized his father's occupation in correspondence, he did state that he was employed by Gorham & Company, silversmiths of Providence, and that his business duties kept him in the Boston metropolitan area for most of the period between his marriage in 1889 and his breakdown in 1893. Winfield Lovecraft's position as a traveling salesman seems to indicate that his duties included primarily representation of his firm to the retail trade rather than to individual purchasers. How he came to meet Sarah Susan Phillips and to win her love is unknown.

In a letter to Maurice W. Moe dated 16 January 1915, Lovecraft stated specifically that his father was an Anglican and was married by the Anglican rite, but it is curious to note that his parents were married at an Episcopal church in

Boston rather than in Providence, which had many Episcopal churches. The witnesses to the marriage were members of the staff of St. Paul's Church. This points toward the possibility that the marriage took place against the wishes of Susie's parents, although this is mere speculation.

Whatever may be said regarding the attitude of Susie's parents toward her marriage to Winfield Lovecraft, they undoubtedly rejoiced at the birth of a first grandchild in 1890 and probably paid a good portion, if not all, of the cost of Winfield Lovecraft's medical care between 1893 and 1898. Despite the tremendous blow that Winfield's illness must have represented to his father-in-law, it must be stated in charity to Whipple Phillips that he permitted his son-in-law to be buried in his own family lot and even erected a marker in his memory.

Lovecraft's own first dim recollections from his childhood were of a family vacation in Dudley, Massachusetts, during the summer of 1892. He could just recall the house where the family stayed, with its frightening attic water-tank and less intimidating rocking-horses at the head of the stairs. He could also remember the plank walks in the town, a wooded ravine, and "a boy with a small rifle who let me pull the trigger while my mother held me" (*SL* 4.354). The recollections of Ella Sweeney, a schoolteacher friend of Mrs. Lovecraft, dramatically confirm Lovecraft's own early memories of the vacation. Sweeney recalled that Mrs. Lovecraft would not eat dinner in the dining room, for fear of leaving her sleeping son alone for one hour on the floor above. Also, when Sweeney took young Howard out for a walk, Mrs. Lovecraft enjoined her to stoop slightly, so as not to pull the boy's arm from its socket.[2] Undoubtedly, Sarah Susan was not an easy person to get along with, given her nervous temperament and overprotectiveness toward her child.

And yet, the early marital life of the couple expanded in expected and normal ways. In the same year, 1892, the Lovecrafts and their young son became boarders in the home of poet Louise Imogen Guiney (1861–1920) and her mother in the Boston suburb of Auburndale. Guiney had been educated in Providence and met Mrs. Lovecraft there. Lovecraft records that he and his parents stayed the entire winter of 1892–93 with the Guineys (*SL* 2.107). Research conducted by L. Sprague de Camp in the Guiney letters to F. H. Day in the Library of Congress appeared to indicate that their stay in the Guiney home lasted only from early June to late July 1892, but subsequent research has revealed that the guests in question were not the Lovecrafts but some German visitors.[3] Because of Howard's long yellow curls—shorn at age six, as his mother wept[4]—Guiney dubbed him "Little Sunshine" (*SL* 1.32).

Lovecraft's own first fully defined memories dated from this period, and he could vividly recall the railway bridge of the Boston and Albany line in Auburndale and the Guiney home, so much so that he walked right to it on Vista Avenue when he paid a return visit in 1908, without any guidance (*SL* 4.355). He could remember not only reciting Mother Goose rhymes on a table for the edification of his parents and the Guineys but also Guiney's favorite St. Bernard dog Brontë's "being ever in attendance on my chariot as my mother wheeled that vehicle through the streets & avenues" (*SL* 1.32). According to Lovecraft, Brontë would snarl if any stranger approached the infant, and would even allow him to place his fist in the dog's mouth.

Doubtless, the Guineys were glad when they were able to return to unfettered control of their household. Nor would Mrs. Lovecraft likely have recalled the period in Auburndale with fondness had a quarrel with the Guineys forced the family to leave. In fact, Lovecraft records that a dramatic step took place in the marriage at this time; Winfield Lovecraft, feeling moderately prosperous, acquired a home site upon which to build in Auburndale (*SL* 1.6, 33). Thus, they were in fact taking another major step in the typical development of a middle-class family: the acquisition of a building site for a home of their own.

One can imagine Susie's elation. Her first memories were doubtless of her father's spacious home in Greene, Rhode Island, but she spent her young adult years in the homes of her father and mother on the fashionable West Side of Providence (1873–81), then in the beautiful home her father built at the corner of Angell Street and Elmgrove Avenue on the East Side (1881–89), which was pulled down in 1961 after spending its final decades as a warren of doctors' offices.

It was H. P. Lovecraft's lifelong dream from 1904 onward to repurchase 454 Angell Street and restore it to its original grandeur. Lovecraft and his aunts, in later years, would shed a tear at each alteration to the basic structure or to the outbuildings and yard. What greater joy for Susie than the prospect of a home of her own, after living in rented quarters for the first four years of her marriage. Surely, the domestic felicity of the home of her parents, to which she would return for the years 1893–1904, was the model for what she herself hoped to achieve in her own marriage. When she celebrated her thirty-fifth birthday on 17 October 1892, perhaps she was still hopeful that she and her husband could fill their own house in Auburndale with more children.

Up to the time of Winfield Lovecraft's tragic collapse in April 1893, there is nothing to point to any severe abnormality in the marriage. In fact, in the birth of a son and the acquisition of a home site, the Lovecrafts had followed a pattern common to many middle-class couples of the day. All seemed auspicious for young Howard to grow up in a parental household as stable and loving as that which his maternal grandparents Whipple and Robie Phillips had provided for their children. However, it was not to be. Before he attained his fortieth birthday, Winfield Lovecraft was admitted to Butler Hospital, where he spent the final five years of his life, and declared legally incompetent on the grounds of insanity.

To the best of my knowledge, Winfield Townley Scott was the first to reveal in print that Lovecraft's father died in "an advanced state of general paresis." Scott states that this is the cause of death shown on the official death certificate on file at City Hill in Providence, while a modern official transcript of the death record on file with the State of Rhode Island Department of Health obtained with family permission indicates only "general paresis." Although Lovecraft's friend Kenneth Sterling, M.D., expressed doubt that Lovecraft's father could have survived five years in the paretic state,[5] it would appear that the cause of death as indicated in the death certificate is definitive as to the nature of his illness. August Derleth eliminated any direct reference to syphilis—the underlying cause of general paresis—from Scott's essay as published in *Marginalia,* but as reprinted in *Exiles and Fabrications* Scott's final comment on Winfield Scott Lovecraft is as follows: "The 'pompous Englishman' of a father, in the phrase of that family friend, we now see by medical evidence was a diseased megalomaniac: a victim of syphilis."[6] Scott concluded his portrait of Lovecraft's father with an assertion of his disbelief in the theory later asserted by David H. Keller, M.D., that the son may have been infected with his father's illness through his mother. Scott closes his account by saying that Winfield Lovecraft was, in fact, "worse than dead" during the final five years of his life spent at Butler Hospital.[7]

The connection of general paresis with syphilis, while the subject of speculation from the mid-nineteenth century onward, was not definitely proven until Noguchi isolated the spirochete in the brains of paretic patients in 1911. General paresis, however, was well known and described during the nineteenth century, even if largely forgotten today because of the success of penicillin therapy. The description of the mental symptoms of the disease from Leland E. Hinsie's and Robert Jean Campbell's *Psychiatric Dictionary* is worth reprinting for the lay reader:

> Mental symptoms may appear in various forms: as (1) simple dementia, the most common type, with deterioration of intellect, affect and social behavior; (2) paranoid form, with persecutory delusions; (3) expansive or manic form, with delusions of grandiosity; or (4) depressive form, often with absurd nihilistic delusions. No matter what the form, intellectual functions show increasing

impairment, with loss of more and more memory, confabulation, disorientation (especially in the area of time), carelessness in personal appearance and hygiene, irritability and restlessness, alcoholic excesses, and sexual aberrations.[8]

One need not be a physician to understand the living hell Winfield Lovecraft endured during the final five years of his life. Nor was he the only member of his family to suffer from this disease. R. Alain Everts has revealed that Winfield's first cousin, Joshua Elliot Lovecraft (1845–98), died insane of paresis in the same year as Winfield.[9] Joshua Lovecraft was the son of Joseph Lovecraft, Jr. (1811–79), the brother of Winfield's father George. Joshua's death certificate reveals that he died on 8 November 1898 at the state hospital in Rochester after having suffered from "general paralysis" for over four years.[10]

In his biography of Lovecraft, L. Sprague de Camp relates an anecdote first committed to paper by Arthur S. Koki, presumably deriving from family sources, that confirms several of the symptoms described by Hinsie and Campbell.[11] According to the anecdote, Winfield had to be placed under restraint while on a business trip to Chicago and returned to Providence. De Camp relates: "Alone in his hotel room, he suddenly began crying out that the chambermaid had insulted him and that his wife was being assaulted on the floor above." Recurring hallucinations resulted in his admission to Butler Hospital on 25 April 1893.

The hallucinations reported by Koki confirm one of the important manifestations of the disease as described by Hinsie and Campbell. In addition, Scott's citation of the recollection of Winfield Lovecraft by a family friend as "a pompous Englishman" also points toward delusions of grandeur. One is led to wonder what engendered the persecutory delusion he suffered in his Chicago hotel room in April 1893. His reported statement that his wife was being assaulted on the floor above certainly points toward a sexual basis, at least in part, for his delusions. The reference to an insult suffered at the hands of a chambermaid suggests the possibility of several types of incident. Perhaps Winfield returned to his room with a prostitute and quarreled with her. Or, alternatively, perhaps he solicited favors from the chambermaid and was rejected. However, his delusions need not have been grounded in any actual incident.

Undoubtedly, the family felt great shame because of Winfield's illness. Susie returned to the home of her parents in Providence with her young son in tow. The site in Auburndale had to be sold. It seems doubtful that either Susie or her son ever visited Winfield in the hospital; perhaps they were given to believe that he had suffered a severe stroke and was in fact comatose and wholly paralyzed. In view of the presence of her son, it is particularly pathetic to note that Susie chose to be listed at her father's address in the Providence City Directories for 1896–99 as "Miss Winfield S. Lovecraft." Only in 1900 did she change her listing to "Mrs. Winfield S. Lovecraft."

The primary evidence concerning the illness of Winfield Lovecraft apart from his death certificate is very slim indeed. A medical expert informed me that the use of the term "general paresis" was, by the last decades of the nineteenth century, restricted to the disease later identified as the tertiary phase of neurosyphilis. The weight of evidence does suggest that Winfield died of the ravages of tertiary neurosyphilis. Perhaps the most important statements are those of H. P. Lovecraft himself, which deserve careful examination. Writing to his good friend Maurice W. Moe on 1 January 1915, Lovecraft stated:

> In 1893 my father was seized with a complete paralytic stroke, due to insomnia and an overstrained nervous system, which took him to the hospital for the remaining five years of his life. He was never afterward conscious, and my image of him is but vague. This of course disrupted all plans for the future, caused the sale of the home site in Auburndale, and the return of my mother and myself to the Phillips home in Providence. Here I spent all the best years of my childhood. The house was a beautiful and spacious edifice, with stable and grounds, the latter approaching a park in the beauty of the walks and trees. (*SL* 1.6)

Writing to another friend, Rheinhart Kleiner, on 16 November 1916, Lovecraft stated:

> In April 1893 my father was stricken with a complete paralysis resulting from a brain overtaxed with study & business cares. He lived for five years at a hospital, but was never again able to move hand or foot, or to utter a sound. This tragedy dissolved all plans for permanent settlement in Auburndale, & caused the sale of the property recently acquired there. Permanently stricken with grief, my mother took me to the Phillips household, thereby causing me to grow up as a complete Rhode-Islander. (*SL* 1.33)

These are the fullest statements by Lovecraft concerning his father's illness that have been published to date. The fact that Lovecraft records mental and nervous symptoms (insomnia and nervous strain) is notable. A sustained disruption of the normal patterns of sleep is particularly suggestive of the possibility of a more serious mental problem.

Did Lovecraft in fact believe that his father's collapse in April 1893 left him completely paralyzed and unconscious? It is impossible to say with certitude.

Perhaps the young boy was given this explanation as to why he and his mother could not visit his father at Butler Hospital. Nevertheless, we can say with near certainty that Winfield was not left paralyzed and unconscious. For on 6 June 1893, Albert A. Baker was appointed guardian of Winfield Scott Lovecraft, "an insane person." This characterization would hardly have been used if Winfield were completely paralyzed and comatose. It also conflicts with the family tradition that Winfield was returned to Providence from Chicago under restraint. If he were paralyzed and comatose as a result of a stroke, restraint would not have been necessary.

While both Winfield and Joshua Lovecraft both survived about five years in the paretic state, longer than normal, this does not offend credulity as much as the assertion that Winfield survived, paralyzed and comatose, for five years. Surely, in those days before antibiotics, Winfield would have perished of one infection or another long before five years had elapsed.

The funeral of Winfield Lovecraft, which took place at the home of his father-in-law on 21 July 1898, was private. Whipple Phillips's wife Robie had been dead for nearly two and a half years. But one wonders, from the following entry in Lovecraft's *Commonplace Book,* whether Lovecraft himself, not yet aged eight, was obligated to pay a final, terrified visit to the casket of his father:

> [159] Certain kind of deep-toned stately music of the style of the 1870's or 1880's recalls certain visions of that period—gas-litten parlours of the dead, moonlight on old floors, decaying business streets with gas lamps, &c.—under terrible circumstances.[12]

This entry suggests several things. First of all, Lovecraft himself, having been born in 1890, could not personally recall funerals from the 1870s or 1880s. There was no funeral in the immediate household of Whipple and Robie Phillips between April 1865, when their third child Emeline E. Phillips died in Greene, Rhode Island, and January 1896, when Robie Phillips died in Providence. By 1870, the older generation of Phillips aunts and uncles had largely passed away. Perhaps there were deaths in Robie's family, the Places, that saddened the Phillips household in the 1870s and 1880s. But the point is that Lovecraft's own first experience of a funeral was likely that of his maternal grandmother in January 1896. This loss brought the boy his first dreams of the terrible "night-gaunts" one finds in his later fiction and poetry, and caused him to try to relieve the gloom of a Victorian mourning period by pinning strips of bright cloth to the dresses of his mother and aunts (*SL* 1.34–35). We can be certain that Lovecraft did not attend the funeral of his paternal grandfather in

Pelhamville, New York, in September 1895, for he states that he never saw his paternal grandfather in person (*SL* 1.31). Thus, the funerals of Lovecraft's maternal grandmother and father would have been his first, and probably most lasting, exposure to Victorian funeral customs.

The following revelatory passage from Lovecraft's letter to Maurice W. Moe dated 5 April 1931 is important for the understanding of Winfield Lovecraft and his influence upon his son:

> My father was constantly warned not to fall into Americanisms of speech and provincial vulgarities of dress and mannerisms—so much so that he was generally regarded as an Englishman despite his birth in Rochester, N.Y. I can just recall his extremely precise and cultivated British voice, and his immaculate black morning-coat and vest, ascot tie, and striped grey trousers. I have myself worn some of his old ascots and wing collars, left all too immaculate by his early illness and death. (*SL* 3.362)

The other concrete memory of his father that Lovecraft left us occurs in his letter to J. Vernon Shea dated 4 February 1934 and is equally moving: "I can just remember my father—an immaculate figure in black coat & vest & grey striped trousers. I had a childish habit of slapping him on the knees & shouting 'Papa, you look just like a young man!'" (*SL* 4.355).

Several things are notable about Lovecraft's recollections of his father. First of all, the visual image he retained of his father undoubtedly derives in large part from the family portrait of the Lovecrafts (c. 1892) reproduced as the frontispiece of *The Shuttered Room and Other Pieces* (1959). No other photograph of Winfield seems to have survived; at least none has been published. Every element of Winfield's typical dress as mentioned by Lovecraft is present in this photograph: wing collar, ascot tie, black coat, gray striped trousers. It seems quite possible that the trauma of her husband's illness caused Sarah Lovecraft, eventually, to destroy many physical mementos of her husband. The photograph may in fact be the sole surviving artifact of Winfield Lovecraft, since no specimen of his handwriting is known to exist, and presumably the articles of clothing once worn by his son perished long ago.

Lovecraft himself never deviated from the point of view that his father was an exemplary provider, left completely paralyzed and unconscious after suffering a stroke on account of overwork and nervous strain. He perpetuated the memory of his father in other ways than by occasionally wearing articles of his clothing. (One wonders whether the famous amateur photograph of Lovecraft in 1915 depicts him wearing one of his father's wing collars.)[13] He never deviated from his lifelong Anglophilism. He even regretted the American Revolution with apparent sincerity, startling his grandfather, mother, and aunts with this position as early as 1896 while his father was still living. He always preferred British spellings and complained when his American editors altered them. Circumstantially, Lovecraft's references to his father's "immaculate" clothing and to his youthful appearance, combined with his lifelong allegiance to things English, certainly point toward a conscious effort to defend his attachment to and identification with his father against any attempt to besmirch his memory.

Nevertheless, Lovecraft certainly knew that Butler Hospital, where both his mother and father ended their lives, was not a place for the care of the paralyzed and the comatose. He knew very well that the institution was a mental hospital. Writing to Frank Belknap Long on 26 January 1921, he stated: "My paternal grandfather had to retire from active life because of a breakdown, my maternal grandfather died of a shock in 1904, my father died in a sanitarium in 1898 after five years of total collapse, and my mother is now in a sanitarium from her second nervous breakdown—1919" (*SL* 1.122). Writing to Maurice W. Moe on 5 April 1931, he acknowledged:

> I didn't inherit a very good set of nerves, since near relatives on both sides of my ancestry were prone to headaches, nerve-exhaustion, and breakdowns. My grandfather had frightful blind headaches, and my mother could run a close second; whilst my father was stricken with paralysis in the early forties. (*SL* 3.368)

Did Lovecraft know that both parents died in the grips of severe mental illness? With virtual certainty, we cay reply: yes. Was he aware that his father was not the victim of a stroke, as was his maternal grandfather? With some degree of probability, we cay reply: very likely so, although whether he knew that syphilis caused his father's physical and mental symptoms is not known. He would have revealed such knowledge only in personal conversation with old and trusted friends like Maurice W. Moe and W. Paul Cook, if at all; and, if he ever participated in such a conversation, his close friends chose not to disclose it.

"Facts concerning the Late Arthur Jermyn and His Family" (1920)—undoubtedly one of Lovecraft's most shocking fictions—contains in the description of Sir Robert Jermyn's madness a snippet that may just be relevant to the madness of Lovecraft's father. Presented with the horrifying evidence of Wade Jermyn's activities in Africa, Sir Robert murders explorer Samuel Seaton and all three of his own children in one terrible incident at Jermyn House on 19 October 1852. Confined to a madhouse, Sir Robert spends his final years thus: "Sir Robert himself, after repeated attempts at suicide and a stubborn refusal to utter any articulate sound, died of apoplexy in the second year of his confinement" (*D* 76–77).

Just possibly, there is an echo of something Lovecraft may have known of his father's illness in this passage. Having been placed under restraint after the real or imagined incident in his Chicago hotel room, Winfield Scott Lovecraft, the immaculately dressed and well-spoken Englishman, was returned to Providence under humiliating circumstances and admitted to the hospital. When his hallucinations abated and he found himself deprived of his freedom and his dignity, perhaps he perversely determined that he would speak no more to mankind.[14]

There are a few other curious hints of the shadowy figure of Winfield Lovecraft lurking in his son's fiction.[15] It is probably no coincidence that several of Lovecraft's stories—most dealing with madness or some sort of hereditary degeneracy—take place in mid-July, the time of Winfield's death. Delapore's downfall begins in "The Rats in the Walls" when he moves into Exham Priory on 16 July 1923. The escape of the narrator of "The Shadow over Innsmouth" from Innsmouth occurs on 16 July 1927, but that escape eventually turns to allegiance with his pursuers. Both "The Whisperer in Darkness" and "The Haunter of the Dark" contain sequences that develop over the summer and include dates from mid-July.

But the most telling of this group of tales is one whose climax occurs on 17–18 July 1935 in the desert of Western Australia. In "The Shadow out of Time," Nathaniel Wingate Peaslee, a man haunted by his past in the most literal meaning of the phrase, develops a strange "amnesia," losing his personality for a time to an alien invader. As a counterpoint to his strange behavior, he assures us, "I would have it known that there is nothing whatever of the mad or sinister in my heredity and early life. This is a highly important fact in view of the shadow which fell so suddenly upon me from *outside* sources" (*DH* 370). His behavior is so strange during the tenancy of the member of the Great Race in his body that his wife, family, and friends leave him:

> Only my second son, Wingate, seemed able to conquer the terror and repulsion which my change aroused. He indeed felt that I was a stranger, but though only eight years old held fast to a faith that my proper self would return. When it did return he sought me out, and the courts gave me his custody. In succeeding years he helped me with the studies to which I was driven, and today, at thirty-five, he is a professor of psychology at Miskatonic. (*DH* 373)

This telling passage finds its roots in the following entry in Lovecraft's *Commonplace Book*:

[167] Boy rear'd in atmosphere of considerable mystery. Believes father dead. Suddenly is told that father is about to return. Strange preparations—consequences.[16]

Lovecraft himself was not quite eight years old when his father died. Surely the father he remembered as having a cultivated and precise speaking voice and mannerisms must have presented a disturbing figure if the boy ever saw him during his final illness. Perhaps young Howard "held fast to the faith" that his father's "proper self would return" eventually, though that was never to happen. Nathaniel Wingate Peaslee did regain his personality and his son matured into an adult with a respectable profession. It would seem that, fictional character though he is, he is the only memento of Winfield Scott Lovecraft that survives, thanks to the loving memory of his son Howard.

II. Sarah Susan Phillips Lovecraft

Having added what little can be added to Winfield Townley Scott's portrait of Lovecraft's father, we must now pass to the consideration of a person of even greater influence in the life of H. P. Lovecraft: his mother, Sarah Susan Phillips Lovecraft. The evidence concerning her is slightly more abundant than the evidence concerning her husband, and it is easy to cite the principal sources of information:

1. Once again, Scott's early biographical work heads the list. As reflected in his pioneering biographical essay, "His Own Most Fantastic Creation," Scott was able to examine Susie Lovecraft's medical records at Butler Hospital. His summary of their contents is basic for an understanding of Lovecraft's mother.

2. Next in importance are undoubtedly Lovecraft's own statements concerning his mother in correspondence. While his grief at her unexpected passing on 24 May 1921 was real (although not abnormal, as was his grief at the death of his maternal grandfather and the loss of the family home in 1904), his statements also make clear that the long years spent with his mother did not fail to cast a long shadow over his life.

3. Thirdly, we have a fascinating reminiscence of Mrs. Lovecraft over a period of perhaps twenty-five years' acquaintance by Clara G. Hess, her erstwhile neighbor on the East Side of Providence, published in

the *Providence Sunday Journal* and reprinted with additions by August Derleth in his essay on "Lovecraft's Sensitivity."

4. Finally, we have a few, but nevertheless remarkable, statements from Sonia H. Davis's correspondence with August Derleth published in the *Arkham Collector,* along with her own more formal memoir, "Lovecraft as I Knew Him."

There is probably no better method to commence a discussion of Susie Lovecraft than to summarize these important sources.

Winfield Townley Scott had several sources for the portrait he painted of Susie Lovecraft in "His Own Most Fantastic Creation." In addition, it was through his book column in the *Providence Sunday Journal* that Clara Hess left her exceedingly important recollection of Mrs. Lovecraft.

Among Scott's sources was family lawyer Albert A. Baker, who served as guardian for both Winfield Lovecraft (1893–98) and H. P. Lovecraft (1899–1911). Since the only survivor of Lovecraft's immediate family was his mother and since his maternal grandfather was nearly seventy years old, it was no doubt considered appropriate that Lovecraft should have a legal guardian after his father expired. Clarke Johnston (1833–1917) had served as Whipple Phillips's attorney for years, but Phillips undoubtedly preferred Baker, as the younger man, for this important charge. One wonders whether Baker was the "family friend" who described Winfield as "a pompous Englishman." In any case, as is the way with many successful legal practitioners, Baker left us with a succinct description of Susie Lovecraft recorded by Scott: "a weak sister."[17]

Scott's most important source, however, was undoubtedly Susie's file at Butler Hospital, to which he obtained access.[18] One of Susie's psychiatrists at Butler was Dr. F. J. Farnell, who described her thus: "A woman of narrow interests who received, with traumatic psychosis, an awareness of approaching bankruptcy."[19] According to Scott, there was only a mention of the death of Winfield Lovecraft in Susie's file, but her psychiatrist remarked mental disorder of fifteen years' duration and mental abnormality of twenty-six years' duration at the time of her admission to the hospital.[20]

Measured from her admission date of 13 March 1919, Susie's psychiatrist established the commencement of her disorder from the death of her father and the loss of her home in the spring of 1904 and the commencement of abnormality from the admission of her husband to Butler Hospital in the spring of 1893. The correspondence of the commencement of Susie's abnormality and disorder with these major traumas in her life can be no coincidence, as Scott properly notes.

On interview, Susie stressed her economic worries and spoke of everything she had done for her son, "a poet of the highest order."[21] Her psychiatrist noted the existence of a "psycho-sexual contact" with her son, but, observing that such an Oedipal relationship generally has more impact upon the son than upon the mother, left the subject.[22] Scott summarized his own evaluation of Susie in the following words: "She suffered periods of mental and physical exhaustion. She wept a good deal under stress. In common phrase, she was a woman who had 'gone to pieces.'"[23]

According to the sources whom Scott interviewed, Lovecraft himself never entered the hospital buildings to visit his mother. Instead, when weather permitted, he would meet her on the hospital grounds, usually at the "grotto," and walk with her along the wooded bluffs overlooking the Seekonk River. Scott maintains that Susie spoke "constantly and pridefully" of her son to her fellow patients, but they never saw him.

The hospital record appears to confirm that Lovecraft never visited his mother in her final illness; the record shows only her elder sister Mrs. Clark as a visitor.[24] However, it should be noted that the death of Mrs. Lovecraft on 24 May 1921 was unexpected. She had had surgery for the removal of her gall bladder on 18 May, and the surgery was believed to be successful. However, when she began to fail on 23 May, her nurse noted that she expressed a wish to die, saying that "I will only live to suffer." She expired the next day.[25]

Scott notes astutely that Winfield's early illness and death threw Lovecraft into an unduly close and overly protective relationship with his mother. He also relates the famous anecdote of Mrs. Lovecraft accompanying her son with her hand on his shoulder as he rode his tricycle down Angell Street.[26] Even so biased an observer as Lovecraft's elder aunt Lillian Clark expressed a fear to W. Paul Cook, after the death of Mrs. Lovecraft, that they had coddled Howard to his own detriment.[27]

Scott presents a portrait of a woman driven by a compelling fear of bankruptcy and a love-hate relationship with her son, so gifted yet so helpless to relieve her financial concerns. Both she and her young son spent many years under the shadow cast by the early illness and death of Winfield Lovecraft. Lovecraft speaks of his mother as being permanently stricken by grief on account of the illness and death of her husband, whereas normal grief would resolve itself within six to twelve months after the loss. Scott's portrait of Lovecraft's mother is a powerful and revealing one, informed both by hospital records and by first-hand recollection. It is unlikely to be supplanted in the future.

While Scott's description of Susie Lovecraft's medical records enables us to pinpoint the most significant events in her mental decline, her son's letters provide enriching detail that can help us understand her better. With the publication of Lovecraft's *Selected Letters*, a fuller portrait of Lovecraft's mother, in the author's own words, than was available to Scott has emerged. Even when a perceived need to express conventional sentiments is factored in, there is no doubt that Lovecraft felt real love for his mother and real grief at her passing.

Lovecraft's descriptions of his mother contain elements of great interest. Writing to Anne Tillery Renshaw on 1 June 1921, soon after the shock of his mother's death, Lovecraft stated:

> My mother was, in all probability, the only person who thoroughly understood me, with the possible exception of Alfred Galpin. She was a person of unusual charm and force of character, accomplished in literature and the fine arts; a French scholar, musician, and painter in oils. I shall not again be likely to meet with a mind so thoroughly admirable. (*SL* 1.134)

In the same letter, he discussed his mother's lack of conventional religious belief and her desire for death:

> The result is the cause of wide and profound sorrow, although to my mother it was only a relief from nervous suffering. For two years she had wished for little else—just as I myself wish for oblivion. Like me, she was an agnostic with no belief in immortality, and wished for death all the more because it meant peace and not an eternity of boresome consciousness. (*SL* 1.133)

Writing to Winifred Virginia Jackson on 7 June 1921, Lovecraft commented upon his mother's unfavorable view of amateur journalism:

> Of amateurdom in general her opinion was not high, for she had a certain aesthetic hypersensitiveness which made its crudeness very obvious and very annoying to her—in fact, she was rather ashamed of my complete absorption in an institution having so many mediocre phases. (*SL* 1.138)

This revelation demonstrates that there was undoubtedly tension between mother and son, not only over Howard's economic uselessness but also over his amateur journalism associations. W. Paul Cook's famous anecdote of his first visit to Lovecraft brings this out vividly.[28] Almost turned away from the door of 598 Angell Street by Mrs. Lovecraft and Mrs. Clark, who protested that Howard had just retired after working through the night, Cook was saved from summary dismissal only by Lovecraft himself, who appeared in his bathrobe and instructed that Cook be admitted. While Lovecraft regaled Cook with his erudite conversation, his mother and aunt popped into his study every few minutes to make sure that Howard had not fainted or shown any signs of undue strain. It is a tribute to Cook's liberal mind and capacity for friendship that he deigned to make Lovecraft one of his fastest friends after such an initial visit. Lovecraft even became involved in the affairs of a local Providence amateur club, consisting mainly of evening high school students, where he met Victor Basinet and John T. Dunn.

In fairness to Mrs. Lovecraft, Rheinhart Kleiner has preserved a more favorable recollection of his own reception at 598 Angell Street.[29] Along with New York City amateurs en route to the national amateur convention in Boston, Kleiner first met Lovecraft, briefly, when he transferred from boat to train in Providence in 1916. However, he returned to Providence in 1917 for the specific purpose of spending several days with Lovecraft. Kleiner recorded that he was greeted at the door by Mrs. Lovecraft, whom he described as "just a little below medium height, with graying hair, and eyes which seemed to be the chief point of resemblance between herself and her son." In contrast to the chilly reception Paul Cook received the same year, Mrs. Lovecraft was "very cordial and even vivacious" with Kleiner and ushered him directly into her son's study.

Kleiner found the small, cramped study lined with books on three sides. Reflecting the occupant's political views, pictures of Robert E. Lee and Jefferson Davis decorated the walls. A copy of the latest *Farmer's Almanac* hung from the wall near Lovecraft's desk. Echoing the same visitations recorded in Cook's memoir, Kleiner remembered: "Every hour or so his mother appeared in the doorway with a glass of milk, and Lovecraft forthwith drank it." Just before suggesting that they take a walk, Kleiner drew his pipe out of his jacket, and while he immediately thought better of his action, Mrs. Lovecraft, looking in at the door, spied the pipe before he could completely conceal it. Far from reprimanding him, she immediately expressed a wish that Kleiner would convince her son to take up pipe-smoking, since it would be "so soothing for him."

Liberated from the stuffy confines of Lovecraft's study at last, Kleiner and Lovecraft toured the historic sections of the city and ended up downtown, where at Kleiner's request they stopped at a cheap restaurant for coffee and cake. Lovecraft had only milk. It seemed quite apparent to Kleiner that his host was not accustomed to take his meals elsewhere than under the roof of 598 Angell Street. While Kleiner received a far more favorable initial reception than Cook, the extent to which Lovecraft was then living under the thumb of his mother is equally evident in the memoirs of two of his oldest amateur friends.

Until 1919, Lovecraft met in person only those amateurs who made a pilgrimage to his residence at 598 Angell Street in Providence, beginning with William B. Stoddard in 1914 (*SL* 1.152). Following his mother's hospitalization in March 1919, however, he began to make day-trips to amateur meetings in Boston. On one notable occasion in late 1919, he attended a lecture by his literary mentor Lord Dunsany at the Copley Plaza Hotel in Boston.[30] By 1920, he was making overnight trips to accept the hospitality of Boston amateurs, and by 1922 he had ranged as far as New York City and Cleveland in pursuit of amateur fellowship.

If any of the immediate Lovecraft family suffered from lack of opportunity to meet the opposite sex in appropriate social settings, it was surely Susie's son Howard. According to R. Alain Everts, Lovecraft once confided to his wife that his sexual feelings were at their height when he was eighteen or nineteen years of age, a period when he was hermetically sealed within the confines of 598 Angell Street.[31] One wonders whether a sexual problem or other adolescent adjustment disorder may have been a contributory cause of the "breakdown" of 1908–09, which forced Lovecraft's withdrawal from school and the abandonment of college plans. Lovecraft's isolation would not have fostered healthy social relationships with members of the opposite sex, even East Side girls whom Susie might have considered suitable wives for Howard.

During most of his life, Lovecraft was more at ease among fellow males than among females. He very probably had at most two or three romantic involvements during his entire lifetime; after the period of his marriage, his relationships with younger women like Helen V. Sully, Eunice French, Catherine L. Moore, and Margaret Sylvester were purely avuncular.

Indeed, George T. Wetzel and R. Alain Everts believe that Winifred Virginia Jackson (1876–1959), formerly Mrs. Jordan, was Lovecraft's first serious romance prior to the development of his relationship with Sonia Greene in 1921–24.[32] That Jackson had not faded entirely from Lovecraft's eye by mid-1921 can be detected from this remarkable passage in his letter to her dated 7 June 1921:

> In case it would interest you to know my mother's appearance during these latter days, I enclose a snap-shot—inadequate enough, I regret to say—which I took a year ago last autumn [i.e., fall 1919]. Her appearance was as handsome as mine is homely, and her youthful pictures could form close rivals to your own in a contest for aesthetic supremacy. Her beauty was of the opposite type—a very fair complexion, but dark eyes and dark brown hair before it became grey. Some of her portraits have, in truth, been mistaken for art studies. (*SL* 1.138)

Written but two weeks after the loss of his mother, during a period of real grief, this letter nevertheless strongly projects Lovecraft's healthy attraction for Jackson, who, like his wife Sonia Greene, was considerably older than he. What Jackson thought of a man who sent her a snapshot of his mother along with praises of her own beauty, history has not recorded; Sonia Greene eventually won Lovecraft's hand. However, this intimate passage alone is sufficient rebuttal to those who believe that Lovecraft was a "touch-me-not" uninterested in the opposite sex.

While Lovecraft was demonstrative of affection in public only with his mother and his aunts, and then only with verbal expressions of his love, he quite evidently had a strong attraction to the opposite sex in the persons of Winifred Jackson and Sonia Greene.[33] One senses strongly from his letter to Miss Jackson of 7 June 1921 that he would have welcomed her embraces in his time of loss. His wife recorded that he was "an adequately excellent lover,"[34] a singular tribute coming from a woman who believed that he had divorced her. These authentic recollections should permanently dispel the idea that Lovecraft was not attracted to women or was impotent in the wake of the long years spent in his mother's shadow.

Once she became a widow, Susie apparently began to manifest at least a façade of pride in her deceased husband. After all, her sisters had not fared so much better than she in marriage. The flighty Annie (1866–1941) had married Edward F. Gamwell (1869–1936) on 3 July 1897, a union from which resulted Lovecraft's cousins Phillips Gamwell (1898–1916), who died in Roswell, Colorado, of tuberculosis on the last day of 1916, and Marion Roby Gamwell, who lived only five days after her birth in February 1900. But Mr. and Mrs. Gamwell separated soon after the beginning of the century, although apparently they were never divorced. Elder sister Lillie (1856–1932), the schoolteacher, finally found a loving husband in Dr. Franklin C. Clark, M.D. (1847–1915), on 10 April 1902, too late to found a family of her own.

Susie, by contrast, had a fine son and the honorable estate of a widow with a home, albeit a humble one, of her own. She even allowed Howard to correspond in 1905 with his great-aunt Sarah Allgood (d. 1908), the sister of Helen Allgood Lovecraft, concerning his paternal ancestors (*SL* 2.179). It never hurt to keep up some connection. When Lovecraft's aunt Mary Louise Lovecraft Mellon (1855–1916) died, she left her nephew an inheritance of $2,000.[35]

Whipple Phillips traveled twice to Europe to promote his business interests. He attended the Paris Exposition in 1878 and spent about a year on the Continent afterward, traveling extensively in Italy. In 1880 he went to London and Liverpool for an extended business trip.[36] He brought back from his travels, particularly those in Italy, paintings and statuary which were used to decorate the spacious home he built at the corner of Angell Street and Elmgrove Avenue in 1881. By the early 1880s he was acquiring water rights in the Snake River valley in Idaho, where his Owyhee Land and Irrigation Company was active from the mid-1880s until the first years of the new century.

Phillips expended much energy in the pursuit of his business endeavors in the far west, making numerous trips to the region between 1883 and 1899. He wrote his young grandson many letters whilst on his business travels in Idaho; one such letter, donated by Mr. Robb Baker, is preserved in the Lovecraft Collection in the Brown University Library.[37] But on 5 March 1890, some months before Howard's birth, the Owyhee Land and Irrigation Company suffered a major loss in the washing away of the dam it had built on the Bruneau River (a tributary of the Snake River) in 1886–87. The company rebuilt the dam, completing it in 1893, but never really recovered from the setback.[38]

All during the 1890s, young Howard noticed the cutbacks in the domestic establishment at 454 Angell Street. Sometime after 1895, the carriage and coachman were disposed of, leaving young Howard in possession of the stable and its loft for his juvenile games. The domestic staff was reduced to just one servant by the time the federal census was taken in 1900.

Nevertheless, Howard enjoyed a privileged childhood, and life's wonders and pleasures continued virtually unabated until the death of his maternal grandfather in 1904. In 1894–95, the family coachman, then still employed, built for Howard a playhouse on the adjoining lot. Within several years, the young boy had developed the playhouse and its lot into a complex playground containing the fort of "New Anvik," where he directed the military operations of his neighborhood playmates, and gardens he designed himself. Even after the forced removal to 598 Angell Street, a second "New Anvik" was built in the vacant lot next door. Only the year 1907, which also marked the discontinuation of Lovecraft's attendance at Hope Street High School, saw the end of New Anvik. Writing in 1920, Lovecraft remarked sadly: "Big boys do not play in toy houses and mock gardens, so I was obliged to turn over my world in sorrow to another and younger boy who dwelt across the lot from me" (*SL* 1.104).

In truth, Lovecraft was also loath to relinquish the reminders of his happy childhood in the home of his grandparents, and his letters are full of recollections of the furnishings of 454 Angell Street, his boyhood interests and games, and his pet cat Nigger-Man. He continued his hectographed juvenile publications—of which the John Hay Library retains a remarkable file—with some regularity until the time he abandoned New Anvik.

Lovecraft's mother and aunts continued to indulge each new interest during his boyhood. When he fell in love with the *Arabian Nights* in 1895, he was soon possessed of an elaborate Oriental set-up, which he described to Robert E. Howard:

> Then again—how many young dream-Arabs have the *Arabian Nights* bred? I ought to know, since at the age of 5 I was one of them! I had not then encountered Graeco-Roman myth, but found in Lang's *Arabian Nights* a gateway to glittering vistas of wonder and freedom. It was then that I invented for myself the name of Abdul Alhazred, and made my mother take me to all the Oriental curio shops and fit me up an Arabian corner in my room. (*SL* 4.8)

The copy of the *Arabian Nights* in his library was given to him by his mother on Christmas Day, 1898.[39] When Lovecraft became interested in science later in the decade, he was soon provided with his own chemical laboratory (1899), and later his own telescope (1903) when his interests shifted to astronomy. While the staff of domestics maintained by the Phillips family at 454 Angell Street decreased between 1890 and 1900 from four full-time employees to one, reduced financial circumstances were hardly a very stark reality for Howard or for his mother.

The death of Whipple Phillips of a cerebral hemorrhage on 28 March 1904 at the age of seventy changed everything. Only a few weeks before, spring floods had washed out the irrigation canal which he and other investors in the former Owhyee Land and Irrigation Company had purchased when the assets of the company were sold at sheriff's sale in 1901. Now his investments were sold, when he himself would have wished to persevere. Many of the crucial financial decisions during this period were doubtless made by Whipple's son Edwin Everett Phillips (1864–1918), who was again associated with his father in business at the time of Whipple's death.

Edwin had been hotel manager at Grand View, the western headquarters of the Owyhee Land and Irrigation Company, in 1886–87, but thereafter returned to Providence. On 30 July 1894 he married Martha Helen Mathews (1868–1916). In 1896 or 1897, he seems to have quarreled both with his wife and with his father. His business connection with his father's offices at 5 Custom House Street was broken, and between 1897 and 1902 he is listed in the directories as a boarder, rather than a householder. However, on 23 March 1903 he remarried Martha, and beginning in 1903 the Providence directory reflects a renewed association with his father's firm. Nevertheless, Whipple's will, drafted in 1903, left a lesser share of the estate to his son Edwin E. Phillips than to any of his three surviving daughters. The entire estate of Whipple Phillips may have amounted to less than $25,000, which left the family, including his widowed daughter and her son, a very modest capital to live upon.

At the time of the death of Whipple Phillips, only Howard and his mother were living with his grandfather in the large home at the corner of Angell Street and Elmgrove Avenue. These spacious quarters could hardly be maintained on their inheritances, especially with no prospect of income other than investment return upon capital for the foreseeable future. The family home was quickly sold, to the distress of both mother and son. They moved several blocks eastward to a cramped flat at 598 Angell Street, where Lovecraft remained until he married in March 1924. Susie's brother Edwin appears to have continued to remain involved in his sister's financial affairs; perhaps she would have prospered more had she entrusted these duties to Clarke Johnston or Albert A. Baker.

While Lovecraft himself was not forced to make any personal economies, mainly in the form of restraint in book-buying, until 1915 or so, he could perceive a steady economic decline from 1904 forward as he and his mother inexorably diminished their capital as their expenditures exceeded the income from their investments. In his letter to Maurice W. Moe dated 5 April 1931, Lovecraft remarked of "several sharp jogs downward, as when an uncle lost a lot of dough for my mother and me in 1911" (*SL* 3.367).

The likelihood that the uncle was Edwin seems very strong. Edwin never attained anything like the success and prosperity of his father or his father's first cousin Theodore Winthrop Phillips. In later years, he seems to have earned his living primarily as a real estate agent and rent collector. For a single year, in 1910, he is listed as manager of the Providence office of the Brunswick Refrigerating Company; thereafter, he returned to his own business. He must have suffered reverses during this period, too, because in 1912 he and his wife removed from the fashionable, and expensive, East Side.

Just what investment by Edwin cost Susie and her son a considerable sum of money, we do not know. Whether Edwin remained involved with his sister's finances after this reverse is also not known. Edwin's wife Martha died on 9 February 1916 of pneumonia, leaving no children, and Edwin himself died of tuberculosis on 14 November 1918, aged fifty-four.

It has not been commonly noted, but Sarah Susan's sharp decline, which ended in her hospitalization, seems to have begun at about the time of Edwin's death, which would have deprived her of the counsel of the last surviving male member of the family apart from her own son. Dr. Clark had died in 1915, and young Phillips Gamwell in 1916. Annie and her husband Edward F. Gamwell were probably separated by that time. From the death of Edwin E. Phillips in

1918, the surviving Phillips sisters—Lillie, Susie, and Annie—were very much on their own. This can only have intensified Susie's financial worries, as she continued to see her own and her son's capital diminished with no prospect of an income to supplement it.

Inadequate notice has been given to the effect upon Susie's mental health of her son's attempted enlistment in the Rhode Island National Guard in 1917, following the entrance of the United States into World War I. Petrified by the news of her son's enlistment, Susie apparently just barely succeeded in having the enlistment revoked on account of his medical condition (he had passed the physical examination). Lovecraft wrote to Rheinhart Kleiner on 23 May 1917:

> The sensation created at home was far from slight. In fact, my mother was almost prostrated with the news. . . . Her activities soon brought my military career to a close. . . . My mother has threatened to go to any lengths, legal or otherwise, if I do not reveal all the ills which unfit me for the army. If I had realised to the full how much she would suffer through my enlistment, I should have been less eager to attempt it; but being of no use to myself it was hard for me to believe I am of use to anyone else. Still, I might have known that mothers are always solicitous for their offspring, no matter how worthless said offspring may happen to be! (*SL* 1.46)

In letters written following his mother's death, Lovecraft stressed the understanding and intellectual communion between himself and his mother; but there is no doubt that his attempted enlistment in 1917 represented a major crisis in their relationship. Grown accustomed to financial worries and worries about her "useless" son, Susie was suddenly confronted with the fear of losing the only progeny of her unhappy marriage in the war. She reacted with panic and shock. Lovecraft wrote of the aftermath to Kleiner on 22 June 1917: "I am feeling desolate and lonely indeed as a civilian. . . . I would try to enter, were it not for the almost frantic attitude of my mother; who makes me promise every time I leave the house that I will not make another attempt at enlistment!" (*SL* 1.48). Perhaps Sarah Lovecraft received her son's attempt at enlistment as a breach of faith on the part of the exemplary young man for whom she had done so much, a betrayal comparable to that committed by her long-dead husband.

By the first weeks of 1919, Susie's mental decline was accelerating. Lovecraft wrote to Kleiner on 18 January 1919 that his mother had gone to the home of his elder aunt Mrs. Clark "for a complete rest" (*SL* 1.78). She had been suffering from stomach trouble, diagnosed as nervous in origin. Considering that she died from complications resulting from inflammation of her gall bladder and bile duct, one wonders whether in fact her mental distress in early 1919 may have derived at least partially from an actual physical ailment.

The situation did not resolve itself. Susie was unable to return home and was admitted to Butler Hospital on 13 March, never to emerge. For Howard, what seemed at first a tragedy became in fact a blessing, resulting in a far wider view upon the world than had been the case during the long years from 1904 to 1919 he spent with his mother at 598 Angell Street. When he began attending amateur meetings in Boston in 1919 following his mother's hospitalization, he had last been in Boston proper in 1916 and in Cambridge in 1910. One is very skeptical that his romances with Winifred Jackson and Sonia Greene could have occurred under his mother's watch.

In truth, Susie's hospitalization many have saved the very sanity of her son. Especially in light of the recollections of Clara G. Hess and of Sonia H. Davis, which we shall review shortly, one wonders whether Lovecraft himself would have escaped spending his final days at Butler Hospital, or worse, a state institution for the mentally ill, if he had had to spend another decade with his mother within the confines of 598 Angell Street. It is virtually inconceivable that he would have married or even have begun traveling widely had his mother survived. Had she died at home in 1931, rather than in the hospital in 1921, the position of her forty-one-year-old son would have been difficult to imagine. The New York experience both toughened and humanized Lovecraft, and enabled him to live out the remainder of his life on his own terms. Had he been left alone in Providence with only a few thousands or hundreds of dollars following the death of his mother a decade later, he would probably have been fortunate indeed to end his life at Butler Hospital!

Perhaps the most remarkable portrait of Mrs. Lovecraft that has come to us is that painted by Clara Hess, who was her neighbor on the East Side of Providence for many years. Hess, then living in Warwick Neck, Rhode Island, came into correspondence with August Derleth after responding to one of Scott's columns discussing Lovecraft and his work in the *Providence Sunday Journal*. Derleth abstracted Hess's recollections in his essay on "Lovecraft's Sensitivity" in *Something about Cats* (1949). Apart from Scott's landmark biographical work in "His Own Most Fantastic Creation," published before he came into contact with Hess, and Lovecraft's letters, Hess's perceptive and insightful recollections, which have the unique ring of foundation in actual life experience, are the most remarkable portrait of Mrs. Lovecraft that we possess. They are thus worthy of quotation in their entirety. The following appeared in the *Providence Sunday Journal* for 19 September 1948:

Howard Lovecraft and I grew up in the same "old time" East Side neighborhood in Providence when there were open fields covered with buttercups and daisies in the Butler Avenue—Angell Street—Orchard Avenue area. Although of a younger generation, I knew Howard's mother better than I knew Howard who even as a young boy was strange and rather a recluse, who kept by himself and hid from other children because, as his mother said, he could not bear to have people look upon his awful face. She would talk of his looks (it seemed to be an obsession with her) which would not have attracted any particular attention if he had been normal as were the other children in the community. They, because of the strangeness of his personality, kept aloof and had little to say to him.

I first remember meeting Mrs. Lovecraft when I was a very little girl at the home of the late Mr. and Mrs. Theodore Phillips on Angell Street where I visited often. At that time Mrs. Lovecraft was living on the corner of Angell Street and Elmgrove Avenue. She was very pretty and attractive, with a beautiful and unusually white complexion—got, it was said, by eating arsenic, although whether there was any truth to this story I do not know. She was an intensely nervous person.

Later when she moved into the little downstairs flat in the house on Angell Street around the corner from Butler Avenue I met her often on the Butler Avenue cars, and one day after many urgent invitations I went in to call upon her. She was considered then to be getting rather odd. My call was pleasant enough but the house had a strange and shutup air and the atmosphere seemed weird and Mrs. Lovecraft talked continuously of her unfortunate son who was so hideous that he hid from everyone and did not like to walk upon the streets where people could gaze at him.

When I protested that she was exaggerating and that he should not feel that way, she looked at me with a rather pitiful look as though I did not understand about it. I remember that I was glad to get out into the fresh air and sunshine and that I did not repeat my visit! Surely it was an environment suited for the writing of horror stories but an unfortunate one for a growing youth who in a more wholesome environment might have grown to be a more normal citizen.

Howard used to go out into the fields in back of my home to study the stars. One early fall evening several of the children in the vicinity assembled to watch him from a distance. Feeling sorry for his loneliness I went up to him and asked him about his telescope and was permitted to look through it. But his language was so technical that I could not understand it and I returned to my group and left him to his lonely study of the heavens.

After a time one did not meet Mrs. Lovecraft very often. . . . Sometimes when going around the corner to mail a letter on an early summer evening, one would see a dark figure fluttering about the shrubbery of her home, and I discovered that it was Mrs. Lovecraft.

Sometimes I would see Howard when walking up Angell Street, but he would not speak and would stare ahead with his coat collar turned up and his chin down. After awhile I heard Mrs. Lovecraft was ill and was away and that the aunts had taken over. I knew nothing more about them until I heard of Howard's marriage which was wondered at by some of those who had known him.

Derleth apparently came in to contact with Hess after reading the above, and he must have asked her additional questions regarding Lovecraft and his mother; Derleth printed Hess's reply in "Lovecraft's Sensitivity":

I do not know that Mrs. Lovecraft ever spoke to her son directly about his "ugliness," but I think he must have known how she regarded him. Howard resembled his mother. She had a peculiarly shaped nose which rather fascinated me, as it gave her a very inquiring expression. Howard looked very much like her.

In looking back, I cannot ever remember to have seen Mrs. Lovecraft and her son together. I never heard one speak to the other. It probably just happened that way, but it does seem rather strange, as we were neighbors for a considerable period of time. I remember the aunts who came to the little house on Angell Street often, as I recollect, quiet, determined little New England women, quite different from Mrs. Lovecraft, although Mrs. Lovecraft was a very determined person herself. I remember that Mrs. Lovecraft spoke to me about weird and fantastic creatures that rushed out from behind buildings and from corners at dark, and that she shivered and looked about apprehensively as she told her story.

The last time I saw Mrs. Lovecraft we were both going "down street" on the Butler Avenue car. She was excited and apparently did not know where she was. She attracted the attention of everyone. I was greatly embarrassed, as I was the object of all her attention. . . . Howard's people were old fashioned gentlefolk, which meant considerable in the old aristocratic Providence East Side neighborhood prior to World War I. He himself had a cultural background and was a real student and a great reader.[40]

The recollections of Lovecraft's wife Sonia H. Davis do not tell us quite as much about Mrs. Lovecraft and her relationship with her son as do Hess's remarkable recollections, which, next to Scott's biographical research, probably constitute the fullest portrait of Susie Lovecraft that we have or are likely to have in the future. Nevertheless, Sonia's recollections add in several ways to our knowledge of Lovecraft's mother and her relationship with her son, because of Sonia's intimate involvement with her son in marriage.

Probably the starkest recorded memories of Sonia Davis occur not in her formal memoir of her husband, but in correspondence to August Derleth from which Derleth selected extracts and published them as "Memories of Lovecraft" in the *Arkham Collector*. Her most cogent memories were these:

> H. P. used to speak of his mother as a "touch-me-not" and once—but only once—he confessed to me that his mother's attitude toward him was "devastating". . . . In my opinion, the older Lovecraft, having been a travelling salesman for the Gorham Silversmiths, and his wife being a "touch-me-not", took his sexual pleasures wherever he could find them; for H. P. never had a sister or a brother, and his mother, probably having been sex-starved against her will, lavished both her love and hate on her only child. . . .
>
> H. P. was inarticulate in his expressions of love, except to his mother and to his aunts, to whom he expressed himself quite vigorously; to all others it was expressed by deep appreciation only. . . . As a married man he was an adequately excellent lover, but refused to show his feelings in the presence of others. He shunned promiscuous association with women before his marriage. . . .
>
> If H. P. L. could not be described as facially handsome, he had an interesting atmosphere about him that attracted people, making them curious to admiration. Unfortunately, he was conditioned by his poor demented mother to believe himself badlooking.[41]

Sonia's comments in her more formal memoir are less telling, but nevertheless several of them are interesting. Writing in "Lovecraft as I Knew Him," she stated:

> Howard's mother had hoped her child would be a girl, and as a baby he looked like a beautiful little girl. A photograph shows him with a mass of flaxen curls until he was about six. When at last he protested, his mother took him to the barber's where she cried bitterly as he was shorn. (These curls were kept: Howard once showed them to me.)[42]

In the same memoir, Sonia made note of Lovecraft's adult query: "How can any woman love a face like mine?" He attributed his plain looks, Sonia explained, to a broken nose suffered in a bicycle accident at fifteen or sixteen and his slightly stooped posture to many years of craning his neck to gaze at the stars through his telescope. Sonia concluded her recollections of her husband's looks as follows:

> Actually, he resembled his mother very much. Though less pronounced in the womenfolk, the entire Phillips family had the prognathous jaw and the ex-

tremely short upper lip. Howard was fond of making caricatures of himself as he would appear when he became old.[43]

While the cancer that killed him at age forty-six never allowed the world to test the accuracy of Grandpa Theobald's self-caricatures, the moving recollections of Clara Hess and Sonia Davis do allow us to form some additional conclusions about Sarah Lovecraft and her relationship with her son. Looking at Lovecraft's handsome amateur portrait of 1915, it is clear that there was a definite pathological process present within the mind of a mother who could find such a son "hideous" and worthy of being hidden from the world. Both Clara Hess and Sonia Davis, commenting from the very different perspectives of former neighbor and daughter-in-law, comment upon the injustice of Mrs. Lovecraft's opinions concerning the appearance of her son and the cross her son had to bear because of the opinions his mother ingrained in his psyche.

All the evidence seems to point toward the likelihood that Susie came to learn of the nature of her husband's illness. That she transferred the fear and loathing caused by the illness of her husband onto her innocent young son seems indubitable. Throughout his adult life, Lovecraft suffered from the minor ailment of ingrown facial hair.[44] Perhaps he considered this disfiguring. When he first experienced the problem as an adolescent, however, his mother's expressed attitude concerning his appearance must have been "devastating." One tends to believe that Lovecraft's own "breakdown" of 1908–09 centered on unresolved adolescent adjustments, compounded by his mother's pathological transference of her fear and loathing of her husband's illness onto her son.

It is nevertheless easy to be much too harsh with Sarah Susan Lovecraft. One does not doubt the accounts of Clara Hess and Sonia Davis, but it is clear that H. P. Lovecraft felt genuine grief at the death of his mother. If indeed he had not visited his mother since the autumn preceding her death, he was probably wracked by tremendous spasms of guilt and loss when the immediate shock of her death and funeral wore off within a few days. Also, we cannot doubt that Lovecraft *did* benefit from his close association with his mother in a number of ways. Lovecraft's finely honed aesthetic sensibilities and seasoned artistic judgment undoubtedly owed something to the early influence of his mother. (One wonders, indeed, how Lovecraft would have grown up had his "pompous Englishman" of a father survived to be a living influence.) The wonderful home that Susie and Howard shared with her parents and sisters at 454 Angell Street during the 1890s must have been truly a delight (one regrets very much the lack of photographs of the interior of the Phillips mansion in its heyday), and there is no reason to doubt Lovecraft's assertions that his child-hood, until 1904, was very happy, if somewhat lonely.

While Whipple Phillips took time out from his business affairs for his young grandson, it must have been Susie who read most to him and provided the necessary stimulation for his precocious mind. How wonderful were Love-craft's discoveries of the vast realms of literature—the *Arabian Nights*, Greek and Roman myths, Poe, Verne, and so much else—and doubtless Susie, with her literary tastes, played a strong role in forming her son's predilections.

While his mother yet lived Lovecraft had no especial motivation to praise her to his correspondents, but he wrote to Kleiner on 6 November 1916: "My mother is a landscape painter of no little skill, while my eldest aunt is still more expert in this direction, having had canvases hung in exhibitions at the Provi-dence Art Club" (*SL* 1.29). Lovecraft treasured his memories of his mother's aesthetic tastes and culture. He recorded proudly in correspondence that she was a graduate of Wheaton Seminary in Norton, Massachusetts. Correspon-dence with officials of Wheaton College in 1972 revealed that Lillie and Susie were both enrolled in the preparatory course for the 1871–72 school year, studying instrumental music in addition to arithmetic, grammar, and geogra-phy. Lillie alone was listed as a member of the junior class (and a pupil in Latin) for the 1872–73 school year).[45] Lillie subsequently graduated from the Rhode Island State Normal School and became a schoolteacher, whereas Susie, insofar as is known, never had an occupation outside the home.

With the assistance of her parents and her sisters, Susie gave her gifted son a fine formation and cultural background. She also managed to preserve for the boy an idealized image of his English father that was emotionally important to him throughout his life, despite any objective questioning that may have arisen in his mind. If the reader seeks for the origin of Lovecraft's meticulous atten-tion to dress and etiquette, despite his own humble circumstances, and of his lifelong Anglophilism, one need look no further than the image he preserved of his father. If in fact Lovecraft had a partial knowledge of the nature of his father's illness, he was nevertheless left with an honorable "turf" to defend, which he did all his life.

On the other side, however, we must also admit that Susie caused her son significant psychological harm. She must have perceived that Howard was lonely and isolated despite his brilliance. Yet she denied him normal social opportuni-ties by convincing him of his abnormality and even denied him normal physical closeness with herself. Through a particularly insidious blend of overprotective-ness and psychological distancing, Susie made an invalid of her son throughout his teens and his twenties, when in fact he could have enjoyed normal health and activity, as proved by his "miraculous" recovery during the 1920s.

In view of Susie's pathological attitudes and fixed false beliefs concerning her son's appearance, one is led to wonder whether Lovecraft had himself physically examined before undertaking marriage. Whether he did or not, he certainly made the wisest decision in breaking the links with 598 Angell Street and deciding to marry. Doubtless, several women wooed him during his period of intense social activity within amateur journalism (1919–24), and at last Sonia Greene won him, although not without competition from rivals like Winifred Jackson.

The period during which he consistently had marital relations with his wife was limited, for they lived together only a little over ten months before Sonia departed for a new job in Cincinnati, in addition to which Sonia spent some weeks during the autumn of 1924 in a New Jersey sanitarium recovering from a "nervous breakdown" of her own. Nevertheless, the physical success of Lovecraft's marriage may likely have exorcised many demons and false beliefs deriving from his 598 Angell Street years. Sonia Davis would have had no good reason to describe her husband as an "adequately excellent lover" had this not been the case; her sharing of her relationship with her husband with posterity, in fact, was remarkably generous, given the unfortunate end of the marriage.

That Lovecraft did not in the last analysis have the emotional flexibility, or the underlying desire, to work to make the marriage succeed needs certainly to be laid at least partially at the door of the pathological relationship between mother and son, which denied him many normal social experiences during his childhood (when he had few friends of his own age) and his young adulthood. Perhaps he would have failed had he accepted the offer of the editorship of a *Weird Tales*–type magazine from J. C. Henneberger in 1924, but at least it would have been a first editorial job on a résumé which could only reflect poorly paid revision work for David V. Bush and other clients. L. Sprague de Camp rightly perceived that editorial work held the possibility of steady employment and a more normal life for Lovecraft, but the author himself rejected probably his best opportunity to enter into such work.

Instead, he expended his considerable editorial and critical talents in unpaid labor for the amateur press associations. This endeavor forever endeared Lovecraft to a generation of amateurs who have now passed entirely from the scene, apart from a few teenagers active in science fiction fandom at the very end of Lovecraft's life now in their nineties. If he had been paid by the word, Lovecraft would have earned many thousands for his writings in amateur journals now accessible in only a few institutional collections.

Should not the offer of a well-paying editorial job in Chicago, with the prospect of continuing his life together with his wife, have attracted Lovecraft, faced with his bleak prospects in New York City? (Lovecraft's failure as sales agent for a collection agency specializing in the garment industry, as told by de Camp, is particularly pathetic.) Perhaps the odor of failure and the unfamiliar masses of New York City were already wearing him down and leading him to regret that he had ever left the asylum of 598 Angell Street. The parallels between his own married life and the failure of his parents' marriage surely must have haunted him. In the end, he sacrificed the embraces of his wife on account of his own fears and prejudices.

As W. Paul Cook perceived, Lovecraft's two years in New York City were a period of testing, a period he barely survived. When he returned to Providence, however, he was a man of broader perspective and greater wisdom. The primary pathological influence in his life had been removed for nearly five years by the time he returned to Providence on 17 April 1926. Restored to his hometown, he could fulfill a sense of family duty by providing protection and companionship for his aunts in their old age. He could spread his wings in travel and literary work, as he was never able to do under the dominance of his mother.

It is notable that while he retained his affiliation with amateur journalism and his amateur friends until the end of his life, amateur journalism occupied less and less of his time in his later years, enabling him to concentrate his energies on more important professional work. While the period 1926–37 was not without artistic frustration on account of self-criticism and rejections from *Weird Tales*, it was nevertheless definitely one of artistic growth for Lovecraft. With just a trifle more flexibility and commercial savvy, Lovecraft could very probably have published a novel with a trade publisher during his lifetime. Indeed, had Lovecraft been able to summon the energy to tackle the typing of the manuscript of *The Case of Charles Dexter Ward*, which remained in holograph during his lifetime, this effort alone might have secured him a professionally published novel, which could have served as the entrée to a more important collection of his shorter fiction.

Instead, Lovecraft devoted most of his efforts to poorly paid revision work and his own masterful essay "Supernatural Horror in Literature," which remains a critical landmark in its chosen field, although it never earned Lovecraft a penny in its initial publication in W. Paul Cook's *Recluse* (1927) or subsequent republications. He also expended inordinate amounts of time in correspondence with his friends.

Despite Lovecraft's failure to attain commercial success as a writer, the experience of his marriage taught him what was important to him in life and ingrained in him the toughness to be able to achieve it. While his final years in Providence were not easy ones, either artistically or financially, Lovecraft had emerged from his marriage a full-fledged adult, determined to live life on his own terms. De Camp and other observers would doubtless contend that he never succeeded in shedding many self-defeating habits from the hermitlike years at 598 Angell Street, but in truth there were many activities, including a generous personal correspondence and the donation of literary work to amateur journalism, which afforded him lifelong pleasure worth more to him than the income he could have been earning in more commercially rewarding activities.

Lovecraft emerged during these years to live much the life he wanted to lead. Although critical judgments as to Lovecraft's later literary work differ, any sober judgment would have to identify his last decade in Providence as the pinnacle of his personal and professional life. Had he died a suicide in New York City in 1925–26, he would doubtless be almost totally forgotten today, another chapter in the sad extinction of the Lovecraft line on the North American continent. Instead, he surmounted incredible obstacles to lead the kind of creative life he wanted to lead. He was no saint, and any objective observer must conclude that Sonia Davis invested far more, emotionally and materially, in their marriage than did her husband. But he overcame the long shadows cast by the mental illness of both parents to leave a lasting body of literary work that will continue to have meaning for thousands of readers for centuries.

Notes

1. I am indebted to Gary Sumpter of Burlington, Ontario for the identification of Winfield Lovecraft in the 1880 U.S. census.

2. Winfield Townley Scott, "His Own Most Fantastic Creation" (1944), *LR* 12.

3. L. Sprague de Camp, *Lovecraft: A Biography* (Garden City, NY: Doubleday, 1975), 14, 450. See Faig, *The Unknown Lovecraft* (New York: Hippocampus Press, 2009), 71.

4. Sonia H. Davis, "Lovecraft as I Knew Him" (1949), *LR* 255.

5. Rebuttal to David H. Keller's "Shadows over Lovecraft," *Fantasy Commentator* 3, No. 5 (Winter 1951–52): 153–54; rpt. *Fresco* 8, No. 3 (Spring 1958): 27–29.

6. Winfield Townley Scott, *Exiles and Fabrications* (Garden City, NY: Doubleday, 1961), 68.

7. Scott, "His Own Most Fantastic Creation," *LR* 23.

8. Leland E. Hinsie and Robert Jean Campbell, *Psychiatric Dictionary*, 4th ed. (New York: Oxford University Press, 1970), 546–47.

9. R. Alain Everts, "The Lovecraft Family in America," *Xenophile* 2, No. 6 (October 1975): 7.

10. A very rich history of the Lovecraft family in America by Richard D. Squires, *Stern Fathers 'neath the Mould: The Lovecraft Family in Rochester,* was published by Necronomicon Press in 1995.

11. de Camp, 15; Arthur S. Koki, "H. P. Lovecraft: An Introduction to His Life and Writings" (M.A. thesis: Columbia University, 1962), 9.

12. HPL, *Commonplace Book* (*CE* 5.229).

13. See frontispiece, *SL* 2.

14. Butler Hospital released the 1893–98 medical record of Winfield Lovecraft to Prof. John L. McInnis III in 1990. It was published in *Lovecraft Studies* 24 (Spring 1991) with commentary by M. Eileen McNamara, M.D. In fact, Winfield Lovecraft was quite vocal during some of the period of his hospitalization at Butler Hospital.

15. I am indebted to David E. Schultz for the following observations.

16. *Commonplace Book* (*CE* 2.229).

17. Scott, "His Own Most Fantastic Creation," *LR* 15.

18. Robert M. Price accomplished a similar coup in the 1980s by obtaining access to HPL's medical records at Rhode Island Hospital, which showed that he had a negative Wasserman test during his final illness in 1937. See Price's "Did Lovecraft Have Syphilis?," *CoC* No. 53 (Candelmas 1988): 25–26. According to my medical sources, a Wasserman test could produce a negative result during a dormant period of a syphilitic infection. Nevertheless, the possibility that HPL suffered from hereditary syphilis is regarded as remote.

19. Scott, "His Own Most Fantastic Creation," *LR* 15.

20. Ibid. (*LR* 16).

21. Ibid.

22. Ibid.

23. Ibid.

24. Ibid. A letter by HPL to his friend J. Vernon Shea dated 29 May 1933 supports the presumption that HPL never visited his mother in her room at Butler Hospital. Replying to Shea's inquiry regarding his exposure to various practical life experiences, HPL replied: "My only experience of a madhouse was last year, when my friend Brobst (a nurse in one) took me over an ideal institution of its kind. I was never in a hospital till 1924—but in that year & 1929 I had occasion to call on patients in a typical institution of the sort" (*SL* 4.191). Unless HPL was intentionally attempting to conceal from Shea the fact that his mother ended her days in a mental hospital, which seems little likely in view of the richness of biographical detail he provided in other letters to Shea, this statement appears to provide conclusive support of Scott's Butler Hospital anecdotes. (HPL's 1924 hospital visits would undoubtedly have been paid to his wife at the New Jersey sanitarium where she

recovered from her nervous breakdown that year. Whom he visited in the hospital in 1929, I do not know.)

25. Ibid. (*LR* 17).

26. Ibid. (*LR* 12).

27. W. Paul Cook, *In Memoriam: Howard Phillips Lovecraft* (1941), *LR* 113.

28. Ibid. (*LR* 110f.).

29. Rheinhart Kleiner, "A Memoir of Lovecraft" (1949), *LR* 195–97.

30. *SL* 1.91–93. HPL noted that his trip to hear Lord Dunsany lecture at the Copley Plaza Hotel, accompanied by Alice Hamlet, her aunt, and "young Lee," was his first trip to Boston since January 1916 and his first to Cambridge since 1910 (the latter probably representing a visit to his cousin Phillips Gamwell). It seems strange that HPL made no visits to the Boston metropolitan area between January 1916 and September 1919, particularly if Annie Gamwell was living in Cambridge during that period. This only shows how constricted HPL's life was while his mother was still living at 598 Angell Street. Until 1919, only the few amateur journalists who traveled to Providence or lived in Providence, like the members of the Providence Amateur Press Club of 1915–16, met HPL in person.

31. R. Alain Everts, "Howard Phillips Lovecraft and Sex; or, The Sex Life of a Gentleman," *Nyctalops* 2, No. 2 (July 1974): 19.

32. George T. Wetzel and R. Alain Everts, *Winifred Virginia Jackson—Lovecraft's Lost Romance* (Madison, Wis.: Strange Co., 1976).

33. Sonia H. Davis, "Memories of Lovecraft: I" (1969), *LR* 275–76.

34. Ibid. (*LR* 275).

35. de Camp, 156.

36. Obituary of Whipple V. Phillips, *Providence Journal* (31 March 1904).

37. Another such letter to HPL by Whipple Phillips from Grand View, Idaho, on 20 February 1899, was catalogued with a photograph of Phillips in *The Undead* (Orange, CA: The Book Sail, 1984), item 427. Yet another letter was in the possession of HPL's cousin, the late Ethel Phillips Morrish (1888–1987).

38. A much fuller account of the involvement of Whipple Phillips and of his son Edwin E. Phillips and of his nephew Jeremiah W. Phillips (1863–1902) in the Owyhee Land and Irrigation Company may be found in Kenneth W. Faig, Jr., "Whipple V. Phillips and the Owyhee Land and Irrigation Company," *Owyhee Outpost* (Owyhee County Historical Society) No. 19 (May 1988): 21–30; rpt. in *The Unknown Lovecraft* 50–55. The entire May 1988 issue of the *Owyhee Outpost* is devoted to the town of Grand View, Idaho, founded by Whipple Phillips. The issue also contains a photograph of the hotel built by the Owhyee Land and Irrigation Company in Grand View, later known as the Rowe Hotel & Store (burned 1920).

39. See S. T. Joshi and Marc A. Michaud, *Lovecraft's Library* rev. ed. (New York: Hippocampus Press, 2002), #38.

40. August Derleth, "Lovecraft's Sensitivity" (1949), *LR* 35.

41. Sonia H. Davis, "Memories of Lovecraft," *LR* 275–76.

42. Davis, "Lovecraft as I Knew Him," *LR* 255.

43. Ibid.

44. Sonia H. Davis, *The Private Life of H. P. Lovecraft* (West Warwick, RI: Necronomicon Press, 1985), 14.

45. Personal communication, Wheaton College Reference Librarian to author, 6 December 1972.

The Cosmic Yankee

Jason C. Eckhardt

One can say not only, "I love these waving grasses and towering elms and brook-threaded valleys and stone-wall'd farmsteads and white village steeples," but "these waving grasses and towering elms and brook-threaded valleys and stone-wall'd farmsteads and white village steeples *are ME, MYSELF, I, THE CONSCIOUS EGO*"! And what more can any guy ask than that? Isn't all art an effort of the artist to *identify himself* with the burning beauty and strangeness he depicts? Why, then, reject such identification as Nature provides? (*SL* 3.31)

The reader will grant that a person is largely a product of his or her environment. We are, indeed, "the Mortal Clay" in this regard, for we move through our lives accumulating marks and additions, scars and growths of all we experience. The self is constantly reshaped and molded by its surroundings. With the creative personality we are met with a paradox in this respect; for the artist must experience *and* stand back from that experience to depict it accurately and truthfully in his art. He must bring familiarity and objectivity to his work in equal proportions. A powerful example of this balance of the soul is the American writer Howard Phillips Lovecraft. He was a man born into the old society and landscape of New England, and anyone who has read much of his work will vouch for his love for the region as manifested in his stories. "How compleatly," he once wrote, "O Mater Novanglia, am I moulded of thy venerable flesh and as one with thy century'd soul!" (*SL* 1.205–6). This is unabashed and fervent love, but it wasn't blind, and it wasn't exclusive. Lovecraft recognized that objectivity was a necessary side of the artist, and wrote that he could "laugh at the piety, narrowness, and conventionality of the New England background which [he loved] so well and [found] so necessary to contentment" (*SL* 3.244). Lovecraft achieved this remove by his "cosmick" point of view, a product of a long interest in science and logic. He put it thus:

There are really two distinct personalities in me—the cosmick & fantastic on the one hand, & the historical, domestic, & antiquarian on the other hand. In my contacts with written literature the fantastic is paramount, but in all contacts with real life or the visible world the old-fashioned, soil-loving, conservative Yankee has full sway. Few persons have ever been as closely knit to New England's rock-ribbed hills as I. (*SL* 2.159)

What sort of place could breed this kind of devotion in a man of Lovecraft's wide reading and scientific realism? Over and over he regales the reader with the wonders of the region; from "hushed stony slopes and low ivied cottages in the lee of huge boulders in Rhode-Island's back country" (*MM* 401) to Maine's "fantastic and forbidding scenery" (*DH* 287). Geographically New England is six states: Vermont, New Hampshire, Maine, Massachusetts, Connecticut, and Rhode Island. Physically it is roughly 450 miles long by 325 miles wide; at 66,600 square miles, it is almost a third again as large as the country for which it was named. Nature herself drew many of its boundaries: to the east and south there is the gray expanse of the Atlantic Ocean; Lake Champlain and the Poultney River separate much of Vermont from upstate New York; the St. Croix and St. John rivers help separate northern Maine from Canada; northeastern Massachusetts once ended at the Merrimack River (its present border with New Hampshire parallels this); Rhode Island's eastern border was once defined by eastern Narragansett Bay; and the Connecticut River, like a great Algonquin snake-spirit, holds Vermont and New Hampshire apart before rushing down through Massachusetts and Connecticut to empty into Long Island Sound. The region claims several mountain chains, including the Green Mountains of Vermont, the White Mountains of New Hampshire, and the Berkshires in western Massachusetts. Eastern Massachusetts and much of Rhode Island are fairly low, rolling land (the highest point in Rhode Island, Jerimoth Hill, is a mere 812 feet), becoming more dramatic the farther west and north one goes. Thus Lovecraft, something of a "flatlander," thought that the hills of central Massachusetts "[rose] wild, and there are valleys with deep woods that no axe has ever cut" (*DH* 53).

One gets a feeling for the rise of the landscape by taking a couple of passages from Lovecraft in sequence. From the hills rising wild, west of Arkham, we proceed toward Dunwich, in north-central Massachusetts, where we encounter "a lonely and curious country. The ground gets higher, and the brier-bordered stone walls press closer and closer against the ruts of the dusty, curving road. The trees of the frequent forests seem too large, and the wild weeds, brambles, and grasses attain a luxuriance not often found in settled regions. . . . Gorges and ravines of problematical depth intersect the way" (*DH* 156). A little ways west and north into Vermont we get into a "hill-crowded countryside with its towering, threatening, close-pressing green and granite slopes" (*DH* 246). There are "dense, unvisited woods on those inaccessible slopes [that] seemed to harbour alien and incredible things" (*DH* 247). Vermonters might not appreciate this last statement, but by and large the description—like all Lovecraft's New England descriptions—is accurate. He would admit to a little artistic license in this regard, that his New England was "a dream New England—the familiar scene with certain lights and shadows heightened (or meant to be heightened) just enough to merge it with things beyond the world" (*SL* 2.130). But what changes he made were to restore to the settings "in vivid freshness all the accumulated wonder and beauty which it has produced in its long continuous history" (*SL* 2.131). Thus he is not so much exaggerating as *expanding* his view of the scene through the three dimensions into the fourth, time. "Poe has his haunted regions nameless, and peopled by mysterious beings with unknown pasts—but I make mine *minutely typical* of old New England" (*SL* 4.31–32; my italics).

I once took a gentleman from Minnesota for a tour of Portland, Maine; pointing out to him various historical sites and recounting what I knew of that city's 350-year history. At the end of our walk I asked him what he thought of it all. "Well," he replied, "the history has its value, of course, but it's not a very *accessible* city." Those 300 years had just been discounted because Portland has no ring-road. Such a road is convenient, I'm sure, and having driven a bit on New England city streets I'll be the first to admit that they're far from easy to negotiate (even many New Englanders would rather swim around Boston than drive through it). But those "endless labyrinths of steep, narrow, crooked streets" (*D* 209) tell volumes of history, and that is the one thing to which Yankee practicality takes a back seat.

First off, remember that New England is *not* flat; where one hill ends another usually begins. Second, many of New England's major cities (Boston, Providence, New Haven, Portsmouth) were settled as ports that spread outward from river-banks or bays. As one of Lovecraft's characters puts it, "'God, man! Don't you realise that places like these weren't merely *made*, but actually *grew*? Generation after generation lived and felt and died there, and in days when people weren't afraid to live and feel and die!'" (*DH* 15). Lovecraft's cities—his Providence, his Boston, Arkham and Innsmouth—are all faithful to this ideal of the old and *living* city. Though the latter two of these are imaginary places, Lovecraft took "pains to make these places wholly and realistically characteristic of genuine New England [cities]" (*SL* 3.433). As for those people who lived and felt and died in these settings, they were as shaped by the landscape as were their cities. They were (and are) "that continuous native life whose deep roots make it the one authentic outgrowth of the landscape" ("Vermont—A First Impression," *CE* 4.13). When the Pilgrims, Puritans, and assorted others first arrived here, they were faced with a wooded wilderness that stretched as far as any dared explore. Fortunes—even bare livings—had to be hacked from the woods, wrenched from the soil, or dragged thrashing from the sea. The weather didn't help much either, often well below zero in winter and hot, muggy, and crawling with insects in summer. (Even this crept into Lovecraft's work: "The fact is . . . that I can't feel the same deep, Gothic horror in any mild and genial region that I can in the rock-strewn, ice-bound, elm-shaded hillsides of my own New England. To me, whatever is *cold* is sinister, and whatever is warm is wholesome and life-giving" [*SL* 5.180–81].) Add to this an unpredictable indigenous population (the Algonquin tribes of the Northeast), with aid from the Mother Country months away by ship, and the cause for the Yankee's no-nonsense character becomes clear.

But *what*, after all, *is* a Yankee? When Lovecraft calls himself an "old-fashioned, soil-loving, conservative Yankee," what does that mean? Ambrose Bierce, grim grin pulled tight on his face, defined a Yankee as "in Europe, an American. In the Northern States of our Union, a New Englander. In the Southern States the word is unknown [See DAMYANK]."[1] The wry comment aside, Bierce is accurate as far as general use of the term is concerned. Within New England the bounds of the term are tightened even more, often defining only those of the "old blood"—descendants of original settlers. But more commonly the term "Yankee" has more to do with attitude and point of view than with latitude and place of birth. Without descending into stereotypes, I feel that there are some features that many of us (today and traditionally) in New England share. Judson Hale, former editor of *Yankee* magazine (who certainly ought to know such things), defines some of these traits:

> New Englanders are inclined to differentiate between good and bad by determining whether it's old or new. Frugality, reluctance to change, reliance on the "tried and true," abhorrence of all things showy or gaudy, pride in the past, a strong need for tradition and continuity.[2]

To this I would add independence, reserve, and a certain amount of Anglophilia (which is, really, an outgrowth of a love of ancestry). All these are evident in Lovecraft, man and work, as some examples will show.

"The past is *real*—it is *all there is*" (*SL* 3.31). The Yankee love of the old pervades Lovecraft's fiction. Its manifestations are almost too numerous to list, but consider for example that most of his horrors emerge from the past. There are those from the recent past ("Herbert West—Reanimator," "Cool Air," "The Colour out of Space"), the historical past ("The Tomb," "The Shunned House," *The Case of Charles Dexter Ward*), and the incredibly distant past ("The Call of Cthulhu," *At the Mountains of Madness*, "The Shadow out of Time"). His settings are full of "antediluvian gables" (*D* 212) and "prehistoric gambrel-roofers" (*MM* 114); and while he seems to pronounce fear of such things, it isn't so much fear as awe. The fear is actually of the "wormy decay" (*DH* 316) that is bearing these old things down into the dust: "I shiver that a town could be so aged and maggoty with subterraneous evil" (*D* 213). Lovecraft himself preferred the old to the new in many ways; on modern writers, he stated: "if that is new-Americanism, I thank the powers of the cosmos I am a Rhode-Island Englishman of the old tradition! Even if my culture-stream be a thinned & effete one, it is at least *something* as distinguished from *nothing at all*" (*SL* 4.200). This love of the old and of tradition is directly related to a New English Anglophilia. As a child Lovecraft would "often [make] Old England's gnarled oaks out of New England's maples" (*SL* 4.150); and late in life he still considered New England to be "a bit of the Old World transferred bodily to the New—a virtual *extension of* Old England itself" (*SL* 5.29–30). The two affections—Anglophilia and Novanglophilia—fed upon each other in Lovecraft. He could love Old England because of the traditions, language, and character that it had given to his homeland; and he could argue that New England, as "a virtual extension" of the Mother Country, was superior to the rest of the United States. He wrote to James Morton in 1923:

> Yes—I guess Ol' New-England can give the rest of America points on historic beauty. But OLD ENGLAND! Honestly, if I once saw its venerable oaks and abbeys, manor-houses and rose gardens, lanes and hedges, meadows and mediaeval villages, I could never return to America. (*SL* 1.210)

This is doubtful, considering that "few persons have ever been as closely knit to New England's rock ribbed hills" as he, but it does make the point. The Anglophilia is manifested in the fiction primarily in choice of settings. Before settling into New England as his fictional home, Lovecraft experimented with different locales, and set three tales ("Facts concerning the Late Arthur Jermyn and His Family," "The Hound," and "The Rats in the Walls") in England, with a possible fourth in that haunting piece, "The Outsider." Still, aside from knighthoods and castles, there is nothing particularly English about the tales. In fact, the narrator of "The Rats in the Walls" describes himself as "a stolid Yankee" (*DH* 27). But now and then one finds a telling reminder of Lovecraft's attachment for England, as in his description of Providence's College Hill as being "crowned by the vast new Christian Science dome as London is crowned by St. Paul's" (*MM* 115).

In keeping with an interest in England is the Yankee's passion for genealogy.

The region is crowded with genealogical and family societies (the D.A.R., Sons and Daughters of the Pilgrims, Piscataqua Pioneers—even one group called Son of a Witch, whose ancestors were hanged during the Salem witch panic of the 1690s). When my family moved to rural Rhode Island in the 1970s, I was told that you couldn't be a native unless your *grandfather* had been born there. Lovecraft was deeply interested in this subject, and his letters bear one after another retelling of his own ancestry, often as far back as the seventeenth century. In one letter (*SL* 2.214) he even stretches the blood-ties a bit to include Arthur Machen, Ambrose Bierce, and Lord Dunsany among his cousins! Even discounting those luminaries, Lovecraft was very proud of his ancestry. "R.I. was more a *family* than a *colony*" (*SL* 2.237), he wrote in a 1928 letter, and considering the state's small size, this is probably close to true. But it also brings up an important point. By the time Lovecraft wrote this, he had lost most of his close family—both parents and grandparents—and it is not too difficult to see this love of ancestry as an attempt to recover a sense of family. The Yankee reserve enters the picture here, for families give us an "instant" group of confidants and friends without the danger of revealing too much of ourselves to strangers. If you're related to someone, you already have something in common. This can be a bad thing, as in cases of clannishness or (worse) incest; but with Lovecraft perhaps it fulfilled the unspoken needs of a lonely man.

In his fiction, blood ties are thick and many. Lovecraft gave his "characters (by implication and sometimes in detail) characteristic New England genealogies" (*SL* 4.32). There is the extensive and detailed family history in "The Shunned House"; the narrator's ichthyic heritage in "The Shadow over Innsmouth"; and most of all, hapless Charles Dexter Ward, a less worldly version of Lovecraft himself, dragged into black magic and ultimately death by his maternal ancestor, Joseph Curwen.

But hold on a second: these last two are hardly respectable lineages. Why should a man as concerned with ancestry as Lovecraft spend so much energy in portraying such degeneration? It was the additional fear that one's heritage was *not* clean and proper. The horror in "The Lurking Fear" or "The Festival" or "The Shadow over Innsmouth" is that there *might* be some taint in the line. "Some fear had been gathering in me," broods the narrator of "The Festival," "perhaps because of the strangeness of my heritage" (*D* 210). Perhaps the most astounding example of this fear of ancestry occurs in *At the Mountains of Madness*, when Dyer and Danforth discover, from the Old Ones' carvings, that early man was originally bred by the Old Ones and "used sometimes for food and sometimes as an amusing buffoon" (*MM* 65). It is retroactively the same as the fear of decay: both threaten to destroy Lovecraft's New England—his extended home and family.

In the mere naming of characters Lovecraft lets us know that they are respectable citizens, often including a family name as middle name. There's Charles Dexter Ward, of course, and his doctor, Marinus Bicknell Willett. Francis Wayland Thurston tells us of the Cthulhu cult that his uncle, George Gammell Angell, uncovered. Richard Upton Pickman may be the cousin that Edward Pickman Derby ("The Thing on the Doorstep") doesn't talk about. Nathaniel Wingate Peaslee ("The Shadow out of Time") passes his middle name—his mother's maiden name—on to his son; and so on. Also note that less savory characters, like Wilbur Whateley ("The Dunwich Horror"), Joe Slater ("Beyond the Wall of Sleep"), and Joe Sargent ("The Shadow over Innsmouth"), have no such qualifications. These coveted heritages are sometimes invoked in times of stress, as when "Marinus Bicknell Willett was sorry that he looked again" (*MM* 207), or the time that, "but for a cry from his recovering wife . . . it is not likely that Theodore Howland Ward could have maintained for nearly a year more his old boast that he had never fainted" (*MM* 172).

I've heard it said that New Englanders are "cold." We are not: we are *cautious*. It takes a while to earn our trust, but once that is done we can be warm and faithful friends. This is another aspect of the Yankee heritage, inherited (by blood or association) from our Puritan forebears. It is a reserve: in England it is propriety; around here it's just manners. But it also stems from this close, crumpled countryside of ours, which didn't allow for very easy travel and communication before the advent of highways. In the hermitic phase of his early manhood, Lovecraft wasn't atypical of his kind. Consider Emily Dickinson, locked up in her grim house and an unrequited love; or Thoreau, shutting himself up alone in the woods. All three lived in areas of some population density; but all three were alone, withdrawn into themselves. They are only extreme cases of this prevalent strain in our regional character. It breeds individualism, but not always of the good kind. Lovecraft recognized the danger of this when he wrote about the secluded and degenerate families of Dunwich, the unnaturally aged cannibal of "The Picture in the House," or the people of Kingsport, whose "drawn curtains" (*D* 209) disturb the narrator so. Thus isolation is manifested not only on a personal level, but in communities as well. New England is small enough, yet there is often strong regionalism *within* this area. There is state-pride, of course, but even beyond this there can be county-pride and town-pride. People will correct you if mistake New Hampshire for Vermont, northern Maine for southern Maine, West Bay of

Rhode Island for East Bay. In Maine they use the expression "from away" for someone not from that state; but to someone up in Bethel, say, it can also include those from Portland, or Auburn—or *anywhere* outside of Bethel. There is an echo of this in the speech of "the stout, shrewd-faced agent" (*DH* 305) in "The Shadow over Innsmouth." First off, he refers to the narrator as "a Westerner" (*DH* 307), though he is only from Ohio. Then he goes on to talk about local Massachusetts gossip on the Innsmouth folk, saying archly "but I come from Panton, Vermont, and that kind of story don't go down with me" (*DH* 306). Last of all there is that gossip itself, recalling the judgment of Daniel Upton, narrator of "The Thing on the Doorstep," on Asenath Waite's servants: "They're her kind—Innsmouth people" (*DH* 293). This from a man from Arkham, which, since Lovecraft in this story based Arkham and Innsmouth on Salem and Newburyport respectively, would be only twenty miles away.

Reserve appears in other ways, too. Lovecraft recognized that good horror fiction depends upon suggestion. That he excelled at this can be at least partly attributed to his close-mouthed forebears, who had to compensate with inference what they lacked in directness. Lovecraft's characters show a certain reticence in their doings: "It is altogether against my will that I tell my reasons for opposing this contemplated invasion of the antarctic . . . and I am the more reluctant because my warning may be in vain" (*MM* 3). No sense in playing the fool unless you have to. And again: "After twenty-two years of nightmare and terror, saved only by a desperate conviction of the mythical source of certain impressions, I am unwilling to vouch for the truth of that which I found in Western Australia on the night of July 17–18, 1935" (*DH* 368). And again: "Let me pray that, if I do not survive this manuscript, my executors will put caution before audacity and see that it meets no other eye" (*DH* 154).

A fine example of reserve in Lovecraft occurs in "Pickman's Model," where the narrator must have *three* glasses of something from a decanter (brandy?), plus a cup of coffee, to break down his reserve during a story which, if read aloud, takes only fifteen to twenty minutes to tell! There is, too, the whiskey the narrator of "The Shadow over Innsmouth" gives Zadok Allen: "After an hour [Allen's] furtive taciturnity shewed signs of disappearing" (*DH* 328). Eventually it takes *two* hours plus the bottle of whiskey.

Coupled with the reserve is a need for proof. As one must prove his worth with a Yankee, so must he defend his statements to overcome the Yankee's caution. Lovecraft was typical in this respect, even exemplary, because of his knowledge of science. He would take nothing on faith; so why should the reader? In "The Whisperer in Darkness," Akeley writes to Wilmarth, concerning their debate on the rumored Mi-Go in the Vermont Hills:

> What I desire to say now is, that I am afraid your adversaries [in the debate] are nearer right than yourself, even though all reason seems to be on your side. They are nearer right than they realise themselves—for of course they go only by theory, and cannot know what I know. If I knew as little of the matter as they, I would not feel justified in believing as they do. I would be wholly on your side. (*DH* 217)

Akeley acknowledges that the idea of these interplanetary fungi is an outrageous one, and he himself would not believe it unless he'd actually seen and heard them. He realizes, too, that he is writing someone of the same mind-set, so he must prove what he is about to say. That is why Peaslee in "The Shadow out of Time" presents us with page after page of his research; why it takes most of the story before Thurston believes what his uncle uncovered about the Cthulhu cult; and why Lovecraft's characters in general seem to be so "thick." The reader and critic alike would do well to remember that the characters of a story are *in* the story: it is their world, and it is as logical and mundane to them as ours is to us. If Lovecraft's characters take their sweet time realizing there *are* shoggoths in Antarctica or dimension-hopping witches in suburban Massachusetts, well, what would *you* think if told of such a thing? They are New Englanders on top of that, and their practical commonsense point of view isn't easily breached.

One famous (or infamous) trait of New England is their thrift. This, too, is a carry-over from colonial days. "As Want was the prime foe these hardy exodists had to fortress themselves against," says Massachusetts native James Russell Lowell, "it is little wonder if that traditional feud be long in wearing out of the stock. . . . Thrift was the first lesson in their horn-book, pointed out, letter after letter, by the lean finger of the hard schoolmistress, Necessity."[3] Lovecraft's own care with money is well known: "I have financial economy worked out to a fine art, and know the self-service lunch room where I can get the best bargains. I never spend more than $3.00 per week on food, and often not even nearly that" (*SL* 4.104). Of course he was living off a dwindling inheritance and meager ghost-writing fees. But still, there's a certain amount of pride in the "fine art" of his careful economy. Lovecraft's characters, when called upon to account for such matters, are no less careful. The protagonist of "The Shadow over Innsmouth" buys a bottle of whiskey and interjects the statement— unimportant to the story—that it was "not cheaply obtained" (*DH* 327). He also tells us that, when dinnertime rolled around, "A bowl of vegetable soup with crackers was enough for me" (*DH* 342). (This statement actually operates on a couple of levels. First, the narrator is voicing his distrust of the "dismal restaurant" [*DH* 320] where he's forced to eat; second, he's pinching his pennies and making the excuse that he's *not really hungry* to cover his stinginess. This rationalization is as much to himself as to the reader.) Then there is Charles Dexter Ward's father, who goes to bring Joseph Curwen's portrait for the boy. Ward, Sr., confers with the owner of the house where the portrait is discovered, and obtains "the whole mantel and overmantel bearing the picture at a curtly fixed price which cut short the impending torrent of unctuous haggling" (*MM* 156). Considering that Mr. Ward "was a practical man of power and affairs—a cotton manufacturer with extensive mills at Riverpoint in the Pawtuxet Valley" (*MM* 155), it is not as though he could not afford to pay a little more, especially since the picture "impressed him mightily with its likeness to his son, and he believed the boy deserved it as a present" (ibid.).

As in much else about the Yankee, his speech is distinctive. In a roomful of North Americans from all regions, there is no mistaking that sharpness, those dropped or added *r*'s (remember Cape Codder John F. Kennedy's concern over "Cuber"?), the understatement and straightforwardness. Again, we must look to England for the origins of this regional feature. H. L. Mencken, in *The American Language*, tells us:

> The early settlers of Eastern New England and the Tidewater region of the South came chiefly from the Southern parts of England, and they brought with them those characteristics of Southern English speech that are still marked today in Standard English and separate the dialects of the Boston area and of the South from the speech of the rest of the United States, *e.g.,* the use of the broad *a* and the elision of *r* before consonants and in the terminal position.[4]

Lovecraft echoes this:

> My speech is simply the ordinary literate medium of Southern & Central (not Northern) New England *outside* Boston—the daily speech of Providence, Hartford, New Haven, Springfield, Worcester, Salem, & so on. . . . We don't sound any final *r* in words like *car, far,* &c. (phonetically, our common pronunciation is indistinguishable from *caa, faa,* &c.), but this is not a Bostonism or a Briticism at all; but merely the ordinary usage along the Atlantic seaboard (with the single exception of the Philadelphia zone) from Maine to Florida. (*SL* 3.420)

This particular aspect of our speech is well represented in Lovecraft's poetry, where "Farmer John" rhymes with "his barn" (*CP* 22). Later in the same poem ("New England Fallen"), Lovecraft tells us that

> Betwixt the trees, a wand'ring lane he *saw;*
> Stone were its walls, and mossy was its *floor.* (*AT* 391)

This one presents us with a choice. Either it's "saw/flaw" or "sawr/floor"—either is perfectly acceptable New England speech. However, it's probably the former, since a lot of stress is laid upon the first of the rhyming words. Of the same type is the following:

> . . . Esmond, D. Copperfield, or *Hiawatha,*
> Or anything from some nice high-school *author.* (*AT* 163)

Is it "Hiawatha/authah" or "Hiawather/author"? At any rate, such was the speech of H. P. Lovecraft. A good way to hear this accent "in action" is by watching films of the 1930s and '40s, as many actors were taught diction with a New England accent (that being considered "proper speech"). Listen, especially, to Bette Davis and Katherine Hepburn, both natives of the region. As this was Lovecraft's speech, it would also have been the speech of many of his characters.

Anyone who has read much of Lovecraft's fiction will know that there are several obvious exceptions to the above statement. The first (chronologically) appeared in "The Picture in the House," in the speech of the incredibly aged resident of said house. He greets the narrator thus:

> "Glad to see ye, young Sir—new faces is scurce arount here, an' I hain't got much ta cheer me up these days. Guess yew hail from Bosting, don't ye? I never ben thar, but I ken tell a taown man when I see 'im—we had one fer de-estrick schoolmaster in 'eighty-four, but he quit suddent an' no one never heerd on 'im sence—" (*DH* 121)

This "eye-dialect" recurs with small variation in "The Silver Key" ("'Mister Randy! Whar be ye? D'ye want to skeer yer Aunt Marthy plumb to death?'" [*MM* 416]), "The Colour out of Space" ("'. . . can't git away . . . draws ye . . . ye know summ'at's comin' but 'tain't no use . . . I seen it time an' agin senct Zenas was took . . .'" [*DH* 71–72]), "The Dunwich Horror" ("'Seth he's gone aout naow to look at 'em, though I'll vaow he wun't keer ter git very nigh Wizard Whateley's!'" [*DH* 178]), and "The Shadow over Innsmouth" ("'Hey, yew, why dun't ye say somethin'? . . . Think the old man's crazy, eh? Wal, Sir, *let me tell ye that ain't the wust!*'" [*DH* 339]). There are elements of this dialect that ring true;

the changing of "Martha" to "Marthy" (Lovecraft had an "Aunt 'Rushy" [*SL* 2.82], Jerusha Foster); the use of "senct" for "since" recalls Lovecraft's own use of "whilst" (*MM* 202) and the use of "acrost" for "across" one hears in these parts; and "rud" (*DH* 120) for "road" can still be heard in parts of Maine.

Now all New Englanders do not speak the same way. Linguist Hans Kurath, with whose work Lovecraft was familiar, divided these six states into almost as many different speech zones, and a trained ear can even differentiate between the accents of Providence and Newport Counties, Rhode Island. But nowhere have I encountered such an accent, nor has anyone (including a student of dialects from central Massachusetts) whom I have asked about this (although Marc A. Michaud reports that certain older residents of New Hampshire retain some similarities to this speech). The "-aow" sound and "keer" for "care" (instead of "kay-uh" or "keah") strike me as particularly non–New English, the former sound more reminiscent of the Philadelphia/Trenton area (Lovecraft himself says so; see *SL* 3.421). But knowing Lovecraft's demand for realism—and the glaringly awkward appearance of this dialect—one must assume that he had an actual basis for it. The following letter added to my confusion:

> As for Yankee farmers—oddly enough, I haven't noticed that the majority talk any differently from myself; so that *I've never regarded them as a separate class to whom one must use a special dialect* [my italics]. If I were to say "Mornin', Zeke, haow be ye?" to anybody along the road during my numerous summer walks, I fancy I'd receive an icy stare in return—or perhaps a puzzled inquiry as to what theatrical troupe I had wandered out of! (*SL* 2.306)

Where did he get it, then, if not from actual experience? The answer lies in his library. Among the books Lovecraft owned was *The Poetical Works of James Russell Lowell,* which includes, among other things, the series of poems entitled *The Biglow Papers.*[5] Better than an explanation from me would be a quotation from a typical section of these poems:

> Want to tackle *me* in, du ye?
> I expect you'll hev to wait;
> Wen cold lead puts daylight thru ye
> You'll begin to kal'late,
> S'pose the crows wun't fall to pickin'
> All the carkiss from your bones,
> Coz you helped to give a lickin'
> To them poor half-Spanish drones?[6]

Lowell's "hev" for "have" is recalled in Lovecraft's "hed" (*DH* 120) for "had"; Lowell's "kal'late" becomes "calc'late" in the same conversation, but otherwise the identity is unmistakable. That "-aow" or "-eow" sound doesn't occur in Lowell's poems, but does occur in the introduction to the first series of *The Biglow Papers*. By way of illustrating the dialect he is about to use, he re-writes a familiar bit of Shakespeare as his poem's narrator might say it:

> Neow is the winta uv eour discontent
> Med glorious summa by this sun o' Yock,
> An' all the cleouds thet leowered upun eour heouse
> In the deep buzzum o' the oshin buried; . . .[7]

And so on and so on. But why did Lovecraft dig up a vanished accent for his characters? To help establish the extreme age of these figures. Of the cannibal in "The Picture in the House" it is said: "His speech was very curious, an extreme form of Yankee dialect I had thought long extinct" (*DH* 120). This implies that Lovecraft never actually heard it spoken, and that he lifted it from Lowell because Lowell's use of it was over fifty years old by then. He continued to use this dialect at times when he wanted to show the great age (as with Zadok Allen) or the isolation (as with the people of Dunwich) of his characters. Lowell himself defends the authenticity of this speech in the very long and fascinating preface to the second series of the poems, tracing many Novanglian speech elements back as far as the sixteenth century. For example, the pronunciation "pizened" for "poisoned" in "The Colour out of Space" is what Lowell calls "a semi-Gallicism, for it is the result of a futile effort to reproduce a French sound with English lips. Thus for *joint, employ, royal,* we have *jynt, emply, ryle.*"[8] Lovecraft is vindicated. One could wish, however, that he had toned down this dialect. Authentic or no, it's often distracting to read. He achieves a comparable but more legible evocation of regional speech with that of "the stout, shrewd-faced agent" mentioned earlier, talking about the Innsmouth bus:

> "Run by an Innsmouth fellow—Joe Sargent—but never gets any custom from here, or Arkham either, I guess. Wonder it keeps running at all. I s'pose it's cheap enough, but I never see more'n two or three people on it—nobody but them Innsmouth folks. . . . Looks like a terrible rattletrap— I've never ben on it." (*DH* 305)

Here is a minimum of spelling change but a true feeling for New English speech. The dropped first words of each sentence remind us that Yankees are busy people, they've got to say what they're saying and get on; and there's a tacit judgment in the tone of *"I've* never ben on it." No one from Arkham rides the bus either, "I guess"—just a little cautious with this "Westerner" from Ohio.

Lovecraft's use of New England as a setting for his works was broad but not static. He did not, for example, immediately make the region his first choice of setting. After "The Tomb" (1917), it was three years before he returned to his native soil in fictional efforts, though when he did so he produced four such stories in one year. But even these (with the exception of "The Picture in the House") are set in a flat New England, a mere backdrop, void of depth; "they are in as much a never-never land as 'The Outsider,'"[9] as S. T. Joshi puts it. They are also outnumbered by non–New England stories during this period. Joshi goes on to say that Lovecraft's use of New England settings stems from his ambitious 1920 reading of the works of fellow New Englander, Nathaniel Hawthorne. Donald R. Burleson stresses this influence:

> Prior to his serious study of Hawthorne, Lovecraft's tales show no particular tendency to concentrate upon New England; but as his style ascends to its maturity in the late 1920s and early 1930s, he weaves the byways and accumulated lore of his native region into the heart of his most sweepingly cosmic conceptions.[10]

But if this influence were as strong as Joshi and Burleson would have us believe, then surely we'd have seen the fruits of it sooner. The year following his reading of Hawthorne (1921) shows only one New England story, "Herbert West—Reanimator," and 1922 has none. Instead, Lovecraft looked to upstate New York ("The Lurking Fear") and England ("The Hound," "The Rats in the Walls"), regions similar to yet different from New England. We see Lovecraft searching for the right setting, casting his imagination back and forth in time and space as the Great Race cast their minds into the future in "The Shadow out of Time." It seems that a stronger jolt was required to bring Lovecraft back home. He finished this "Searching Period" with two New England stories, "The Unnamable" and "The Festival." These come closer than previous works to capturing a New England mood. "The Unnamable" mentions Cotton Mather, is set in a typical New England churchyard, and boasts a character "born and bred in Boston, and sharing New England's self-satisfied deafness to the delicate overtones of life" (*D* 201). Obviously, Lovecraft was still not entirely satisfied with his home region. "The Festival" is full of true New England images—"ancient vanes and steeples, ridgepoles and chimney-pots, wharves and small bridges, willow trees and graveyards" (*D* 209)—inspired by a visit to Marblehead, Massachusetts, "the most powerful single emotional climax experienced during [his] nearly forty years of existence" (*SL* 3.126).

The next period of his career is defined by his two years in New York. During this period he produced only two New England tales as opposed to three others; their quality tells where his heart lay. "The Shunned House" is well developed and original in its premise and execution; "The Horror at Red Hook" is mostly a shriek of rage at New York's immigrants and modern, bustling character, and its horrors are textbook demons. The horror to Lovecraft wasn't so much the supernatural element, but the depths to which he felt New York had fallen. It was his nightmare; for New York was as old as New England, and he recognized that the same thing could happen to his beloved Providence or to Boston. "He" is an attempt to draw inspiration from New York's past, but by the end the narrator has "gone home to the pure New England lanes up which the fragrant sea-winds sweep at evening" (*D* 276). "In the Vault" is traditional but tightly written, and is notable as much for its clear depiction of a New England scene as for its savage horror. The best of his New York efforts is the short piece, "Cool Air," which embraces (as much as Lovecraft cared to) the modern feeling of the city. The fact that the horror in it is precipitated by the mere failure of a cooling system is far different from the detailed history of deaths in "The Shunned House," caused by the buried, gelatinous thing under the house. Both tales are successful in their own ways, as different as they are.

Like the narrator of "He," Lovecraft returned to New England in the spring of 1926, and the effect upon his work was staggering. Before the calendar turned up 1927, he had produced four stories, all set in New England, and most of a fifth, the novel *The Dream-Quest of Unknown Kadath*. If the first era of his writing career was the Searching Period and the second the New York Period, the next could perhaps best be called the Reconstruction Period. The horrors of New York, real or imagined, had made Lovecraft appreciate his homeland all the more; and he set about mentally putting everything back in place. He rebuilt New England around him, from Providence's "queer dark courts on the precipitous hillside" (*DH* 126) to Boston's "crumbling-looking gables, broken small-paned windows, and archaic chimneys" (*DH* 17); from "the rushing Miskatonic" (*MM* 415) to "the pleasant hearths and gambrel-roofed taverns of Kingsport" (*D* 285). Lovecraft peeked in all the corners, adjusted this thing, changed that, and sat back satisfied that all was as it should be, "line for line, detail for detail, proportion for proportion" (*SL* 2.47).

The last work of this period, *The Dream-Quest of Unknown Kadath*, although it seems at first glance to be a non–New England story, offers us quite an interesting array of Novanglian elements upon closer scrutiny. There is, most obviously, the fact that the story begins and ends in the bedroom of Bostonian Randolph Carter, and the long, lyrical lecture that Nyarlathotep gives him before sending him back home. Lovecraft himself says of the story:

> All genuine art, I think, is local and rooted in the soil; for even when one sings of far incredible *twilight lands* [my italics] he is merely singing of his homeland in some gorgeous and exotic mantle. It is this point which I seek to emphasize in my 110-page effort "The Dream-Quest of Unknown Kadath." Take a man away from the fields and groves which bred him—or which moulded the lives of his forefathers—and you cut off his sources of power altogether. (*SL* 2.131)

The memory of the New York years died hard.

The Novanglian presence is there in the form of the artist Pickman, who helps Carter on his quest. It is there in Ulthar, where "old peaked roofs and overhanging upper stories and numberless chimney-pots and narrow hill streets" (*MM* 311) might be just up the road from Kingsport's "unwholesomely archaic houses having peaked roofs and overhanging gables" (*D* 212), "ridgepoles and chimney-pots . . . endless labyrinths of steep, narrow, crooked streets" (*D* 209). But an even more startlingly New English region lies far to the north of Ulthar, in the realm called "Inganok." The very name of this realm—home of the children of the gods—recalls Algonquin place-names like Sagadahoc (a county in Maine), Naugatuck (Connecticut), and most startlingly Monadnock (a New Hampshire mountain that inspired one of Lovecraft's poems). It may not be consciously derived from such roots (as his Miskatonic and Manuxet rivers were), but it's certainly very reminiscent of such names. Note, too, that the only other such names in the story (Mt. Ngranek and Ilarnek) are closely associated with Inganok. Compare these to the exotic Celephaïs, the fluid Serennian, the ethereal Dylath-Leen. The location of Inganok, too, is revealing. It is the furthest north—excepting Kadath, actual home of the gods—of all the dream-world lands; and its description as a "cold twilight land" (*MM* 350) not only could be a fair description of New England, but also echoes almost exactly the above quotation about "incredible twilight lands."

The Inganokians themselves provide several clues as to their origins. They are described as talking "little with the other folk . . . but would gather in groups in remote corners and sing among themselves" (*MM* 357). Carter is put off by their reserve, for "he did not know how much of pride and secrecy and dim supernal memory might fill these children of the Great Ones" (ibid.). Tradition and ritual are stronger in Inganok than elsewhere in the dream-world. In the city bearing that land's name is a great Temple, from which the city's streets radiate "as spokes from a wheel's hub" (*MM* 361). A bell sounds periodically from its central tower, and is answered by peals of music. All the Inganokians drop whatever they are doing to listen, "for the priests and people of that city were wise in the primal mysteries, and faithful in keeping the rhythms of the Great Ones" (*MM* 359). There would be no getting the priest drunk here as Carter had done in Ulthar (cf. *MM* 312). Reserve, pride in ancestry, respect for tradition—all clearly indicate the earth-bound inspiration for the Inganokians. That these dream-world Yankees are the children of the gods says much about Lovecraft's estimation of his fellow New Englanders.

Having put New England in order, Lovecraft plunged into a veritable ecstasy of writing about the region. This was his Regionalist Period, typified by strong local character, detailed descriptions of scenery (unlike the "never-never land" of his earlier New England works and interminable "list-descriptions" of fantasy worlds), and the use of dialect. He began with the short novel *The Case of Charles Dexter Ward* (1927), which expands on the portrayal of Providence begun in "The Shunned House" and "The Call of Cthulhu." Again, it is a portrayal in three dimensions plus time; for a large part of the story takes place in the eighteenth century, involving several actual historical figures (the Brown brothers, Stephen Hopkins, Lovecraft's own ancestor Abraham Whipple, etc.). The living past of New England is given human form in the person of the evil Joseph Curwen, revived by his guileless descendant Ward. It is a victory cry of New England; the apex of its expression in Lovecraft's work; a poem in prose and history of all that was dear to him. Here is his Providence:

> At the high square where Broad, Weybosset, and Empire Streets join, [Ward] saw before and below him in the fire of sunset the pleasant, remembered houses and domes and steeples of the old town; and his head swam curiously as the vehicle rolled down to the terminal behind the Biltmore, bringing into view the great dome and soft, roof-pierced greenery of the ancient hill across the river, and the tall colonial spire of the First Baptist Church limned pink in the magic evening light against the fresh springtime verdure of its precipitous background. (*MM* 165)

Here we encounter an image that occurs three times in Lovecraft's fiction in widely different settings; it might be termed "Road into Staircase." It first occurs in the 1921 tale, "The Music of Erich Zann." The street Zann lives on, the Rue d'Auseil, is described as "almost a cliff, closed to all vehicles, consisting in several places of flights of steps" (*DH* 84). This image appears next in *Dream-Quest*, where Randolph Carter and his Inganokian guide "climbed up an alley that was all steps" (*MM* 362) towards the Veiled King's garden; and finally, in *The Case of Charles Dexter Ward*, Lovecraft tells us of Meeting Street (an actual street on Providence's College Hill) and "the arched flight of steps to which the highway had to resort in climbing the slope" (*MM* 114). Clearly this was an image that caught Lovecraft's fancy, and he tried to use it in different settings. The first was somewhere that was *not* New England (France); the second was an imaginary place based upon New England (Inganok); and finally, like Lovecraft, the image comes home.

The next three New England stories, "The Colour out of Space," "The Dunwich Horror," and "The Whisperer in Darkness," take the reader out into the wild woods of Massachusetts and Vermont. The first two make extensive use of the dialect discussed earlier in this paper; and all three warn against the dangers of isolation, whether the surly, ignorant seclusion of the Whateleys, the vulnerable loneliness of the doomed Gardner family, or the stubborn reclusiveness of Henry Akeley. Lovecraft followed this period with a period of expansion, an Exploration Period. Here are voyages to Antarctica (*At the Mountains of Madness*), Australia ("The Shadow out of Time"), and other dimensions ("The Dreams in the Witch House"). There is even something of an exploration of a different type of fiction in the form of his collaboration with R. H. Barlow, "The Night Ocean." Its subtlety and stress upon introspection rather than an actual horror make it something novel in Lovecraft's *oeuvre*. Its use of New England is unspecified but can be inferred by the fact that, "there being no fireplace," the beachside cottage the narrator rents "stood empty and alone from October until far into the spring" (*HM* 432). This certainly wasn't Barlow's Florida, anyway. The contemplative and sometimes melancholy tone recalls other hermitic Yankees searching for their souls. It is set by a wide and changing body of water that influences and reflects the moods of the narrator—it could be considered Lovecraft's *Walden*.

Among the exploratory tales are two examples of the Yankee character taken to curious lengths. I refer to the nature of the Old Ones in *At the Mountains of Madness* and the Great Race in "The Shadow out of Time." With the Old Ones we are told that "Their preternatural toughness of organisation and simplicity of natural wants made them peculiarly able to live on a high plane without the more specialised fruits of artificial manufacture" (*MM* 62). The Old Ones were, in a way, the Puritans of their time, coming from a far distant home with little hope of aid from that home should their toughness prove insufficient to the demands of the new environment. This relationship extends further: "The beings multiplied by spores" (*MM* 64). This makes them sexless, a state the early New Englanders might have welcomed in their search for piety. Like the Pilgrims, the Old Ones did not have a clear path to occupation of their new lands. As the Yankee had the Indian, so did the Old Ones have their "cosmic octopi," the spawn of great Cthulhu, who had to be subdued in order for the Old Ones to establish ocean cities:

> New land cities were founded [after the war]—the greatest of them in the antarctic, *for this region of first arrival was sacred* [my italics]. From then on, as before, the antarctic remained the centre of the Old Ones' civilisation, and all the discoverable cities built there by the Cthulhu spawn were blotted out. Then suddenly the lands of the Pacific sank again, taking with them the frightful stone city of R'lyeh and all the cosmic octopi, so that the Old Ones were again supreme on the planet except for one shadowy fear about which they did not like to speak. (*MM* 66)

This passage is quite revealing. In it we are told that the Old Ones, like the New Englanders, hold sacred their "region of first arrival"—their Plymouth Rock, if you will. In a broader sense, New England is that region for the whole United States, the so-called "Cradle of Liberty." The passage also details the subjugation of the Cthulhoids, with intimations of treaties, that (like those of the victimized Indians) are later null and void. At the end of the passage is the curious statement that there was something "about which [the Old Ones] did not like to speak." Imagine a civilization capable of interplanetary travel, that rears monstrously huge cities both beneath the sea and on land; has a highly developed artistic and technological foundation; is unchallenged in its supremacy of the earth and can even *create life*. So Lovecraft would have us believe of the Old Ones, and yet there is something about which even *they* cannot talk. Lovecraft is, of course, trying to pile horror on top of horror by having the "monsters" of the tale themselves afraid of something. But that they wouldn't even make specific mention of something so hideous seems incredible. This, I feel, is another reflection of the Yankee element in these otherworldly beings. Lovecraft obviously has a lot of respect for them by the end of the story ("God, what intelligence and persistence! What a facing of the incredible, just as those carven kinsmen and forbears had faced things only a little less incredible! Radiates, vegetables, monstrosities, star-spawn—whatever they had been, they were men!" [*MM* 96]) and he brings to them admirable attributes with which he was familiar. They are, in a sense, "super-Yankees," living a sexless and rigorous life in a new frontier.

Like the Old Ones, the Great Race of Yith in "The Shadow out of Time" are sexless and reproduce through "seeds or spores" (*DH* 399). Even so, "ties among persons of common descent were recognised, and the young were generally reared by their parents" (ibid.), recalling the strong family ties of New England society. These beings, like the Puritans, have little patience for wrong-doing:

> Crime was surprisingly scant, and was dealt with through highly efficient policing. Punishments ranged from privilege deprivation and imprisonment to death or *major emotion wrenching* [my italics], and were never administrated without a careful study of the criminal's motivations. (*DH* 400)

Theirs is, like the Old Ones' society, a kind of intellectual utopia for Lovecraft to envision as an ideal. And in addition to the aesthetic opportunities provided, this society boasts several things that Lovecraft admired in his own society: the freedom from sexuality (exaggerated to a biological level), the family bond, the strict and proper social mores, the suppression of emotion. But even this fantastic society, which had leapt from planet to planet and life-form to life-form, had a fear. Like the mountains the Old Ones furtively hinted at, the Great Race fear certain basalt ruins and sealed trapdoors among their cities. This fear is so acute that "everything specific which bore on it was significantly absent from such books as were on the common shelves" (*DH* 400). This is a Great Race, remember, which "had learned all things that ever were known or ever would be known on the earth" (*DH* 385)—yet they simply will *not* speak of the thing. Lovecraft's own opinion of the Yitheans is that they were "the greatest race of all because [they] alone had conquered the secret of time" (ibid.). New Englanders, too, had "conquered time" in a way; preserving the past in many of its visible and less tangible forms—and Lovecraft's opinion of *them* is well documented. It is surely a hint (if only a subconsciously given one) that Peaslee, near the site of the Great Race's city, feels a "persistent and perplexing illusion of memory" about "the general northeasterly direction" (*DH* 408). Finally, Peaslee spells it out for us: "For this was no chance or remote resemblance. Definitely and absolutely, the millennially ancient, aeon-hidden corridor in which I stood was the original of something I knew in sleep as intimately as I knew my own house in Crane Street, Arkham" (*DH* 417).

H. P. Lovecraft's place among writers of the bizarre is secure; but where, exactly, is that place? A place is so much of nothing without other places to define it. Lovecraft *was* New England; and New England, physically and psychologically, is midway between two ends of the spectrum, England and California. To understand Lovecraft more clearly, consider representatives of these two opposite shores: M. R. James, master ghost-story teller of Cambridge, and the literary scourge of San Francisco, Ambrose Bierce. The ghost stories of James, while raising that specific type of tale to an art, are highly traditional, his ghosts acting "in ways not inconsistent with the rules of folklore."[11] Bierce, while also using ghosts for his horrors, injects them with a terrible potential for violence. James's ghosts skulk or leap in the shadows; Bierce's specters throttle their sons, are born of gunfights, tear the living into rags. James's spirits arise from a long-settled land and are discovered by well-read, well-bred gentlemen in the comfort of panelled libraries. Bierce's spirits appear in a hostile land not yet tamed, waylay the average Joe in rugged canyons and raw frontier towns, and writhe in a cycle of violence.

Lovecraft comes between these two types; for as New England is not as sedate as Old England but far more set in its ways than the West Coast, so are Lovecraft's horrors more physical than those of James and less so than those of Bierce. Lovecraft's entities often have a historical depth comparable to those of James; but the noxious shoggoth of *At the Mountains of Madness* has far more potential for harm than, say, the hideous sheet-faced ghost of "'Oh, Whistle, and I'll Come to You, My Lad.'" Neither is as brutal as "The Damned Thing" of Bierce. The violence of the Englander and the New Englander takes place "off-stage."

To define even further, take Lovecraft in context with his fellow New Englanders. In his own opinion, "The best exponents of New England I can think of are Hawthorne and Mary E. Wilkins" (*SL* 2.140). The similarities of these two to Lovecraft are readily apparent. The commonality of images between Lovecraft and Hawthorne are nicely enumerated by both Donald R. Burleson ("H. P. Lovecraft: The Hawthorne Influence") and Peter Cannon ("H. P. Lovecraft in Hawthornian Perspective"); and Lovecraft shared a use of dialect and local color with Wilkins-Freeman. But there are important differences as well. The horror stories of Mary E. Wilkins-Freeman are simply and effectively drawn, but they are almost all of the traditional ghost-story type. There are two important exceptions: "Luella Miller," about a young woman who draws the life out of anyone who cares for her (a novel treatment of the vampire theme), and "The Hall Bedroom," about a room whose limits disappear into a strange dimension every night, only to reappear with the switching on of the light. Wilkins-Freeman's stories are given their power more by realistic portrayal of characters (often Yankee spinster-ladies living gray lives) and setting than by any originality in conception.

The differences between Lovecraft and Hawthorne are more complex. As the difference between Lovecraft and Bierce can be equated to that between New England and California, so can the difference between these two New

Englanders be compared to that of the historical character of their respective home-states, Rhode Island and Massachusetts. Massachusetts was established by Puritans, self-exiled fanatics who came to the New World to set up a theocracy. Theirs was a collective separatism. Rhode Island, on the other hand, was founded by Roger Williams and others who did not conform to the rigid Puritan ethic. Their colony was established for those who sought the religious freedom simultaneously sought and destroyed in the Puritan's New Jerusalem. They were personal individualists. They no doubt bore with pride the sobriquet that Massachusetts gave to their state, "Rogue Island." In "Endicott and the Red Cross," Hawthorne defends his Puritan forefathers, saying: "Let not the reader argue, from any of these evidences of iniquity, that the times of the Puritans were more vicious than our own."[12] These "evidences of iniquity" were cropped ears, slit nostrils, confinement in stocks and pillories, and the mark of the branding iron, all for such serious "crimes" as toasting the then-Catholic king of England, gossiping, or interpreting Holy Writ. Hawthorne's portrayal of Massachusetts Governor Endicott is of a man of "stern and resolute countenance," while that of Roger Williams is merely "mild." Overall the depiction of Williams in this piece is that of an ineffectual old man, as opposed to the charismatic and merciless Endicott. Compare this to Lovecraft's statement that "Massachusetts always remained a definitely hostile neighbour [in colonial times], though glad enough to secure Roger's [Williams] good offices with the Injuns in times of trouble" (*SL* 3.353). Or his opinion that Puritans were "warp'd in mentality by isolation and unnatural thoughts" (*SL* 1.222). The difference between the two is one of the group versus the individual. This difference manifests itself definitely in these two authors' respective works.

In Hawthorne's "Ethan Brand," for instance, the "Unpardonable Sin" for which Brand searches is, ironically, his own rejection of human company during the search. The moral is: join in. But Lovecraft's protagonists go it alone, often conducting their researches unaided. Hawthorne's "Footprints on the Seashore" is similar in basic idea to Lovecraft's and Barlow's "The Night Ocean." In both cases a man goes to the shore to find rest. But whereas Hawthorne's narrator ends up joining a group of people gathered by a fire on the beach, happy of the company, Lovecraft's remains alone, content to continue speculating on the mysteries around him. Further, in Hawthorne, "abominations" are things contrary to religious (group) conscience; in Lovecraft, "the ultimate abomination" (*D* 207) is that which conflicts with natural law. His focus is personal, but his scope is cosmic.

And this, finally, is Lovecraft's importance as a horror writer and as a New England regionalist. Perhaps Wilkins-Freeman handled characters better and Hawthorne delved more deeply into human drives. But Lovecraft was able to take their common foundation—New England, its physical state, its history and mind-set—and *extend* it beyond the everyday. What is "The Dunwich Horror," after all, but a story of rural family decay writ large? or "The Call of Cthulhu," but a ghost story on a cosmic scale? Deep in the Antarctic super-plateau, a crazed explorer chants "'South Station Under—Washington Under—Park Street Under—Kendall—Central—Harvard'" (*MM* 100)—the stops of the Boston subway. The familiar cobbles of Providence and Newport pave the streets of Ulthar and Inganok. Super-Yankees from interstellar space erect fantastic cities in the waste places of the world. By the method of cosmic exaggeration, the world and thoughts of the cosmic Yankee are made *more real.* Nyarlathotep, the Crawling Chaos and messenger of the gods, was speaking to Lovecraft as much as to Randolph Carter when he told him of New England's wonders:

> "These, Randolph Carter, are your city; for they are yourself. New-England bore you, and into your soul she poured a liquid loveliness which cannot die. This loveliness, moulded, crystallised, and polished by years of memory and dreaming, is your terraced wonder of elusive sunsets. . . .
>
> "Look! through that window shine the stars of eternal night. Even now they are shining above the scenes you have known and cherished, drinking of their charm that they may shine more lovely over the gardens of dream." (*MM* 401)

Lovecraft saw both the terraced wonder *and* the stars of eternal night. He transcended his heritage, his very *self,* and steered a course for the stars. But, heeding Nyarlathotep's warning to steer for them "'only till you hear a far-off singing in the high aether'" (*MM* 402), he kept a part of himself forever rooted in the rocky Rhode Island soil. "'Higher than that lurks madness'" (ibid.)—do not lose sight of your beginnings. As did Charles Dexter Ward, Nathaniel Wingate Peaslee, and Randolph Carter, this cosmic Yankee always returned home.

Notes

1. Ambrose Bierce, *The Devil's Dictionary,* in *Collected Writings of Ambrose Bierce* (New York: Citadel Press, 1946), 390.

2. Judson Hale, *Inside New England* (New York: Harper & Row, 1982), 141.

3. James Russell Lowell, "Introduction" to *The Biglow Papers, The Poetical Works of James Russell Lowell* (Boston: Houghton Mifflin, 1882), 166.

4. H. L. Mencken, *The American Language: An Inquiry into the Development of English in the United States* (1919; 4th ed. New York: Alfred A. Knopf, 1936), 357.

5. See S. T. Joshi and Marc A. Michaud, *Lovecraft's Library*, rev. ed. (New York: Hippocampus Press, 2002), #553.

6. Lowell, 170.

7. Ibid., 167.

8. Ibid., 214.

9. Joshi, *H. P. Lovecraft* (Mercer Island, WA: Starmont House, 1982), 25.

10. Donald R. Burleson, "H. P. Lovecraft: The Hawthorne Influence," *Extrapolation* 22 (Spring 1981): 262.

11. M. R. James, *The Penguin Complete Ghost Stories of M. R. James* (Harmondsworth: Penguin, 1984), 5.

12. Nathaniel Hawthorne, *Twice-Told Tales*, in *Tales and Sketches* (New York: Library of America, 1982), 544.

H. P. Lovecraft and the Pulp Magazine Tradition

Will Murray

The universally accepted view of H. P. Lovecraft the writer is that he was an amateur who wrote for his own amusement and through an accident of publishing history—the birth of *Weird Tales* in 1923—found a receptive market for his work in a lowly pulp magazine. It is a view that Lovecraft himself fostered. Writing to the "Transatlantic Circulator"—a group of amateur writers who exchanged and criticized works in manuscript—Lovecraft said, "For the endorsement and interest of the public I care not at all, writing solely for my own satisfaction. Writing for any other motive could not possibly be art—the professional author is the ultimate antithesis of the artist" (*CE* 5.62).

This is a view supported by Lovecraft's *Selected Letters,* in which his ongoing dealings with *Weird Tales* are recorded in minute detail. But in his still unpublished letters, principally to his fellow pulp magazine contributor and later publisher August Derleth, another Lovecraft emerges—one who avidly pursued a host of professional fiction markets, who evidently saw acceptance by those markets as a validation of his literary worth, and whose self-confidence and motivation suffered immeasurably—his protests to the contrary aside—whenever ephemeral pulp magazines like *Strange Tales* or *Ghost Stories* politely declined his work.

To read his published letters, one comes away with the feeling that Lovecraft abhorred the pulp magazine as a class of periodical—a distaste that did not exclude even the now-venerated *Weird Tales.* The traditional perception is that Lovecraft considered himself to be "slumming" when he deigned to be published by "The Unique Magazine." This assessment might appear to be borne out by the earliest reference to the pulp field that occurs in his *Selected Letters.* Writing to Rheinhart Kleiner on 16 November 1916, Lovecraft haughtily remarked:

> In 1913 I formed the reprehensible habit of picking up cheap magazines like *The Argosy* to divert my mind from the tedium of reality. One of the authors in that periodical so much excited my contempt, that I wrote a letter to the editor in quaint Queen-Anne verse, satirising the offending novelist. This letter, which was printed in the September number, aroused a veritable tempest of anger amongst the usual readers of the magazine. I was assailed & reviled by innumer-

able letters, which appeared in the editorial department. Among these hostile compositions was a piece of tetrameter verse by one John Russell, of Tampa, Fla., which had in it so much native wit, that I resolved to answer it. Accordingly I sent *The Argosy* a 44-line satire in the manner of Pope's *Dunciad*. This was duly printed in January, 1914, & it created an immense sensation (of hostile character) amongst the *Argosy* readers. The editorial department had nothing but anti-Lovecraft letters the following month! And then I composed *another* satire, flaying all my tormenters in stinging pentameter. This, too, was printed, till the storm of fury waxed high. Russell's replies were all rather clever, & well worth answering. Finally I sent Russell a personal communication which led to an ultimate peace—a peace established just in time, for T. N. Metcalf, the editor of *The Argosy*, had intimated that the poets' war must end soon, since correspondents were complaining of the prominence of our verses in their beloved magazine. They feared we were usurping all the extra space! So Russell & I officially closed the affair with a composite poem—my part of which was in heroics; his in anapest. This farewell to *The Argosy* took place in October, 1914, & I have never since beheld that worthy organ of popular literature. (*SL* 1.41–42)

The degree of detail in which Lovecraft relates this episode, his first brush with a national magazine—as opposed to the nationally distributed amateur press—is quite revealing and indicates the importance he placed on it.

This is more than borne out by the discovery that, in disavowing his then-three-year past interest in the *Argosy*, Lovecraft was being disingenuous. More than merely engaging in a rebuff of Fred Jackson, one of the *Argosy*'s most popular writers, Lovecraft had been a faithful reader of the *Argosy* and its companion, the *All-Story Magazine*, for a much greater length of time than he indicated to Kleiner.

Probably Lovecraft felt that to admit to reading pulp magazines at the age of twenty-six was too lowbrow for one who boasted of having read Virgil in Latin; but in later years, as Lovecraft was drawn into the pulp field as a contributor, he admitted to some very surprising extracurricular reading. In a letter to J. Vernon Shea, written on 4 February 1934, he allowed:

By the time of the first cinema shows (March, 1906, in Providence) I knew too much of literature & drama not to recognise the utter & unrelieved hokum of the moving picture. Still, I attended them—in the same spirit that I read Nick Carter, Old King Brady, & Frank Reade in nickel-novel form. Escape—relaxation. It was not till later that I got fed up & no longer enjoyed such mentally juvenile performances. (*SL* 4.355)

Lovecraft also read popular boy's book series like the Rover Boys, but it is especially fascinating to think of him reading the much-reviled dime novels of his teenage years, for they were widely considered even more inferior than the pulp magazines, which in 1906 were just beginning to come into popularity.

What is remarkable about Lovecraft's attitude toward the pulp magazines he read as a young man is that the pulps of that era were on a much higher literary plane than *Weird Tales* and others that flourished in the post-World War I period.

The pulp magazine field was an outgrowth of one ambitious publisher, Frank Munsey, whose career began with the publication of the *Golden Argosy* in 1882. It was a slim pamphlet-sized magazine of children's stories, less lurid than a pulp magazine but not as sensational as the dime novels. The magazine was at first unsuccessful, and Munsey attempted to improve its fortunes by retitling it the *Argosy* and aiming it at a slightly older audience, primarily young adults.

It was not until 1891 and the launching of a companion magazine, *Munsey's,* that Frank Munsey hit upon a successful formula. *Munsey's* was a thick magazine of fiction, printed on rude paper called "pulp" and devoid of illustrations. Within a comparatively short time it was selling a half-million copies each month. In short order, Munsey revamped the *Argosy* into this format and added two more companion titles—the *All-Story,* begun in 1905, and the *Cavalier* in October 1908.

For the first two decades of the twentieth century, Munsey was the premier publisher of pulp magazines. The format of all his magazines was identical. They published novels—often serialized—as well as novelettes and short stories. There were no restrictions as to theme or subject matter, except within the assumed boundaries of good taste. A detective story might precede a romance. A western might be juxtaposed to a story with a professional sports background. These magazines were cornucopias of fictional variety and owed some of their success to the waning interest in the dime novel and, of course, to the very variety of their contents. The early pulps were known as "all-fiction" magazines for this reason. Copies were assumed to pass from friend to friend or within the family circle so that each person could read only the stories that appealed to his or her tastes.

It was a very successful package and, within the Munsey chain especially, allowed for some experimentation. At Munsey, under editor Robert H. Davis, this led to the creation of a special category Davis dubbed the "different" story. As defined by Davis, the different stories came from "the queer, *outré,* unusual, bizarre, exotic, misfit manuscripts that we get occasionally."[1] Many different stories were fantasies or science fiction, but others were so termed because of their then-daring sexual content.

Lovecraft became a reader of these magazines during this period. As he wrote to the *All-Story* letter column for 7 March 1914:

> Having read every number of your magazine since its beginning in January, 1905, I feel in some measure privileged to write a few words of approbation and criticism concerning its contents.
>
> In the present age of vulgar taste and sordid realism it is a relief to peruse a publication such as *The All-Story*, which had ever been and still remains under the influence of the imaginative school of Poe and Verne.
>
> For such materialist readers as your North-British correspondent, Mr. G. W. P., of Dundee, there are only too many periodicals containing "probable" stories; let *The All-Story* continue to hold its unique position as purveyor of literature to those whose minds cannot be confined within the narrow circle of probability, or dulled into a passive acceptance of the tedious round of things as they are.[2]

Clearly, Lovecraft was attracted to these magazines in part because of their heavy fantasy content. As he recalled to James F. Morton on 23 February 1936, "I used to buy [the *Black Cat*] reg'lar-like, and recall the swell weird stuff it had. That and the old *All-Story* were the first sources of *contemporary* weird material I ever stumbled on!" (*SL* 5.227). But in his letters to the *All-Story*, Lovecraft admitted to enjoying western writer Zane Grey as well as Edgar Franklin, Albert Payson Terhune, and others whose work might be assumed to be as far afield from Lovecraft's outré tastes as it would be from his literary concerns. Even Lovecraft's dislike of Fred Jackson's work, and others like De Lysle Ferrée Cass, indicates that he read a great deal of it. For by no means did every issue of any of the magazines Lovecraft admitted to reading—the *Argosy*, the *All-Story*, or the *Cavalier*—feature imaginative fiction. Regardless, he appears to have read them from cover to cover.

It is interesting to note that all these magazines were monthly and each contained a minimum of 100,000 words of fiction spread over 240 pages. The *All-Story* became a weekly in 1914, the year after Lovecraft claimed to have stopped reading the *Argosy* and its companion magazine. As Lovecraft wrote in the 15 August 1914 *All-Story Cavalier Weekly* (the two magazines had been combined):

> Ever since last August I have been engaged in a wordy warfare with some of the readers of *The Argosy* concerning an alleged author whose erotic, effeminate stories fill me with the most profound disgust. This author was one of the principal contributors to *The Cavalier*; in fact his tales formed the reason for my ceasing to read the latter periodical. Now he is to be inflicted upon the readers

of *The All-Story*. For my somewhat severe criticisms of this writer, I have received every imaginable sort of ridicule and opposition, both in prose and in verse, through *The Argosy* "Log-Book."

Lovecraft's attacks upon Fred Jackson forced him into what seemed to be at first a playful exchange—one carried out largely in verse. It had a profound effect upon the *Argosy*'s editor, for the magazine stopped carrying Fred Jackson stories. The January 1914 editorial promised "you won't get too much Fred Jackson in 1914."[3]

It may be that Lovecraft, at first stimulated by the sensation he had triggered in one of his beloved magazines, ultimately was stung by the vituperative anti-Lovecraft tone that grew more pointed as the controversy roared on. The following was a typical retort: "I get sore at people like H.P.L. I will pay his fifteen cents a month if he will quit reading *Argosy*. . . . I am a cow-puncher, and would certainly like to loosen up my .44-six on that man Lovecraft."[4]

Such a furious response could explain why Lovecrafts transferred his epistolary comments, which he signed with his initials, to the *All-Story Weekly*,. Rather than being a mere adventure, this entire affair could very well have been a pivotal experience for Lovecraft, one that affected him so much so that he forswore reading the *Argosy* for years after and which, in a way, foreshadowed an event that may have dealt his fictional writing career a brutal blow.

It was pivotal in another way. Lovecraft's *Argosy* letters brought him to the attention of Edward F. Daas of the United Amateur Press Association, who invited Lovecraft into the amateur press—an involvement that focused and energized his previously desultory writing interest and laid the groundwork for more ambitious work.

By 1920, the year the *Argosy* and the *All-Story* were combined under the title *Argosy All-Story Weekly*, the pulp world Lovecraft was familiar with was undergoing dramatic change. Other publishers sprang up to rival Munsey, chief among them Street & Smith, a former dime novel house that entered the pulp field in 1903 with an *All-Story* rival called the *Popular Magazine*. Seeing that the dime novel was on the wane, Street & Smith began converting their dying dime novel titles into pulp magazines. In 1919 *Nick Carter Stories* was reincarnated as the first truly specialized pulp magazine, *Detective Story Magazine*. It was a risky venture, a magazine devoted only to detective stories and thus of interest only to detective story readers, but it was an immediate success. Street & Smith followed it with *Western Story Magazine, Love Story Magazine,* and even *Sport Story*

Magazine. In 1920 another publisher launched *Black Mask*, later to become famous for fostering the hard-boiled school of detective writing much in the way *Weird Tales* would come to nurture a certain school of fantasy writing markedly influenced by Lovecraft himself.

The 1920s were an incredibly active period for the pulp magazine field. It was the decade of specialization. The early specialized pulps were patterned on the popular genres. They enjoyed high circulations and, while they tended to be less literary than the all-fiction titles, they were not as blatantly sensational as the pulps would later become.

One exception was the highly unusual early specialized pulp launched in 1923, *Weird Tales.* Whether Lovecraft, who was deeply involved with the amateur journals and enjoying correspondence with writers like Frank Belknap Long and Clark Ashton Smith, continued to purchase pulp magazine cannot be said with certainty. That his interest in the weird remained undiminished is evidenced by his return to writing weird fiction in 1917 following a lengthy hiatus. (It is noteworthy that among his early tales was a lost dime-novel pastiche called "The Mystery of Murdon Grange," which attests to the powerful hold popular fiction exerted on Lovecraft's imagination.) When, late in 1921, Lovecraft was asked to contribute to his first professional market, he seized upon the chance, however grudgingly, perhaps as relief from the tedious revision work he was doing for clients like David Van Bush. As he wrote to Rheinhart Kleiner:

> Another business opportunity recently appearing is that afforded by St. Julian's [George Julian Houtain's] new magazine, *Home Brew.* He wants a series of six ghastly tales to order. . . . I doubt if any story from my pen could please the clientele of an essentially popular magazine, and have so informed the jovial publisher. However—if he will be satisfied with some frankly artificial hackwork, in no way related to my normal output, I will do my best for him. (*SL* 1.152)

Lovecraft's "Herbert West—Reanimator" was duly published in six parts, and was followed by "The Lurking Fear." He considered both, amazingly enough, to be "of insufficient merit for amateur use" (*SL* 1.157). Yet something of the experience must have encouraged him, for, prodded by James F. Morton, he offered two earlier stories to professional pulp magazines. "The Tomb" was submitted to, and rejected by, *Black Mask.* The *Black Cat*, a small magazine that often published weird stories and whose contributors were usually fledgling writers, spurned "Dagon." Lovecraft's published letters are silent on his reaction, but he seems not to have been terribly stung by the dual rejection, for upon the appearance of *Weird Tales* in March 1923, once again urged by Morton and others, he submitted five stories to editor Edwin Baird.

Baird accepted all five stories, but only after Lovecraft retyped his single-spaced typescripts. Although the money was welcome, Lovecraft evinced only tepid interest, and his attitude toward the magazine might well be summed up in thoughts he shared with Clark Ashton Smith in a letter dated 12 November 1922, as "stuff done to order for a vulgar magazine, & written down to the herd's level" (*SL* 1.201). Yet in the same letter he encouraged Smith, who was to illustrate "The Lurking Fear": "One need not be ashamed to write or draw for such magazines—Poe & Bierce, I believe, used to write for any old thing" (ibid.).

Perhaps Lovecraft considered *Weird Tales* to be a cut above *Home Brew* (which he denigrated as "positively beastly but now happily defunct" in a letter to August Derleth dated 7 November 1926),[5] although its garish covers and crude packaging made it seem cheap when compared to the Munsey titles. As a result, he encouraged both Smith and Frank Belknap Long to contribute to it. For a man who reviled pulp magazines, at least publicly, Lovecraft seemed perfectly willing to lead his literary friends into their clutches.

The first two years of *Weird Tales* were exciting ones for Lovecraft. He had a story in most of the early issues, was instrumental in convincing Baird to break his no-poetry rule and publish some of Clark Ashton Smith's verse, and revised several stories for his friend C. M. Eddy that Baird also published. Lovecraft was clearly *Weird Tales*'s star writer during its formative period. So taken was Lovecraft by his new-found acceptance in the magazine field that he undertook an original story, at 8,000 words the longest he had ever undertaken up to that time, and the first written specifically for a professional pulp as opposed to being an amateur journal cast-off. The story was "The Rats in the Walls," and upon accepting it, Baird's publisher, J. C. Henneberger, called it the best story *Weird Tales* had ever received. When informed of the compliment by Baird, Lovecraft remarked, in a letter dated 3 February 1924, "I wish he'd tell sister Bob Davis that!" (*SL* 1.295). For, astonishingly, Lovecraft, who seemed so timid about offering his work to professional markets, had passed up the near-certainty of a sale to *Weird Tales* for the more prestigious and better-paying *Argosy*.

He seemed to take the manuscript's return in stride, although he was still amateur enough to share the rejection letter with Frank Belknap Long:

> It will interest you to observe the professional rejection of this piece by R. H. Davis, Esq. of the Munsey Co., to whom I sent it at the insistence of . . . [C. M.] Eddy. You will note that the contention of [Arthur] Leeds appears to be justify'd; since Davis, tho' admitting it hath some merit, holds it too horrible

for the tender sensibilities of a delicately nurtured publick. Leetle Bairdi is becoming a very great friend of mine and designs to publish my efforts with much regularity. I will enclose an epistle of his, which please return. He hath since accepted "Arthur Jermyn", and I am not without hopes for "Hypnos" and "The Rats in the Walls", which I am this day sending him. (*SL* 1.259)

Lovecraft seemed to be a cheerful, if sometimes testy, regular contributor to *Weird Tales*, remarking at one point to Baird: "Are you giving me a vacation for March, or are the *Rats* to gnaw their uncanny course through that issue?" (*SL* 1.294–95).

At about this time, Henneberger asked Lovecraft to write a novel for *Weird Tales*. Lovecraft told Baird he contemplated a novel to be called *The House of the Worm*, "which I shall be happy to send when I finish it" (*SL* 1.295). Lovecraft did neither. The culmination of Lovecraft's early *Weird Tales* experiences came when Baird invited him to collaborate on a story with the renowned illusionist and escape artist Harry Houdini. It was heady stuff, and Lovecraft's veiled distaste for popular magazines didn't seem to extend to *Weird Tales*—or if it did, his letters are noticeably silent on that score.

Lovecraft's enthusiasm for the magazine, despite his comments to others that it was desperately in need of truly unconventional weird fiction, is no more clearly expressed than in a letter to James F. Morton dated 19 February 1924:

> *Weird Tales?* Boy—what I told yuh afore was only the beginnin'! I'm hearin' damn near every day from Henneberger—the owner of the outfit—and just had a special delivery order to collaborate on an Egyptian horror with this bimbo Houdini. . . . Well . . . it's all jake with me if dey's any jack wit'in reach o' me lunch-hooks! I'm a practical man, and ya kin get anyt'ing outa me if ya flashes a fat enough roll! (*SL* 1.312–13)

Lovecraft the amateur author had clearly made the transition to Lovecraft the professional fiction writer; but he had only one market, one he felt was probably short-lived. As he remarked in that same letter: "This sort of blah is a flash in the pan, and w'en W.T. goes blooey you kin' find Old Theobald hangin' out at the same ol' blind pig on the corner" (*SL* 1.313).

Lovecraft's foresight would prove on the mark but not in the way he thought, for within weeks *Weird Tales* suspended publication. No May or June issue appeared. Regular monthly publication did not resume until the November 1924 issue, and by then Edwin Baird was replaced by Farnsworth Wright, a man of peculiar editorial attitudes who was afflicted with Parkinson's disease. Wright's rejection of the very first story Lovecraft sent him, "The Shunned

House," as too long and wordy marked the beginning of a pattern that was to estrange Lovecraft from the only steady fiction market he would ever have. In 1924 *Weird Tales* truly was, as it was subtitled, "The Unique Magazine." It would not have a serious rival for another decade, and the first true science fiction magazine—its nearest equivalent—did not come into being until 1926, when Hugo Gernsback launched *Amazing Stories*.

For a brief period during the *Weird Tales* upheaval, Henneberger considered the idea of starting a new magazine in the *Weird Tales* vein, and offered the editorship to Lovecraft. Recently married to Sonia H. Greene, Lovecraft considered the offer but, because it entailed moving to Chicago, resisted Henneberger's entreaties. The magazine never materialized.

In the fall of 1925 Lovecraft had a flurry of creativity resulting in three stories: "The Horror at Red Hook," "He," and "In the Vault." A year had passed since the rejection of "The Shunned House," and Lovecraft would later admit that "The Horror at Red Hook" was written specifically to meet *Weird Tales's* editorial requirements. The others may have been as well. Lovecraft did attempt to sell "Red Hook" and "The Shunned House" to Edwin Baird's *Detective Tales,* and actually contemplated a detective story set in Salem, but Baird's rebuffs proved fatal to his plans. Wright accepted "Red Hook" and "He" but rejected "In the Vault." He also rejected Lovecraft's next effort, "Cool Air."

Although Lovecraft characterized these rejections as absolute, more than likely this was not the actual situation. Unlike professional pulp editors, who simply accepted and rejected stories purely on their merits—only rarely asking for a rewrite with a borderline manuscript—Wright seems to have returned the majority of submissions with the suggestion that a rewrite might bring a favorable verdict. Wright went so far as to tell one *Weird Tales* contributor that the only story he ever accepted without asking for an automatic revision was A. Merritt's legendary short story "The Woman of the Wood." The offering was too fortuitous to risk losing, for Merritt was a major Munsey writer, highly popular, and normally beyond the reach of a paltry penny-a-word market like *Weird Tales*. *Argosy* had rejected the story and it became Wright's good fortune to acquire it. Wright was no doubt exaggerating when he made his claim, but many *Weird Tales* contributors during the Wright period complained of the constant rejection-with-suggested-revision experience. Why Wright conducted himself so unprofessionally is difficult to determine.

For most of its thirty-year existence, *Weird Tales* was the only outlet for writers of weird fiction, and was a magazine virtually without the usual pulp formula requirements. It was a place where writers, professional or not, could publish material not saleable elsewhere. Wright understood his monopoly, of course. He may have felt that it allowed him to make extra demands on his essentially captive stable of writers. Or he may have felt that with his payment policy—comparatively low and only on publication—his writers were simply giving him tossed-off stories while writing for the better-paying magazines that invariably paid on acceptance. It is more likely, however, that the relative crudeness of the submissions he received dictated this policy. The imaginative pulp fiction of this time—even science fiction titles like *Amazing Stories* and *Astounding*—was incredibly wooden and lifeless, especially compared with the better pulp titles. Many pulp writers simply did not consider *Weird Tales* a serious market. It was a haven for oddballs and dabblers, not true professionals, who considered it, in the parlance of their time, a "dump market" for their rejects. The writing quality of much of the first two decades of *Weird Tales* bears this out. Wright may have felt it necessary to return most of the potentially acceptable submissions on the assumption that his hungry writers would be forced to give their work an additional smoothing draft it would not otherwise receive. Pulp writers were notorious for submitting first drafts, albeit usually acceptable first drafts.

Most *Weird Tales* contributions slavishly followed Wright's urging, but a number reported that they simply resubmitted after several months without actually making revisions. This ploy worked surprisingly often. It did not work, however, with H. P. Lovecraft. Still clinging to his amateur status while automatically submitting stories, he refused to revise his work.

A rival of sorts came into existence in 1926 when Bernarr Macfadden brought out the first issue of *Ghost Stories*. It was not by any stretch of the imagination a serious threat to *Weird Tales*'s uniqueness. It was a rotogravure magazine of fictional ghost stories written in the confession-story style and illustrated with staged photographs of supposed true-life hauntings. The tepid style and mundane subject left Lovecraft unimpressed. As he remarked to Frank Belknap Long on 16 October 1926: "You will find it quite hopeless—even worse than *Weird Tales*. Indeed, its chief merit is to me the proof it affords that a magazine can be worse than Brother Farnie's" (*SL* 2.79). What Lovecraft did not mention is that he had submitted three stories to the magazine, all of which were returned. It is not difficult to see why they were rejected. A typical *Ghost Story* ghost story might be titled "I Married a Ghost," "John Kelly's Christmas Ghost," or "The Thing That Paid the Rent." Tame stuff when compared to "In the Vault," which was turned down by *Ghost Stories* after *Weird Tales* had rejected it as too strong for its supposedly thrill-hungry readers.

In an exchange of letters with August Derleth, Lovecraft's attitude toward writing for the magazine goes from fatalistic expectation to a game determination not to give up, something quite at variance with the accepted Lovecraftian dilettante image. "Yes—I suppose I'll get my stuff back from *Ghost Stories,*" he confided on 2 September 1926. "It hasn't improved—& is about as poor as a magazine can be. I know the Macfadden junk is altogether impossible—in fact, I've never so much as opened one of these publications with the exception of that named! A man I know, however, picks up quite a little cash by deliberately catering to their needs."[6] Yet he later told Derleth in a letter dated 11 October: "*Ghost Stories* has rejected two of my tales & will probably reject the third, but I rather expected that. To land anything with them, one would have to study a special technique suited to the crude minds of half-baked readers. Since the pay is 2¢ per word, I may yet try it!"[7]

Lovecraft toyed with submitting "Pickman's Model," which he was then working on, telling Derleth on 8 September 1926, "not that it's of their moronic type, but that the style happens to be somewhat colloquial." Lovecraft appears, however, to have sent the story directly to *Weird Tales* and there is no record of his attempting to crack *Ghost Stories* again until 1931, when it changed ownership and was converted to a pulp. Lovecraft mentions submitting "In the Vault" and "From Beyond" to the new editor. Both were rejected.[8]

In submitting to *Ghost Stories,* Lovecraft believed that his work might elevate the level of contributions. It was a misguided notion. *Ghost Stories* had an ironclad slant and it sold respectably for many years. It was not interested in stories out of tune with its intended audience, which would seem to have been primarily women interested in spiritualism and astrology—much the same readers who bought Macfadden's confession titles.

Lovecraft was left with only one market. Rejections continued to plague him. When he penned his classic "The Call of Cthulhu" in 1926, he duly submitted it to Wright. As he explained to Frank Belknap Long on 26 October 1926:

> Little Farnie rejected Grandpa's "Cthulhu" story on the grounds that it was too slow and obscure for his zippy morons—but I guess I'll send along his note and let you see for yourself. If I could get plenty of good revisions to do, I'd never write another tale for these cheap commercial caterers. It ruins one's style to have a publick of tame-souled half-wits hanging over one's head as one writes. (*SL* 2.79)

Yet Lovecraft evidently felt "The Call of Cthulhu" too important to allow Wright's capriciousness to sink it. He resubmitted it to an obscure semi-horror magazine called *Mystery Stories,* whose editor Robert Simpson, according to

Lovecraft, "rejected [it] on the ground that it was 'too heavy' for his airy & popular publication."[9]

Lovecraft's first tirades against pulp commercialism seem to date from the rejection of "The Call of Cthulhu." But many of his pronouncements seem to have been defensive and not philosophic in nature. He continued to court *Weird Tales* by offering poetry and old stories that had previously appeared in amateur journals, and when new markets appeared, he often leapt at them with the same scattershot multiple-submittal approach that had worked well with the Baird *Weird Tales* and failed miserably with *Ghost Stories.*

It is not surprising then that Lovecraft would approach it *Amazing Stories* when it appeared in 1926. While his old prejudices were resurfacing, and he had not given up on *Weird Tales*—"Pickman's Model" had been accepted early in 1927—he declined to submit "The Colour out of Space" to Wright and instead sent it to *Amazing Stories.*

"The Colour out of Space" was a departure from anything Lovecraft had written before. He later pointed to its composition as the beginning of his "realistic period." It was also the first story he had written that could remotely be considered acceptable to a science fiction magazine. Given his previous patterns of submittal and the fact that he did not first offer the story to *Weird Tales,* it must be seriously considered whether "The Colour out of Space" was written expressly for *Amazing Stories.*

Amazing Stories was the first magazine market Lovecraft had succeeded in breaching since *Weird Tales.* Unfortunately, although the story garnered Lovecraft much attention and notice outside the magazine, editor Hugo Gernsback paid him, belatedly, an insulting $25.00—about one-fifth *Weird Tales*'s low rates. This was a business practice typical of Gernsback, and it effectively precluded *Amazing Stories* as a market for Lovecraft's fiction. It wasn't the slim payment, Lovecraft later explained, it was the misrepresentation. After all, Lovecraft was receiving as little as $20.00 for his revisions of his clients' weird stories.

Within days of hearing that *Amazing* had accepted the story, Lovecraft received a letter from Wright asking to see "The Call of Cthulhu" again. Wright evidently realized, nearly a year after first rejecting the story, that Lovecraft was not about to revise and resubmit it. Wright took the story, but Lovecraft's pleasure was tempered by Wright's simultaneous turndown of two new stories, "The Silver Key" and "The Strange High House in the Mist." True to form, Wright would later change his mind and ask to see both stories again—and accept them.

A false ray of hope came in 1927 in the form of Edwin Baird's announcement of a new weird magazine. Evidently hoping that lightning would strike twice, Lovecraft submitted six unidentified stories in May, but while Frank Belknap Long met with an immediate acceptance of two submissions, Baird asked Lovecraft if he could hold his stories for a later decision. Lovecraft agreed, but the magazine, which had been scheduled for a late 1927 release, never came to pass.

The first evidence of Lovecraft's demoralization is the fact that in 1927 he produced two short novels, *The Dream-Quest of Unknown Kadath* and *The Case of Charles Dexter Ward*, and made no attempt to polish or market them. In 1928 his only new fiction was a revision for Zealia Bishop and one major story of his own, "The Dunwich Horror." Wright accepted the latter at once.

Lovecraft might never have written "The Dunwich Horror" but for a series of positive incidents occurring in December 1927. First, "The Horror at Red Hook" appeared in the anthology *Not at Night*, the first appearance of a Lovecraft story in hard covers. Then Edward J. O'Brien listed "The Colour out of Space" in his *Best Short Stories of 1928* anthology. It was not Lovecraft's first such notice, but it was his first three-star listing. Then there was the acceptance of "Cool Air," a story once rejected by *Weird Tales*, by the new *Tales of Magic and Mystery*. Although the sale earned Lovecraft the modest sum of $18.00, it was potentially a step forward, for *Tales of Magic and Mystery* was not a pulp but a rotogravure magazine. Unfortunately it expired with the issue following the appearance of "Cool Air."

Tales of Magic and Mystery might never have developed into a reliable outlet for Lovecraft, however. Editor Walter B. Gibson accepted "Cool Air" only after rejecting seven other stories Lovecraft had submitted simultaneously—including "The Strange High House in the Mist" and "The Nameless City." When word reached Lovecraft that Gibson had been replaced, he considered resubmitting the rejected stories, but it is not known if he followed through. Lovecraft seems to have responded to this minor boost by undertaking a new revision, "The Curse of Yig." Then came "The Dunwich Horror," which Wright accepted immediately. It paid him the largest amount he had seen so far from a pulp sale—$240.

Other events were occurring to motivate Lovecraft. His first hardcover book, *The Shunned House*, was planned in 1928 (it was printed but the sheets were never bound), and "The Call of Cthulhu" appeared in T. Everett Harré's anthology *Beware After Dark!* in 1929. Earlier Lovecraft stories were reprinted in *Weird Tales* and he began his sonnet-cycle *Fungi from Yuggoth*, many of which were taken by *Weird Tales*. Other anthology appearances occurred with regularity into 1931.

After writing "The Dunwich Horror," Lovecraft became preoccupied with revisions, most of which were placed in *Weird Tales* by the nominal authors.

Eventually he resumed writing original fiction. In October 1930 Wright accepted his new story, "The Whisperer in Darkness," prompting Lovecraft to confide to Clark Ashton Smith, "This quick landing certainly pleases me mightily, & encourages me to cut down revision long enough to grind out a whole series of tales as I used to do in 1919 & 1920" (*SL* 3.193).

Unfortunately, acceptance of "The Whisperer in Darkness" was followed by an announcement only two months later that *Weird Tales* was having financial difficulties and was retrenching to bimonthly publication. Lovecraft seemed to take this philosophically, telling Wilfred Blanch Talman in a letter dated 21 January 1931: "Too bad W.T. has curtailed, but it's not a bad market even now. Actually, the change will affect very few of us—for we have scarcely ever had things in except at long intervals" (*SL* 3.280–81).

Part of *Weird Tales*'s retrenchment included a curtailing of serials and longer stories. A truly professional writer, conscious of his editor's needs and difficulties, would respond by producing only shorter stories. Not Lovecraft. Amazingly, he undertook the longest, most ambitious story he had attempted to market to date, *At the Mountains of Madness*. This was after Wright had earlier in the year turned down "The Mound," which Lovecraft had ghost-written for Zealia Bishop. Rather prophetically, Lovecraft remarked to Derleth in an undated letter from early 1930:

> That damned fool has just turned down the story I "ghost-wrote" for my Kansas City client, on the ground that it is too long for a single publication, yet structurally unadapted to division. I'm not worrying, because I've got my cash; but it does sicken me to watch the caprices of that editorial jackass! I'll bet ten bucks he turns down the first really signed story I send him, too; notwithstanding his insistent urging that I write one.

"The Mound" was the longest story Lovecraft would ghost. *At the Mountains of Madness* was more than ten thousand words longer. Lovecraft may not have been exhibiting creative stubbornness here, for two new markets for fantastic fiction were looming to challenge *Weird Tales* and *Amazing Stories*.

First, William Clayton launched *Astounding Stories* with a January 1930 cover date, saying "We want fantastic pseudo-scientific fiction, especially meccano-fantasy with good story and human interest values." He was paying a handsome two cents a word on acceptance, and sought long serials. Hard on Clayton's heels, publisher Harold Hersey of the Good Story Publishing Company announced a similar new magazine, entitled *Astonishing Stories*. He solicited novels as long as 50,000 words and especially favored novelettes of 25,000 words.

Lovecraft was made aware of these new prospects but appeared more excited by *Astonishing*, probably because August Derleth was selling regularly to Hersey. As HPL wrote Derleth in March 1930:

> Thanks immensely for the Hersey tip! I think I shall send him "The Nameless City" & perhaps one or two others—although I fear none of these has the publick appeal demanded by the "pulp" press. The remark about interplanetary stuff, though, sounds encouraging. It's time for somebody to write the tale of a voyage to the 9th planet discovered at the Lowell Observatory.

Lovecraft alludes to "The Whisperer in Darkness," which he had begun composing in February, before the discovery of the planet Pluto. While the timing is tight, an additional impetus for this work may have been the opening up of these promising new markets. Or at least, it emboldened Lovecraft to slant this tale toward their expansive editorial visions.

Unfortunately, the depression delayed *Astonishing Stories*, which was ultimately released the following spring as *Miracle, Science and Fantasy Stories*. It expired with its second lackluster issue. It's unknown if Lovecraft completed "Whisperer" in time to submit it, even if that were his intention. Or if "The Nameless City" were ever considered for this title. But during the course of the year he continued to express to Derleth strong interest in *Astounding Stories* as well as *Amazing Stories*, saying:

> I note the data on various magazines, & am glad that *Astounding Stories* is still going. What, by the way, is the present address of *Amazing Stories?* Before long I may try some old MSS. on some of these scattered markets—especially the new Hersey venture you spoke about.

Could Lovecraft's 1930–31 shift toward pseudo-science themes have been partly influenced this mini-boom of SF magazines? It seems both probable and practical, inasmuch as any rejection by one would still permit a sale to another. With its science fictional premise, *At the Mountains of Madness* fit the boom perfectly. But no evidence exists that it or any other Lovecraft story was offered to any of these magazines. In the end, Lovecraft did submit *At the Mountains of Madness* to *Astounding*, long after Wright initially had expressed a willingness to consider the story. When faced with the short novel, Wright turned it down with regrets.

At first, Lovecraft seemed to take the rejection in stride, telling J. Vernon Shea in a letter dated 7 August 1931:

Yes—Wright "explained" his rejection of the "Mountains of Madness" in almost the same language as that with which he "explained" other recent rejections to Long & Derleth. It was "too long", "not easily divisible into parts", "not convincing"—& so on. Just what he said of other things of mine (except for length)—some of which he has ultimately accepted after many hesitations. Those once-rejected & later accepted things include "Cthulhu", "The Tomb", & many others. It is very possible that I am growing stale—that is for readers of the "Whisperer" & "Mountains of Madness" to judge—but if so it merely signifies the end of my fictional attempts. There is no field other than the weird in which I have any aptitude or inclination for fictional composition. (*SL* 3.395)

Coupled with this rebuff was the rejection by editor Winfield Shiras of a proposed collection of Lovecraft tales for the hardcover publisher G. P. Putnam's Sons, which Lovecraft blamed on Wright in the same letter to Shea:

The grounds for rejection were twofold—first, that some of the tales are not subtle enough .... too obvious & well-explained—(admitted! That ass Wright got me into the habit of obvious writing with his never-ending complaints against the indefiniteness of my early stuff.) & secondly, that all the tales are too uniformly macabre in mood to stand collected publication. The second reason is sheer bull—for as a matter of fact unity of mood is a positive asset in a fictional collection. But I suppose the herd must have their comic relief! (*SL* 3.395–96)

It was at virtually the same time that the first serious rival to *Weird Tales*'s supremacy appeared. News of the appearance of the September 1931 issue of *Strange Tales*, published by the formidable William Clayton Company, must have shaken Farnsworth Wright when he heard it. Clayton was one of the many pulp chains that came into being during the financially expansive twenties. Boasting several healthy titles and a starting payment rate of two cents a word (with regular raises thereafter for its better writers), Clayton had the ability to attract the best writers in the pulp field and in theory raid Wright of his star contributors. At best, *Strange Tales* represented a true editor's nightmare. Since it paid significantly more than Wright could afford, it was virtually certain that *Weird Tales*'s writers would submit first to *Strange Tales*, leaving Wright dependent on Clayton's rejects. A virtually overnight leveling of *Weird Tales*'s story quality was assured, if not the magazine's very existence, which was already threatened by the worsening world depression.

Wright's fear that he would lose Lovecraft to *Strange Tales* was a realistic one. Lovecraft must have seen in *Strange Tales* not only an alternative to Wright's peculiar editorial foibles but also a lucrative market for himself. Until that time, Lovecraft had never written for one of the better-paying pulp magazines. *Strange Tales,* were it to accept his work, would give him a taste of a true pulp writer's earning ability.

Lovecraft pounced on this opportunity upon hearing of a pre-publication announcement of its first issue and contacted editor Harry Bates. "I sent Bates four old yarns—'Sarnath', 'Nameless City', 'Beyond the Wall of Sleep', and 'Polaris'—together with a request for information as to whether material of that sort would be totally unacceptable from its very nature," Lovecraft wrote Derleth on 16 April 1931. "You will see his courteous reply—which only confirms my original opinion that nothing of mine could ever find lodgment in a Clayton magazine."[10]

The day Lovecraft received Bates's letter, he also had a form-letter rejection from *Ghost Stories.* As he told Clark Ashton Smith, "The latter bunch did not condescend to a personal note, but Bates covered three closely-typed pages with friendly comment and outlining of his needs."[11]

His pessimism notwithstanding, Lovecraft was sufficiently encouraged to send Bates one of the stories just bounced by *Ghost Stories.* It was to no avail. "Bates promptly rejected 'In the Vault'," he reported to Derleth on 9 May, "but said that a better story of that kind might be rather in his line. I doubt that I shall ever make a Clayton magazine—they obviously want something in a mood & vein essentially alien to anything which could be mine."[12] Harry Bates's specific reasons for rejection are not known, but *Strange Tales* was by no means a clone of *Weird Tales.* The Clayton chain preferred stories of action. In fact, with the exception of *Weird Tales*—which had always been a pulp backwater untouched by trends of popular fiction—action was the byword of the pulp field during the depression. For the industry was undergoing one of its periodic dramatic transformations. In the trade, the editors called this new slant "bang-bang," a synthesis of the old dime novel heroics and the terse Hemingwayesque writing style fostered by Dashiell Hammett, Erle Stanley Gardner, Carroll John Daly, and other writers of *Black Mask* magazine's hard-boiled school of writing. H. P. Lovecraft could not have been more ill-suited for the new trend if it had required him to write in Esperanto.

Lovecraft realized this eventually and declined to submit further offerings to Bates despite hints sent to Lovecraft by way of August Derleth that Bates was interested in seeing more Lovecraft pieces. The only Lovecraft prose ever to grace the magazine's pages was his uncredited collaboration with Henry S. Whitehead of 1932, "The Trap."

By the time Lovecraft admitted defeat in a February 1932 letter to Derleth, his opinion of Bates and *Strange Tales* had soured:

> I have just finished the new S.T., & think it almost uniformly rotten. . . . It is leagues below the low-enough average of W.T.—for Handsome Harry's fatal intelligence spies out & rejects all too readily any item with the abhorred traces of sincere emotion or passable originality! I could never make that rag if I tried from now till Edmond Hamilton gets a new plot![13]

The rejection by *Strange Tales* obviously dealt Lovecraft a severe emotional blow. Until that time, he could in clear conscience blame Wright's capriciousness for his frequent rejections. But he approached *Strange Tales* with a solid reputation and a clean slate. The wholesale declining of his submittals could only be interpreted as a rejection—no doubt without the sweetener suggestion of revising and resubmitting—of Lovecraft by a serious pulp publisher, and it meant that should *Strange Tales* ultimately replace *Weird Tales*, Lovecraft would lose his only market.

It was at this time that Lovecraft began to rail against the pulp field's growing action trend, as seen in his letter to Clark Ashton Smith dated 20 November 1931:

> In choosing which direction to take for further efforts, I have little difficulty. Repugnance—and the lack of natural cleverness and adaptability—definitely debars me from the popular "eckshun" field, so all I can do is to try honestly to write really better stories or give up the whole mess as a bad job—though possibly pulling off consciously mediocre yarns now and then for sheer amusement. (*SL* 3.436)

Although Lovecraft would probably not have admitted it for fear of seeming to contradict his frequently vented distaste for pulp magazines, the Clayton experience may have been as important as, if not more important than, the Putnam rejection, which had in fact been tendered with the suggestion that a different story collection from the one Lovecraft had submitted might work. Lovecraft, ever sensitive to rejection, preferred to drop the matter rather than face a second Putnam turndown. Subsequent book opportunities also bore no fruit.

By this time Lovecraft's opinion of Farnsworth Wright and *Weird Tales* was sinking, even as Lovecraft's circle of friends, including Clark Ashton Smith and Frank Belknap Long, was growing around it. Lovecraft was in the peculiar position of seeing the friends he had encouraged to submit to *Weird Tales* appear more often than he himself did! These included new, young writers like August

Derleth and Robert Bloch, whom he mentored, even when he felt their writing was not up to his own exacting standards.

In January 1932, Lovecraft had learned of a new weird fiction magazine, *Galaxy,* and submitted two stories to editor Carl Swanson. Swanson asked for permission to reprint some of Lovecraft's earlier *Weird Tales* stories as well, but when Farnsworth Wright refused to release second-serial rights to the stories he controlled and hinted that he would look unfavorably on Lovecraft's allowing earlier *Weird Tales* stories to appear in *Galaxy,* Lovecraft told Wilfred Blanch Talman, "Well—what I did was to give him the civilised Rhodinsular equivalent of that curt injunction so popular in his own tempest-swept cosmopolis— 'go jump in the lake'!" (*SL* 4.27).

Nevertheless, Lovecraft declined to cut all ties with Wright and assured him that, as he told Talman, "I'd give him a first look at any extra short or conventional specimen I might happen to evolve." This was wise, inasmuch as *Galaxy* never materialized.

It was during this time that Lovecraft began revising stories for Hazel Heald, one of which—"Winged Death"—was rejected by *Strange Tales.*[14] There is every reason to believe that most—or all—of the five Heald stories were commissioned by Heald with the high-paying *Strange Tales* market in mind. Unfortunately, none sold to *Strange Tales,* even though the stories were clearly "written down" to the market mentality as Lovecraft perceived it.

One submission nearly made it, however. Lovecraft had suggested revisions to an Egyptian reincarnation fantasy by E. Hoffmann Price, entitled "Tarbis of the Lake." It had previously been bounced by *Illustrated Detective Magazine.* Price then tried it on *Strange Tales,* reporting to Lovecraft on 27 September 1932 the following:

> I got a rare break on "Tarbis": Bates said he liked it very much, and would buy it, only, he had orders to discontinue Strange Tales! (Chant me a page from the Necronomicon! Foul & filthy, please!) So I did some revising and am mailing it to the surviving master of spectral fancies, Satrap Pharabozus. I trust that there have been no rumors about our joint composition of this masterpiece, as that might prejudice it.[15]

Ultimately, *Weird Tales* did take it, but only after Farnsworth Wright had wrung from Price a rewrite that severely diluted the Lovecraftian contributions.

Lovecraft's letters become increasingly bitter and despondent over these matters, yet there always remained that stubborn hope expressed at the end, as in his letter to Carl Jacobi dated 27 February 1932:

Your versatility is decidedly greater than my own for I can never hit the popular formula well enough to land anywhere but in *Weird Tales*. . . . Moreover, I think my days of contribution to W.T. are decidedly numbered, for Wright rejected my best story last year, & is likely to do the same with my later work on account of its greater length & slower motion as compared with my earlier stuff. I can no longer be satisfied with the glib, machine-clipped type of tale which editors demand—& unfortunately there is no likelihood of editors ever being satisfied with the kind of story I now write. Repeated rejections began to get on my nerves so badly last autumn that I was almost unable to write anything at all—so now I have resolved to let professional magazines alone for a while & write to please myself only; letting the results pile up for whatever ultimate disposition the Fates may provide. Of course, though, I would probably try my professional luck with any especially short or obvious story which might happen to drop from my pen in the course of varied composition. (*SL* 4.24)

This fatalistic surrender of control over the fate of his writing activities greatly annoyed August Derleth. Derleth, who considered himself the consummate professional writer, was busily writing fiction that catered to editorial demands and urged Lovecraft to reconsider. Lovecraft's slow draining of self-confidence is reflected in a letter to Derleth dated 4 March 1932:

Glad the literary work still goes on. . . . As for my own latter-day attitude toward writing & submitting—I can see why you consider my anti-rejection policy a stubbornly foolish & needlessly short-sighted one, & am not prepared to offer any defence other than the mere fact that repeated rejections *do* work in a certain way on my psychology—rationally or not—& that their effect is to cause in me a certain literary lockjaw which absolutely prevents further fictional composition despite my most arduous efforts. . . . There are times when the experience of repeated rejections would mean little to me, but other times when the symbolism of the process grated harshly—& now is one of these other times. [16]

As the months passed, the rejection of *At the Mountains of Madness* loomed larger in Lovecraft's mind as an irrecoverable blow. He wrote:

Last year Wright rejected my best story . . . and in so doing revealed such a purely commercial attitude that I have not felt like sending him anything since. He has no sympathy with any story not calculated to please the herd of crude and unimaginative illiterates forming the bulk of his readers—and repeated rejections have such a bad psychological effect on me that I have thought it best to pause for a while. Moreover—my subconscious efforts to meet the Wright standard were having a bad effect on my work. When Putnam's rejected a book-form collection which I had submitted upon their own request, they gave as one of their objections the fact that my tales had an over-explanatory quality—a lack of subtlety—indubitably caused by the influence of the cheap-magazine standard. On reflection, I concurred in this objection—even though I have always (at least since 1925) sought to repudiate the popular commercial tradition. Without doubt, the constant early thunderings of Wright against my debatable endings and obscure implications have had an insidious tendency to make me tone such things down—largely without knowing it. Actually, my stuff falls between two stools. It is not intrinsically good enough for high-grade publication, and it is not cheaply popular enough to suit the vendors of pulp rags. Thus I am left high and dry as a misfit. (*SL* 4.53–54)

Shortly after the rejection of *At the Mountains of Madness*, Lovecraft began another story, "The Shadow over Innsmouth." Although long, "The Shadow over Innsmouth" was an extended chase story possessing action elements hitherto alien to Lovecraft's work; it was also almost entirely devoid of Cthulhu Mythos impedimenta that might be unfamiliar to the Clayton readership. This strongly suggests that the story was specifically written with the *Strange Tales* market in mind. However, Bates apparently never saw it.[17] As Lovecraft wrote to Derleth on 10 December 1931:

> I have been paying too much attention to the demands of markets & the opinions of others—hence if I am ever to write again I must begin afresh; writing only for myself & getting into the old habit of non-self-conscious storytelling without any technical thoughts. No—I don't intend to offer "The Shadow over Innsmouth" for publication, for it would stand no chance of acceptance.[18]

But Lovecraft was missed by *Weird Tales* readers who repeatedly asked for more of his work in letters directed to its letters page, called "The Eyrie," prompting Wright to ask Lovecraft about his fictional endeavors. Responding to Wright's inquiry on 18 February 1932, Lovecraft said with evident and uncharacteristic sarcasm:

> Sorry to say I haven't anything new which you would be likely to care for. Latterly my tastes have run to studies in geographical atmosphere requiring greater length than the popular editorial fancy relishes—my new "Shadow over Innsmouth" is three typed pages longer than "Whisperer in Darkness," and conventional magazine standards would undoubtedly rate it "intolerably slow", "not conveniently divisible", or something of that sort. (*SL* 4.17)

Even this biting retort ends with a note of hoped-for reconciliation: "But of course—if by chance I turn out anything short and apparently conventional I may try my luck at it now and then; and if I do, I shall certainly send it to *Weird Tales* first of all." Clearly, this was a low point for Lovecraft, as a letter to Wilfred Blanch Talman from early 1932 shows:

> I have virtually abandoned the idea of attempting professional fiction contributions. The repeated rebuffs I receive from capricious asses like Wright, Babbitesque dolts like that drivelling Clayton, and conventional namby-pamby's like Shiras of Putnam's have about paralysed me into a helpless and disgusted inarticulateness; so that I resolved some time ago to chuck the whole loathsome mess and return to the purely non-professional basis of the pre-1923 days, when I wrote spontaneously and without expectation of marketing. (*SL* 4.27–28)

Oddly, despite this seeming low point, Lovecraft immediately followed "The Shadow over Innsmouth" with "The Dreams in the Witch House" in early 1932. But when Lovecraft let Derleth read the story, the latter criticized it so severely that Lovecraft put aside any thought of submitting it. Months later, at the end of 1932, Derleth perversely sent a typescript he made of the story to Wright without Lovecraft's knowledge, and the story was accepted.

Lovecraft wrote no other original fiction in 1932. He was kept busy revising stories for Hazel Heald, all presumably first offered to Clayton. Four of these—including the one known *Strange Tales* rejection, "Winged Death"— ended up in the pages of *Weird Tales*, some of them several years after composition. A fifth, "The Man of Stone," appeared in *Wonder Stories*, Hugo Gernsback's successor to *Amazing Stories*.

Lovecraft could not have been happy to see his work in a Gernsback magazine, even if under another name, but at least he had been paid in advance by his revision client. He collaborated on a sequel to "The Silver Key" with E. Hoffmann Price—but only because Price took his polite acquiescence over a proposed collaboration more seriously than Lovecraft had intended. He labored through the task of revising Price's original story only to have Wright reject it. Wright was later cajoled into reconsidering, and Lovecraft acknowledged this in a letter to Wright dated 21 November 1933, in which he revealed his dissatisfaction with the current state of *Weird Tales* and did what no professional writer would ever dream of doing: tell an editor how he ought to edit his magazine:

> I am indeed glad that the collaboration has finally proved acceptable, and hope that no epistolary alarms of outraged illiterati may cause you to regret the decision. For my part, as I have often said, I think that a restriction of con-

tributions to the sort of thing the densest clods like would alienate nearly as many readers as an all-literate policy would. I know surely a dozen or more followers of the magazine who would certainly not continue to follow it if its contents uniformly represented the lifeless, mechanical, stock-figure, diagrammed type of hack-work so dearly beloved by the *Eyrie*-bombarding proletariat—and that dozen can scarcely be altogether unrepresentative. The trouble is, that the readers who do the most letter-writing—in eagerness to publicise themselves—tend to reflect a stratum of taste distinctly lower than that of the best (and by no means negligible) part of the magazine's clientele. There seems to me little doubt but that *Weird Tales* is bought and read by large numbers of persons infinitely above the pulp-hound level—persons who relish Machen and Blackwood and M R James, and who would welcome a periodical of the Machen-Blackwood-James degree of maturity and fastidiousness if such were published. Naturally, they tolerate the hack stuff merely for the sake of the occasional real stories—Clericashtoniana, Howardiana, Caneviniana [here Lovecraft refers to the work of Clark Ashton Smith, Robert E. Howard, and Henry S. Whitehead], etc.—which accompany it, and would certainly drop off if not assured of at least a fair supply. (*SL* 4.322)

This is nothing less than a plea by a nearly desperate writer that *Weird Tales* be reconfigured so that his own stories might become more acceptable. What Lovecraft failed to recognize or admit is that even if Wright had raised the magazine's standards, comparatively few Machens and Blackwoods existed and could hardly be expected to create highly polished and crafted pieces of work for a mere penny per word. Further, if *Weird Tales* readers—as opposed to Lovecraft and the dozen or so other writers in his circle—truly disliked most of its contents, they would not long be steady readers and *Weird Tales* would simply collapse.

Lovecraft clearly understood this, as seen in his letter to Vincent Starrett of 11 April 1927:

I certainly agree that the lack of a market for spectral material over the penny-dreadful grade is a very unfortunate circumstance. Yet I fear it is an irremediable one, since the actual number of persons to whom such things appeal is apparently small indeed. I have had a fair assortment of stories in the crowd-cultivating *Weird Tales,* but believe this market is gradually closing to me on account of the editor's deference to a clientele demanding simple, understandable ghostliness with plenty of "human interest" & a brisk, concrete, cheerful, & non-atmospheric style. (*SL* 2.124)

What had really happened—the repeated estrangements aside—was that creatively, H. P. Lovecraft had outgrown *Weird Tales* and what little pulp weird fiction he continued to enjoy. He had outgrown his markets, but there was no higher market or outlet to which he could aspire. There was no such thing as a "slick" weird fiction magazine of the caliber of the *Saturday Evening Post* or *Collier's*. Hardcover publication would have been the next logical step but, except for his increasingly frequent anthology appearances, Lovecraft never pursued it even though he had one perfectly publishable novel, *The Case of Charles Dexter Ward*, in his files. Given his temperament, Lovecraft's only outlet for fictional expression remained the weird short story, and in his imaginative growth he was expanding its very parameters with stories like *At the Mountains of Madness*, which married horror and science fiction in ways no writer had ever before contemplated.

Frustrated, Lovecraft continued with revision work, invariably landing in *Weird Tales* more often as a ghost-writer than under his own name. For all his protestations about being unable to write to a formula, he hit the mark most often when hacking second-rate stories for Hazel Heald, Adolphe de Castro, and others.

The specialization of the pulp magazine in the late 1920s and early 1930s, almost single-handedly engineered by Street & Smith, flowered into an incredible profusion of narrow-interest titles, among them *Gangster Stories, Underworld Love, Ranch Romances, Courtroom Stories*, and *Fire Fighters*. This trend had its most bizarre expression in titles like *Submarine Stories* and *Zeppelin Stories*. But some titles, like *Spicy Detective Stories*, and dime-novel throwbacks featuring heroic characters like *Nick Carter, Doc Savage, Secret Agent X*, and others, were tremendously popular. Ironically, the magazines featuring single heroes came into being in 1931 when the ex-editor of *Tales of Magic and Mystery*, Walter B. Gibson, began writing the long-running pulp adventures of the The Shadow for Street & Smith. Like Lovecraft, Gibson had ghost-written material for Harry Houdini.

When the Fiction Publishing Company released the first issue of the highly specialized *Far East Adventure Stories* in October 1930, Clark Ashton Smith brought this to Lovecraft's attention. A very pointed and accurate assessment of the increasing juvenilization of the pulp industry is seen in Lovecraft's letter to Smith from January 1931:

> Specialised fiction magazines are certainly multiplying & entering narrow fields to an extent almost unbelievable. I wouldn't be in the least surprised to see *Undertaking Stories* or *True Plumber's Tales*—to say nothing of *Garbage-Collecting Adventures* & *Real Newsboy Mysteries*—on the stands any day now. How many of these things survive, I'm sure I have no idea; for I make no attempt whatever to keep track of them. If the geographic idea gains ground, we shall see such things as *Northwestern*

California Stories, True Southern Massachusetts Crimes, Newfoundland Fishing Tales, & so on. *Far East Adventure Stories* is a new one on me! (*SL* 3.247)

By coincidence, the same month saw the premiere of *Oriental Stories,* a companion magazine to *Weird Tales.* Apprised of the coming magazine, Lovecraft at first considered it a potential market, even though it was edited by Farnsworth Wright, but apparently he never pursued it. After little more than a year, *Oriental Stories* was retitled the *Magic Carpet Magazine* in the vain hope of expanding its disappointing circulation base. It expired after a few more issues. This was the fate of virtually every specialized pulp magazine, with the notable exception of the long-running *Ranch Romances.*

The year 1933 is generally considered the worst of the depression. It had a huge impact on the pulp industry. Author payment rates dropped. Circulations plummeted. Magazines, even whole chains, expired, some virtually overnight. Among them was the seemingly rock-solid Clayton chain, which killed *Strange Tales* and its companion title, *Astounding Stories,* which Lovecraft seems never to have considered a serious market for his work. (When E. Hoffmann Price suggested aiming their planned collaboration, "Through the Gates of the Silver Key" at *Astounding,* Lovecraft told Derleth he was agreeable, but "only if he leaves my name off."[19]) The surviving all-fiction titles fell on hard times. By the mid-1930s only a handful like *Argosy, Adventure,* and *Short Stories* remained.

All over the nation, men and women were thrown out of work. With jobs scarce, many of them took to less traditional ways of earning a living. Quite a number who, had there not been a depression, would have remained in business or industry looked to the perpetually story-hungry magazine field as a way to make money. Among them were giants like Raymond Chandler, Lester Dent, Walter B. Gibson, and others.

The sudden influx of young, bright, and eager writers revitalized the pulp story. While the pulps of the 1930s are sometimes justifiably criticized as garish, sensational, and juvenile—this was the era when they became known as the "Bloody Pulps"—they also became more vital. Even *Weird Tales* saw important new contributors like Robert Bloch and Henry Kuttner bring new life to its pages. As new talent with boundless energy entered the field, older pulp writers were pushed out. Many of the titans of the all-fiction magazine era, like Edgar Rice Burroughs and J. Allan Dunn, unwilling to accept the reduced word-rates and unable to retool their somewhat archaic styles, fell by the wayside. Only the prolific thrived. No one dreamed that H. P. Lovecraft, quite literally at the height of his creative expression, would become one of those pulp casualties.

In 1933 Lovecraft continued his revision work. After more than a year of fictional inactivity, he produced a story seemingly well-suited to *Weird Tales*'s current requirements—"The Thing on the Doorstep." It may in fact have been written with another market in mind. For Street & Smith had just announced plans to revive *Astounding* as a weird magazine. Writing to August Derleth just after completing "The Thing on the Doorstep," Lovecraft said: "Time will tell what I can do—but if I do get started again, I think the revived *Astounding* will form a splendid market."[20]

Unfortunately, Lovecraft was unsatisfied with the story and declined to submit it anywhere. Perhaps encouraged by the new market, he attempted several new stories, only to abandon them after a few pages.

That summer, Donald Wandrei contacted *Astounding* associate editor Desmond Hall, suggesting that he reach out to Lovecraft for story material, which Hall promptly did. Writing to Wandrei on 19 August 1933, Lovecraft revealed that a promising exchange had already begun.

> Thanks tremendously for mentioning me to *Astounding*. Hall sent me a form letter a week ago, & I replied—stating that I could not supply the essentially conventional material his specifications seemed to indicate. He came back at once with a personal response in which he said that the rubber-stamp stuff was not by any means necessary, & that his policy would include many stories of an individual, non-orthodox type if well-written. This sounds distinctly encouraging & I really think that if it can get around to writing more tales, I shall send them to *Astounding* first of all. At present I have nothing within the prescribed space-limits which seems to me good enough for submission. However—it may be that my type of tale will not "click" with Hall after all; for I notice that he lays stress on *characterisation*, whereas my efforts deal primarily with *phenomena* & *moods*—the characters being purely incidental."[21]

Lovecraft seemed to be wavering between rekindled interest and fear of rejection. Twelve days later he told Richard F. Searight on 31 August 1933:

> The revival of *Astounding* promises to be a great thing for weird writers— though of course its policy in practice may not be quite as ideal as it now sounds from the lips of its optimistic associate editor. I shall try to secure an entry as soon as I have anything fit to send—I am trying to get time now for some new tales; though I won't preserve or exhibit anything below a certain level, & I don't always hit the level when I try.[22]

Lovecraft fails to mention that among the unfinished stories begun and abandoned at this time, he drafted "The Thing on the Doorstep" between August

21 and 24. With its unusual female character, this throwback to pre-Mythos stories may very well have been composed with Hall's stiff requirements in mind. But unless he did so when he called on Hall in New York the following January, Lovecraft appears never to have shown it to him. Facing an uncertain market, Lovecraft could produce no work suitable to *Astounding* and satisfactory to himself.

When the new *Astounding* appeared late in the year, its weird slant swiftly gave way to science fiction, causing Lovecraft to write if off as a lost market. It was not until early 1935 that Lovecraft produced a finished story of his own, the ambitious "The Shadow out of Time"; but once again uncertain of its merit, he declined to market it.

A major potential turning point in Lovecraft's fiction-writing career occurred ca. October 1935, when Julius Schwartz of the Solar Sales Service, acting as Lovecraft's agent, sold *At the Mountains of Madness* to the new *Astounding*. Lovecraft reported an unexpected sequel to this event in a letter to Lee White dated of 20 December 1935:

> Thanks for the congratulations—& you can double 'em if you like, for no sooner had the "Mts. of Madness" incident sunk into my consciousness than I was given a *second* pleasant surprise . . . in the form of *another* cheque from Street & Smith. It seems that Donald Wandrei, to whom I had lent my newest novelette, "The Shadow out of Time", had taken the liberty of submitting the MS. to *Astounding* without my knowledge—& through some inexplicable coincidence the editor was favourable again! This certainly was a life-saving windfall, & it is needless to say that I feel tremendously encouraged by the incident. I know that such "winning streaks" don't keep up—but the impression is pleasant while it lasts. This dual stroke gave me such a psychological boost that I've written a new tale—a short specimen called "The Haunter of the Dark".[23]

"The Haunter of the Dark" was as much inspired by the dual acceptance as it was by Robert Bloch's short story "The Shambler from the Stars," in which Bloch killed off a character inspired by Lovecraft. "The Haunter of the Dark" was Lovecraft's reply, in which Lovecraft extinguished a Bloch *doppelgänger*.

Encouraged by the *Astounding* sales—and by Schwartz's offer to place a Lovecraft story collection in Great Britain—Lovecraft dusted off "The Thing on the Doorstep," which had never been submitted in the two years since he wrote it and, with "The Haunter of the Dark," offered it to Farnsworth Wright in July 1936 with unsurpassed backhandedness:

Young Schwartz has persuaded me to send him a lot of manuscripts for possible placement in Great Britain, and it occurs to me that I'd better exhaust their cisatlantic possibilities before turning them over to him. Accordingly I am going through the formality of obtaining your official rejection of the enclosed—so that I won't feel I've overlooked any theoretical source of badly-needed revenue. In the absense of other American markets for purely weird material, I won't need to try them elsewhere—hence, if you don't mind, you might send them on after rejection to *Julius Schwartz* . . . instead of returning them to me. (*SL* 5.274–75)

In spite—or perhaps because—of the tone of Lovecraft's letter, Wright accepted both stories with alacrity.

The *Astounding* development considerably brightened Lovecraft's outlook, and his subsequent letters indicate that the *Astounding* sales especially might trigger a new phase of intensive writing. Street & Smith's generous and prompt payments were indeed "a life-saving windfall," and the news prompted a third correspondent, amateur publisher William Crawford, to submit another of his stories to *Astounding*.

Writing to Duane Rimel on 12 November 1935—just weeks after the earlier *Astounding* acceptances—Lovecraft revealed:

I am letting Crawford try "Innsmouth" on *Astounding* as he suggests, though there really is almost no chance of its acceptance. This tale can hardly be gauged as "science fiction" in any stretch of the term—and in addition S&S now has two long novelettes of mine in their hands. But it's perhaps well to leave no stone unturned.[24]

Lovecraft does not record the result of this third third-party submittal, but the assumed rejection of "The Shadow over Innsmouth" does not appear to have discouraged him. Especially since Crawford simply offered Street & Smith a magazine serialization of a story he himself had been planning to bring out in hardcover under his Visionary Press imprint. Although the novelette was ultimately published in a very limited edition by Crawford's tiny amateur press and produced no royalties, it would be Lovecraft's first true book. Unfortunately both experiences ultimately proved crushing. *The Shadow over Innsmouth* was a typographical nightmare. Lovecraft might not have been so sensitive on the matter but for the horrendous changes *Astounding* made in his two novelettes.

"Hell & Damnation!" complained Lovecraft in a letter to R. H. Barlow. "In brief, that goddamn'd dung of a hyena Orlin Tremaine has given the Mts. the worst hashing-up any piece of mine ever received. . . . I'll be hanged if I can consider the story as published at all—the last instalment was a joke, with whole passages missing." [25] Lovecraft's comments to F. Orlin Tremaine are lost, but they must have been heated and, to Tremaine, blatantly unprofessional. For months afterward, any writer who complained of changes in his copy was denigrated by Street & Smith editors with the pejorative of being "Lovecraftish."[26]

Far more debilitating was the reader reaction to the stories. It was a virtual replay of the traumatic Fred Jackson controversy of twenty years before, with the negative side again in the majority. Comments like "I am glad to see the conclusion to *At the Mountains of Madness* for reasons that would not be pleasant to Mr. Lovecraft"; "Why in the name of science fiction did you ever print such a story as *At the Mountains of Madness* by Lovecraft? Are you in such dire straits that you must print this kind of drivel?"; and "Lovecraft's 'The Shadow out of Time' was very disappointing. Like his *At the Mountains of Madness*, the yarn was all description and very little else" could only demoralize the sensitive Lovecraft, and they did.[27]

Lovecraft began to express a growing sense of failure over his work. By this time *Weird Tales* was reprinting earlier Lovecraft stories because it had no new ones. Lovecraft now complained even about his old material, as in this letter to M. F. Bonner, dated 22 May 1936:

> No—weeding out poor work is not a very painful process. Far more painful is the ordeal of beholding a stilted, bombastic piece of junk and being forced to admit that one wrote it oneself. Now and then the magazine *Weird Tales* drags out some early atrocity which I have long since repudiated, and reprints it for the benefit of a gaping yokelry. (*SL* 5.260)

His dissatisfaction with his recent fiction, especially the *Astounding* serials, continued to plague him. Writing to E. Hoffmann Price on 16 March 1936, he said:

> Yes—I'd be pleased to hear opinions on the trouble with my writing, although my own tripartite view seems to me pretty valid. That is (a) lack of general ability (my stuff *never was* much good—its appeal, such as it was, being largely meretricious) (b) too much reading of pulp fiction, whereby I acquired mental patterns fatal to genuine expression, and (c) the fact that *fiction* is *not* the medium for what I *really want to do*. (Just what the right medium would be, I don't know—perhaps the cheapened and hackneyed term "prose-poem" would hint in the general direction.) (*SL* 5.230)

The comment about reading too much pulp is very telling. Lovecraft here indicates that his voracious consumption of the *All-Story, Argosy*, and the other

pulps during his formative years ruined his literary sensibilities. It could have
no other meaning, for by 1936 he had long since stopped reading pulps regularly, with the sole exception of *Weird Tales*, which must have loomed larger
and larger as an old familiar house in which he was no longer welcome. For despite his problems with Wright, *Weird Tales* remained a kind of social nexus for
Lovecraft. Many of his correspondents were by now *Weird Tales* contributors,
who were appearing in its pages far more frequently than he. It was not that
they were rejected less often than Lovecraft, but that they were more prolific
and more willing to revise and submit to Wright's tyranny.

Lovecraft's bitterness and even envy took expression in his occasional de-
nunciation of his friends in private letters, as in these comments to C. L.
Moore in October 1936:

> What is valued & insisted upon by commercial editors is precisely what has no
> place whatever in authentic literary expression. Whoever consents to aim for
> the tawdry effects demanded by commerce, is deliberately checking & perhaps
> permanently injuring his ability in an effort to achieve certain cheap results
> alien & antagonistic to literature. The literary ruin of brilliant figures like Long,
> Quinn, Price, Merritt, & Wandrei speaks for itself. (*SL* 5.327)

In a letter from February 1937 he continued his caustic analysis:

> I disagree violently with your belief in making concessions in writing. One con-
> cession leads to another—& he who takes the easiest way never comes back.
> They all say they *mean* to come back some day—but they never do. Belknap is
> gone. If Sultan Malik [E. Hoffmann Price] ever pulls out of charlatanry it will be
> purely the individual & non-representative triumph of a singularly keen objective
> intellect. Abe Merritt—who could have been a Machen or Dunsany or de la Mare
> or M. R. James . . . if he had but chosen—is so badly sunk that he's lost the criti-
> cal faculty to realise it. . . . The road does *not* lie through any *magazines* . . . that is,
> the road for a fantastic writer. The "slicks" are just as tawdry and insincere as the
> "pulps". . . . The road to print for the serious fantaisiste is through *book-publication*
> alone—save for those *incidental* magazine placements that lie along the way. And
> if one can't make the book grade in the end, he is better off with his work largely
> unpublished—able to look himself in the face & know that he had never cringed
> nor truckled nor sold his intellectual & aesthetic integrity. He may go down, but
> he'll go down like a free & unbroken gentleman with sword untarnished & col-
> ours flying. Britons shall never be slaves! (*SL* 5.400)

Lovecraft's mock-heroic defiance is an embarrassing throwback to his youthful Anglophilia and is all the more transparently pitiful when one realizes that he

had been reduced to sending his unsold stories—the constantly spurned "Nameless City" went to *Fanciful Tales* around this time—to non-paying fanzines in these, the final months of his life. When Standard Magazines took over *Wonder Stories* in 1936 and approached Lovecraft for contributions, he turned them down with ill-disguised sadness, but in a letter of 30 November 1936 made an astonishing statement to Henry Kuttner that "I may try things on them under a pseudonym if I ever get to writing again."[28] And when Popular Publications launched *Terror Tales* and *Horror Stories,* Lovecraft—correctly—recognized that their brand of sadomasochistic Grand Guignol pulp was so far removed from his approach that he never bothered with the futility of formal submittal. He seems to have at last surrendered to the inexorable sea-changes in the pulp industry and, perhaps as a last gesture to his vanity and ego, wrapped himself in the same mantle as his favorite weird writers of the pre-pulp era for protection. His letters at this time are full of praise of giants like Machen and Blackwood and of his own virtual blanket repudiation of his own fiction.

This period was clearly the nadir of nadirs for Lovecraft. Writing to Wilfred Blanch Talman on 10 November 1936, he said:

> The *commercial or financial* side of fiction is of course simply ridiculous to me. I am no garage mechanic or merchant tailor to use materials of literature in an occupation not only alien but antagonistic to literature—and I have not the happy luck to produce things spontaneously which are likewise marketable. As a source of dependable revenue, original writing is simply *out* with me. I *couldn't* become a successful hack even if I *would.* My growing economic plight is an absolutely *separate* question, on which fiction writing has no possible bearing. As time passes, I must indeed find some source of the $10.00 to $15.00 per week which I require for subsistence—but this source can never be original fiction. I don't care what it is so long as it is honest—but it *can't* be literary whoredom. . . . The remedy lies in some sort of job-hunting outside writing. I may run an elevator, but I'll never write a hack-story! (*SL* 5.347–48)

This remark, coming from a proud man who in his better days styled himself a gentleman unfit for physical labor, is telling. He is no longer the youthful, energetic man who remarked to Rheinhart Kleiner after finishing his 1918 dime-novel pastiche, "Really, I think I could have been a passable dime novelist if I had been trained in that noble calling!" (*SL* 1.68).

The death in June 1936 of Robert E. Howard, his friend and one of the two *Weird Tales* writers—the other being Clark Ashton Smith—who he felt still upheld the highest standards in weird fiction, was another in a relentless succession of blows. Lovecraft was unaware of it at the time, but he himself was dying of intestinal cancer. His illness became grave in February 1937, but he continued writing letters, reading *Weird Tales*, and working on what was probably his last feeble fiction effort, a revision of a story for his friend Duane Rimel.[29] He entered the hospital in March and expired within a few days.

Just months before his death, he was in contact with a young aspiring writer named Fritz Leiber and his wife, Jonquil, who dreamed of launching a truly revolutionary weird fiction magazine, which they wanted Lovecraft to edit. Writing to Jonquil on 20 December 1936, Lovecraft was a resigned man:

> I shall probably be available a decade hence—if still living at so advanced an age—for that good-weird-magazine editorship which Mr. Leiber has in mind! Such a magazine would surely be welcomed by a limited and devoted circle—though in harsh fact I gravely doubt its practicability as a commercial or even self-sustaining venture. The old W.T. group has many a time discussed something of the sort—pointing out that virtually all of the world's first-rate authors (for example—Henry James, Rudyard Kipling, Edith Wharton, F. Marion Crawford, Theodore Dreiser, Guy de Maupassant, etc., etc., etc.) have at one time or another written weird material, and arguing that they would probably produce a great deal more if a definite and dependable market existed. With this potential source of contents . . . argued the optimists, the right sort of publisher might float a weird magazine of the very highest grade, commanding a select and dependable public, and reaching persons who would toss aside a cheap rag like W.T. with contempt. A pleasing picture! But there were not lacking pessimists to point out that this select and faithful public would of necessity be woefully small. After all, a taste for fantasy in large doses is a rather unusual thing. (*SL* 5.379–80)

These were prophetic comments. Only three years later, Street & Smith would launch just such a magazine with *Unknown*. Literate, iconoclastic, and unconventional, it would feature many then up-and-coming *Weird Tales* writers, among them Fritz Leiber, and showcase new and experimental types of fantasy. There was a double irony in this. First, Lovecraft would not live to see the magazine. Second, even if he had, his work would have been decidedly unwelcome in its pages.

Writing to Jack Williamson on 6 January 1939 preparatory to launching *Unknown*, editor John W. Campbell outlined his new magazine's requirements, making it very clear he saw H. P. Lovecraft as a relic of the near past:

> I do not want old-fashioned, 19th century writing, the kind that has burdened fantasy fiction steadily in *Weird Tales*. I do not want unpleasant gods and god-

lings with penchants for vivisection, and nude and beauteous maidens to be sacrificed. I do not want reams of phoney atmosphere. I do not want the kind of stuff Lovecraft doted on. He was immensely liked—by the small clique that read *Weird* regularly. It still wasn't good writing.[30]

Unknown instead featured humorous fantasies somewhat in the manner of Thorne Smith as well as serious but thoroughly modern treatments of traditional supernatural themes. Neither approach would have suited Lovecraft's style or tastes.

In the months and years after Lovecraft's death, *Weird Tales* scrounged up every possible Lovecraft story it could print and reprint—including virtually every story Farnsworth Wright had ever rejected during Lovecraft's lifetime. Arkham House came into being in 1939, realizing the Lovecraftian dream of hardcover publication, and with subsequent collections of his poetry, essays, and correspondence created and fostered the image of a genteel writer who happened to be published in a magazine like *Weird Tales* because it was the only avenue of publication open to him. This is only partly true, since Lovecraft's *Selected Letters* have been purged of virtually every mention of his attempts to sell to pulp magazines other than *Weird Tales*—perhaps deliberately so.

For as Lovecraft's unpublished correspondence shows, despite all his pretensions to literature, he was, to use his own pejorative term, a "pulphound"—a voracious pulp fan and reader. After he made the transition to pulp writer, he became as industrious and conscientious as any of the hacks he came to denigrate. It was only after several pulp markets began to reject him that he turned increasingly bitter. He was a man who had achieved a dream and was ultimately betrayed by that same dream, in part because he refused to acknowledge it as his.

Lovecraft could be said to have outgrown his pulp markets but never successfully aspired beyond them during his lifetime. He was not really akin, except in spirit, to the pulp writers of his day, who in the depression were expected to be enormously prolific to be able to survive on the low word-rates they were paid. He could, of course, have adapted to any of these markets—the ready acceptance of lesser stories he ghost-wrote proves this—but he chose not to do so. Unable to adapt or move on, he perished. It was a failure he seems to have predicted during his first year of writing for *Weird Tales*, but forgot or ignored in his desperate attempt to achieve recognition and remuneration for his work. As he wrote in "The Professional Incubus" (1924):

I do not think any meritorious short story could be sold to an average professional magazine of the popular class except by accident. He who strives to
produce salable fiction is lost as an artist, for the conditions of American life
have made art impossible in the popular professional field. . . . Editors and
publishers are not to blame. They cater to their public, and would suffer ship-
wreck if they did not. . . . If any magazine sought and used artistically original
types of fiction, it would lose its readers almost to a man.[31]

The ultimate irony of H. P. Lovecraft the writer was that he was just as much
of an outsider—even an outcast—in the very fiction arena that, curiously, both
nourished and starved his creativity as he was in everyday life.

Notes

1. Sam Moskowitz, *Under the Moons of Mars* (New York: Holt, Rinehart & Winston,
1970), 402.

2. *Uncollected Letters* (West Warwick, RI: Necronomicon Press, 1986), 1–2.

3. Moskowitz, 377.

4. L. Sprague de Camp, *Lovecraft: A Biography* (Garden City, NY: Doubleday, 1975), 77.

5. *Essential Solitude: The Letters of H. P. Lovecraft and August Derleth* (New York: Hippocampus Press, 2008), 1.47.

6. *Essential Solitude*, 1.34.

7. *Essential Solitude*, 1.40.

8. HPL to Clark Ashton Smith, 15 April 1931 (ms., JHL).

9. HPL to August Derleth, [21 October 1927]; *Essential Solitude*, 1.110.

10. *Essential Solitude*, 1.330.

11. HPL to Clark Ashton Smith, 15 April 1931 (ms., JHL).

10. *Essential Solitude*, 1.334.

11. HPL to August Derleth, [13 February 1932]; *Essential Solitude*, 2.453.

14. HPL to August Derleth, [mid-August 1932]; *Essential Solitude*, 2.497.

15. Will Murray, "Lost Lovecraftian Pearls: The 'Tarbis' Collaboration." *The Fantastic
Worlds of H. P. Lovecraft.* James Van Hise, ed. Yucca Valley, CA 1999. p. 44.
16. *Essential Solitude*, 2.460–61.

17. Wright did, however. August Derleth has surreptitiously submitted the story to
Weird Tales, since HPL himself refused to. Wright told Derleth he could not accept
the story because of its length and inability to be divided into two parts for serialization. Derleth did not tell HPL of the matter, but HPL certainly learned of the
rejection, for in a letter to Henry Kuttner dated 16 February 1936, he said: "This is
one of the things Wright rejected." *Letters to Henry Kuttner* (West Warwick, RI: Necronomicon Press, 1990), 8.

18. *Essential Solitude*, 1.419–20.

19. HPL to August Derleth, [April 1933]; *Essential Solitude*, 1.559.

20. HPL to August Derleth, [1 September 1933]; *Essential Solitude*, 1.604.

21. HPL and Donald Wandrei, *Mysteries of Time and Spirit*, pg 329.

22. HPL, *Letters to Richard F. Searight*, pg. 12.

23. HPL to Lee McBride White, Jr., 20 December 1935; "Letters to Lee McBride White," *Lovecraft Annual* 1 (2007): 46.

24. Unpublished letter to Duane Rimel (ms., JHL).

25. HPL to Barlow, 4 June 1936; *O Fortunate Floridian: H. P. Lovecraft's Letters to R. H. Barlow* (Tampa: University of Tampa Press, 2007), 335.

26. Will Murray, "The Man Who Edited Lovecraft," *CoC* No. 48 (St. John's Eve, 1987): 3–5.

27. Robert Weinberg, "Lovecraft in *Astounding*," *Nyctalops* No. 10, (January–February 1975): 5.

28. *Letters to Henry Kuttner*, 27.

29. The title of this story is "From the Sea" (see HPL to Duane W. Rimel, [20 February 1937]; ms., JHL). It was apparently not published.

30. Jack Williamson, *The Reign of Wizardry* (West Bloomfield, MI: Fantasia Press, 1979), 5.

31. *National Amateur*, 46, No. 4 (March 1924): 35–36.

II
Thematic Studies

On Lovecraft's Themes: Touching the Glass

Donald R. Burleson

Over the two decades of his career in fiction writing, H. P. Lovecraft progressed from relatively modest beginnings to final creations of high artistic power and employed a number of fictional themes repeatedly reworked at increasing levels of sophistication; yet in the broadest sense he remained faithful to the one thematic precept with which he began, clarifying and magnifying it as the corpus of his writing grew. He was a writer of the *idée fixe*. He started with a premise, and he finished with it; yet he reiterated and reinscribed it over the years with such refreshing narrative variety that the idea never grew old—it grew large.

After producing a few earlier tales (stories that, while perhaps minor, adumbrate the thematic posture of later works), Lovecraft in 1921 wrote "The Outsider" and gave us the central apocalyptic moment at the mirror, the moment of terrible revelation when the Outsider, trying at first to believe the carrion horror in the frame to be a separate entity, reaches out and touches the polished glass and knows the abominable form to be his own. In a sense, the fateful mirror is also a lens, in that the moment at the glass brings to focus what is going to be the broad thematic concern of Lovecraft's entire oeuvre: the nature of self-knowledge, the effects of learning one's own nature and one's place in the scheme of things. The rotting finger that touches the glass sets ringing a vibration that will endure, will continue to resonate in varying pitches and intensities, throughout the whole experience of Lovecraft's fiction. While Lovecraft himself came to regard "The Outsider" as overwritten and stylistically too dependent upon Poe, this early tale, besides being rich in critical interpretability, remains metaphorically central to an understanding of Lovecraft's thematic continuity. The grand theme of the soul-shattering consequences of self-knowledge is the one defining notion into which Lovecraft's other themes feed in confluence, rivers running to a common sea. As Lovecraft's stories follow one another, other Outsiders, under other names and with other faces, reach out and touch other sorts of mirrors; but the ultimate philosophical effect is always the same, the original Outsider's loathsome form standing forever as a metaphor for the revelations of humankind's self-discovery. Further Lovecraftian Outsiders merely gaze into larger mirrors.

Aside from (but connected to) the grand theme just described, one may discern five major themes in Lovecraft's fiction. They may be listed and characterized as follows:

1. The theme of denied primacy: the theme that as human beings on this planet we were not first, will not be last, and have never really been foremost.

2. The theme of forbidden knowledge, or merciful ignorance: the theme that there are some types of knowledge only by the avoidance or suppression of which can humankind maintain a semblance of well-being.

3. The theme of illusory surface appearances: the theme that things are not as they seem, that surface appearances mask a deeper and more terrible reality.

4. The theme of unwholesome survival: the theme that some things, and some beings, outlive what would be from the ordinary human viewpoint their rightful existence, producing circumstances in which it must be concluded that the present is no place where we can hide from an encroaching past that can reach forward to find us.

5. The theme of oneiric objectivism: the theme that there is at best an ambiguous distinction between dreaming and reality—that the world of deep dream may be as real as, or more real than, the waking world; the suggestion is strongly present that the shared dreamworld of humankind holds awesome secrets about the ultimate nature of things.

All these themes are recurrent, and they often mingle with one another in a given work. Indeed, they conceptually overlap somewhat, presenting patterns of mutual implication. The theme of forbidden knowledge, for example, often operates in a work because the knowledge that is "forbidden"—the knowledge of which humankind is mercifully ignorant—is the knowledge that the human race is the least of earth's sentient races (the theme of denied primacy), or the knowledge of an unwholesome survival (in that ancient races still lurk nearby, beyond or beneath our traveled paths), or the knowledge that, for one reason or another, things are not as they seem (the theme of illusory surface appearances), or the knowledge that there are terrible conduits of accessibility, unthinkable connections, in a shared world of dream open to the human psyche (the theme of oneiric objectivism). Lovecraft's major fictional themes thus form a sort of conceptual web, interlacing to provide a potential for expression of the one major idea that always emerges; they form a web on which scutters the inevitable Lovecraftian spider—the idea that self-knowledge, or discovery of one's position in the real fabric of the universe, is psychically ruinous.

We may proceed to observations on the thematic content of some of Lovecraft's major works.

Groundwork was laid even prior to "The Outsider." Lovecraft employed the theme of unwholesome survival as early as 1908, in a limited form, in "The Alchemist," writing of unnatural longevity and introducing (in Charles Le Sorcier) a character-type that would develop (by way of Robert Suydam in "The Horror at Red Hook") eventually into a grand fruition with Joseph Curwen in *The Case of Charles Dexter Ward.* The larger notion of collective survival does not come into play in "The Alchemist," but it is suggested in "Dagon" (1917), Lovecraft's first story to be published in *Weird Tales.* In "Dagon," the hieroglyph-covered monolith that has risen from the waters suggests that the aquatic monstrosity who comes to worship at the shrine is not the only one of its kind, but rather a member of an entire race of ancient beings. By suggesting his own madness, the narrator of course creates the possibility that the entire experience is delirium; in thematic terms it matters little either way, because at least on the symbolic level Lovecraft has here employed the theme of unwholesome survival, as well as the theme of denied primacy (in an inchoate form to be fleshed out in later tales), as well as a question about the distinction between reality and illusion.

In general, one may say that many of the early stories show thematic concerns that prefigure those of tales to come, though they often do so in a partial or fragmentary way. "The Terrible Old Man," written in early 1920, reveals two of the primary themes: that of illusory surface appearances (the old man appears weak and helpless to the robbers but turns out to be nothing of the kind) and that of unwholesome survival (the old man, like certain other Lovecraft characters, is older than anyone should naturally be); but the cosmically vast thematic concern of later stories is missing here, in that in this fascinating but limited tale there is no notion of ancient races or large-scale bodies of forbidden lore. (Lovecraft may well have derived his title from Melville's *Moby-Dick*, in which Starbuck at one point thinks of his own unknowable sea-captain, Ahab, as "Terrible old man!") Similarly, in "Facts concerning the Late Arthur Jermyn and His Family" (1920), a story of tainted ancestry, the discovery that Arthur Jermyn's family tree contains certain non-human elements (a notion to be elaborated upon later, in a much different and much more effective way, in "The Shadow over Innsmouth") smacks of the theme of unwholesome survival—the potentially atavistic element—and of illusory surface appearances (see the story's opening statement: "Life is a hideous thing, and from the background behind what we know of it peer daemoniacal hints of truth . . ." [D 73]) but only on the very low level of individual or family involvement, without any broader implications. Likewise, Lovecraft in the same year gave us "The Picture in the House," in which the theme of unwholesome survival surfaces in the form of a cannibalistic character of unnatural longevity, without any more ambitious thematic consequences. Clearly, Lovecraft in this period had some fictionally intriguing matters on his mind, but it would take him time to give them their larger conceptual unfolding.

Late in that same year, however, Lovecraft did take something of a thematic step forward with "From Beyond," a story that, although it is rather unimpressive in terms of style, presents the theme of illusory surface appearances in a more strongly implicative way than the way it appears in, say, "The Terrible Old Man." In Crawford Tillinghast's experiments we have no mere account of a strange individual or family, but rather an exploration of the illusory (or at least incomplete) nature of appearances on a large scale, an exploration that calls into question the very nature of the fabric of reality. In having Tillinghast speak of the narrowness of that portion of the spectrum that humans can perceive, Lovecraft is well on the way to a more cosmic thematic treatment of humankind's feeble position in the universe, a universe that in truth is not as it appears, and is not partial to humankind.

In the following year Lovecraft wrote "The Nameless City," magnifying again his fictional concerns, this time with regard to the theme of denied primacy. Evidently inspired by Thomas Moore's *Alciphron,* this tale employs what will come to be a common Lovecraftian device: the desperately rationalizing narrator, the human observer who resists "looking in the glass," as it were; who resists confronting the truth until he can resist no longer. Finding the remains of ceremonially preserved semi-reptilian creatures far beneath the desert sands of Arabia, he insists on seeing these remains as the religious fetish of an early human society, until he is forced to recognize the brutal fact that "the crawling reptiles of the nameless city" were that city's real inhabitants—that, as a consequence, humankind as a sentient species has been preceded by another race of beings. If the narrator's senses are to be believed at the end, those beings have also survived to the present time, so that Lovecraft is here making early use of the theme of unwholesome survival on the collective level. These themes will be played out in grander form later, but it is interesting to see them on Lovecraft's mind as early as 1921.

That same year saw the writing of "The Outsider" itself, with its moment at the mirror in the lighted hall. Lovecraft's ill-fated narrator in "The Nameless City" has already in a sense reached out and touched the glass—touched the mirror of the world as it is, the mirror that shows humankind its own transient face—and when the Outsider touches the glass, he is no mere individual figure of carrion horror; by extended implication of the imagery, he is ourselves, discovering our disillusioning reality. Arthur Jermyn has merely discovered himself in touching the mirror of his blighted ancestry; the Outsider, as a synecdochical figure, has discovered what is inevitable for us all—the actual reference to a mirror (which was expressly missing in the Outsider's ancestral chamber) makes it clear that Lovecraft, unconsciously as likely as not, was here bringing the image into high focus and making it a metaphorical adumbration of all that was to come, thematically, in the later tales. Texts, after all, are patterns of reflection of themselves and each other; they are mirrors.

Yet even after the appearance of this compelling image, Lovecraft would take a good deal of time to give his fictional concerns full force; he wrote, following "The Outsider," a number of tales in which the central themes are present, but present in lesser forms than would eventually be the case.

It should be noted at this point that both before and after "The Outsider," the "Dunsanian" stories, such as "The Quest of Iranon," "Celephaïs," and "The Other Gods," often stray from what we have called the central themes, in that these stories primarily portray, with great beauty of language it must be said, the mythic quest. ("Celephaïs" does deal with the question of oneiric objectivism, but with less far-ranging implications than later tales employing the theme.) Lovecraft in his early productive years seems to have stayed closer to what would evolve as his themes when he wrote in his own manner, rather than in the manner of Dunsany. "The Outsider" was of course heavily influenced by Poe in terms of diction and style, but thematically, as we are in the process of seeing, it was very much Lovecraft himself; Poe, with his psychological mind-set involving the tragically isolated narrator alone with his horrors, never produced, for all his great narrative power, the sort of cosmic implications that would come to characterize Lovecraft at the height of his creative life.

Indeed, even when he was writing largely under the stylistic influence of Poe, Lovecraft was capable of his own unique thematic vision, and not just in "The Outsider." In "The Music of Erich Zann," for example, written in late 1921, Lovecraft experiments with the themes of forbidden knowledge and illusory surface appearances while employing a story setting (in France) and a psychological framework (the isolated narrator) reminiscent of Poe. Near the end of that tale, the narrator, in the garret room of Erich Zann on the Rue d'Auseil (presumably in Paris), gazes from the window, expecting to see the city lights: "Yet . . . I saw no city spread below, and no friendly lights gleamed from remembered streets, but only the blackness of space illimitable; unimagined space alive with motion and music, and having no semblance to anything on earth" (*DH* 90). This vista is a species of forbidden knowledge, since earlier Zann has gone to great pains to prevent the narrator's gazing from the window; but the narrator has looked, has found not what prosaic life would have led him to expect to find, but rather a different reality. He has reached out, he has touched the glass—because any such look outward into the chaos of the abyss is also a look inward; the window becomes a mirror in which the narrator sees himself for what he really is: a frightened and ignorant figure not prepared to deal with the nature of things. It is symbolically significant that Zann's own handwritten notes, which would have tried to explain everything, have been carried out the window into the void; the void refuses to submit to being explained or known or understood; Erich Zann's music is the music of the impenetrable abyss.

Also somewhat in the manner of Poe, but with thematic content that is Lovecraft's own, is "The Rats in the Walls," written in 1923. Here the themes of merciful ignorance and unwholesome survival come into play as Lovecraft gives us a tale of atavism, a story whose narrator discovers dreadful facts about the activities of his ancestors and finds that the family tendencies in fact survive down to himself, the present scion. (Here we find also the theme of oneiric objectivism in a narrow form, in that the narrator's dream of the twilit grotto prefigures his actual discovery of such a place beneath the priory. The theme functions here on the relatively limited level of oneiric precognition; Lovecraft at this point has yet to pursue it in a broader way.)

In such early fictional efforts as these, Lovecraft clearly is already at work on some of the thematic fixations that will color his later work, but at this point the themes in question take the expressive form of horrors coming to isolated characters. While it is true that even in later stories the horrors come to individual, isolated characters, the horrors of the later and more mature works also have more global implications for humankind generally. In thematic terms, Lovecraft, in the early and middle 1920s, is merely warming up.

He employs the themes of illusory surface appearances and unwholesome survival again in 1923 in "The Festival," and the latter theme in 1924 in his famous Hawthorne-and-Poe-influenced novella "The Shunned House," and in 1925 in his New York stories "The Horror at Red Hook" and "He," but again the horrific survivals in these tales are of a relatively limited sort, lacking the cosmic scope of implication that would come later.

By the time Lovecraft was through with his New York period, ending his brief and unsuccessful marriage and moving back to his native Providence, he seems to have been ready to settle down to more substantial writing. For all the variegated appeal of some of the early stories, one must view Lovecraft as a developing artist, and it is in terms of his post–New York works that one most discerns in him what is uniquely Lovecraft—what stands out as the really memorable playing out of his cherished themes. It is not without significance that one sees Lovecraft's fictional efforts from this point growing in length, his post–New York stories often tending toward the novella form, his writing on three occasions even edging over into the short novel; for a more meaningful exploration of his chosen themes, Lovecraft simply needed more room—he was beginning to enact his dramas upon a thematically larger stage, and this fact, together with the fact that he was beginning to find it increasingly important to provide the reader with emotional preparation to "suspend disbelief," meant that a story-length like that of (say) "The Music of Erich Zann" was no longer sufficient. He was not merely waxing verbose; rather, his works were growing more adequately expressive of the inner vision that demanded to be let out, and growing more responsive to the needs of the reader.

Even before moving back home to Providence, Lovecraft was already drawing up plans for "The Call of Cthulhu," finished in the summer of 1926 in Rhode Island, and that story's opening statement gives vent to as clear an articulation of the theme of forbidden knowledge as one could want: "The most merciful thing in the world, I think, is the inability of the human mind to correlate all its contents. We live on a placid island of ignorance in the midst of black seas of infinity, and it was not meant that we should voyage far" (*DH* 125). Some day, the narrator continues, the chance juxtaposition of disparate bits of knowledge will open up "terrifying vistas of reality, and of our frightful position therein." Here we have also the related theme of illusory surface appearances; if new and dangerous knowledge can open up new "vistas of reality," then beneath the patina of superficial appearances, the world is not as it seems. Curiously, in saying that "it was not meant that we should voyage far," unless the language is heavily metaphorical or merely expressive of an idiosyncratic narrative stance or persona, the suggestion comes close to being one of a teleological view of the universe, which view would run counter to the usual philosophical stance discernible in Lovecraft's fiction, and counter to his personal view; but the statement in any case remains a powerful expression of some important Lovecraft themes.

Further, the story itself broadens the view considerably and begins an enduring expression, on Lovecraft's part, of an unprecedentedly far-flung level of thematic concern. As the story's events unfold, the themes of forbidden knowledge and illusory appearances shade off into, and mingle with, the theme that had been prefigured as early as 1917 in "Dagon"—the theme of denied primacy. The frame-narrated disclosure of the preceding of humankind by the Old Ones begins a series of fictional treatments, increasingly powerful treatments, in which the mirror of the cosmos is held up to human eyes so that they may glimpse their own evanescence and insignificance. Unwittingly, Lovecraftian narrator after narrator will reach out and touch the glass. At the end of "The Call of Cthulhu," though great Cthulhu has sunk again beneath the waters, the suggestion is clear that the problem for humankind is ineluctable and eternal: "What has risen may sink, and what has sunk may rise" (Lovecraft reverting to the chiasmus form by which he so often expresses such apocalyptic views)—"loathsomeness waits and dreams in the deep" (*DH* 154). Dreams play a heavy role in the tale, though they are dreams telepathically generated and not the quite the archetypally universal dreams by which Lovecraft will a short time later more thoroughly explore the theme of oneiric objectivism.

In 1926, Lovecraft produced a short story called "The Silver Key," a tale whose broodingly introspective and penetratingly philosophical narration gives vent to a definitive statement of the theme of oneiric objectivism. Lamenting Randolph Carter's worldly ennui, the narrator remarks that "he had forgotten that all life is only a set of pictures in the brain, among which there is no difference betwixt those born of real things and those born of inward dreamings, and no cause to value the one above the other" (*MM* 408). Later that same year Lovecraft, in his first experiment with the novel form (or at least of novel length), would explore this oneiric notion much further in *The Dream-Quest of Unknown Kadath*, in which the same Randolph Carter, here a sort of Lovecraftian Odysseus, explores realms of dreamland assumed common in access at least to privileged, deep dreamers, and does battle with a variety of denizens of this dream world in his quest to win favors from the gods of Kadath; like Alice, the dreamer has touched the glass, this time to find a whole realm of wonder commonly hidden from humankind, a realm calling into question humans' real understanding of the nature of reality and thus involving also the theme of illusory surface (or waking) appearances. The notion that some of the inhabitants of the realm of deep dream correspond to primal entities in some sense really existing in the world's past also smacks of the theme of denied primacy and raises provoking questions about the relations between conscious and unconscious perception, between the external world and the internal machinations of the human mind, between mythic archetypes as history and mythic archetypes as current presences in the deep psyche.

Lovecraft in early 1927 would venture again into novel length with *The Case of Charles Dexter Ward*, where this time the thematic concern centers upon forbidden knowledge and unwholesome survival. The young Charles Ward, a kind of Faust figure whose yearning for knowledge leads to disaster, unearths (somewhat as does the narrator of "The Call of Cthulhu," with, however, the tragic difference that the motive this time is a pure love of learning) scattered bits of information that culminate in the resurrection of his long-dead ancestor, a character-type that has evolved through a number of earlier works as a sort of Lovecraftian obsession. (Lovecraft, like Charles Ward, has gone to considerable trouble to get Joseph Curwen reborn.) There are suggestions in the text that the "sorcery" of old Curwen involves access to remote spheres of being, primordial sources of influence and power. Clearly at this point Lovecraft's treatment of his cherished themes is no longer entirely on the level of Poe's isolated character alone with private horrors—now there are cosmically vast implications. The Outsider's mirror is also a lens on the great Outside itself.

And as if to allow the reader to gaze farther into this bottomless pit of externality without delay, Lovecraft immediately afterward (in March 1927) wrote one of his most memorable stories, "The Colour out of Space," in which the ineffable Outside presents the glass for humankind to touch yet again. In their ruinous encounter with the poisonous effects—the "grey brittle death"—of the meteorite that has fallen on their farm, the Gardners of the tale (gardeners indeed, with a very strange crop) discover something monstrous to know—that to live safely ensconced in a little corner of the planet is to live mercifully shielded from knowledge of the cosmos and of our position in it. Humankind, the Gardners find, can in no way live juxtaposed with the uncaring powers that the universe has in its bag of tricks, once that bag gapes open. The thematic concern here—forbidden knowledge—is one by which the story catapults itself straight into the central Lovecraftian theme: that self-knowledge, knowledge of where one stands in the whole picture, is consummately disastrous.

A year later, in the summer of 1928, Lovecraft would find another colorful articulation for his particular thematic agenda, in one of his most widely read tales. "The Dunwich Horror," full of curious in-jokes about its western Massachusetts setting, is nonetheless a text that stands central to the expression of that fictional worldview that has come to be known as the Lovecraft Mythos, the expression of those themes with which the author began and ended his career. Inspired in part by Arthur Machen's "The Great God Pan," the story, treating as it does of a monstrous pair of twins sired by the "god" Yog-Sothoth upon a deformed woman in the backwater western Massachusetts village of Dunwich (really an amalgam of North Wilbraham, Athol, and North New Salem), forces the confrontation of humankind once again with the great Outside. In its portrayal of the twins, who textually give us symbolic death and rebirth and thus partake ironically of the mythic qualities of the questing hero, the story manages to create a sardonic reversal of roles; humankind "touches the glass" to find a reflection of its own evanescence, yet (in the buffoonlike character of Henry Armitage) does not even understand what it sees. Here we have not only the theme of denied primacy, but also, in the form of human failure to comprehend the implications of the confrontation, the theme of merciful ignorance.

In 1930 Lovecraft explored the effects of the themes of denied primacy, illusory appearances, and unwholesome survival in his Vermont tale "The Whisperer in Darkness," an account of ancient beings that have inhabited the wild, unpeopled hills of Vermont from prehuman times, beings that dwell there still, as the hapless Henry Wentworth Akeley discovers. By arranging the narration so that the narrator Wilmarth (an epistolarian like Lovecraft and many of his friends) is in contact with the besieged Akeley only by mail, Lovecraft reproduces the sort of isolated sufferer, the character alone with unbearable horrors, who would have been worthy of Poe—yet with a breadth of implication far exceeding Poe's fictional scenarios. When Akeley encounters his timeless predecessors, and when the narrator learns of the encounter, humankind has again touched the glass, has again known the horror of self-discovery, discovery of self as superseded. The hands and face on the chair at the story's end can clearly be read as symbolic of this ruination; the loathsome entity that has even masqueraded as Akeley has worn the face as a mask, metaphorically suggesting the illusory nature of the notion that the cosmos puts on a human face to care for humankind—in effect, the great Outside "looks human" only to self-deluded humans. As if to underscore this presence of the theme of illusory surface appearances (and the themes of forbidden knowledge and unwholesome survival, with even a whiff of the theme of oneiric objectivism), the narrator has even remarked of the physical setting of the tale that "the very outline of the hills themselves held some strange and aeon-forgotten meaning, as if they were the vast hieroglyphs left by a rumoured titan race whose glories live only in rare, deep dreams" (*DH* 247). The world is a cryptogram best left unsolved.

The themes of denied primacy and unwholesome survival come in for even a more ambitious treatment in 1931, with Lovecraft's third and last (and in many ways most successful) experiment with novel length, *At the Mountains of Madness*. Here the narration supplies horrors beyond horrors: the Antarctic explorers discover not only the lingering presence of the ancient, barrel-shaped Old Ones, whose mighty prehuman city still stands behind a range of mountains (the term "mountains of madness" being borrowed from Dunsany), but the lingering presence as well of those gelatinous creatures that the Old Ones had come to have reason to fear, the shoggoths. Similarly, one learns that the fearsome mountain range masking the city from the outside (a striking instance of Lovecraft's fictional penchant for the motif of masks) is not the ultimate such range, a glimpse of which threatens madness indeed. The humans who happen upon the ancient stone city learn not only of the previously unsuspected existence of the elder race (a race hinted at only in folklore); reading that race's historical murals, they learn the most devastating fact of all—that the ancient race, experimenting with life forms, created people as a sort of jest. Here humankind has looked into the most cruelly candid mirror, has touched the glass and come away forever scarred.

Late in the same year, Lovecraft wrote "The Shadow over Innsmouth," a long story in which the themes of denied primacy, forbidden knowledge, illusory appearances, and unwholesome survival all loom large, in an account of a Massachusetts seacoast town where there is literally something fishy. The vacationing narrator (who, significantly, and unlike some other first-person narrators in Lovecraft's fiction, is unnamed in the final, published form of the tale) comes to understand that the town's denizens, with their unblinking eyes and distorted features, are the results of interbreeding with aquatic creatures of great antiquity. The town is riddled with underground passages (hence illusory appearances, even given the unsavoriness of the surface appearance: horror beyond horror again), and the inhabitants go to great pains to protect the town's secrets (forbidden knowledge). In this tale the narrator quite literally looks into the glass and finds the "Innsmouth look" staring back. Like the original Outsider, the narrator (whose namelessness symbolizes his ambiguous identity or nature—Lovecraft named him Robert Olmstead in an early draft of the story but later dropped the name) after a fashion accepts his lot, as an individual. But the implications for humankind remain: there are older tenants of the earth, and a melding of the races leaves no question as to which race has the capacity for dominance and survival.

After writing two stories that were competent but relatively modest in the scope of their implications—"The Dreams in the Witch House," involving the themes of forbidden knowledge and unwholesome survival, and "The Thing on the Doorstep," involving these same themes as well as that of illusory appearances—Lovecraft finally wrote his most powerful thematic statement, the novella "The Shadow out of Time" (1934–35), a work through which one may trace all the major themes. The narrator, Nathaniel Wingate Peaslee, suffers a period of "amnesia" that really stems from a mind-transfer by which a prehuman race in Australia has drawn his consciousness back many millions of years: thus the theme of denied primacy. During the transfer, his body is host to an alien mind: the theme of illusory surface appearances. His experience is masked from his mind (forbidden knowledge), but he has dreams that increasingly seem more like memories (a form of oneiric objectivism). Most terribly of all, he discovers, upon flicking on a light in a buried crypt and seeing his own handwriting in a prehistoric book, that the experience has been real—this is the ultimate moment in the Lovecraft Mythos, the moment at which humankind (for Peaslee is nothing less than ourselves) most poignantly "touches the glass." In his rush to escape this place of unthinkable confirmation of all his fears, Peaslee hears sounds suggesting that the darker inhabitants of the Great Race's far-off age, inhabitants feared even by the Great Race, are still alive and lurking underground: again, horror beyond horror.

While Lovecraft would write one more major story involving the themes of forbidden knowledge and unwholesome survival—"The Haunter of the Dark" (1935)—he would never again produce a work expressing his characteristic themes so powerfully as in "The Shadow out of Time," where all the themes coalesce to affirm the grand Lovecraftian theme: that self-knowledge, knowledge of humankind's vanishingly motelike position in the uncaring scheme of the cosmos, is psychic ruin. The tale's narrator even remarks, when about to recall the events of his experience, "If the thing did happen, then man must be prepared to accept notions of the cosmos, and of his own place in the seething vortex of time, whose merest mention is paralysing" (*DH* 368). There could be no more succinct summary of the informing notion at the heart of the Lovecraft Mythos.

The overall effect, then, of the thematic content of Lovecraft's fiction is to cleave reality into a bipolar opposition: the hope of humankind to have dignity and worth and meaning on the one hand, and, on the other, the dashing of those hopes in the contemplation of a cosmos blindly indifferent to the presence of humans. Time after time, in various ways, the Outsider reaches forth to touch the glass, and suffers the agony of self-discovery. To be human is to be the Outsider, a meaningless speck adrift in the sea of stars. This "ironic im-

pressionism" (as I have termed it)—this fictional effect of making human consciousness the conduit for experiencing the reality of the cosmic scheme while
showing that that consciousness is uniquely capable of reduction to suffering in
its self-understood insignificance—is an effect unprecedented in literature. The
effect is impressionistic in that what is important is the mental life of those
who gaze into the fateful mirror; the irony is that humankind is just sufficiently
well developed to suffer, uniquely among earth's acknowledged creatures, the
awful knowledge inhering in self-discovery. The old saying is that "it shouldn't
happen to a dog," and indeed it could not; dogs are unreflective on their lowly
status in the universal scheme, while *Homo sapiens*—ironically, the knowing
animal—can know its debasement, a debasement not even so elevated as true
tragedy, since humankind has no genuinely tragic dignity, no dignity of great
beings brought low, to fling back at the mocking stars.

Yet the complexity of the matter does not rest there. In the binary opposition into which Lovecraft thematically carves reality—the dichotomy of worth-
seeking humankind versus the uncaring cosmos—one discerns that in a sense
each pole of the opposition necessarily contains the other.

When one considers the indifferent cosmos, one can only characterize it as
"indifferent" in the sense that it is indifferent to (toward, and from the viewpoint of) humans; in the total absence of human consciousness, the universe
could not be "indifferent," for indifference amounts to the opposite of a collective human expectation. The universe can only be thought to be indifferent
to (and by) a consciousness that has had loftier expectations, so that in a paradoxical way, humans subvert themselves to contribute to their own insignificance; on the cosmic canvas, the human face is missing precisely because it is
present—it paints its own absence.

Conversely, humankind, even in its self-deluding and futile quest for worth
and recognition, is still made of star-stuff; humankind is still an interwoven
part of the universe by which it is ignored, a universe that amounts to a cosmic
complementation without which there could be no question of worth or position to begin with. A solipsist whose solipsism was fact could not be either significant nor insignificant, for these descriptions presume a universe standing
beyond oneself for comparison—a universe, as it turns out, standing in a relation of mutual inclusion with the beholder. When humans collectively behold
themselves, then in a sense the cosmos beholds itself as well. As Nietzsche has
said, gaze into the abyss and it will gaze back into you—you may discover, in
fact, that you are the abyss, the one twitching nerve-end of the cosmos that
writhes against itself. The experience of Lovecraft's fiction is an eternally fro-

zen yet living moment of gazing into one's own face in a mirror of devastating self-revelation. The Lovecraftian dichotomy deconstructs itself into, and reinscribes itself as, a perpetual aporia of mutual and self-reflection.

In literary theorist M. H. Abrams's well-known *The Mirror and the Lamp*, the mirror is a metaphor for mind, mind viewed (in pre-Romantic or Neoclassicist terms) as a mimetic reflector of externality, in contrast with the "lamp" metaphor of mind as a radiant contributor to what it perceives. For Lovecraft (in such a scheme decidedly the pre-Romantic) the mind is more mirror than lamp. But for Lovecraft the mirror is also a metaphor for the cosmos itself that reflects back humankind's true face, the face of a lost and nameless soul. Self-referentially, Lovecraft's career-long text itself is a sprawling hall of mirrors, mirrors mirroring mirrors, a labyrinth of iterated thematic reflections through which wanders the Outsider who forever reaches forth, in hope against hope, to touch the glass.

Letters, Diaries, and Manuscripts: The Handwritten Word in Lovecraft

Peter Cannon

Like any author worthy of the name, H. P. Lovecraft was both a prodigious reader and writer. During his years of artistic maturity, as a free-lance "revision-ist" with no family obligations other than to his two independent if elderly aunts, he could devote ample time to literary pursuits. But while reading had formed an essential part of Lovecraft's intellectual development since his youthful immersion in the eighteenth-century tomes that filled his grandfa-ther's library, the act of putting fountain pen to paper would become for him a far more characteristic gesture than picking up a book.

One typically imagines Lovecraft variously engaged in writing: closeted in his study far into the night attending to his voluminous correspondence; lodged at a YMCA or other cheap hostelry making notes on his latest antiquar-ian tour; seated on a bench on Prospect Terrace or in the woods outside Providence working through a briefcase full of papers, among which might be the draft of an original tale. In his hand he holds his 1906 Waterman—or per-haps the free-flowing Parker that he was so pleased to receive from his amateur colleague Ernest A. Edkins. In a 1931 letter to his young correspondent J. Vernon Shea describing his search for the perfect writing instrument, he could claim that "honest, old-fashioned script is the only medium of expression in which I feel absolutely at home" (*SL* 3.395).

Certain mechanical exigencies prompted Lovecraft naturally to value the written word over the printed word. Never advancing beyond the two-finger typing method, he boasted in 1935 that he "couldn't possibly write anything im-portant on a typewriter" (*SL* 5.267). He often persuaded others, like his friend and revision client C. M. Eddy, to type his stories for him in exchange for edito-rial services. In "The Loved Dead" (1923), one of the tales that he touched up for Eddy, Lovecraft changed the last paragraph from a typed note to a hand-written one ending, "I can—write—no more . . . ." (*HM* 357).[1] Two of his two short novels, *The Dream-Quest of Unknown Kadath* and *The Case of Charles Dexter Ward,* remained in manuscript until after his death largely because he would not bother to type them. Much of the despair that he felt after *Weird Tales* rejected *At the Mountains of Madness* can be attributed to the enormous effort he put into typing it. He evidently never even considered typing his longest work, his Quebec travelogue, which remained unpublished until 1976.

Apart from a few anthology appearances, Lovecraft's tales never achieved the dignity of mainstream hardcover publication in his lifetime. Misprints and typos in their pulp magazine appearances were a common complaint of their author. He considered his one book-form story, a small-press edition of *The Shadow over Innsmouth,* "a lousily printed mess" (*SL* 5.359). Without a collection of stories to his name, he became fixated on the tools of the preproduction process. A chronological survey shows just how pervasive is the handwritten word in his fiction—notably in the shape of letters, diaries, and manuscripts.

"I am writing this under an appreciable mental strain," declares the narrator in the opening sentence of "Dagon" (1917), a conventional example of the story itself constituting a manuscript. Presumably found in the protagonist's room after he had cast himself "from this garret window into the squalid street below" (*D* 14), the text shows him to have recorded events to the very end: "I hear a noise at the door, as of some immense slippery body lumbering against it. It shall not find me. God, *that hand!* The window! The window!" (*D* 19). Melodramatic his final words may be, yet in such persistence the narrator of "Dagon" establishes the pattern for future Lovecraftian heroes who will likewise tend to write rather than run in the face of supernatural threat.

In contrast, Karl Heinrich, the cold, iron-willed U-boat commander in "The Temple" (1920), soberly sets down his strange tale, which ultimately reaches the reader in the same manner as Poe's "MS. Found in a Bottle," as the descriptive line below the title reveals: "(Manuscript found on the coast of Yucatan.)" (*D* 59). "I shall seal the manuscript in a bottle and entrust it to the sea" (*D* 72), Heinrich announces near the close of his diarylike account before his exit from the submarine to seek the ineffable horror that has been plaguing him and his crew. While "The Temple" may be a more subtle story than "Dagon," it too follows the familiar first-person confessional mode in its guise of posthumous document.

Writing first figures as an act integral to plot, indeed as an essential means of communication between characters, in "The Music of Erich Zann" (1921), a first-person narrative not explicitly framed as a document.[2] When the narrator initially visits his mute fellow lodger, the old viol-player pencils a note, "an appeal for tolerance and forgiveness" (*DH* 87). At the climax, Zann prepares what promises to be a "full account in German of all the marvels and terrors which beset him" (*DH* 89). At the end, the narrator is not "wholly sorry" for the loss in "undreamable abysses of the closely written sheets which alone could have explained the music of Erich Zann" (*DH* 91). Here is the first instance in Lovecraft's fiction of an important document going astray, intercepted before it can reach the eyes of its intended recipient. By giving no hint of Zann's revelations, Lovecraft would seem to err on the side of suggestiveness, though such vagueness suits the elusive, dreamlike quality of the short tale. In his longer, more realistic works, he will not shy away from providing full quotations or paraphrases.

In "The Rats in the Walls" (1923), Delapore speaks of the information "recorded in the sealed envelope left before the Civil War by every squire to his eldest son for posthumous opening" (*DH* 27). Although the packet was consumed in the fire that destroyed the family home during the Civil War, Delapore obtains "some very circumstantial accounts of the final tragedy and flight of Walter de la Poer" that he believes to be "the probable contents of the hereditary paper" (*DH* 32). (Had he seen the actual letter, might he have decided not to go to England and restore Exham Priory and thus avoided the family curse?) Here, in keeping with the realism of the story, Lovecraft conveys the substance of the document in question, striking a perfect balance between suggestion and revelation. Not a major element like the lost pages in "The Music of Erich Zann," the ancestral envelope serves as one of a number of subtle touches that add to the air of Gothic mystery that suffuses this finest of Lovecraft's early tales.

In "Cool Air" (1926), as in the two previous stories, written communications do not tend to survive. The narrator says of the stranger, Dr. Muñoz, who lives in the same rooming-house, "He acquired a habit of writing long documents of some sort, which he carefully sealed and filled with injunctions that I transmit them after his death to certain persons whom he named. . . . As it happened, I burned all these papers undelivered and unopened" (*DH* 205). The narrator also sets a match to "the stickily smeared paper" that he retrieves from the remains of Dr. Muñoz, though he does conclude his tale by quoting the text of "that noisome scrawl" (*DH* 207). Where a supernatural agency had swept up Zann's pages or the Yanks had burned Carfax and the secret, here a protagonist acts deliberately to suppress information. This may be merely a passing detail within a concise narrative, yet it helps set Lovecraft's horrors on a global scale. Unlike Dr. Herbert West, Dr. Muñoz is no lone fanatic; like Joseph Curwen, he corresponds with those who share his aims, "including a once celebrated French physician now generally thought dead, and about whom the most inconceivable things had been whispered" (*DH* 205). Again, Lovecraft will expand on the possibilities inherent in this document motif given a large enough canvas.

"The Call of Cthulhu" (1926) stands as Lovecraft's first tale to articulate his pseudomythology in depth and also has the distinction of being the first story to employ a complex structure of nested narratives.[3] Like "Dagon," "The Call of Cthulhu" purports to be a manuscript, as the line below the title indicates: "(Found Among the Papers of the Late Francis Wayland Thurston, of Boston)" (*DH* 125).[4] Thurston, like Erich Zann, is privy to terrible secrets. But here Lovecraft is bold enough to reveal the worst, as filtered through the narrator's summaries of certain documents found in a locked box belonging to his late grand-uncle and written "in [Professor Angell's] most recent hand" (*DH* 127). The main document, headed "CTHULHU CULT," divides into two sections: the account of the artist Henry Wilcox; and the narrative of Inspector Legrasse of New Orleans, which incorporates the oral reports of Professor Webb and Old Castro.[5] Newspaper cuttings and Wilcox's dream-inspired bas-relief also point to the existence of Cthulhu, but it is primarily through the handwritten word, representing a multiplicity of fragmented viewpoints, that the narrator comes to accept the reality of that cosmic monstrosity.

For the sake of drama, Lovecraft does not place every document of consequence in the late professor's possession. Thurston must travel to Norway to claim the final manuscript of the story, Johansen's narrative, which "was a simple, rambling thing—a naive sailor's effort at a post-facto diary—and strove to recall day by day that last awful voyage." Lovecraft wisely does not have Thurston attempt "to transcribe it verbatim in all its cloudiness and redundance" (*DH* 149). No doubt the original lacks the images from modern art and classical myth that make Cthulhu's climactic rise from R'lyeh so powerful. In addition, such paraphrasing contributes, as it does in earlier sections, to the overall economy of the tale.

Like the narrator of "Dagon," Thurston realizes by the end that death is near. Having the time to ponder the implications of his research, he decides that his account should be restricted: "Let me pray that, if I do not survive this manuscript, my executors may put caution before audacity and see that it meets no other eye" (*DH* 154). The purpose of his exercise has been not to warn the world but at most to persuade others that it is in the world's best interest to suppress the terrible knowledge he has pieced together. Perhaps Thurston's executors disregarded his advice because they had only his (handwritten) word for it.

The Case of Charles Dexter Ward (1927), Lovecraft's longest work of fiction, contains a rich assortment of holographs. Some receive passing mention, like Ezra Weeden's notebooks, Eleazar Smith's "none too coherent diary," and the accounts of "other diarists and letter-writers" (*MM* 130) from which Ward reconstructs Joseph Curwen's last days; others appear in full, like the various letters between Curwen and his henchmen, Charles Ward's plea to Dr. Willett for help, and Dr. Willett's explanation to Charles's father. From a purely mechanical standpoint, these quoted documents, together with newspaper extracts, provide the narrative texture conventionally supplied by dialogue. By writing at short-novel length, Lovecraft could quote substantially from the kinds of papers whose contents could only be hinted at in shorter tales. *The Case of Charles Dexter Ward* shows in particular his skill at imitating the prose of the eighteenth century.

The most extraordinary written communication in the novel, however, dates from a far earlier period. This is the note that Dr. Willett obtains from one of Curwen's resurrected victims, who composes it "in such Latin as a barbarous age might remember" using "the pointed Saxon minuscules of the eighth or ninth century A.D." (*MM* 220). (Lovecraft provides both the crude original text and a translation.) Confined for nearly two centuries to a pit and presumably fired by revenge, the note's author remains sane enough to urge Curwen's destruction. No matter how grotesque or difficult the circumstances, Lovecraft's characters are able to rise above them and scrawl final, level-headed missives.

In the end the tip from this uncanny source contributes only slightly to Curwen's downfall, since it is the fiend's own handwriting that mainly leads to his undoing. As heedless as Lovecraft himself on the consequences of his letters reaching an audience beyond the persons to whom they are addressed, Joseph Curwen freely discusses his nefarious schemes in correspondence with his co-conspirators, thereby alerting his enemies who intercept his mail in both the eighteenth and twentieth centuries. In addition, Curwen leaves behind a wealth of handwritten papers, which Ward finds behind his ancestor's portrait. One text "was in a hand which he had learned to recognise at the Essex Institute, and proclaimed the volume as the *Journall and Notes of Jos. Curwen, Gent., of Providence Plantations, Late of Salem'*. . . . All the other papers were likewise in Curwen's handwriting" (*MM* 156). Dr. Willett too becomes sufficiently familiar with "Curwen's intricate and archaic chirography" (*MM* 158) to see that "the strained and awkward signatures of the cheques" (*MM* 191) bearing Ward's name are clumsy forgeries. Although Curwen can raise the dead, he proves singularly inept at disguising his writing. Here, as elsewhere in the later Lovecraft, one's handwriting would seem to be the one reliable test of personal identity.

Like *The Case of Charles Dexter Ward*, "The Dunwich Horror" (1928) is an omniscient third-person narrative, punctuated by speech (chiefly rustic dialect) that in places approaches dialogue and by various printed material, like the epigraph from Charles Lamb, the extract from the Reverend Abijah Hoadley's sermon, and the lengthy passage from the *Necronomicon*. The tale features one substantial manuscript, "written in a huge ledger and adjudged a sort of diary because of the spacing and the variations in ink and penmanship" (*DH* 176). This coded document turns out to be Wilbur Whateley's diary, which Dr. Armitage deciphers only after great effort but in time to take the necessary steps to eradicate the Dunwich horror. As in *The Case of Charles Dexter Ward*, the villain's own written words contribute to the thwarting of his evil designs.

Of course, to call Wilbur a villain is somewhat misleading, for as Donald R. Burleson has shown,[6] the Whateley brothers may be regarded as the real heroes of the story. Indeed, insofar as he develops into a "scholar of really tremendous erudition" and is "quietly known by correspondence to many librarians in distant places where rare and forbidden books of old days are kept" (*DH* 167), Wilbur is Lovecraft's parody of himself, a secluded prodigy who maintains contact with the outside world through letter writing.[7] For all the horror of the diary entry quoted for 26 November 1916, written "by a child of three and a half who looked like a lad of twelve or thirteen" (*DH* 184), Wilbur is perhaps to be admired for taking up his pen at so early an age.

With "The Mound" (1929–30) Lovecraft once more puts a manuscript at center stage, devoting the bulk of the story to a paraphrase of "The Narrative of Pánfilo de Zamacona y Nuñez, gentleman, of Luarca in Asturias, *Concerning the Subterranean World of Xinaián, A.D. 1545*," whose "wretched and ill-punctuated script," as the unnamed ethnologist narrator notes, is written in "the formal, pompous Spanish of a long-departed day" (*HM* 113). Zamacona's scroll provides a full and terrifying glimpse into the underground world of K'n-yan, yet like R'lyeh it surfaces only briefly. By foolishly taking the manuscript below the mound the day after he reads it, the narrator in effect ensures its loss for what could well be another few centuries if not forever. The contents of such documents may be conveyed, but for the sake of leaving a rational out— again the reader has only the narrator's word for the mysteries he has unearthed—the physical evidence cannot survive.

When he first settles in K'n-yan, Zamacona finds that his apartment includes all the amenities that a writer could wish for: "Desks with great stacks of membrane-paper and pots of the prevailing green pigment were in every room—each with graded sets of pigment brushes and other odd bits of stationery. Mechanical writing devices stood on ornate golden tripods" (*HM* 146). Though he would seem to have a choice between pen and typewriter, the intrepid Spaniard naturally prefers the former. By the time of his last escape attempt, his handwritten account has become more precious to him than gold:

"Of course he could not bear away any gold, but mere escape was enough. He would, though, dematerialise and carry away with him his manuscript in the Tulu-metal cylinder, even though it cost additional effort; for this record and proof must reach the outer world at all hazards" (*HM* 154). Despite his grotesque and tragic end, Zamacona triumphs insofar as his story, as relayed by the narrator, does ultimately reach an audience. In "The Mound" Zamacona's setting down his personal history and observations, rather as Lovecraft did daily in his prolific correspondence, assumes especially heroic proportions.

Correspondence, together with the narrator's reflections on its significance, dominates all but the final section of "The Whisperer in Darkness" (1930). Professor Albert Wilmarth quotes from memory the complete texts of two long letters that he receives from the recluse Henry Akeley. The first letter to reach Wilmarth is "in the cramped, archaic-looking scrawl of one who had obviously not mingled much with the world during his sedate, scholarly life" (*DH* 216). Akeley's subsequent letters are also handwritten, except for the last: "the signature as well as the body of the letter was typed—as is frequent with beginners in typing" (*DH* 238). Unlike Curwen after he disposes of Ward, the fungi from Yuggoth do not even attempt to forge the signature of their victim but trust that this shift in format will not arouse the narrator's suspicions. In the event their faith is justified. Just as the ethnologist in "The Mound" had taken along Zamacona's scroll in his descent, so even more naively does Wilmarth carry "the entire file of Akeley's correspondence" (*DH* 244) to his friend's Vermont farmhouse; at the climax he too flees in panic leaving all behind. Here script is a true guide to character, whereas typing is an act of treachery and deceit.

No handwritten communications of consequence appear in the two major tales Lovecraft produced in 1931, *At the Mountains of Madness* and "The Shadow over Innsmouth." The narrator of the former states that he is "forced into speech" (*MM* 3) because scientists have refused to follow his advice, while that of the latter says that the "mere telling" (*DH* 305) helps him to restore confidence in his own faculties; otherwise neither comments on the form of his story.

After Randolph Carter returns to earth in "Through the Gates of the Silver Key" (1932–33), he disguises himself as one Swami Chandraputra, sending "inquiries to various mystics in 1930–31–32" (*MM* 457). Like Dr. Muñoz and Joseph Curwen, he strives to keep in touch with like-minded souls by mail. At the meeting to settle Carter's estate, his friend De Marigny says that "since 1930 I have received letters from the Swami which tally with his account" (*MM* 453). The Swami offers as proof of Carter's existence "some papers obviously written since 1930, and in the unmistakable style of Randolph Carter," adding,

"Of course the handwriting is almost illegible—but remember that Randolph Carter now has no hands well adapted to forming human script" (*MM* 454–55). Here Lovecraft introduces the idea that one's handwriting, even after one's mind has been transferred into a foreign body, remains constant. By this stage the handwritten word not only indicates individual identity but also is the one sure sign of humanity.

Under certain circumstances a character whose personality has been displaced may lack even handlike appendages, though this handicap can be overcome, as the experience of Thomas Slauenwite, M.D., suggests in "Winged Death" (1932). The investigators who examine the late doctor's journal note that "the entries were in a fine handwriting, which, however, grew careless and nervous-looking toward the last" (*HM,* 243). At the end they see something strange on the ceiling of the victim's hotel room, "a series of shaky, straggling ink-tracks, such as might have been made by the crawling of some ink-drenched insect." These inky smudges prove to form "definite letters of the alphabet—letters coherently arranged in English words . . . scrawled in a place no human hand could reach" (*HM* 263). After finding his consciousness in the body of a fly, Slauenwite evidently dipped himself in ink and wrote a message confirming the implications of his journal, his final gesture before drowning himself in a bottle of ammonia. Had the doctor possessed a typewriter, his fly alter ego could conceivably have leapt upon the keys, rather like Archie the cockroach of *Archie and Mehitabel,* but in Lovecraft the written word is always the preferred means of communication, no matter how awkward the act.

In "The Thing on the Doorstep" (1933) the narrator, Daniel Upton, gets a lesson in the immutability of handwriting from his friend Edward Derby: "'Listen, Dan—do you know why my wife always takes such pains with that silly backhand writing? Have you ever seen a manuscript of old Ephraim's? Do you want to know why I shivered when I saw some hasty notes Asenath had jotted down?'" (*DH* 289). These remarks help prepare the ground for the climax, perhaps the most shocking instance in the fiction of a character persisting to write in extremity. Upton rejects the theory that Derby's servants forged the handwriting of the text presented at the close of the story. Beyond question, the "large, closely written paper impaled on the end of a long pencil" that the thing on the doorstep thrusts at him "was in Edward's script" (*DH* 301). Trapped in the rotting corpse of the wife he has murdered, Derby summons the same courage and determination that the author of the Saxon minuscules displayed in *The Case of Charles Dexter Ward* to write a message calling for the death of an impostor in a madhouse.

Derby's letter includes the sentence: "I'm too far gone to talk—I couldn't manage to telephone—but I can still write" (*DH* 302). The spoken word may fail but not the written word. Civilized man reduced to his essentials is a creature that writes.

In "The Thing on the Doorstep" dental work positively identifies the body as Asenath's, but in "The Shadow out of Time" (1934–35) handwriting alone confirms the truth of everything the narrator has experienced, both in waking and in dream. As a captive mind among the rugose, cone-shaped members of the Great Race, Peaslee observes that "the tops of the vast pedestals were littered with books, papers, and what seemed to be writing materials—oddly figured jars of purplish metal, and rods with stained tips" (*DH* 380). Like Zamacona in K'n-yan, he discovers that his masters have provided him with all the resources he needs for recording the history of his own age.

In his visions Peaslee finds himself "writing for hours at the great tables with a stylus managed by the green tentacles that hung down from my head" (*DH* 394). Despite such utterly alien appendages, Peaslee, unlike Randolph Carter in his Yaddithian form, readily writes in his normal human hand. In the final sentence of the tale, as the reader has long anticipated, he reveals that what he saw in the volume beneath the ruins in the Australian desert were "the letters of our familiar alphabet, spelling out the words of the English language in my own handwriting" (*DH* 433). Thus the small intimate strokes of the narrator's script serve to underscore the awesomeness of time and space and to shatter any illusions about man's place in the cosmic scheme. A printed page would not have had the same poignant impact. Like Lovecraft himself, the most advanced beings in the universe are sentimental enough to regard the written word (whether by hand or tentacle) as superior to mere technical efficiency. Here the motif reaches its imaginative pinnacle.

Peaslee calls attention to his narrative as a manuscript—"These pages . . . are written in the cabin of the ship that is bringing me home" (*DH* 369)—which he intends to give to his son Wingate. So powerful is the story that Lovecraft need not identify it as a posthumous document. The letter from the narrator's Australian correspondent, Robert B. F. Mackenzie, was presumably typed, though Peaslee appears not to have held this against him.

In "The Diary of Alonzo Typer" (1935), the title character leaves behind a diary that "has been proved by handwriting experts to be genuine. The script shews signs of increasing nervous strain as it progresses toward the end, in places becoming almost illegible" (*HM* 305). In his diary Typer refers to a bound manuscript "in Low Latin, and full of the strange, crabbed handwriting

of Claes van der Heyl—being evidently the diary or notebook kept by him between 1560 and 1580" (*HM* 313), as well as a second diary or notebook by the
demonic van der Heyl and a key in a "wrapping of dried skin . . . which bore a
Low Latin message in the same crabbed writing as that of the notebooks I
found" (*HM* 319). Such details, however, do little to redeem this perfunctory
ghost-written tale, whose fevered diarist undergoes a formulaic series of random supernatural events in the haunted-house tradition of William Hope
Hodgson's *The House on the Borderland*. Indeed, as Robert M. Price has commented,[8] the ending verges on the ludicrous. Typer's last entry reads: "Too
late—cannot help self—black paws materialise—am dragged away toward the
cellar" (*HM* 322). Lovecraft seems here to be parodying the impulse of his
typical hero to keep writing at all costs.

"The Haunter of the Dark" (1935), composed shortly after "The Diary of
Alonzo Typer," also focuses on a diary, but here an urbane third-person voice
like that in *The Case of Charles Dexter Ward* summarizes its contents (apart from
the dramatic excerpt that closes the story), while maintaining a skeptical distance: "the entries in [Blake's] diary are clearly the result of a fantastic imagination aroused by certain local superstitions and by certain old matters he had
uncovered" (*DH* 92). Where in the ghost-written "Winged Death" or "The Diary of Alonzo Typer" Lovecraft was content to present unedited diary tran-
scripts within a conventional frame, in "Haunter" he weaves a paraphrase of the
central document into a rich narrative that draws on the reports of others, from
the ignorant Italians on Federal Hill to the youths living in the fraternity houses
on College Hill. As in "The Mound," this economy of structure contributes
greatly to the success of this, the most cosmic of the late shorter stories.

In the course of investigating the Starry Wisdom Church, Blake finds assorted
written materials, ranging from the Pnakotic Manuscripts and "a small leather-
bound record-book filled with entries in some odd cryptographic medium" (*DH*
100) to a crumbling leather pocketbook containing "a paper covered with pen-
cilled memoranda" (*DH* 103), the notes of the unfortunate reporter Edwin M.
Lillibridge, whose curiously charred skeleton lies amid the debris in the church
steeple. Lovecraft suggests primarily through the parallels between the writings
of the two men that Blake will suffer a similar fate. The "disjointed text" (*DH*
103) of the reporter's notes anticipates the form of the fantaisiste's final diary entries, which were "highly disjointed, and legible only in part." Furthermore,
"Blake had prolonged his frenzied jottings to the last, and the broken-pointed
pencil was found clutched in his spasmodically contracted right hand" (*DH* 114).
Sixteen months after depicting Blake's demise, too weak to hold a pen, Lovecraft

himself would resort to pencil, making notes on his fatal illness as bravely as any of his characters facing approaching doom.[9]

"In the Walls of Eryx" (1936), a collaborative excursion into science fiction, stands as Lovecraft's last tale to feature a diary. When Kenton J. Stanfield finds himself trapped in the maze of the Venusian man-lizards, he acts as heroically as Zamacona to ensure the survival of his account, hoping it will serve as a warning to others. (Like Blake, he comes across the body of a predecessor whose fate foreshadows his own.) One of his last entries reads: "I am growing numb and cannot write much more" (*D* 319). The head of the operatives who find Stanfield remarks: "He had a record scroll in his left hand and a pen in his right, and seemed to have been writing when he died" (*D* 320). Like the Great Race, man will forever ply the pen, regardless of the advances of technology.

By the end of his life Lovecraft clearly had come to regard the act of writing as one of the most noble of human endeavors. The anxiety his characters so often express over the survival of their various manuscripts reflects his own insecurity about his work, which to his disappointment received almost no attention from the literary establishment of his day. Happily, the wide publication in the decades since his death of his handwritten words—literally millions of them, preserved mostly in letters but also in stories and miscellaneous prose—has gained him the immortality he at some level knew his art deserved. No doubt Lovecraft would have delighted in the cosmic irony of his being saluted by the wordprocessor generation in the year of his centenary.

Notes

1. See Eddy's remarks on this episode as quoted by August Derleth in *The Dark Brotherhood* (Sauk City, WI: Arkham House, 1966), 98.

2. A slightly later instance of the mute communicating in this fashion occurs in "The Festival," where the narrator's host writes "a quaint and ancient welcome with the stylus and wax tablet he carried" (*D* 210).

3. See S. T. Joshi, "The Structure of Lovecraft's Longer Narratives," in *Selected Papers on Lovecraft* (West Warwick, RI: Necronomicon Press, 1989), 28–29.

4. HPL identified one other story as a posthumous document, "Out of the Aeons" (1933), perhaps the best of his ghostwritten jobs for Hazel Heald, which likewise features a horror with a South Pacific origin.

5. During the middle period covering his return to Providence from New York, HPL mastered the art of oral narrative as well. Both "In the Vault" (1925) and "Pickman's Model" (1926) are addressed to a specific listener. Quoted speech figures prominently in a number of later tales. In "The Dunwich Horror" the locals

talk over a party line about the horror's progress; Wilmarth overhears the fungi from Yuggoth converse in "The Whisperer in Darkness"; de Russy recounts his melancholy family history in "Medusa's Coil" (1930); the bibulous Zadok Allen holds forth in "The Shadow over Innsmouth" (1931); and Swami Chandraputra fills in those interested in Randolph Carter's whereabouts in "Through the Gates of the Silver Key."

6. See Donald R. Burleson, "The Mythic Hero Archetype in 'The Dunwich Horror,'" *LS* No. 4 (Spring 1981): 3–9.

7. There are a number of sardonic parallels between the Whateley and the Lovecraft families, as I demonstrate in my study, *H. P. Lovecraft* (Boston: Twayne, 1989), 87.

8. See Robert M. Price, "Famous Last Words," *CoC* No. 8 (Michaelmas 1982): 28–29.

9. HPL sometimes used pencil under ordinary circumstances. Earlier in the year he had written the pretyped draft of "The Shadow out of Time" in pencil, and in 1932 he had complained to a correspondent: "Having abandoned all hope of getting a fountain pen to suit my ageing claw and crabbed cacography, I have returned to the pencils of my infancy" (*SL* 4.28).

Outsiders and Aliens: The Uses of Isolation in Lovecraft's Fiction

Stefan Dziemianowicz

> There was thunder in the air on the night I went to the deserted mansion atop Tempest Mountain to find the lurking fear. I was not alone, for foolhardiness was not then mixed with that love of the grotesque and the terrible which has made my career a series of quests for strange horrors in literature and in life. With me were two faithful and muscular men for whom I had sent when the time came; men long associated with me in my ghastly explorations because of their peculiar fitness. (*D* 179)

As any reader of H. P. Lovecraft's fiction knows, the passage above is an expression of misplaced bravado at best. Just as it is a given that Lovecraftian narrators grossly underestimate the forces they face on their excursions into the unknown, it is also a given that Lovecraftian horrors abhor crowds. An aura of inevitability overshadows the trio of characters from the moment they are introduced in the opening chapter of "The Lurking Fear," and it is no surprise that several thousand words later the narrator awakens to find his two stalwart companions mysteriously plucked from his side during the night. The chapter closes with the narrator in a physical and emotional state that is a direct contrast to the one he enjoyed in the opening scene: "alone in the accursed mansion, shivering and gibbering" (*D* 184). To drive the point home, Lovecraft deprives the narrator of companionship in the face of horror yet one more time.

Lovecraft never again isolated his narrators so blatantly, but by doing so in "The Lurking Fear" he acknowledged one of the unwritten rules of supernatural fiction: horror is most effective when it comes to a solitary character in a solitary place. This convention is so generally accepted that very few studies of supernatural literature consider it worthy of comment, yet the history of supernatural horror fiction is a virtual study in techniques of character isolation: the remote castle in Horace Walpole's Gothic novel *The Castle of Otranto*, the voyage to a distant land in Poe's *The Narrative of Arthur Gordon Pym*, the haunted forests and hills where terrors lie in wait in the fiction of Algernon Blackwood and Arthur Machen—these, and the variations wrought upon them in countless other works of horror literature, are convenient devices for abstracting characters from familiar surroundings. Such isolating techniques serve a simple but important function: they lay the foundation for the reader's suspension of disbelief by suggesting that the supernatural flourishes in the terra incognita of the rational world. However, they go beyond the realm of simple geographic displacement, for in depriving the narrator of witnesses to corroborate his experience, they make the reader's belief an important part of the isolating technique. The reader finds himself in the same position as the wedding guest in Coleridge's *Rime of the Ancient Mariner*: he may believe the testimony of the lone survivor and abide his warning, or he may dismiss the account as the fantastic ravings of a madman, thus further isolating the character.

The tension between the belief and doubt such a situation creates is one of the yardsticks by which we measure the effectiveness of horror fiction. Lovecraft admitted as much when he wrote "One cannot, except in immature pulp charlatan-fiction, present an account of impossible, improbable, or inconceivable phenomena as a commonplace narrative of objective acts and conventional emotions" (*CE* 2.177). He held that "all a wonder story can ever be is a vivid picture of a certain type of human mood," and as story after story in the Lovecraft *oeuvre* demonstrates, he felt there was no better way to express that mood than through the narrative of the individual confronting by himself the vastness of the unknown.

Lovecraft's work has been characterized as almost pathological in its use of characters alienated from normal human society. Donald R. Burleson reminds us that "Lovecraft protagonists are virtually always placed in the position of facing their horrors alone, without consolation or even corroborating witnesses to the reality of their perceptions."[1] But if Lovecraft repeatedly isolated his characters, he did not do so in quite the same fashion in every story. Just as the nature of Lovecraft's fiction changed considerably with his growth as a writer and thinker between 1917 and 1937, so too did the means he used to articulate his horrors. The relationship between his characters, their society, the world at large, and the universe was dynamic and changed as he labored to clarify his unique perspective on supernatural horror. Considering the significance that solitude and isolation play in all Lovecraft's stories, an analysis of how he used them as ends in his fiction, even as he transformed the means by which he arrived at them, can help us trace the evolution of what we know today as "Lovecraftian fiction."

I

The earliest and most lasting influence on Lovecraft's fiction was the work of Edgar Allan Poe, which Lovecraft praised as "a literary dawn" for the supernatural horror story. Lovecraft credited Poe with overcoming "empty literary conventions" to get at "the psychological basis of the horror appeal."[2] Indeed, he found this aspect of Poe's fiction so compelling that he tried his own hand at it in his first mature story. In "The Tomb" (1917), Lovecraft equates character psychology with the isolation of the outsider. The narrator professes an innate alienation from the world around him:

> My name is Jervas Dudley, and from earliest childhood I have been a dreamer and a visionary. Wealthy beyond the necessity of a commercial life, and temperamentally unfitted for the formal studies and social recreations of my acquaintances, I have dwelt ever in realms apart from the visible world; spending my youth and adolescence in ancient and little-known books, and in roaming the fields and groves of the region near my ancestral home. I do not think that what I read in these books or saw in these fields and groves was exactly what other boys read and saw there. (*D* 3–4)

Dudley is a familiar character in fantasy fiction, the sensitive soul excluded by his temperament from the vulgar world around him. Yet his alienation from the world seems to have its compensations, for it opens to him a realm from which his peers are excluded. His is a personality not merely detached from the world around him, but also poised somewhere between this world and another world he longs for.

We glimpse that other world when Dudley assures us that, despite his detachment from the world, he does not dwell alone. "This no human creature may do; for lacking the fellowship of the living, he inevitably draws upon the companionship of things that are not, or are no longer, living" (*D* 4). When we learn those companions reside in a "lone tomb in the darkest of the hillside thickets; the deserted tomb of the Hydes, an old and exalted family whose last direct descendant had been laid within its black recesses many decades before my birth" (*D* 4), our suspicion that Dudley is much more alienated from the normal world than most dreamers is confirmed. When Dudley finally gains entrance to the tomb, he finds the spirits of the deceased Hydes a surprisingly lively crew who welcome him as one of their own. He begins to feel more at home with the Hydes than with the living, an antisocial attitude that is contrary not merely to the social norms by which his family raised him, but also to his very nature as a living being. Concerned about their son's peculiar behavior and the gossip of neighbors, Dudley's parents apprehend him one evening at the tomb and deliver him to the insane asylum, where he writes his narrative.

Up to this point, we have had no reason to disbelieve Dudley's accounts of his adventures, no matter how bizarre they sound. Dudley acquires a good deal of knowledge on the history of the Hydes that, presumably, is gotten first-hand from the Hydes themselves. We even see how his "socializing" with the Hydes changes him from a withdrawn person to something of an extrovert. The discovery of a cameo in the tomb that bears a striking resemblance to him and the initials "J. H."—presumably for "Jervas Hyde"—and of an empty coffin with the single name "Jervas" on it is offered as further proof that Dudley is a true scion of the Hydes, whose life was uncannily anticipated years before he was born. But at the end of the story Dudley's father reveals a damning piece of evidence to the contrary, declaring that "at no time did I pass the chained portal [of the tomb], and swear[ing] that the rusted padlock had not been touched for fifty years when he examined it. He even says that all of the village knew of my journeys to the tomb, and that I was often watched as I slept in the bower outside the grim facade" (D 12–13). As for the obscure historical knowledge Dudley acquires, his father dismisses it as "the fruits of my lifelong and omnivorous browsing amongst the ancient volumes of the family library" (D 13).

These revelations create tension between the believable and unbelievable elements of Dudley's narrative that Lovecraft does not attempt to resolve. For readers who feel they point to Dudley's madness, the doubts they engender cast his opening remarks—made in hindsight, we now realize, from the confines of an asylum—in a new light: "Men of broader intellect know that there is no sharp distinction betwixt the real and the unreal; that all things appear as they do only by virtue of the delicate individual physical and mental media through which we are made conscious of them; but the prosaic materialism of the majority condemns as madness the flashes of super-sight which penetrate the common veil of obvious empiricism" (D 3). Dudley offers this insight as a rational explanation for his behavior, in the hope it will exonerate him of accusations that he is mentally unbalanced, but his words paradoxically reinforce what the reader has suspected all along: that he is incapable of distinguishing the real from the unreal.

In "The Tomb" we meet a character-type that appears in much of Lovecraft's early fiction: the person who is by nature an outsider. Whether presented as a dreamer or a madman, he is generally so withdrawn that it is no easier for the reader to distinguish the point where the internal landscape of the character's imagination gives way to the external landscape of the "real" world than it is for the character himself. From this perspective, Dudley's trips to the tomb take on the eerie symbolism of a madman's retreat into the suffocating recesses of his own mind.

Lovecraft found that it was not necessary to present characters as totally mad to isolate them from the rest of world. Like Poe, he simply exaggerated a perverse personality trait or taste to such grotesque extremes that it is difficult to think of the character as psychologically "normal." The horror hunters of Lovecraft's early fiction are good examples of another favorite outsider figure. These leftovers from the Gothic tradition are not cut from the same cloth as the "eminently respectable individuals, descended from the oldest families in New England: university professors . . . reputed doctors, worthies surrounded by general consideration"[3] who in Lovecraft's later work go in search of the unknown. Rather, they display an unnatural obsession with the ghoulish and gruesome that almost sets them as far apart as Jervas Dudley from the rest of mankind. In "The Statement of Randolph Carter" (1919), the title character tells of his friend, Harley Warren, who conducts "terrible researches into the unknown." Carter has been "a partial sharer" of those researches and pursued "terrible studies . . . more through reluctant fascination than through actual in-clination" (*MM* 300). For all the weak protestations of his genuine reluctance to delve into forbidden knowledge, Carter proves an apt pupil. He returns in "The Unnamable" (1923) as a writer of horror stories who has "a preoccupa-tion with the mystical and the unexplained" (*D* 201). "Herbert West—Reanimator" (1921–22), Lovecraft's variation on the Frankenstein story, con-cerns a doctor whose obsession with revivifying the dead takes him from the charnel houses of New England to the blood-soaked battlefields of Europe to find subjects for his experiments. In "The Lurking Fear," the narrator pro-fesses more stoutly than Randolph Carter did a "love of the grotesque and ter-rible which has made my career a series of quests for strange horrors in literature and in life" (*D* 179). This extraordinary personality-type reaches its unsavory nadir in "The Hound" (1922), the story of two men "wearied with the commonplaces of a prosaic world" (*D* 171) who become "neurotic virtu-osi," robbing graves to fulfill a "frightful emotional need" (*D* 172). Perhaps the best that can be said about such characters is that their excursions into the su-pernatural usually end with fitting retribution. It is possible to see then as nas-cent forms of the serious investigators of the supernatural who dominate Lovecraft's later work, but one thinks of them just as easily as variations on Jervas Dudley who lack a fantasyland into which they can withdraw to pursue their prurient interests.

Not all of Lovecraft's early outsider figures are as objectionable as Jervas Dudley or the horror hunters. Especially in his Dunsanian fantasies, Lovecraft usually made his protagonists romantics or visionaries who find the real world too crass and uncompassionate for their sensitive natures. In "Celephaïs" (1920), Kuranes, an unappreciated writer who refuses to cater to modern tastes, "did not think like others who wrote. Whilst they strove to strip from life its embroidered robes of myth, and to shew in naked ugliness the foul thing that is reality, Kuranes sought for beauty alone. When truth and experience failed to reveal it, he sought it in fancy and illusion" (D 81–82). Not surprisingly, Kuranes finds that "the more he withdrew from the world about him, the more wonderful became his dreams." Though not as grotesque as Dudley's fate, Kuranes's flight from reality inevitably leads to suicide. In "The White Ship" (1919), the idealistic Basil Elton says of his life at the North Point lighthouse "that I sometimes feel strangely alone, as though I were the last man on our planet" (D 36). While in this mood, the ship of his dreams comes to take him on a journey to exotic lands, another flight from reality in which the ports of call constitute "an allegorical odyssey, a journey through the human mind."[4]

Lovecraft's dreamland fantasies fall outside the bounds of discussion of his supernatural horror fiction, but they share with it a similar theme: outsideness associated with the internal disposition, alienation as a quality inherent in a character's personality and temperament. Like Jervas Dudley, the characters in the dreamland stories so long to escape the real world that their desires momentarily sustain the illusion of a fantasy world that is a more pleasant alternative to reality. Invariably, these stories end in despair or horror, with the narrator's painful recall to the world he has tried to escape.

"Hypnos" (1922) begins with the narrator lamenting the loss of his "only friend" (D 165). We know little of the friend, except that his Grecian features were so striking that the narrator was inspired to sculpt a bust of him. The two explore the numinous worlds of drug-induced dreams, but after a particularly harrowing nightmare in which the friend is rescued from some nameless horror only at the last minute, his character changes. "Heretofore a recluse so far as I know—his true name and origin having never passed his lips—my friend now became frantic in his fear of solitude" (D 168). The friend tells the narrator that if they cherish their lives, they must never fall unconscious again—but of course they do, and after a second encounter with the nightmare, the narrator awakens to find himself alone with the marble bust of his friend beside him. However, neighbors summoned by the narrator's screams claim that he never had a friend, and point out to him that "that haunting memory-face [on the bust] is modelled from my own, as it was at twenty-five" (*D* 170). The implication is that the narrator, like Jervas Dudley, has been living a fantasy. His "friend" may have been no more than an idealization of himself. Also like Dudley, he cannot accept the final truth of his madness when he is forced to confront it. To soften the intrusion of reality upon his private illusion he rationalizes that the claims his friend never existed are proof that "not only was my own mind unseated by the strange and hideous thing, but others were tainted with a forgetfulness which can mean nothing if not madness" (*D* 170).

If the narrator of "Hypnos" resembles Jervas Dudley in his abstraction from the world around him and in his final retreat into the safety of paranoid rationalization, he differs in that part of him truly wants to live in the world outside his mind. In relating how he and his friend had tried to avoid falling asleep, the narrator recalls that "At night he would not be alone, nor would the company of a few friends calm him. His sole relief was obtained in revelry of the most general and boisterous sort; so that few assemblies of the young and gay were unknown to us" (*D* 168). By his admission that "Our appearance and age seemed to excite in most cases a ridicule which I keenly resented, but which my friend considered a lesser evil than solitude," the narrator seems to hint that the part of his psyche that manifests itself as "his friend" wants to integrate itself with the world at large, but ultimately is unable because it cannot overcome the part of him that disdains that world. Unlike Lovecraft's other early fantasies, in which the main character is at odds with the world of his fellow humans, "Hypnos" offers a character crushed by self-alienation: upon withdrawing from the world, his quarrel is less with others who would forcibly bring him back and make him conform than with the part of himself that longs to return.

By the time Lovecraft wrote "Hypnos," he had achieved a complexity in his portrait of the solitary character. He deepened the sense of alienation by showing a character waging a war of loneliness on two fronts—against the world and against himself—and in doing so made his character a more sympathetic figure. Before he wrote "Hypnos," Lovecraft had taken the same approach to its most horrifying extreme to produce his masterpiece of alienation, "The Outsider" (1921). The most notable difference between "The Outsider" and most of Lovecraft's earlier fiction is that, for once, Lovecraft presents a character who actively wishes to belong the real world but is rejected by it. As a result, Lovecraft deprives his narrator of the opportunity to take comfort in his own madness. Whereas the narrators of "The Tomb" and "Hypnos" are left rationalizing their fates at the hands of an ignorant, or mad, society, the Outsider must confront his desires as the self-mocking delusions they are; but rather than helping him to become a part of the real world, the cold realization of what he must accept proves so oppressive that it renders him incapable of returning to the world. Unfit to live in the world of human beings, unable to live anymore in the world he once knew, he is forever trapped between two worlds—"an outsider; a stranger in this century and among those who are still men," a creature who welcomes "the bitterness of alienage" (*DH* 52).

"The Outsider" was not the first story in which Lovecraft portrayed a character possessed of an unbearable awareness. In "Dagon" (1917), he told of a man so horrified by the import of his discovery of a race of fishlike creatures that he takes his life. In "Facts concerning the Late Arthur Jermyn and His Family" (1920), the title character, besides having a "poetic delicacy" (*D* 78) that sets him apart from others, has a hidden defect of nature that makes his separation so irrevocable that it drives him to suicide. But "The Outsider" is cruelly ironic in that its narrator is not even afforded the escape route of last resort left open to Lovecraft's other characters, since he is already dead. The strong sense of alienation that results from having to live with a horrible truth known to no one else was to become a hallmark of Lovecraft's later fiction.

Before leaving Lovecraft's early stories, we should note that his writing style does much to enhance the sense of "outsideness" of the "inside" of his characters. He wrote most of his tales in the first person and, as might be expected, the landscapes easily take the imprint of his narrators' perceptions. Indeed, the entire effect of "The Outsider" is predicated on the reader's seeing the world through the narrator's eyes and, like him, not realizing that the decorations and landmarks he takes for normal are actually those of the graveyard.

Dream imagery abounds in "Hypnos" and "The Tomb," to the point where characters are in danger of being lost in their solipsistic fantasies. Randolph Carter describes the events leading to Harley Warren's death as a sort of dreamy trance in which consciousness is divorced from physical action:

> My first vivid impression of my own presence in this terrible necropolis concerns the act of pausing with Warren before a certain half-obliterated sepulchre, and of throwing down some burdens which we seemed to have been carrying. I now observed that I had with me an electric lantern and two spades, whilst my companion was supplied with a similar lantern and a portable telephone outfit. No word was uttered, for the spot and the task seemed known to us. (*MM* 301)

It is also common for Lovecraft's characters to be left uncertain whether they had experiences that drove them mad or whether some temporary insanity induced waking nightmares for them. "Often I ask myself if it could not all have been a pure phantasm," says the narrator of "Dagon," "a mere freak of fever as I lay sun-stricken and raving in the open boat after my escape from the German man-of-war" (*D* 19).

The possible unreliability of these characters' subjective narratives is abetted by Lovecraft's dependence on the pathetic fallacy to build mood. Jervas Dudley tells how he is spurred on by "the hideous soul of the forest" (*D* 5). Among the artifacts in the collection of the narrators of "The Hound" are "nauseous musical instruments" (*D* 172). From the point of view of the Outsider, the coffins in the crypt are "odious oblong boxes" (*DH* 48). Such descriptions permit little objective analysis of the narrator's story, although ultimately they say a good deal about the narrator's state of mind. Lovecraft was never to give up descriptive extravagances of this type entirely, but in his early stories, where the point of view of the character-as-outsider is crucial, they serve a more important function than they ever would for him again.

II

It would be wrong to characterize all Lovecraft's early fiction as tales told by neurotic narrators alienated from their fellow men. To the contrary, stories like "Dagon" (1917), "The Temple" (1920), "The Nameless City" (1921), and "The Moon-Bog" (1921) are accounts of relatively ordinary characters forced into extraordinary circumstances. Even so, each story involves a journey to a secluded locale, as though Lovecraft tried to compensate for the lack of an intrinsic isolating factor in the personality of the narrator.

Lovecraft chose geographically isolated settings for the same reason other supernatural fiction writers stranded protagonists in remote locations: to suggest that things beyond human ken occur in places outside the familiar avenues of life. He turned the tables on this traditional narrative device in the opening paragraph of "The Picture in the House" (1920):

> Searchers after horror haunt strange, far places. For them are the catacombs of Ptolemais, and the carven mausolea of the nightmare countries. They climb to the moonlit towers of ruined Rhine castles, and falter down black cobwebbed steps beneath the scattered stones of forgotten ancient cities in Asia. The haunted wood and the desolate mountain are their shrines, and they linger around the sinister monoliths on uninhabited islands. But the true epicure in the terrible, to whom a new thrill of unutterable ghastliness is the chief end and justification of existence, esteems most of all the ancient lonely farmhouses of backwoods New England; for there the dark elements of strength, solitude,

grotesqueness, and ignorance combine to form the perfection of the hideous. (*DH* 116)

Lovecraft may have been poking fun at himself here—"sinister monoliths on uninhabited islands" seems to refer to "Dagon," and he may already have been playing with the ideas for "The Nameless City" (which takes place "beneath the scattered stones of forgotten ancient cites in Asia") and "The Outsider" (which appears to involve a "climb to the moonlit towers of ruined Rhine castles"), both of which he wrote in 1921. Clearly he sought new venues for horror fiction, settings where qualities ("strength, solitude, grotesqueness, and ignorance") rather than distance or exotic distinctions created a sense of solitude. As Peter Cannon has written, "with this manifesto, Lovecraft serves notice that he will rely less upon stock horror backgrounds and will turn more and more to his own New England as a source for horror."[5] One could even go so far as to say that Lovecraft announces his decision to leave the confines of his narrators' minds and seek "outsideness" in the external world.

The settings of Lovecraft's early stories initially played a minor role, serving mostly as adjuncts to his narrators' imaginations. The dark, brier-choked grove of the "The Tomb" seems merely an extension of the narrator's disturbed mind, and Randolph's Carter's fuzzy descriptions of the graveyard make it seem like the setting of a waking nightmare rather than the backdrop for a real experience. In contrast, the house in "The Picture in the House" has an important presence and serves a crucial purpose. On the one hand, it is *just* a house, a common piece of scenery that connects the slightly out-of-the-way countryside to the everyday world known to the narrator; on the other hand it is part of a special environment with a particular history—the Arkham countryside—for which it serves as a focus:

> In such houses have dwelt generations of strange people, whose like the world has never seen. Seized with a gloomy and fanatical belief which exiled them from their kind, their ancestors sought the wilderness for freedom . . . and in their isolation, morbid self-repression, and struggle for life with relentless Nature, there came to them dark furtive traits from the prehistoric depths of their cold Northern heritage. . . . Only the silent, sleepy, staring houses can tell all that has lain hidden since the early days; and they are not communicative, being loath to shake off the drowsiness which helps them forget. (*DH* 117)

It is the narrator's misfortune to discover that one of those "strange people" still lives in the house, and that the "furtive traits" of his heritage, stimulated by the isolation the house and countryside enjoy, have atavistically resurfaced.

Thus, the house serves as a portal through which the narrator steps from the normal outer world into a world greatly at variance with it. Like the narrators of Lovecraft's early stories, it is isolated at a point between two worlds—one familiar and the other extraordinary—of neither of which it is completely a part.

With "The Picture in the House," Lovecraft indicated interest in recreating the mood of "outsideness" articulated in his psychological horror stories but in the outside world. Especially in the stories set in his imaginary towns of Arkham and Kingsport, Lovecraft began to associate out-of-the-way places with abnormal phenomena. It is significant that the setting of "The Picture in the House" is *not* as remote as the setting for a story like "The Nameless City" but only slightly off the beaten path. By remaining in the realm of the familiar, Lovecraft reminds us that, "at a laughably short distance from the great industrial centers, from the most respected universities, from the tourist sites—amid smiling civilisation—[there exists] an abominable region where evils are practiced."[6] The incongruous juxtaposition of the natural and the supernatural heightens the sense of isolation in a story by creating a pocket of mystery in which characters discover that the rules of the regular world do not obtain. In such situations, it is the normal character—the traveler, the student, the visitor—who finds himself at the greatest disadvantage. Thus, as Lovecraft began to explore the horror potential of the isolated setting, he began to de-emphasize the importance of the alienated narrator.

Lovecraft's preferred means for setting a particular locale apart from the world around it was to suggest that distortions of space and time took place within its borders. Thus, even though he presumably set "The Music of Erich Zann" (1921) in France, the geographic distance is negligible compared to the vast gulf between the different realities the narrator crosses in it. "I have examined maps of the city with the greatest care," he says at the opening of the story, "yet have never again found the Rue d'Auseil." The loss of a geographically fixed location seems unusual until the narrator recalls

> peculiarities which could hardly be forgotten by anyone who had been there. . . .
>
> The Rue d'Auseil lay across a dark river bordered by precipitous brick blear-windowed warehouses and spanned by a ponderous bridge of dark stone. It was always shadowy along that river, as if the smoke of the neighbouring factories shut out the sun perpetually. The river was also odorous with evil stenches which I have never smelled elsewhere, and which may some day help me to find it, since I should recognise them at once. . . .

> I have never seen another street as narrow and steep. . . . It was almost a cliff. . . . The houses were tall, peaked-roofed, incredibly old, and crazily leaning backward, forward, and sidewise. . . .
>
> The inhabitants of that street impressed me peculiarly. At first I thought it was because they were all silent and reticent; but later I decided it was because they were all very old. (*DH* 83–84)

These impressions create a vivid picture of the Rue d'Auseil as a dark, chaotic corner of the world. They set the mood for the narrator's story of his encounter with Erich Zann, who plays unearthly music with an almost unhealthy intensity and who agrees to let the narrator listen to him play as long as he does not look out Zann's window. The narrator disobeys, and what he sees boggles the mind:

> It was very dark, but the city's lights always burned, and I expected to see them there amidst the rain and wind. Yet when I looked from that highest of all gable windows, looked while the candles sputtered and the insane viol howled with the night-wind, I saw no city spread below, and no friendly lights gleamed from remembered streets, but only the blackness of space illimitable; unimagined space alive with motion and music, and having no semblance to anything on earth. (*DH* 90)

"No semblance to anything on earth," that is, except to the dark, chaotic Rue d'Auseil itself. Lovecraft does not make it clear whether the void outside Zann's window inspires his music or whether his music opens a window on that void, but in either interpretation the Rue d'Auseil is a nexus between the regular world and "the blackness of space illimitable," as though a small fragment of the void had condensed temporarily into a piece of the normal world, only to be reabsorbed by the void.

In "The Music of Erich Zann" Lovecraft abstracted his setting from the normal world by depicting it as a place without fixed dimensions, only a point on the surface of unfathomable spaces and distances. He pursued the idea further in "The Festival" (1923), another story in which the borders of a seemingly fixed setting are revealed to be insubstantial. "The Festival" opens with the narrator telling us (with more than a little irony) "I was far from home" (*D* 208). He hints at just how far in the next sentence, in which he describes the road to Kingsport as one that "soared lonely up to where Aldebaran twinkled among the trees" (ibid.). Although he is describing merely a simple trick of perspective, his impressions establish at the outset a correspondence between Kingsport and the cosmos.

Lovecraft reinforces the impression throughout the story, giving it slightly more sinister overtones with each passing reference. Several moments later the narrator views the city from a nearby summit and remarks:

> I saw . . . snowy Kingsport with its . . . endless labyrinths of steep, narrow, crooked streets, and dizzy church-crowned central peak that time durst not touch; ceaseless mazes of colonial houses piled and scattered at all angles and levels like a child's disordered blocks; antiquity hovering on grey wings over winter-whitened gables and gambrel roofs; fanlights and small-paned windows one by one gleaming out in cold dusk to join Orion and the archaic stars. (*D* 209)

His emphasis on the antiquity and chaotic layout of Kingsport makes the town seem a benign version of the Rue d'Auseil, and his likening of the window lights to starlight once again links the town and the heavens above. Twice more his descriptions help to obliterate the boundary between the town and the heavens: when he observes "beside the road at its crest a still higher summit . . . a burying-ground where black gravestones stuck ghoulishly through the snow like the decayed fingernails of a gigantic corpse" (*D* 209) reaching up to the sky, and when he later recalls the view of "a great white church . . . [where] Aldebaran had seemed to balance itself a moment on the ghostly spire" (*D* 212). This concatenation of impressions is not a random one, for as the narrator discovers, the church and the graveyard of Kingsport are linked to each other through the ceremonies he has been summoned to attend. Those ceremonies are held in underground caverns of seemingly limitless dimensions that have a disturbing import for the narrator: "I knew we must have passed down through the mountain and beneath the earth of Kingsport itself, and I shivered that a town should be so aged and maggoty with subterranean evil" (*D* 213). Thus, Kingsport is not only in touch with the infinite spaces above, it is also undermined by a vast, dark emptiness—it is literally an island in the void.

To amplify the atmosphere of isolation of Kingsport's aberrant geography, Lovecraft also displaces the town in time. The narrator says he has been summoned to attend a festival "that men call Christmas though they know in their hearts it is older than Bethlehem and Babylon, older than Memphis and mankind" (*D* 208). The discovery that the ceremony is not simply a recapitulation of rituals past, but one actually conducted by the corpses of the narrator's ancestors, reveals an unnatural continuity of the "dead" past into the present. In Kingsport the progression of time is denied; it is both out of space and out of time. Small wonder that Lovecraft was to write of his beloved New England locales that "landscapes like this have a deeply ingrained character, & exude a positive kind of antiquity. To enter one is almost like walking at will through time and space, or climbing through some strange picture on the wall."[7]

Lovecraft's increasingly greater use of secluded landscapes and the strange events that take place in them to suggest grand vistas of space and time marks the beginning of the cosmic viewpoint we associate with his best and most influential work. As he explained in "Notes on Writing Weird Fiction," distortion of time sense is significant to this viewpoint because "this element looms up in my mind as the most profoundly dramatic and grimly terrible thing in the universe. *Conflict with time* seems to me the most potent and fruitful theme in all human expression" (*CE* 2.175). Lovecraft expressed an interest in time indirectly in "The Tomb" and "Dagon," where the past encroaches menacingly on the present. He developed the idea further in "The Shunned House" (1924), in which a physical embodiment of the past siphons life from the present, and in *The Case of Charles Dexter Ward* (1927), in which a person from the past usurps the body of a man living in the present. Lovecraft was also intrigued by the possibility that the present could collapse back into the past, destroying all sense of linear historical progression. Atavism was first given expression in "Facts concerning the Late Arthur Jermyn and His Family," in which a man discovers that his ungainly physique and looks have been inherited from an ape grandmother. It was with "The Lurking Fear" (1922), though, that Lovecraft set out the worst implications of devolution.

The narrator of "The Lurking Fear" is frustrated by his inability to determine the cause of the monstrous carnage on Tempest Mountain every time there is a thunderstorm. Faced with having to consider that there may be some truth in the legends surrounding the horror, he puts his trust in history instead. "History, indeed, was all I had after everything else ended in mocking Satanism" (*D* 190), he says with a sense of desperate assurance. Yet it is history that proves the greatest mockery, for even as the historical truths revealed to him dispel the myths of Satanism, they also subvert the very idea of historical procession.

Lovecraft's fascination with the past's inescapable hold on the present continued in "The Rats in the Walls" (1923). The narrator, Delapore, moves into Exham Priory, a family home abandoned centuries before for mysterious reasons. The priory has a "peculiarly composite architecture; an architecture involving Gothic towers resting on a Saxon or Romanesque substructure, whose foundation in turn was of a still earlier order or blend of orders—Roman, and even Druidic or native Cymric, if legends speak truly" (*DH* 27). With its accretions of additional levels and wings over the centuries, the priory stands as both a monument to the forward march of time and a symbol of time standing still.

After the priory has been renovated, Delapore begins to hear the nightly scurrying of rats in the walls. He traces them to a subcellar, beneath which he finds a passageway leading down to a bone-filled grotto. The crushing truth that Delapore's forebears practiced cannibalism overwhelms him. Before the reader's eyes, his words degenerate progressively to proto-human grunts, in a descent that mirrors his actual physical descent through the priory from the contemporary furnishings upstairs to the prehistoric caverns below. Lost in time, he develops the same appetites as his ancestors, and so he must be institutionalized.

Lovecraft's interest in time was not limited solely to these abstract expressions. Even as he manipulated the past and present to create an atmosphere of historical stagnation, he used specific historical events to undermine the certainty of the historical record. In "The Lurking Fear" he deliberately places the building of the Martense mansion in 1670, six years after the British takeover of New Amsterdam and the decline of the Dutch influence in the colony. The death of Jan Martense, the event that precipitates investigation into the Martense family's bizarre withdrawal from the world, is put at some time between 1760 and 1763, following his six years of campaigning in the colonial army and a return to a family that has changed so much during his absence that "he was hated as an outsider by his fathers, uncles, and brothers" (*D* 191). Likewise, in "The Rats in the Walls" we are told that the flight of the Delapores from Exham Priory occurred during the reign of James I, that the family fought in the American Civil War, and that Delapore's own son returned from World War I a maimed invalid. In both instances, the integration of real history with the imagined genealogical history of the characters imparts a convincing realism to the horrible events that follow. This storytelling technique also informs us that the events leading to the revelation of the final horror, though embedded in the historical record, are not recognized when they occur as hideous portents of what is to come. Lovecraft appears subtly to suggest that the conflicts with time and space perceived by his characters are not so much distortions of reality but parts of reality that have been selectively ignored. Insofar as these conflicts reveal hitherto unimagined historical possibilities, two conclusions are possible: that the otherwise normal worlds inhabited by Lovecraft's characters are just a fluke of perspective based on mankind's inability or unwillingness to admit events it cannot explain; or, worse, that what Lovecraft's characters consider to be the normal world is itself just an isolated point in the void, a sort of papering over of the chaos that occasionally rips and lets the horrible truth come through.

Lovecraft explored these ideas most confidently in his later "mythos" fiction, but he gave them their most acute treatment in "The Horror at Red Hook" (1925) and "He" (1925), written during his years in New York. Lovecraft described "The Horror at Red Hook" to Frank Belknap Long as dealing with "hideous cult-practices behind the gangs of noisy young loafers whose essential mystery has impressed me so much. . . . It represents at least an attempt to extract horror from an atmosphere *to which you deny any qualities save vulgar commonplaceness*" (*SL* 2.20; my italics). In "He" Lovecraft describes a New York where the illusion of beauty and order can be sustained only briefly. The narrator recalls his first view of New York romantically: "Coming for the first time upon the town, I had seen it in the sunset from a bridge, majestic above its waters, its incredible peaks and pyramids rising flower-like and delicate from pools of violet mist to play with the flaming golden clouds and the first stars of evening" (*D*, 266). The city soon reveals its true self:

> Garish daylight shewed only squalor and alienage and the noxious elephantiasis of climbing, spreading stone where the moon had hinted of loveliness and elder magic; and the throngs of people that seethed through the flume-like streets were squat, swarthy strangers with hardened faces and narrow eyes, shrewd strangers without dreams and without kinship to the scenes about them. (*D* 267)

Though minor stories in the Lovecraft canon, "He" and "The Horror at Red Hook" are important insofar as they are set in New York, and not one of Lovecraft's isolated New England towns. Their portrayal of horrors revealed to lurk behind the hustle and bustle of everyday life must be accounted a turning point in Lovecraft's approach to supernatural horror fiction.

III

In March 1926 Lovecraft wrote "Cool Air," a story whose opening observations contrast almost directly with those made at the beginning of "The Picture in the House":

> It is a mistake to fancy that horror is associated inextricably with darkness, silence, and solitude. I found it in the glare of mid-afternoon, in the clangour of a metropolis, and in the teeming midst of a shabby and commonplace rooming-house with a prosaic landlady and two stalwart men by my side. (*DH* 199)

Although "Cool Air" is a minor tale, the last of Lovecraft's "Poe pieces," in hindsight its opening paragraphs could not have been written at a more important time in Lovecraft's life. Just as the "The Picture in the House" signaled his growing fascination with the isolated towns of New England as potential sources of horror, so do these sentences anticipate his new perspective on horror, one that seems almost to contradict the "darkness, silence, and solitude" that heretofore had characterized his fiction. Lovecraft's next story, "The Call of Cthulhu," articulated this new perspective, but showed that far from giving up his earlier narrative strategies, Lovecraft had synthesized them to create a wholly original approach to horror, one that is generally referred to as Lovecraftian horror or "the Lovecraft Mythos."

The significance of "The Call of Cthulhu" cannot be overemphasized. It is the first story to articulate clearly the cosmic perspective he had only suggested in earlier stories and that would henceforth dominate his fiction. There is perhaps no better explication of this viewpoint than the well-known opening passage:

> The most merciful thing in the world, I think, is the inability of the human mind to correlate all its contents. We live on a placid island of ignorance in the midst of black seas of infinity, and it was not meant that we should voyage far. The sciences, each straining in its own direction, have hitherto harmed us little; but some day the piecing together of dissociated knowledge will open up such terrifying vistas of reality, and of our frightful position therein, that we shall either go mad from the revelation or flee from the deadly light into the peace and safety of a new dark age. (*DH* 125)

The island metaphor was an appropriate choice of images, considering Lovecraft's earlier concentration on specific geographic locales as focuses of "outside" forces. In his early New England stories Lovecraft had presented towns like Arkham and Kingsport as small breaches in the fabric of our world through which the terrors of the void occasionally vent themselves. Here, though, the old perspective is inverted, and we are asked to consider the incomprehensible void a sort of greater reality, a "sea" in which our small world of limited knowledge is but an island. This telescoped point of view presents an image of mankind as an isolated presence on the "black seas" of an infinite cosmos, a figure dwarfed into insignificance by the vastness of the universe.

The way Lovecraft intended to express this alienated viewpoint is implicit in his opening paragraph. By saying it is "merciful" that the human mind cannot correlate its contents, Francis Wayland Thurston, the narrator, implies that he himself has already made such a correlation. Something he has discovered has given him a burden of knowledge not shared by other men, and so he stands apart from the rest of mankind, just as Lovecraft's earliest narrators were outside their own society. Thurston describes his devastating, newly acquired knowledge as something "flashed out from the piecing together of separated things" (*DH* 126), echoing his remark about the inability of mankind to piece together the separate contents of its collected knowledge. By drawing a parallel between Thurston's personal experience and the fate of the human race, Lovecraft makes it clear that Thurston is not merely a character in a horror story. He is a symbol for mankind itself, alone in the void, piecing together random bits of information in an effort to find greater meaning. Thus, Thurston's internal alienation reflects humanity's greater external alienation as a consciousness aware of its own insignificance in the cosmic scheme of things.

The knowledge that has so devastated Thurston and left him poised between the madness and ignorance that he sees as mankind's only possible fates comes from his discovery that three seemingly unrelated events—two documented in his late grand-uncle's papers, one chanced upon by himself—not only fit together but also suggest a whole greater than the sum of their parts, a truth more horrifying than any of them yields individually. This is nothing less than "the awesome grandeur of the cosmic cycle wherein our world and human race form transient incidents" (*DH* 126).

Probably the most important aspect of "The Call of Cthulhu" is the means by which Thurston pieces together the clues and extrapolates what they imply. He is never an active participant in any of the story's three episodes. Although he travels to the places mentioned in the three accounts and sometimes interviews survivors, his discoveries mostly confirm what has already been recorded. His is basically a job of armchair deduction, from newspaper clippings that were no doubt read by others but that no one recognized as fitting a pattern. All these stories are described in such realistic, mundane detail (so mundane that Lovecraft was later to criticize his story as "cumbrous" [*SL* 5.348]) that anyone could have verified them had he seen the need to do so. This is Lovecraft's inversion of the transcendentalist notion that "there are sermons in stones." He says, in effect, that one does not need to investigate the dark corners of the universe to uncover mind-shattering cosmic truths; they may be evident in the events of the day if one knows the perspective from which to view the right events. The narrator's despair comes about simply through the *realization* of the pattern these events fit. In a sense, Lovecraft is expressing his belief that each one of us teeters on the brink of alienation along with Thurston.

"The Call of Cthulhu" stands as a watershed story that synthesizes many of the elements of Lovecraft's previous tales. First, it revives the figure of the narrator-as-outsider, although the narrator is not a psychological deviant but a man among men, alienated by his knowledge rather than his nature. Second, it suggests portents that go unrecognized and horrors that lurk beneath banal facades in much the same way as Lovecraft's early New England stories did. Third, it proposes horrors of the same magnitude as those found in exotic and faraway settings where such monstrosities are expected to grow out of proportion. With this in mind, it is interesting to consider the three accounts that make up the trail of clues followed by Thurston. The story of Wilcox, which tells of "a thin, dark young man of neurotic and excited aspect . . . [whom] the staid folk of the ancient commercial city dismissed . . . as merely 'queer'" (*DH* 128), superficially resembles Lovecraft's early characters who are isolated by their neurotic dispositions. The tale of Inspector Legrasse, who finds a survival of ancient rites in the wilds of Louisiana, corresponds to the stories in which Lovecraft suggests "the perfection of the hideous" (*DH* 116) lurks just off the beaten path of the normal world. Finally, the story of Gustaf Johansen, the sailor who sees Cthulhu emerge from R'lyeh, is almost a direct continuation of a story in which horror is found in a remote and unexplored terrain. Lovecraft seems to be commenting subtly on his previous work, saying that none of his earlier approaches to horror fiction is as powerful as the new one that embraces all three.

"The Call of Cthulhu" might be called "an unholy marriage of inside and outside,"[8] a joining together of the alienated perspective of the solitary character with the alienating perspective of the earth's irrelevance in the gulfs of space and time to create an integrated image of mankind's isolation in the universe. The narrative possibilities inherent in this relationship between the internal and external, the individual mind and the world around it, clearly intrigued Lovecraft, and he used it to stunning effect in a story written the following year.

"The Colour out of Space" (1927) opens with one of Lovecraft's most evocative descriptions of an isolated landscape:

> West of Arkham the hills rise wild, and there are valleys with deep woods that no axe has ever cut. There are dark narrow glens where the trees slope fantastically, and where the thin brooklets trickle without ever having caught the glint of sunlight. On the gentler slopes there are farms, ancient and rocky, with squat moss-coated cottages brooding eternally over old New England secrets in the lee of great ledges; but these are all vacant now, the wide chimneys crumbling and the shingled sides bulging perilously beneath low gambrel roofs.
>
> The old folk have gone away, and foreigners do not like to live there. French-Canadians have tried it, Italians have tried it, and the Poles have come

and departed. It is not because of anything that can be seen or heard or handled, but because of something that is imagined. The place is not good for the
imagination, and does not bring restful dreams at night. (*DH* 53)

Not only is the landscape west of Arkham naturally secluded, it has become
associated with an "outsideness" that crosses the border from the external
world to infect the internal world of the mind.

This invasion of the interior (the imagination) by something from outside
(the strangeness of the landscape) mirrors the actual events of the story. The
influence that causes the uneasy dreams in people who have tried to settle the
land was first felt when the meteorite fell on Nahum Gardner's land in 1882.
The meteorite, which is made of a material unknown to human science, re-
leases something that quickly begins to leech the life from Gardner's crops,
livestock, and family. The lifeless "blasted heath" it produces conjures up the
image of something alien taking over a part of the earth and turning it into a
semblance of the void whence it came. As one observer exclaims, "Good God!
What eldritch dream-world was this into which he had blundered?" (*DH* 70).

The narrator does not observe these events himself, learning of them only
through the recollections of a local citizen. Ammi Pierce witnessed the final night
of the Gardner family, when the presence living in the soil had absorbed enough
vitality to attempt its return to outer space. While the others watch its cataclysmic
departure from the earth, Pierce "had had an added shock the others were
spared, and was crushed forever by a brooding fear he dared not even mention
for many years to come. . . . He had seen something feebly rise, only to sink
down again upon the place from which the great shapeless horror had shot into
the sky" (*DH* 79). And because Pierce alone "knew that this last faint remnant
must still lurk down there . . . he has never been quite right since" (ibid.).

Like Thurston, Pierce is the only person to digest fully the implications of
what he has witnessed, and he finds the knowledge almost impossible to bear.
In telling what he knows, he brings the consequences of that awareness full circle. The narrator comes to realize that the meteorite was "a frightful messenger
from unformed realms of infinity beyond all Nature as we know it; from
realms whose mere existence stuns the brain and numbs us with the black ex-
tra-cosmic gulfs it throws open before our frenzied eyes" (*DH* 81). He ends his
story concerned that Ammi's proximity to the blasted heath, which creeps "little by little, perhaps an inch a year" (*DH* 80), leaving him vulnerable to the fate
that befell Nahum Gardner, to become "the grey, twisted, brittle monstrosity
which persists more and more in troubling my sleep" (*DH* 82). Thus, the "out-

sideness" that the heath represents spreads not only physically from Arkham but also metaphorically into the narrator's mind. As Donald R. Burleson has noted:

> The horror is not really some unspeakable external reality, but rather the protagonist's emotional reactions to his glimpses of that reality, and his realization of the awesome implications for mankind. In "The Colour out of Space" . . . it is not so much the "blasted heath" that one finds horrific; rather, it is the narrator's ponderous fear of that site and its implications, in his mind, of unspeakable alienage. . . . The "blasted heath" is not so much a physical phenomenon as a psychological process, a fear-response and an awe, in a mind that by the very experience discovers its own minuteness and precariousness in a cosmos far vaster, far more indifferent to human concerns than that mind has ever imagined.[9]

Some months after writing "The Colour out of Space," in the letter that accompanied his second submittal of "The Call of Cthulhu" to *Weird Tales* editor Farnsworth Wright, Lovecraft wrote his manifesto for the type of horror fiction "The Call of Cthulhu" and "The Colour out of Space" represented:

> Now all my tales are based on the fundamental premise that common human laws and interests and emotions have no validity or significance in the vast cosmos-at-large. . . . To achieve the essence of real externality, whether of time or space or dimension, one must forget that such things as organic life, good and evil, love and hate, and all such local attributes of a negligible and temporary race called mankind, have any existence at all. Only the human scenes and characters must have human qualities. (*SL* 2.150)

Lovecraft knew that the best way to achieve the ends of cosmic horror was to populate his stories with human beings who cling to such notions as "good and evil" and "love and hate." By dwelling on these characters' all-too-human reactions to phenomena that exceed their understanding, he would achieve "the essence of externality" and a more profound sense of isolation than his work had hitherto expressed: his characters would gaze into the void and realize that their lives, their interests, and their pretensions to significance were merely the finite foreground to an infinitely expanding background. Their new self-awareness of their true place in the vast design of the universe would cut them adrift from earlier certainties about themselves and humankind. As Burleson has pointed out, "This ironic capability to *sense* one's own vanishingly small place in the universe is the central feature of the Lovecraft Mythos."[10]

If this was to be the case, one might ask, then how do we explain a story like "The Dunwich Horror" (1928), which, with its professors from Miskatonic University heroically saving the earth from terrible "things from outside," seems to flout these very ideas of human insignificance and impotence? Perhaps we should begin by giving Lovecraft more credit for subtlety than is usually allotted.

This well-known story concerns Wilbur Whateley, a child born of a human mother and the extra-dimensional entity Yog-Sothoth, and "the Dunwich horror," an invisible monstrosity that rampages through the countryside and is eventually identified as Wilbur's twin brother. Dr. Henry Armitage is called in to perform the equivalent of an exorcism of Wilbur's brother, something unthinkable in the Lovecraft Mythos—yet he succeeds. Savoring his "triumph," Armitage seems a far cry from the usual figure in the Lovecraft Mythos who is left dazed by the truths he has uncovered and frustrated by the knowledge that he alone has grasped their full meaning.

The key to Lovecraft's intentions in this story seems to be Armitage's description of the monstrosity he has dispatched: "We have no business calling in such things from outside, and only very wicked people and very wicked cults ever try to" (*DH* 197). The triteness of this comment indicates that Armitage either is oversimplifying matters for the benefit of his audience, or more likely that he has failed to apprehend the full import of what has taken place. Lovecraft lays the foundation for the latter conclusion early in the story, in his opening description of the Dunwich countryside: "When a traveller in north central Massachusetts takes the wrong fork at the junction of the Aylesbury pike just beyond Dean's Corners he comes upon a lonely and curious country," we are told. In this country, one encounters strangely overgrown vegetation, summits that are "too rounded and symmetrical to give a sense of comfort and naturalness," and solitary figures "so silent and furtive that one somehow feels confronted by forbidden things" (*DH* 155–56). Findings like these, along with the seeming decrepitude of the land, the inbreeding of the natives, and the native legends about the surrounding countryside, are the reasons why "outsiders visit Dunwich as seldom as possible," and indeed why "people shun it without knowing exactly why" (*DH* 157).

The descriptions of Dunwich resemble those of the Arkham countryside in "The Colour out of Space." Both are examples of how "geographic space is substituted by a malefic space"[11] in Lovecraft's fiction, and it is significant that in "The Dunwich Horror" Lovecraft devotes the entire first chapter solely to establishing that the ominous qualities of Dunwich that set it apart from the normal world are a natural part of its history. The intrinsic unhallowedness of the place, onto which the Christians, the Indians, and perhaps even the cult of Yog-Sothoth have grafted their mythology, is the backdrop against which Armitage's exploits are projected. It is this larger context that escapes Armitage's awareness and makes his final "victory" seem puny indeed. His experience is like the experience of one of the three people whose accounts comprise "The Call of Cthulhu"; it is only a part of an incomprehensibly bigger picture. The enormousness of that for which Dunwich stands preceded Armitage and will certainly outlast him.

Although there were to be no more "heroes" like Henry Armitage in the Lovecraft Mythos, there was to be at least one more display of human emotion leading to an underestimation of the realities man must face regarding his existence. "The Whisperer in Darkness" (1930), one of Lovecraft's coldest commentaries on the inanity of "human laws and interests and emotions" in the universe at large, opens a window on the abyss to show how "the abyss progressively overpowers [a] sense of individual heroism, until . . . man's last virtue is to survive with a sardonic sense of the inevitable end, of personal and cosmic apocalypse."[12] The story begins with the washing downstream of several "organic shapes" (*DH* 209) during a Vermont flood. These shapes recall to the townspeople folk legends of "a hidden race of monstrous beings which lurked somewhere in the remoter hills" (*DH* 210). Even though the narrator, a literature instructor and folklore enthusiast named Albert Wilmarth, concedes that "it would have been less uncomfortable if the stray accounts of these things had not agreed so well" (*DH* 211), his rationalism convinces him to dismiss any link between the legends and the carcasses as pure superstition. This invites a reply from one Henry Akeley, who claims that he has empirical proof the creatures—the fungi from Yuggoth—do exist. He has been battling them from his mountain home for years, and he makes a believer of Wilmarth by sending him proof of their reality. As Wilmarth and Akeley exchange letters the creatures become more adamant in their efforts to prevent Akeley from spreading news about them.

The more Wilmarth learns about the creatures, the more curious about them he becomes, a human weakness that ultimately leads to his downfall. A particularly harrowing series of letters in which Akeley describes the onslaught of the fungi is quickly followed by a curious letter in which Akeley reverses his opinions. He says he has made friends with the creatures and he wants Wilmarth to come and learn from them what he has learned. Wilmarth is puzzled by Akeley's new attitude, but his jubilation is unbounded:

Mad or sane, metamorphosed or merely relieved, the chances were that Akeley had actually encountered some stupendous change of perspective in his hazardous research; some change at once diminishing his danger—real or fancied—and opening dizzy new vistas of cosmic and superhuman knowledge. My own zeal for the unknown flared up to meet his, and I felt myself touched by the morbid barrier-breaking. To shake off the maddening and wearying limitations of time and space and natural law—to be linked with the vast *outside*—to come close to the nighted and abysmal secrets of the infinite and the ultimate—surely such a thing was worth the risk of one's life, soul, and sanity! (*DH* 242–43)

But Wilmarth's enthusiasm also blinds him to a fact that is painfully obvious to the reader—that the change of tenor in the Akeley's letter signals that he has finally been dispatched by the creatures, and that *they* are inviting Wilmarth in the hope of luring him to the same fate. The dissociated bits of evidence are all before Wilmarth, but his emotions neutralize his objectivity and render him incapable of piecing them together. He rationalizes limply, "Did not the invitation—the willingness to have me test the truth of the letter in person—prove its genuineness?" (*DH* 242). This is exactly the sort of response the fungi are counting on.

Wilmarth's trip to Akeley's mountain home is a virtual journey into the heart of darkness—not of the human heart, but of the infinite void. The solitude of the menacing woods, the peculiar circumstances under which Akeley has arranged the meeting with Wilmarth—all these would have put other Lovecraft characters on their guard. But Wilmarth's emotions betray his common sense, and it is only by chance that he discovers he has committed the one sin Lovecraft considered unforgivable—he has expected to find his "local human passions and conditions and standards" reciprocated in creatures from outside who are totally beyond human conception. The very attributes that affirm Wilmarth's humanity are what render him vulnerable and alone in the domain of the fungi. The price he pays for his folly is the discovery of the fate that has befallen Akeley and the awareness that he must forever bear this knowledge alone.

As Lovecraft explored the possibilities of his cosmic perspective, he strove to find original ways to have the alienation of his characters and their environments reflect humanity's isolation on a cosmic level. One of the cleverest instances of this occurs in "The Shadow over Innsmouth" (1931). The story opens with its nameless narrator traveling through New England. His curiosity is piqued by what he hears of the shunned town of Innsmouth, and he decides to investigate. From a drunken vagrant, he learns Innsmouth's incredible history. The narrator escapes from Innsmouth with this knowledge and divulges enough information to the authorities to instigate a government-sponsored destruction of the town. This smacks of the same brand of heroism displayed by Henry Armitage during his questionable triumph in "The Dunwich Horror"— that is, until the narrator discovers that he has begun to develop "the Innsmouth look" and is himself descended from an Innsmouth family. This is the same sort of revelation that led Lovecraft's Arthur Jermyn to commit suicide rather than live a life of self-loathing, but here the narrator undergoes an extraordinary internal transformation. Before the reader's eyes, the character who was petrified by the horrors of Innsmouth begins eagerly to anticipate the changes overtaking him. He even speaks of his plans to liberate a cousin undergoing a similar transformation so that they both can return to the sea:

> I shall plan my cousin's escape from that Canton madhouse, and together we shall go to marvel-shadowed Innsmouth. We shall swim out to that brooding reef in the sea and dive down through the black abysses to Cyclopean and many-columned Y'ha-nthlei, and in that lair of the Deep Ones we shall dwell amidst wonder and glory forever. (*DH* 367)

Ironically, Lovecraft creates an extraordinarily alienating climax through a conclusion that shows the narrator's lack of alienation. As Maurice Lévy says, "The reader is left adrift, *disoriented* in the most material sense of the term. Amid the multiple constituents that make up the impossible definition of the fantastic event, nothing is, we believe, more basic than this ultimate questioning of what has remained so long uncontested: the adherence of the narrator, the 'witness,' to the norm."[13] With its appalling conversion of the narrator into the very thing he has inspired the reader to fear, "The Shadow over Innsmouth" stands as the Lovecraft story that comes closest to bringing the reader into contact with the conceptual horrors that only Lovecraft's characters come to know.

Disorienting as "The Shadow over Innsmouth" may be, it is yet another example of Lovecraft relying on a horrifying impact on the emotions to communicate a feeling of alienation. Lovecraft knew the impossibility of expressing the horrors of the unknown directly, owing to the inadequacy of human expression to articulate what lies beyond human ken. As he told Farnsworth Wright, "When we cross the line to the boundless and hideous unknown—the shadow-haunted *Outside*—we must remember to leave our humanity and terrestrialism at the threshold" (*SL* 2.150).

In most of his later stories Lovecraft tried to put his terrestrial prejudices behind him when describing the unknown. "The Dreams in the Witch House" (1932) begins in the same vein as stories like the "The Tomb" and "Hypnos" by focusing on the breakdown between fantasy and reality. After several nights spent in the former home of Keziah Mason, a condemned witch who managed a miraculous escape from her prison cell in 1692, student Walter Gilman begins to have bizarre dreams of visits to alien worlds. He accidentally pockets an object during one of those dreams and discovers later that he has brought it back with him into the waking world. By giving Gilman physical proof that his dream world is not fantasy but a different form of reality, Lovecraft dissipates the dramatic tension he built in his earlier stories by leaving the reality of events in question. Gilman's dream travels, like Keziah Mason's witchcraft, are both made possible through a system of mathematics that is related to the non-Euclidian calculus and quantum physics that Gilman studies. Thus, Lovecraft uses the point at which his earlier stories would have ended—with objective validation of the supernatural—as a point of departure.

In "The Dreams in the Witch House" Lovecraft sets a horror story of witchcraft and haunted houses against a background of abstract science and mathematics, with the idea of showing how remote human superstitions (the human foreground of the story) are from cosmic truths (the larger background). Yet only a year before he all but dispensed with the foreground story in an effort to overpower the reader with the scale of his background. *At the Mountains of Madness* (1931) is written as a warning by William Dyer, a member of the ill-fated Miskatonic University Antarctic expedition of 1930–31. The story is a virtual case study of character alienation that begins with Dyer lamenting: "It is an unfortunate fact that relatively obscure men like myself and my associates, connected only with a small university, have little chance of making an impression where matters of a wildly bizarre or highly controversial nature are concerned" (*MM* 4). The expedition's voyage to Antarctica is an isolating technique, reminiscent of similar journeys in "The Temple" and "The Nameless City" where the distance of the setting and the singularness of the narrator's experiences make it impossible either to prove or disprove his account. However, Lovecraft's least intention is to exploit the distance between Antarctica and the normal world to create doubtfulness in the reader. To the contrary, Lovecraft chooses the Antarctic because its vast size permits him to explore wonder and terror within the same landscape.

Shortly after the expedition arrives at its destination, one of its teams finds what it assumes to be the fossilized remains of creatures so ancient that their very existence upsets conventional geological time scales. By the time the rest of the expedition catches up with them, though, the team has been slaughtered and some of the remains have disappeared. While the rest of the expedition concocts a phony story to tell the rest of the world, Dyer and a student named Danforth agree to search for clues to the mystery beyond the visible mountain ranges. There, the pair discovers a city millions of years old that was once inhabited by the Old Ones, the race whose remains they discover. The city is impressive not only for its age and its size, but also for its "infinite bizarrerie, endless variety, preternatural massiveness, and utterly alien exoticism" (*MM* 51). A series of decorative bas-reliefs reveal the historical truth behind the city: eons ago, the creatures who built it migrated from the stars; man, it appears, was one of their accidentally created biological specimens.

Lovecraft's depiction of the absolute alienness of this part of the earth exceeds his achievements in depicting the alien "invasion" of the Arkham countryside in "The Colour out of Space." Here, though, horror is transmuted into awe: "Looking back to our sensations, and recalling our dazedness at viewing this monstrous survival from aeons we had thought pre-human, I can only wonder that we preserved the semblance of equilibrium which we did," writes Dyer. "Of course we knew that something—chronology, scientific theory, or our own consciousness—was woefully awry" (*MM* 47). With the foundations of his science knocked from beneath him, Dyer finds human concepts and expressions inadequate to give a sense of what he and Danforth see: "My imagination sometimes escaped all bounds and roved aimlessly in realms of fantastic associations—even weaving links betwixt this lost world and some of my own wildest dreams" (*MM* 47); "Only in fantastic nightmares could any human beings but Danforth and me conceive such optical effects" (*MM* 50); "There came a point, though, when our sensations could not be conveyed in any words the press would understand" (*MM* 28).

The literal "unspeakableness" of what Dyer and Danforth find is all the more appropriate when one considers the ending of the story. Lovecraft has suggested that, for all their awesomeness, even the Old Ones feared, with an almost worshipful intensity, an indescribably dreadful *something* beyond a distant mountain range. When a shoggoth lurking in the caverns beneath the city forces the pair to flee in their airplane, Danforth gazes for just a moment beyond the far mountain range, and what he sees drives him mad. Thus, Lovecraft creates levels of alienation in the face of cosmic truths that correspond perfectly to the physical isolation of the characters: the world in general knows nothing of the truth of what the expedition has found, the expeditionary team knows only that something inexplicable has happened to several of its members, Dyer and Danforth know that the slaughter was committed by the alien creatures who built the titan city beyond the mountains of madness, and Danforth alone knows of something lying beyond the city so inconceivable that that it shatters his mind.

Lovecraft expanded the scope of his cosmic vision even further in "The Shadow out of Time" (1934–35) with his portrayal of a Great Race who came to our planet 150 million years ago in the usurped bodies of another race of creatures (suggesting a potentially incalculable real age for them). The Great Race has mastered time travel, and it investigates the future by exchanging minds with individuals of different races on different planets. The story is presented as the narrative of Nathaniel Wingate Peaslee, who awakens from a five-year bout of amnesia. Gradually, as memories come back to him in dreams, he comes to the realization that he was one of the Great Race's mind-exchange victims.

Lovecraft achieves extraordinarily alienating effects in this story, not the least of which is Peaslee's discovery that he represents only one of untold numbers of races who have been probed by the Great Race (reinforcing the image Lovecraft creates in "The Call of Cthulhu" of human knowledge being only a small island "in the midst of black seas of infinity"). To create a powerful metaphor for the alienating potential of what Peaslee learns of the Great Race, Lovecraft resorted to an idea that had intrigued him at least from the beginning of his professional writing career: possession and loss of identity.[14] We see Peaslee broken into four different personalities by his experience: the pre-mind-exchange self, the post-mind-exchange self, and two intermediate selves—one that recalls through dreams his life spent in the body of a member of the Great Race, and the other, his body inhabited for five years by the mind of a member of the Great Race, of whom Peaslee is made aware through the accounts of friends and family. The torment Peaslee feels through his inability to integrate these four selves, coupled with his shattering realization at the story's climax, suggest that Lovecraft is saying that the knowledge he bears is simply too much for a single human mind to assimilate.

Not surprisingly, two other stories, "The Thing on the Doorstep" (1933) and "The Haunter of the Dark" (1935), concern the displacement of the mind by a force greater than that of the individual human personality. Robert Blake, a grown-up version of the neurotic characters who appear in Lovecraft's earliest stories, is a writer of weird fiction who tends to let the inscape of his mind seep into the outside world and transform it. When he looks out over the city of Providence, we are told he "had a curious sense that he was looking upon some unknown, ethereal world which might or might not vanish in dream if he ever tried to seek it out or enter it in person" (*DH* 94). The rapport Blake has with worlds beyond the visible one, combined with hints of the past experiences that drove him to Providence, suggest that he is more sensitive than others to influence from the unknown. His vulnerability ultimately leads him to the boarded-up Starry Wisdom Church, where he unwittingly opens the gateway for a monster that can only be destroyed by light. To Blake's horror, he discovers an "unholy rapport he felt to exist between his mind and that lurking horror in the distant steeple" (*DH* 109). As Blake comes more and more under the control of the creature's consciousness, his grasp of reality and ability to know when he is functioning on his own begin to slip away.

At the climax of the story, the monster escapes during a blackout and pursues Blake. His diary details his losing battle as his mind is taken over:

> . . . The thing is taking hold of my mind . . .
>
> Trouble with memory. I see things I never knew before. Other worlds and other galaxies . . . Dark . . . The lightning seems dark and the darkness seems light. (*DH* 114)

The final image of the monster merging with Blake's mind as it is struck by lightning—even as superstitious people swarm the streets below trying in their own way to light the darkness—is emblematic of the sense of alienation Lovecraft sought to create in all his cosmic horror stories: one's sense of isolation is not merely a function of geographic space, but also of mental space; it can occur just as easily amongst a crowd and in the "light" as in solitary out-of-the-way places if one is possessed of a knowledge that is sufficiently disorienting. The final image of Blake's corpse, with "glassy, bulging eyes and the marks of stark, convulsive fright on the twisted features" (*DH* 113), is the perfect symbol of the alienation that characters come to know in Lovecraft's stories: Blake's human features betray his inability to assimilate the dehumanizing knowledge that has taken hold of his mind.

IV

In tracing the evolution of Lovecraft's horror fiction, it is much easier to show how Lovecraft changed his approach to a particular theme over the years than to explain why. One can surmise that the development of his cosmic perspective from the alienated characters and isolated settings of his earlier fiction was influenced by both his personal experiences and his professional life.

When Lovecraft began writing fiction, he was still strongly under the influence of Poe. Far too many critics choose to see the neurotic, self-loathing outsiders of his earliest stories as autobiographical representations without at least conceding that young writers tend to emulate their models. "A rather neurotic narrator around whom the tale centers and who is subject to much psychological analysis"[15] is a mainstay of both Poe's and Lovecraft's fiction. Around 1920, Lovecraft read Hawthorne extensively. Hawthorne's work is thought to be the inspiration for his tales of New England and other locales. However, when Lovecraft was reading as preparation for writing his essay "Supernatural Horror in Literature" (1925–27), he studied the fiction of many other more modern authors. Among them was Algernon Blackwood, whose story "The Willows" Lovecraft praised as the best work of supernatural horror ever written. One can only surmise what must have been triggered in Lovecraft's mind when he read the following passage, in which the two characters in the story confront the awesomeness of nature: "'There are forces close here that could kill a herd of elephants in a second as easily as you or I could squash a fly. Our only chance is to keep perfectly still. Our insignificance perhaps may save us.'"[16]

The changes in Lovecraft's approach to supernatural horror also correspond to three easily marked stages in his life. His earliest fiction was written at the time when he was most withdrawn from the greater world around him. The point where the external world begins to play an increasingly larger role in his fiction occurs when Lovecraft himself came into greater contact with the world through his years spent in New York and his reputation as a respected author. As Lovecraft grew intellectually in the years following his return to Providence, so did the sweep of his cosmic fiction.

Yet it is interesting to note that no matter how mature Lovecraft became as a writer, he was ever recycling and embellishing themes from his earlier fiction. At the very end of his life, Lovecraft was looking from a fresh perspective at ideas first conceived in the days before he was a professional writer: the horrors of a lost identity; the terrors of heredity and atavism; the past that will not die; the figure of the outsider. In particular, it is interesting to note that ideas for "The Call of Cthulhu," the story that would announce Lovecraft's new cosmic perspective and inspire an entire subgenre of fiction dealing with man's isolation and alienation in the universe, came to Lovecraft in nascent form in a dream in 1920, while he was still in the midst of his Dunsanian and Poe period.[17] As he explored new forms of expression for his horror fiction, he added details to the picture the story was creating in his mind, but he did not tackle it head-on until 1926, when the ideas used in his previous works began to coalesce into that single coherent perspective which we now recognize as Lovecraft's greatest contribution to the literature of supernatural horror. One might say that for Lovecraft, as for the narrators of his stories, it was all a matter of fitting and refitting all the pieces together until the right pattern emerged.

Notes

1. Donald R. Burleson, *H. P. Lovecraft* (Westport, CT: Greenwood Press, 1983), 22.

2. HPL, "Supernatural Horror in Literature" (*D* 394–95).

3. Maurice Lévy, *Lovecraft: A Study in the Fantastic* (Detroit: Wayne State University Press, 1988), 41.

4. Burleson, 26–27.

5. "Arkham and Kingsport," *LS* No. 6 (Fall 1987): 71.

6. Lévy, 41.

7. HPL to Lillian D. Clark, 12 June 1930 (ms., JHL); quoted in Lévy, 127.

8. Barton Levi St. Armand, *The Roots of Horror in the Fiction of H. P. Lovecraft* (Elizabethtown, NY: Dragon Press, 1977), 4.

9. Burleson, 14.

10. Ibid.

11. Lévy, 37.

12. St. Armand, 51.

13. Levy, 74.

14. In HPL's *Commonplace Book,* "Transposition of identity" first appears in entries HPL made before 1920, recurs throughout his notes and memoranda, and is present in the next to last entry, written some time in 1934.

15. S. T. Joshi, *H. P. Lovecraft* (Mercer Island, WA: Starmont House, 1982), 44.

16. Blackwood, *Best Ghost Stories of Algernon Blackwood,* ed. E. F. Bleiler (New York: Dover, 1973), 39–40.

17. Steven J. Mariconda, "On the Emergence of 'Cthulhu,'" *LS* No. 6 (Fall 1987): 54–58.

Lovecraft's Cosmic Imagery

Steven J. Mariconda

H. P. Lovecraft's weird tales are distinguished by their unique cosmic orientation—the horror stems not from traditional supernatural themes, but from the concept of an indifferent and unknowable universe. During his career Lovecraft evolved a characteristic set of imagery to convey cosmic horror, imagery reflecting his view of the universe as a vast, purposeless machine. Before we examine that imagery, let us consider how the central tenet of Lovecraft's worldview—that the universe is governed by an immutable and only partially knowable set of laws—provided both the motivation for his art and an infinite canvas upon which to create it.

First, the laws governing the universe are fixed. There is no purpose or direction to the cosmos, for it is only a well-oiled Newtonian machine. Lovecraft accepted this concept intellectually, but found it imaginatively stifling, insisting that "a highly organised man can't exist endurably without mental expansions beyond objective reality" (*SL* 3.140). He was therefore compelled to create fiction which, by incorporating his imaginings as extensions rather than negations of reality, accommodated both his intellectual and his emotional needs.

Lovecraft had the opportunity to create such fiction because of the second part of the proposition above, that the universe's laws are only partially knowable: "Absolute reality is forever beyond us—we cannot form even the vaguest conception of what such a thing would be like, for we have no terms to envisage entity apart from those subjective aspects which reside wholly in our own physiology and psychology" (*SL* 2.301). This gave his imagination free reign to create the alien realms and entities that are the sources of his horror. "If one must weave cobwebs of empty aether," he said, "let them supply a decorative element to those cosmic spaces which would otherwise be an ambiguous and tantalizing void" (*SL* 3.147).

Lovecraft did not seriously attempt weird fiction until he was twenty-six, when his philosophy was solidly established. It is clear from a letter of September 1932 that his aesthetic of the weird was a direct outgrowth of the worldview outlined above:

> It is true that we no longer credit the existence of discarnate intelligence & superphysical forces around us, & that consequently the traditional "Gothick" tale of

spectres and vampires has lost a large part of its power to move our emotions. But in spite of this disillusion there remain two factors largely unaffected—& in one case actually increased—by the change: first, a sense of impatient rebellion against the rigid & ineluctable tyranny of time, space, & natural laws—a sense which drives the imagination to devise all sorts of plausible hypothetical defeats of that tyranny—& second, a burning curiosity concerning the vast reaches of unplumbed and unplumbable cosmic spaces which press down tantalizingly on all sides of our pitifully tiny sphere of the known. (*SL* 4.70)

But Lovecraft the philosopher had set Lovecraft the artist a formidable task: to depict with mere words that which forever lies beyond the sphere of the known. Over the course of his twenty-year career he made great strides in his attempt to imagine the unimaginable, to describe the indescribable. From the clumsy attempts at conveying the outré in "Dagon" (1917) to the magnificent cosmic montage in "The Haunter of the Dark" (1935), he shows substantial artistic progress, refining and expanding the imagery he used to achieve his purpose. Examining these image patterns will lend the reader a greater understanding of Lovecraft's intent and a greater appreciation both of the scope of his imagination and of his skill as stylist.

We should pause to note Lovecraft's assertion that imagery played a central role in art. Fiction and poetry, he said, "must be read wholly for imagery and not for ideas" (*SL* 2.118). His own motive for authorship was "a literary ambition confined altogether to the recording of certain images connected with bizarrerie" (*SL* 2.111). Lovecraft also wrote of "a wish to get on paper some of the images . . . constantly running through my mind" (*SL* 2.107). We will see that he drew upon his conception of the universe in his fiction to create imagery conveying its vastness, its magnificence, and ultimately, its terror.

The narrator of "Hypnos" (1922) may have been speaking for Lovecraft when he decried "that chief of torments—inarticulateness" (*D* 166). The author was captivated by the wonders of the universe from adolescence, but he never ceased refining and clarifying his imaginative vision. Throughout his life, Lovecraft's letters to more traditionally inclined correspondents are filled with passages describing his conception of the cosmos. The universe is simply "blind force operating according to fixed & eternal patterns inherent in entity" (*SL* 2.124–25). In another early letter he described the cosmos as a "ceaseless and boundless rearrangement of electrons, atoms, and molecules which constitute the blind but regular mechanical patterns of cosmic activity" (*SL* 2.41).

This mental picture of the cosmos is the basis for one of the most pervasive motifs in the fiction, that of kaleidoscopic imagery. The technique of showing a rapidly shifting panorama of images first appears in "Beyond the Wall of Sleep" (1919), Lovecraft's earliest attempt to depict the vast Outside. The story is mediocre, but the narrator's dream-visions have impressive impact: "Walls, columns, and architraves of living fire blazed effulgently. . . . Blending with this display of palatial magnificence, or rather, supplanting it at times in kaleidoscopic rotation, were glimpses of wide plains and graceful valleys, high mountains, and inviting grottoes" (*D* 32). Note that Lovecraft pauses to clarify the way in which these visions are perceived, a rhetorical device that both adds to the prose realism and enforces the meaning. In a story written the following year, "From Beyond" (1920), there is a similar exponent. Here an experimental machine invokes a vision that "was wholly kaleidoscopic, . . . [a] jumble of sights, sounds, and sense-impressions" (*D* 95).

More impressive than these stories is "The Shunned House" (1924), in which Lovecraft successfully grafts a transdimensional entity onto a homely Providence dwelling. This entity is reminiscent of a vampire in that it saps the life-force of other beings; but, in an innovative twist, it is also mentally invasive upon its victims. The narrator speculates upon the far-reaching nature of the phenomenon, using the language of Einsteinian physics and quantum mechanics. Near the climax of the tale, during the vigil of the narrator and his uncle in the house's basement, the elderly man experiences a disturbing dream-vision that again embodies Lovecraft's conception of the universe as characterized by "kaleidoscopic pattern-seething" (*SL* 3.230):

> There was a suggestion of queerly disordered pictures superimposed one upon another; an arrangement in which the essentials of time as well as space seemed dissolved and mixed in the most illogical fashion. In this kaleidoscopic vortex of phantasmal images were occasional snapshots, if one might use the term, of singular clearness but unaccountable heterogeneity. (*MM* 255–56)[1]

The wording of this descriptive passage recalls numerous passages in Lovecraft's letters, notably his pronouncement to the Gallomo correspondence club that "the cosmos is a mindless vortex" (*SL* 1.156). Happily, he here does not offer a succession of architectural and landscape images (cf. "Beyond the Wall of Sleep") as examples of what Elihu Whipple saw. Instead, he implies a disturbing *diversity* of possibilities with the closing antithesis. The device of the kaleidoscope enabled Lovecraft to convey both the meaningless, never-ending interactions of matter and the incomprehensible extent of the universe.

Lovecraft grew more and more adventurous in the use of his cosmic kaleidoscope. The hallucinatory "ride on a comet's tail" that the sailor Johansen experienced during his return voyage from R'lyeh in "The Call of Cthulhu" (1926) is a notable example. Even this is exceeded by the "bizarre conceptions" that composed Danforth's ravings at the end of *At the Mountains of Madness* (1931). Lovecraft's bold use of a kaleidoscopic coda for this most far-reaching of tales (a use about which colleagues and editors alike expressed reservations) indicates how central this motif was to his imagination. It also reminds us of the astonishing and surrealistic sequence of visions that concludes his experiment in the prose poem "Nyarlathotep" (1920):

> Screamingly sentient, dumbly delirious, only the gods that were can tell. A sickened, sensitive shadow writhing in hands that are not hands, and whirled blindly past ghastly midnights of rotting creation, corpses of dead worlds with sores that were cities, charnel winds that brush the pallid stars and make them flicker low. Beyond the world vague ghosts of monstrous things; half-seen columns of unsanctified temples that rest on nameless rocks beneath space and reach up to dizzying vacua above the spheres of light and darkness. (*MW* 34)

It may be noted that Lovecraft's boundless kaleidoscopic excursions take place largely within the human consciousness itself: "As I gazed, I perceived that my own brain held the key to these enchanting metamorphoses" ("Beyond the Wall of Sleep," *D* 32).[2] This approach represents the defeat of those sensory limitations that Lovecraft the dreamer found so repressive. Perhaps the Providence gentleman secretly hoped, like Lord Northam in the fragment "The Descendent" (1926?), that "he held within his own half-explored brain that cryptic link which would awaken him to elder and future lives in forgotten dimensions; which would bind him to the stars, and to the infinities and eternities beyond them" (*D* 362).

Both in association with kaleidoscopic imagery and independently of it, Lovecraft often employs sound to convey horror. This thread is evident in his *Commonplace Book*; for example:

> [14] Hideous sound in the dark.

> [39] Sounds—possibly musical—heard in the night from other world or realms of being. (*CE* 5.220, 221)

Certainly Lovecraft's enthusiasm for M. P. Shiel's "The House of Sounds" —with its famous enigma, "Can you not hear the *sound of the world?*"—stems from his imaginative affinity for sound imagery.

Just as Lovecraft's unfortunate protagonists do not see the word-pictures above with their eyes, they do not hear the outré sounds with their ears. Perception takes place in the brain, and is not derived from information gathered through the usual sense-organs. Karl Heinrich, commander of the German submarine and discoverer of an antediluvian undersea city in "The Temple" (1920), is the victim of an "aural delusion." A sedative removes his impression that a "wild yet beautiful chant or choral hymn" (*D* 70) is coming from the temple outside his ship. The narrator of "Beyond the Wall of Sleep," similarly, experiences "a weird lyric melody" of "chords, vibrations, and harmonic ecstasies" (*D* 32) to accompany his dream-vision.

Sometimes Lovecraft's sounds take the form of a simple drone: for example the "infinitely faint, subtly vibrant, and unmistakably musical" sound that held "a quality of surpassing wildness" (*D* 93–94) in "From Beyond." Similar images appear in both "The Music of Erich Zann" (1921) ("an exquisitely low and infinitely distant musical note" [*DH* 89]) and "Hypnos" ("a low and damnably insistent whine from very far away" [*D* 169]). Note the adjectives associated with sound in these stories: faint, low, vibrant, droning, wild, insistent, deliberate, purposeful, clamoring, mocking, calling. This is Lovecraft's music of the spheres, but it is more of a discord—an aural representation of a chaos of atoms.

It is this chaos, indeed, that echoes symbolically in the voice of great Cthulhu—"a subterrene voice or intelligence shouting monotonously in enigmatical sense-impacts uninscribable save as gibberish" (*DH* 129). We cannot understand the import of these sounds. To us they can never have meaning, for we do not possess the "sense-equipment" (a term Lovecraft was fond of using in letters)[3] to interpret them.

In the later fiction, Lovecraft modified his sound exponent, introducing the element of rhythm.[4] Fictional imagery again echoes the author's conception of the universe, here as explained in a letter to Elizabeth Toldridge of 26 November 1929:

> One of the fixed conditions of this infinite & eternal entity [i.e., the cosmos] is pattern or rhythm—certain regular relationships of part to part within the fabric of the unchanging whole; & specialized aspects of this rhythm appear to be the basis of our notions of time, space, motion, matter, & change. (*SL* 2.86)

The rhythm motif is explicated and fully worked out in "The Dreams in the Witch House" (1932). This story is best thought of as Lovecraft's Magnificent Failure—its uneven execution is not equal to its breathtaking conceptions, which are some of the most original in imaginative literature. Walter Gilman has a fever, one symptom of which is hearing so sensitized that it gives him a sense of "strident pandemonium" (*MM* 261). The choice of the noun, with its overtones of cosmic chaos, is no accident. Soon Gilman experiences strange dreams (actually entries into other dimensions) accompanied by a "shrieking, roaring confusion of sound . . . past all analysis as to pitch, timbre, or rhythm" and having "obscure, relentlessly inevitable fluctuations" (*MM* 268). In the same way that he connects Keziah Mason's witchcraft with non-Euclidian mathematics, Lovecraft links sound—again symbolic of the "sound" of the universe itself—with the ritual of the Black Mass: "the chants of the Sabbat were patterned on this faintly over-head pulsing which no earthly ear could endure in its unveiled spatial fulness" (*MM* 293). One of the things Gilman dreads most of all is experiencing "the monstrous burst of Walpurgis-rhythm in whose cosmic timbre would be concentrated all the primal, ultimate space-time seethings which lie behind the massed spheres of matter and sometimes break forth in measured reverberations that penetrate faintly every layer of entity" (*MM* 291).

Even more important to Lovecraft's fiction than the rhythm motif was the other component he mentioned to Toldridge: that of *pattern*. The idea of pattern, and the related ideas of proportion, symmetry, and geometry, combine to form the most important motif of Lovecraft's cosmic imagery. In *The Case of Charles Dexter Ward* (1927), Dr. Willett is sent temporarily insane by something he sees in Joseph Curwen's underground laboratory. For this reaction Lovecraft offers the following explanation: "There is about certain outlines and entities a power of symbolism and suggestion which acts frightfully on a sensitive thinker's perspective and whispers terrible hints of obscure cosmic relationships and unnamable realities behind the protective illusions of common vision" (*MM* 207). Similarly, "the *general outline*" of the bas-relief of Cthulhu is the "most shockingly frightful" (*DH* 127) aspect of the object. The "general shape" of the black stone in "The Whisperer in Darkness" (1930), too, "almost defies the power of language" (*DH* 222). Of the ichthyic designs on a piece of bizarre jewelry in "The Shadow over Innsmouth" (1931), the narrator notes that "every contour" invoked "the ultimate quintessence of unknown and inhuman evil" (*DH* 312).[5]

What could make a simple outline so disturbing? An outline is simply a line bounding a geometrical figure. It is geometry, indeed, that is the very source of these objects' horror. The black stone's cutting was guided by unknown and "outlandish geometrical principles," while on the jewelry "the patterns all hinted of remote secrets and unimaginable abysses in time and space."

The issue of geometry and symmetry in Lovecraft is a complex one. Let us begin by recalling Lovecraft's belief that humankind's aesthetic sense consists of two elements: "one absolute and objective, and based on rhythm and symmetry; and the other subjective" (*SL* 2.229). In his essay "Some Causes of Self-Immolation" (1931), Lovecraft lists eleven instincts and their associated emotions (e.g., nutrition and hunger). To this classification, credited to William McDougall, he adds: "The present writer feels convinced that one basic instinct . . . ought to be added to this list; namely, an instinct for symmetry in the abstract, based upon habituation to the ceaseless rhythms and regularities (astronomical and otherwise) of the terrestrial environment" (*CE* 5.79).

Lovecraft, then, thought that a craving for symmetry was inbred in the human race. He also believed that the universe itself is possessed of symmetry, that it operates in a predictable way. Recall his description of the cosmos to Elizabeth Toldridge—"regular relationships of part to part." Such fixed relations imply order and symmetry. Perhaps as a result, Lovecraft tended to envision the universe in terms of geometry. Relating a dream in which he was a participant in a sort of séance, Lovecraft wrote that his vision "began to take in vast vistas of space—represented by aggregates of gigantic cubes scattered along a gulf of violet radiation."[6] The use of the word "represented" is insightful, revealing that Lovecraft did not literally believe the universe was a collection of cubes; rather, this image is a mental construct or metaphor that helps us envision the universe. Using related imagery, the crablike space beings in "The Whisperer in Darkness" (1931) reveal to a startled Albert Wilmarth the place of our cosmos in "the unending chain of linked cosmos-atoms" (*DH* 256).[7] Walter Gilman's alternate dimensions, too, are populated by "prisms, labyrinths, clusters of cubes and planes, and Cyclopean buildings" (*MM* 267).

If geometry informs the universe, then mastery of geometry is the key to the universe's domination. Keziah Mason uses the unusual angles of her room in the Witch House to enter other dimensions. Wilbur Whateley of "The Dunwich Horror" (1928) needs to "learn all the angles of the planes" in preparation for his attempt to "clear off the earth" (*DH* 184).

The discoveries of Max Planck and Albert Einstein did not move Lovecraft, "a mechanistic materialist of the line of Leucippus, Democritus, Epicurus, and Lucretius—and in modern times, Nietzsche and Haeckel" (*SL* 2.160), away from his position that the universe operated in an orderly fashion. Lovecraft contended (as did Einstein) that the irregularities indicated by quantum physics need not mean the universe operates randomly:

> What most physicists take the quantum theory, at present, to mean, is *not that any cosmic uncertainty exists* as to which of several courses a given reaction will take; but in certain instances *no conceivable channel of information can ever tell human*

beings which course will be taken, or by what course a certain observed result came about. (*SL* 3.228)

More than one hundred years after Lovecraft's birth, scientific thought tends to disagree. But Lovecraft's mechanistic universe was intact—except in his fiction, where he used asymmetry to symbolize "that most terrible conception of the human brain—a malign and particular suspension or defeat of those fixed laws of Nature which are our only safeguard against the assaults of chaos and the daemons of unplumbed space" (*D* 263). If the universe operated according to an intelligible Euclidian geometry, then the existence of objects adhering to non-Euclidian geometry was profoundly unnatural.[8]

The Old Ones of *At the Mountains of Madness* possess both knowledge of higher mathematics and experience in transcosmic voyaging. Their architectural designs, Lovecraft tell us, "displayed a profound use of mathematical principles, and were made up of obscurely symmetrical curves and angles" (*MM* 56). The spectacular description of the city itself that opens chapter five, too, revolves around its geometrical characteristics: "The general shape of these things [the buildings] tended to be conical, pyramidal, or terraced; though there were many perfect cylinders, perfect cubes, clusters of cubes, and other rectangular forms, and a peculiar sprinkling of angled edifices" (*MM* 46). But a violation of known natural law is immediately evident to Dyer and Danforth, because the designs embody "monstrous perversions of geometrical laws" (*MM* 30). Similar to this is the city of R'lyeh—whose geometry was "*all wrong*" (*DH* 143)—as well as the Great Race's city in "The Shadow out of Time." These edifices are not designed using the familiar geometry we know, but are instead made up of "geometrical forms for which even an Euclid could scarcely find a name" (*MM* 51). Even the physiology of these cities' inhabitants does not follow familiar bilateral symmetry but instead adheres to a five-pointed radial plan.[9] Non-Euclidian geometry is also evoked in "The Dreams in the Witch House"; this is both what Walter Gilman is studying and what Keziah Mason had used to move among dimensions.

It is insightful to note how Lovecraft bemoaned the movement of modern (terrestrial) architecture away from familiar forms and toward purely geometrical forms. In "A Living Heritage: Roman Architecture in Today's America" (1935), he protested these "new decorative designs of cones and cubes and triangles and segments" as "problems in Euclid" (*CE* 5.123). His rationale helps to explain why his fantastic cities are so disturbing:

> Our longing for familiar symbols—our homesickness, as it were, of things we
> have known—is in reality the most authentic possible expression of the [hu-
> man] race's persistent life-force. It is the pitiful struggle of the ego against that
> ineluctable change which means decay and engulfment in the illimitable dark.
> (*CE* 5.121)

Just as Lovecraft railed against Picasso, Brancusi, Modigliani, the architect
Raymond Mathewson Hood, and other modernists in his letters, he used modern art as a cue for otherworldly intrusions in his fiction. The Cthulhu bas-
relief recalls "the vagaries of cubism and futurism" (*DH* 127); and when the
unfortunate Johansen described the undersea city "without knowing what futurism is like, [he] achieved something very close to it" (*DH* 150).

The elements of asymmetry, otherworldly sound, and kaleidoscopic vision
all fuse in Lovecraft's concept of Ultimate Chaos. Ultimate Chaos is the Hell of
the Lovecraftian cosmology, the essence and center of his cosmically indifferent universe. This concept mutated as Lovecraft developed it. Its embryonic
appearance was in the climactic final sentence of "Nyarlathotep":

> And through this revolting graveyard of the universe the muffled, maddening
> beating of drums, and the thin, monotonous whine of blasphemous flutes from
> inconceivable, unlighted chambers beyond time; the detestable pounding and
> piping whereunto dance slowly, awkwardly, and absurdly the gigantic, tene-
> brous ultimate gods—the blind, voiceless, mindless gargoyles whose soul is
> Nyarlathotep. (*MW* 34)

A variant of this imagery is found in "The Rats in the Walls" (1923). (Nyarlathotep is later supplanted by Azathoth, the blind idiot god that is the symbolic fig-
urehead of Lovecraft's cosmos.) Lovecraft returns to this verbal icon in several
stories, as well as in the sonnet "Azathoth" (1930), always to invoke the very
nadir of terror. Of all the secrets that Wilmarth learns from the Outside Ones
about time and space, nothing evokes in him more "loathing" than the revelation about "the monstrous nuclear chaos beyond angled space which the *Necronomicon* had mercifully cloaked under the name of Azathoth" (*DH* 256).

Lovecraft most fully explored this important motif in "The Dreams in the
Witch House." Keziah Mason insists Gilman must go "to the throne of
Azathoth at the centre of ultimate Chaos" (*MM* 272). Lovecraft ventures to
depict this abortive journey:

> There were suggestions of the vague, twilight abysses, and of still vaster,
> blacker abysses beyond them—abysses in which all fixed suggestions of form

were absent. He had been taken there by the bubble-congeries and the little polyhedron [Keziah Mason and Brown Jenkin, respectively] which always dogged him; but they, like himself, had changed to wisps of milky, barely luminous mist in this farther void of ultimate blackness. . . . Eventually there had been a hint of vast, leaping shadows, of a monstrous, half-acoustic pulsing, and of the thin, monotonous piping of an unseen flute—but that was all. (*MM* 282)

We can see a hierarchy of horrors here: first certain bizarre phenomena are perceived; then all form itself is lost, and there is only blackness and chaos. This progression is maintained and used to powerful advantage in Lovecraft's fictional swan song, "The Haunter of the Dark" (1935). Robert Blake, writer and painter of fantasy, discovers a church used by a strange cult. The latter worships the entity of the story's title, which shows them other worlds and galaxies and is invoked by staring into an oddly angled stone called the Shining Trapezohedron. As Blake first examines the stained-glass windows of the church, he notices that "one seemed to shew merely a dark space with spirals of scattered luminosity scattered about in it" (*DH* 100). When Blake discovers the Shining Trapezohedron in the bell tower room, he makes a kaleidoscopic mental excursion to the center of the Lovecraftian universe:

> Before he realised it, he was looking at the stone again, and letting its curious influence call up a nebulous pageantry in his mind. He saw processions of robed, hooded figures whose outlines were not human, and looked on endless leagues of desert lined with carved, sky-reaching monoliths. He saw towers and walls in nighted depths under the sea, and vortices of space where wisps of black mist floated before thin shimmerings of cold purple haze. And beyond all else he glimpsed an infinite gulf of darkness, where solid and semi-solid forms were known only by their windy stirrings, and cloudy patterns of force seemed to superimpose order on chaos and hold forth a key to all the paradoxes and arcana of the worlds we know. (*DH* 104)

Perhaps it is this same "infinite gulf of darkness" past even Ultimate Chaos that Crawford Tillinghast experienced as his visions from beyond "gradually gave way to a more horrible conception; that of utter absolute solitude in infinite, sightless, soundless space" (*D* 93). Certainly it is the same "chaos and pandemonium" that the music of Erich Zann invoked, finally causing the narrator to flee from "the blackness of space illimitable; unimagined space alive with motion and music, and having no semblance to anything on earth" (*DH* 90).

We have seen that Lovecraft's worldview provided both the motivation to write supernatural fiction and the opportunity for unlimited speculation as to the vistas that lie forever beyond our ken. It also set him the challenge to envision and describe such vistas. The resulting cosmic imagery in Lovecraft's fiction is a natural and cohesive outgrowth of his philosophical position as expressed in letters and essays. Kaleidoscopic visions, weird sounds, alien rhythms, disturbing outlines and proportions, geometrical figures and patterns, asymmetry, and Ultimate Chaos and the black void beyond: all are motifs he wove through his fiction to convey cosmic horror. Such imagery is the concentrated essence of Lovecraft's unique artistic achievement, the purest expression of his imaginative genius.

Notes

1. The importance of this passage was first pointed out by David E. Schultz in his essay "The Lack of Continuity in *Fungi from Yuggoth*," *CoC* No. 20 (Eastertide 1984): 15. Schultz contends that HPL's sonnet sequence is not a connected narrative but "a congeries of dreams and memories." He supports this ingenious theory by citing this passage and also the passage from "Beyond the Wall of Sleep" above.

2. Cf. Crawford Tillinghast's boast in "From Beyond" (1920): "'We shall overleap time, space, and dimensions, and without bodily motion peer to the bottom of creation'" (*D* 91).

3. S. T. Joshi has noted the influence of Hugh Elliot's *Modern Science and Materialism* (New York: Longmans, Green & Co., 1919) on HPL's thought regarding man's sensory limitations. Cf. pp. 2–3: "Let us first ask why it is that all past efforts to solve ultimate riddles have failed, and why it is that they must continue to fail. It is, in the first place, due to the fact that all knowledge is based on sense-impressions, and cannot, therefore, go beyond what the senses perceive. . . . Now, supposing that we happened to have a thousand senses instead of five, it is clear that our conception of the universe would be extremely different from what it now is."

4. An early precursor of this rhythm element is found the section of "The Poe-et's Nightmare" (1916) called "Aletheia Phrikodes" ["The Hideous Truth"]: "A touch of rhythm celestial reach'd my soul, / Thrilling me more with horror than with joy" (*AT* 24).

5. Note also the disturbing "contours, dimensions, [and] proportions" (*MM* 56) of the Old Ones' city in *At the Mountains of Madness*. The city's layout, like its counterparts in "The Nameless City" (1921) and "The Shadow out of Time" (1934–35), here reflects the non-human nature of its builders.

6. *Dreams and Fancies* (Sauk City, WI: Arkham House, 1962), 38.

7. We might note that Henry Akeley, who allows himself to be lured by the aliens, was (like Walter Gilman) "a notable student of mathematics" (*DH* 215). This aptitude is amusing when we recall HPL's comment to Frank Belknap Long on

22 November 1930—less than a month after finishing the tale—that "only train'd mathematicians are able to conduct original research into the question of 'what is anything?'" (*SL* 3.223).

8. Donald R. Burleson, a Lovecraft scholar who also holds a master's degree in mathematics, explains the idea of non-Euclidian geometry this way: "Non-Euclidian geometry involves eschewing the Euclidian Parallel Postulate—which is independent of the other postulates of Euclid and states given a line and a point not on the line, there is exactly one line through the given point parallel to the given line—in favor of some other axiomatic assumption, e.g., that there are *two* such lines, or none at all, giving rise to such alternative geometries as the Lobachevskian or the Riemannian." ("A Note on Lovecraft, Mathematics, and the Outer Spheres," *CoC* No. 4, [Eastertide 1982]: 23–24.)

9. I owe this observation to David E. Schultz.

From Microcosm to Macrocosm: The Growth of Lovecraft's Cosmic Vision

David E. Schultz

Looking back on it now, I think I have never strayed beyond that book [*Fervor de Buenos Aires*]. I feel that all my subsequent writing has only developed themes first taken up there; I feel that all during my lifetime I have been rewriting that one book.

Jorge Luis Borges on his first book[1]

In the long run each author has to write exactly what's in him.

H. P. Lovecraft[2]

H. P. Lovecraft's fame rests on but a handful of stories. This we must admit. He wrote scores of essays, hundreds of poems, and tens of thousands of letters, but it is primarily his stories that have captured the imaginations of readers around the world. His original fiction amounts to perhaps sixty stories; by his own reckoning, only forty-five could be admitted as compositions worth preserving,[3] and even then he professed dissatisfaction to some degree with most of them.

We probably would not remember Lovecraft if his stories had never been published professionally, if his work had not begun to appear in *Weird Tales* in 1923. Nor would we recognize Lovecraft as a great writer and thinker if, in despair, he had died by his own hand during his so-called exile in New York City, with only a dozen competent but mostly undistinguished short stories published in a pulp magazine as his legacy. Had Lovecraft's literary legacy consisted of only his "amateur" writings, he might be remembered by the few scholars interested in the history of the amateur journalism movement. And we would probably know Lovecraft not at all if he had chosen to write only stories in the vein of his "dreamworld" tales. The name *H. P. Lovecraft* would mean nothing in the twenty-first century if the author's literary heritage consisted of such stories as "The Tomb," "The Temple," and "The White Ship" and such verse as "Nemesis."

The inescapable truth is that Lovecraft's fame lies in only a dozen or so stories written between 1926 and 1935; that only his late fiction contains the elements by which we characteristically refer to his work as *Lovecraftian*. His early minor tales receive our attention primarily because they anticipate the later works. They contain the seeds that may have withered and died following a homecoming that could have remained only Lovecraft's humiliation but which instead became his triumph.

Nearly all Lovecraft's stories express his worldview. In so doing, they are *true* stories. That is not to say that they relate events that actually happened; rather they express intimately Lovecraft's understanding of his world. The same can hardly be said of the hundreds of forgotten pulp writers and amateur journalists of Lovecraft's day. The vast bulk of stories published in amateur journals and pulp magazines will remain unread in our day because their authors have told us nothing to make us wonder. But Lovecraft's later work beckons us to read and reread it because it alone attained the full realization of his cosmic outlook.

The growth of Lovecraft's cosmic vision is most evident in comparing his early stories to his later stories. Many critics have rightly noted that the stories from the latter half of Lovecraft's career basically are rewritten versions of his earlier tales, and that the late incarnations are superior in their handling of themes expressed clumsily or cursorily in the earlier stories. Such themes as "dream-life, strange shadow, and cosmic 'outsideness',"[4] madness, revivification of the dead, the survival of the ancient in modern times, decay and degeneration, the loss of, change in, or transposition of identity, the relative unimportance of humans (or any entities, for that matter) when seen from a cosmic point of view, and his unique antimythology and key and gateway theme permeate the corpus of his fiction. They were always part of Lovecraft's personal and literary makeup and are evident throughout his work, but over time they assumed an ever-broadening view of the cosmos. Why did Lovecraft, either consciously or unconsciously, rewrite his early stories into new tales with the same essential themes but with greater power and scope? The reason, quite simply, lies in the emotional awakening, the profound change in outlook that occurred as a result of his New York exile of 1924–26.

The changes that worked to temper Lovecraft's fiction may be separated into four categories:

1. Changes in Lovecraft's personality
2. Changes in point of view in his stories
3. Changes in the subject matter of his stories
4. Changes in his writing style

Of course, these areas do not have sharply defined boundaries, and exceptions and overlapping will be seen. Few people change so much as they mature that their former selves disappear entirely. The same is true of H. P. Lovecraft. Let us begin by examining how changes in personality affected Lovecraft's writing.

The first step in Lovecraft's reaching out had begun when he joined the amateur journalism movement in 1914. At that time, a young man of twenty-four, Lovecraft was still under his mother's protective wing. For most of his early years he had been reclusive and subject to nervous strain. But in joining the movement he began to make new friends, to get out and experience the world, to embark cautiously on his famous travels. As Lovecraft once remarked:

> When the kindly hand of amateurdom was first extended to me, I was as close to the state of vegetation as any animal well can be. . . . With the advent of the United [Amateur Press Association] I obtained a renewed will to live; a renewed sense of existence as other than a superfluous weight; and found a sphere in which I could feel that my efforts were not wholly futile. For the first time I could imagine that my clumsy gropings after art were a little more than faint cries lost in the unlistening void. . . . What Amateur Journalism has given me is—life itself.[5]

Lovecraft, with his laureateships and presidencies, became a conspicuous and respected figure among his many new friends and colleagues. As exhilarating as amateur journalism was for Lovecraft, he found later professional publication to be an even more heady experience. He was pleased to see his work in professional magazines, even if only in the lowly pulps, as evidenced by the way he carried on about being paid and having his name in print,[6] despite his professed disdain for both.

The death of Lovecraft's mother in 1921 both forced him into the real world and freed him to grow, but for a time Lovecraft remained a rather naive fellow; a man of great intellect but one who was ignorant of the ways of the world. Lovecraft, upon later reflection, recognized how long his immaturity perdured. He was chagrined in January 1937 to read the transcript of a letter he had written in 1924 to Edwin Baird,[7] editor of the new *Weird Tales* magazine, from his days as a novice entering the world of professional writing. Lovecraft's comments on that letter, written a few months before his death, are telling:

> Well—about that damn letter—I gape with mortification at its egotistical smugness, florid purple passages, ostentatious exhibitionism, ponderous jauntiness, and general callowness. It wouldn't be so bad if I had written it at thirteen

or twenty-three—but at *thirty-three!* What a complacent, self-assured, egocentric jackass I was in those days! . . .

Well, the excuse, if any, is this: that the invalidism and seclusion of my earlier years had left me, at thirty-three, as naive and inexperienced and unused to dealings with the world as most are at seventeen or eighteen. As you see by the letter, I had only just burst out of a shell of retirement, and was finding the external world as novel and fascinating as a kid finds it. I was drunk with a sense of expansion, as it were—fascinated by new scenes (I'd just been to New Hampshire, Salem, Marblehead, New York, and Cleveland for the first time) and allured by the will o' the wisp of literary success (first *Weird Tales* placements the year before, and the future rosily imagined)—so that my whole psychology was that of a belated adolescence, with the usual egotism, pompous writing, jauntiness, and show-off tendencies of the callow. It is hard for me to recapture the mood of that far-off age—but very obviously, I thought I was quite a guy. Probably—in fact, certainly—I had a better time then than I have now . . . but only because I didn't realise what a vacuous, snobbish, and complacent ass I was.[8]

As Lovecraft noted, in 1924 he was getting his first taste of professional publication. He married shortly after he wrote his letter to Baird and moved to New York City with his bride, Sonia Greene, to start a new life. But the success that Lovecraft hoped to achieve did not come. The spectacle of the New York skyline observed from afar stirred the imagination of a young man who had lived his entire life in history-shadowed Providence; but when visitor became resident, the squalid atmosphere of the city repelled him and stifled his imagination. He was unable to find a means to support himself and his wife, and eventually his marriage dissolved, for what he called monetary reasons but surely for his inability to relinquish the freedom of his bachelorhood. The experience that might have remained a mere personal disgrace proved to be one of the most important positive experiences of Lovecraft's life, for as W. Paul Cook, one of Lovecraft's closest friends, observed:

Lovecraft never became thoroughly humanized, he never became the man we love to recall, until his New York experience. . . . It took the privations, trials and testing fires of New York to bring his best to the surface. And it took personal contact with those cultured, clever, sophisticated (if somewhat blasé and bored) New York amateurs and semi-amateurs to make him look out and not in, to broaden him so that he could cultivate an artistic tolerance, if not entirely altering his viewpoint. . . . He came back to Providence a human being—and *what* a human being! He had been tried in the fire and came out pure gold.[9]

Now, Lovecraft did not undergo a radical change in his personality or his fundamental beliefs; he did not have a "conversion" experience, abandoning his former beliefs and way of life to adopt another. As Lovecraft noted, amateur journalism had given him a new will to live, but his New York exile showed him how to live. But it was not until Lovecraft returned to his native soil that the altered viewpoint to which Cook refers could achieve authentic expression.

The change in Lovecraft's personality was due in part to his many new friends. The frequent Kalem Club meetings, to say nothing of his lively friendship with Frank Belknap Long, Jr., made Lovecraft a new man. Perhaps Lovecraft's short marriage also awakened a dormant part of his personality. By simply surviving the New York experience, Lovecraft matured. He became less self-absorbed, less egocentric. He became able to "look out and not in."

W. Paul Cook modestly does not mention that he personally played a significant role in the transformation of Lovecraft into a "human being." It was Cook who invited Lovecraft, in November 1925, to write a history of the weird tale in literature for his publication the *Recluse*. Lovecraft's writings from his New York days at first expressed homesickness, as seen in "The Shunned House" and the poem "Providence," and later profound distaste and failure, as seen in "The Horror at Red Hook" and "He." In accepting Cook's challenge, Lovecraft was required to undertake a reading program that caused him to consume ravenously the writings of the great fantaisistes. To be sure, Lovecraft had read Poe and Machen and Blackwood before. But along with rereading his favorite authors, he read many he had not previously known. He was exposed to them in so concentrated a way that he could define what separated successful writers of weird fiction from the unsuccessful. Lovecraft was also forced to reexamine the effectiveness of his own work.

Steeped in the writings of the titans of fantastic fiction, the faltering Lovecraft was renewed, so that when he was finally free of New York, he set about writing tales with new vitality. The new Lovecraft was soon evident in his fiction, particularly in the point of view of his narrators. Lovecraft's early amateur writing, the source of his first real encounter with the outside world, had been stuffy and pedantic. Still, it was genuine, because Lovecraft explored ideas he was fond of and resolved them as only he could; but those stories were shrill at times, often verging on self-parody. Lovecraft spoke in his own voice, but like an immature youth growing to adulthood, the voice sometimes broke, at times in embarrassing moments.

Many of Lovecraft's early stories showed off his intellectualism. Since they were written for publication in amateur journals, they showed Lovecraft's disdain for the shallow thinking of the average amateur writer. "The Temple"

(1920), "The Tree" (1920), "The Outsider" (1921), "The Hound" (1922), "Hypnos" (1922), and other stories contain characters who are thinly disguised copies of their author. In reading such stories, one cannot help but feel that Lovecraft is very pleased with his attempts to confound the low-brows and that he sometimes mocks them. Even Lovecraft's dreamland stories have a smug preciousness about them.

Lovecraft's research for what became "Supernatural Horror in Literature" lasted well into 1926. He began writing the essay while still living in Brooklyn, completing the section on Poe (which influenced his final Poe-esque story, "Cool Air") and getting into the section on the modern masters—Machen, Blackwood, Dunsany, and M. R. James, a quadrumvirate whose praises he sang for the rest of his life—in April, at which time he turned his back on New York and resumed life in his beloved Providence.

We cannot say with certainty whether Lovecraft would have found his voice had he not endured his exile in New York City. Nevertheless, in Lovecraft's post–New York work, we see new maturity and a broader outlook. The transformation can be seen in comparing the stance of the respective narrators of "He" (1925) and "Cool Air" (1926). His work came to bear the earmark of "outsideness," as he called it, that made his fiction noteworthy, and that outsideness coincides with the new confidence heard in the voice of the Lovecraftian narrator. Lovecraft explored the human mind and the nature of personal identity in most of his work; but in the stories from his later period, individual characters are no longer as self-centered as their earlier counterparts. Fritz Leiber's brilliant epithet for Lovecraft—"a literary Copernicus"—captures perfectly the radical change in viewpoint typified in Lovecraft's late fiction.

Lovecraft's maturation, both as a person and as a writer, can be traced by examining the stories in *Dagon and Other Macabre Tales,* an aptly titled collection of much of his early fiction.[10] All the original Lovecraft stories in *Dagon* save "The Strange High House in the Mist" were written before April 1926, the date of his homecoming and the beginning of the flood of cosmic stories from his pen in the following eleven months. The word *macabre* in the title of the book is particularly fitting, for it means "gruesome, grim and horrible, ghastly," describing precisely the themes of Lovecraft's early stories. With the exception of the dreamland stories, Lovecraft's apprentice work is a catalogue of gruesomeness. The pre-1926 stories exhibit an almost morbid fascination with tombs and cemeteries, exhumation of the dead, reanimation of the dead, cannibalism, grave-robbing, degeneration of various kinds, and so on. In those stories, Lovecraft seemed obsessed with the grave. Many of his early tales—"The

Tomb" (1917), "The Statement of Randolph Carter" (1919), "The Temple," "Herbert West—Reanimator" (1921–22), "The Hound," "The Rats in the Walls" (1923), "The Loved Dead" (1923), "In the Vault" (1925), "Cool Air" (1926)—focus upon uncanny events relating to death. These themes recur frequently in the entries his *Commonplace Book* that date from 1919 to 1926.

In those early years, Lovecraft considered himself a specialist in the writing of macabre stories. Describing in February 1924 his assignment from *Weird Tales* to ghost-write a story for Harry Houdini he wrote, "It will be my job to invent [an] incident, and give it my most macabre touches" (*SL* 1.312). Nevertheless, stories with these themes are rarely excursions into terror but instead smug expressions of decadent ennui sometimes marred by sophomoric humor. Lovecraft delighted in writing about shocking themes, but instead of frightening us, he gives a knowing wink and nudge.

The Lovecraft who emerged from the exile in New York is no longer a denizen of the tomb, and thus, no longer a mere caricaturist of horror. He soon realized that he had been something of a parodist, as seen in "Pickman's Model" (1926):

> It takes profound art and profound insight into Nature to turn out stuff like Pickman's. Any magazine-cover hack can splash paint around wildly and call it a nightmare or a Witches' Sabbath or a portrait of the devil, but only a great painter can make such a thing really scare or ring true. That's because only a real artist knows the actual anatomy of the terrible or the physiology of fear— the exact sort of lines and proportions that connect up with latent instincts or hereditary memories of fight, and the proper colour contrasts and lighting effects to stir the dormant sense of strangeness.
>
> . . . In ordinary art, there's all the difference in the world between the vital, breathing things drawn from Nature or models and the artificial truck that commercial small fry reel off in a bare studio by rule. . . . The really weird artist has a kind of vision which makes models, or summons up what amounts to actual scenes from the spectral world he lives in. Anyhow, he manages to turn out results that differ from the pretender's mince-pie dreams in about the same way that the life painter's results differ from the concoctions of a correspondence-school cartoonist. (*DH* 13–14)

The Lovecraft who wrote these words had not long before completed the fore-running story showing his new way of thinking, "The Call of Cthulhu" (1926). The fact that Lovecraft described in "Pickman's Model" an artist instead of a writer like himself does not negate the significance of his observation. Late in life he wrote, "Art is not what one resolves to say, but what insists on saying itself through one" (*SL* 5.19), and indeed, the themes that insisted on expressing themselves in Lovecraft's stories did so over the length of his career. As Lovecraft told Henry Kuttner, "In the long run each author has to write exactly what's in him." And that is what Lovecraft finally did in his late work—he summoned actual scenes from the spectral world he knew, not the tomb about which he could only speculate.

"The Call of Cthulhu," "Pickman's Model," and "The Silver Key" represent the immediate products embodying the "new" Lovecraft following his New York exile; "Supernatural Horror in Literature" became his manifesto. In tempering his cosmic outlook, Lovecraft adopted a stance that might at first glance seem contradictory but which in fact was necessary: he became a fantaisiste who was now an avowed realist, like his Pickman. When Lovecraft's New York experience was little more than a vague dream, he no longer returned to his dreamland stories and his macabre stories. He did not stop writing either story entirely. He wrote a few stories in the quasi-Dunsanian vein before he abandoned it entirely, but those were no longer set apart from the world of everyday experience as the early Dunsanian stories were. The dreamers Randolph Carter ("The Silver Key"; *The Dream-Quest of Unknown Kadath*) and Thomas Olney ("The Strange High House in the Mist") are transformed by their experiences. Just as the Olney who returns from his climb "was not wholly the man who went up" (*D* 284), so too was the Lovecraft who returned from New York not wholly the man who went there.

Lovecraft's early macabre stories took place in such pedestrian settings of horror as castles, tombs, and cemeteries. He had once been content to stage stories in such trite locales, but in the long run realized that cemeteries simply would not do. In his mature stories, Lovecraft has burst free of the confines of the vault. The entire space-time continuum becomes the stage for his stories, and there are frequent forays into the unreal world of dream, memory, and imagination.

For example, "The Picture in the House" (1920) takes place in a room in a cabin. There are only two characters. The action is narrow and confined. Lovecraft points us toward the vast world beyond the cabin when he introduces a real book from another age and place and we learn that the old man is several centuries old. The threat the old man and his book pose, however, is to the narrator alone. We know the old man has had many other victims, but we remain distant observers to macabre events. "Dagon" takes place on an island in the Pacific Ocean and concludes in the narrator's apartment in San Francisco. The island and the room are small areas. The Pacific Ocean is vast, as is the sense of history implied by the ancient stone carvings on the newly risen island. Nevertheless, the marine creature pursues the narrator and there is nothing more to the story. It is in later tales that explore the themes first discussed in "The Picture in the House" and "Dagon"—*The Case of Charles Dexter Ward* (1927) in the former case, "The Call of Cthulhu" (1926) and "The Shadow over Innsmouth" (1931) in the latter—that the events of the story cover broader expanses of time (to embrace the history of the planet) and space. They undeniably will affect the future history of the planet and all mankind—if not at first, then eventually. The reader now recognizes a threat to himself, even though the story does not address itself to him. This is the key characteristic of Lovecraft's mature stories. They, like Lovecraft, look out and not in. The events they chronicle have significance not to isolated individuals but to all mankind.

Another indication of the expansiveness of Lovecraft's later stories is that they take place not in the hoary abode of dead individuals but in the ruins of eon-dead civilizations or even in the midst of our everyday existence. In these settings, Lovecraft achieves potent heights of horror. Even though events may continue to occur in confined areas (the attic in "The Colour out of Space" or the room in "The Dreams in the Witch House"), the cosmos now looms large in the background and its presence is palpable. Lovecraft plants us squarely in the world that we know, the modern, twentieth century—a world of science and knowledge, not myth—and then paints around us a world we *seem* to know but which we know not at all; a world populated by creatures contrary to everything that we have known in our short history on this planet—not as individuals but as a race. His stories imply that humans are not the crown of creation but helpless pawns or worse—creatures of no significance whatsoever. Religions and mythologies in the West espouse the belief that supernatural entities act directly in our lives. The situations Lovecraft poses suggest that God does not act in our lives; they are directed by chance.

In "The Shadow over Innsmouth," Lovecraft skillfully keeps the action of the story geographically limited to Innsmouth, Massachusetts. However, the narrator of the story (and eventually also the reader) comes to realize that the events he has witnessed did not occur in isolation from the rest of the world. We may find that we, too, have Innsmouth blood, or may be related to someone who does. The tendency toward this point of view is evident in most of Lovecraft's later stories. In "The Colour out of Space," the surveyor stumbles upon a dimly remembered event, whose repercussions spread, slowly and almost unnoticeably, through the Arkham countryside. We recognize clearly that even though the Dunwich Horror has been eradicated, it can return as easily as it first came and we could be powerless to do anything about it. It is only by mere chance that Cthulhu is released from R'lyeh, and it is by mere chance that he is re-imprisoned. Even though the cities of the Old Ones and the Great Race were discovered and lost, they may surely be rediscovered, and we could again be exposed not only to their wonders but also to their perils. Joseph Curwen may have been eradicated, but his accomplices still live on, somewhere.

Lovecraft used the word "cosmic" to describe his new genus of stories, but what did he mean by that? "Cosmic" is defined as "of or belonging to the universe considered as an ordered system or totality; relating to the sum or universal system of things"; or "characteristic of the vast scale of the universe and its changes; applied to the distances between the heavenly bodies [and] the periods of time occupied in their cycles." Lovecraft meant that his stories looked at human existence differently from the fiction of other writers, as he stated in his famous letter to Farnsworth Wright of *Weird Tales* that accompanied the weary resubmittal of "The Call of Cthulhu."[11] Consider what Lovecraft is saying: against the vast scale of the entire universe, the planet Earth is like a grain of sand; and since billions of us stand upon that grain of sand, we must be small and insignificant indeed. Yet we cannot deny our place in the cosmos: "What lies *ultimately* beyond the deepest gulf of infinity is the very spot on which we stand" (*SL* 3.388).

The word "cosmic" is not a word Lovecraft carelessly bandied about, but one he used quite appropriately to express a new-found realization of our place in the cosmos in such statements as "insidious cosmic fear" (*MM* 225) and "obscure cosmic relationships and unnamable realities behind the protective illusions of common vision" (*MM* 207). Lovecraft forces us to shift the focus from the immediate and humanocentric to the point of view taken by the vast uncaring cosmos. Cosmic fear must surely penetrate far deeper and with greater persistence than any short-lived personal fear, and obscure cosmic relationships cannot be perceived by shortsighted humans.

To be sure, Lovecraft's early stories had elements of the cosmic, just as his later stories have their macabre moments. Consider the opening paragraph from his macabre tale of cannibalism, "The Picture in the House":

> Searchers after horror haunt strange, far places. For them are the catacombs of Ptolemais, and the carven mausolea of the nightmare countries. They climb to the moonlit towers of ruined Rhine castles, and falter down black cobweb-bed steps beneath the scattered stones of forgotten cities in Asia. The haunted wood and the desolate mountain are their shrines, and they linger around the

sinister monoliths on uninhabited islands. But the true epicure in the terrible, to whom a new thrill of unutterable ghastliness is the chief end and justification of existence, esteems most of all the ancient, lonely farmhouses of backwoods New England; for there the dark elements of strength, solitude, grotesqueness, and ignorance combine to form the perfection of the hideous. (*DH* 116)

Here we see Lovecraft straining toward the cosmic, yet still seemingly unable (or unwilling) to get beyond the "thrill of unutterable ghastliness [as] the chief end and justification of existence." He recognizes the potency of terror and wonder, yet he sees no farther than certain places imbued with characteristics that stimulate mere thrills, and forbidden thrills at that. Many of Lovecraft's characters are thrillseekers, like the narrators of "The Tomb," "The Statement of Randolph Carter," "The Hound," and "The Loved Dead," and it seems that Lovecraft must be one himself for the stance he takes in narrating his early horror tales. Still, Lovecraft evinced early recognition of his cosmic outlook:

. . . my aim is merely self-expression. I could not write about "ordinary people" because I am not in the least interested in them. Without interest there can be no art. Man's relations to man do not captivate my fancy. It is man's relations to the cosmos—to the unknown—which alone arouses in me the spark of creative imagination. The humanocentric pose is impossible to me, for I cannot acquire the primitive myopia which magnifies the earth and ignores the background. Pleasure to me is wonder—the unexplored, the unexpected, the thing that is hidden and the changeless thing that lurks behind superficial mutability. To trace the remote in the immediate; the eternal in the ephemeral; the past in the present; the infinite in the finite; these are to me the springs of delight and beauty. (*CE* 5.53)

Man's relation to the cosmos always interested Lovecraft. Nevertheless, 1926 marks a watershed in his career, for his literary expression swung from the primarily macabre to the primarily cosmic. Lovecraft acknowledged this himself in 1928, when he wrote that his "serious literary efforts [were] *now* confined to tales of dream-life, strange shadow, and cosmic outsideness, notwithstanding skeptical rationalism of outlook and keen regard for the sciences" (*CE* 5.286; my italics).

Lovecraft's fiction contains many themes that recur throughout his career. Just as Borges continually explored the themes expressed in his first book, Lovecraft returned again and again to themes found in his earliest stories. Certain themes, images, and plots are found from the most primitive of his juvenilia through his final story written at age forty-five. Although Lovecraft returned to those themes, images, and plots, his application of them changed over time and their use grew both more expansive and more subtle.

Lovecraft's early stories are focused inward; that is, the narrators' attentions are turned nearly exclusively on themselves, and their stories are the culmination of their reflections upon their condition. Lovecraft's "outsider" might be considered the typical figure in stories written before 1925. Jervas Hyde, Randolph Carter, Herbert West, Arthur Jermyn, and others are all social outcasts. But the outsiders of the early 1920s have no parallel in Lovecraft's later stories. The jaded, self-absorbed, decadent thrillseekers of "The Hound" and "The Loved Dead" are not seen again. Lovecraft's narrators are no longer self-indulgent "sensitive" types, but respected professionals—not gregarious fellows by any means but sympathetic, caring men who interact daily with others.

First-person narrators populate Lovecraft's later stories with about the same frequency as in his early stories (mostly because Lovecraft felt first person was the ideal voice for expression of the personal experience of fear), but the new Lovecraftian personae recognize that the predicaments in which they find themselves have implications not for them alone but for the entire human race. For example, in "The Call of Cthulhu," Francis Wayland Thurston reflects:

> We live on a placid island of ignorance in the midst of black seas of infinity, and it was not meant that we should travel far. The sciences, each straining in its own direction, have hitherto harmed us little; but some day the piecing together of dissociated knowledge will open up such terrifying vistas of reality, and of our frightful position therein, that we shall either go mad from the revelation or flee from the deadly light into the peace and safety of a new dark age. (*DH* 125)

Lovecraft conspicuously uses the word "we," acknowledging that his narrator is a member of human society, that he has a place in it, and that he makes real contributions to it through his profession. In piecing together the bits of information about the Cthulhu Cult found among his uncle's papers, Thurston realizes that he has assumed a kind of responsibility to his fellow human beings.

The same can surely be said of other characters in Lovecraft's later stories. The surveyor who narrates "The Colour out of Space" recognizes that the spawn of the meteorite poses far-reaching implications not only for the Arkham folk or even himself, but for all mankind. Dr. Willett in *The Case of Charles Dexter Ward* recognizes a far greater peril in store for humanity than the peril that threatens him personally, as do Henry Armitage, Albert N. Wilmarth, Nathaniel Wingate Peaslee, and others. Only "The Thing on the Doorstep" is a dismal exception to this pattern, and Lovecraft recognized his failure in settling for the cheap thrill instead of striving for a story of greater cosmic import.

Lovecraft learned that to be truly convincing in his work he needed to lead readers through territory they could recognize instead of continuing to push them into the landscapes of diseased minds or through dreamworlds so personal that only their creator could fully appreciate their beauty. He intended "The Call of Cthulhu," *The Case of Charles Dexter Ward,* "The Colour out of Space," "The Dunwich Horror," *At the Mountains of Madness,* "The Shadow over Innsmouth," "The Shadow out of Time," and "The Haunter of the Dark" to be read as bona fide *real* events. In fact, the events of those stories are corroborated in newspapers, other publications, and notes written in books held in libraries, as if to tell the reader he could establish the veracity of each tale if he so wished.

The new realism of Lovecraft's late fiction is its hallmark. Each of the late cosmic stories has its origin in an earlier story of considerably narrower focus. Lovecraft seems almost discontented with the premature execution of his early ideas (see table). Thus, "Dagon" is recast larger, more profoundly, and more convincingly, in "The Call of Cthulhu." "The Shadow out of Time" becomes a more deeply unsettling version of "Beyond the Wall of Sleep" and gives a profounder sense of personal alienation than "The Outsider." *The Case of Charles Dexter Ward* is a sophisticated retelling of Lovecraft's tired "mad doctor" and graverobber stories, penned earlier in the form of "The Alchemist," "Herbert West—Reanimator," "From Beyond," "The Hound," "In the Vault," and "Cool Air"—some of these being mere gruesome tales with a trite revenge motive. *The Case of Charles Dexter Ward* has no such theme, and although Lovecraft first conceived of the story as a tale of a man who sells his soul to the devil, the story transcends what could have been simple mediocrity.[12]

"The Dunwich Horror" is a story of teratological monstrosities, about which Lovecraft never tired of writing (see his earlier "The Nameless City" and "Under the Pyramids"), and his other late stories abound with creatures of unparalleled bizarrerie—creatures founded on biological principles unlike those characteristic of life on earth. *At the Mountains of Madness* is a far more ambitious version of "The Nameless City." "The Shadow over Innsmouth" is a masterful retelling of "Facts concerning the Late Arthur Jermyn and His Family" and, with its theme of immortality, "Cool Air"; however, we now see immortality as the hideous, self-chosen prolongation of life instead of the clinical reanimation of cadavers by mad experimenters—a frequent theme in early stories and seen even in that novel of perverted immortality, *The Case of Charles Dexter Ward.* Lovecraft's epic "The Shadow out of Time" is a great amalgam of a handful of earlier stories, containing elements with quite different cosmic emphases in their earlier incarnations, such as "Polaris," "Beyond the Wall of Sleep," "The Statement of Randolph Carter," "The Doom That Came to Sarnath," and "The Nameless City."

Lovecraft's "Cosmic" Rewrites

Old Version	*New Version*
"[The Picture]" (?)	"Pickman's Model"
"The Alchemist," "The Tomb," "From Beyond," "The Picture in the House," "Herbert West—Reanimator," "The Hound," "In the Vault," "Cool Air"	*The Case of Charles Dexter Ward*
"Dagon"	"The Call of Cthulhu"
"Polaris," "The Cats of Ulthar," "The Doom That Came to Sarnath," "Celephaïs," "The Other Gods," "The White Ship"	"The Silver Key," *The Dream-Quest of Unknown Kadath*
"Beyond the Wall of Sleep"	"The Dreams in the Witch House"
"Polaris," "Beyond the Wall of Sleep," "The Statement of Randolph Carter," "The Doom That Came to Sarnath," "The Nameless City"	"The Shadow out of Time"
"The Doom That Came to Sarnath"	"The Shadow over Innsmouth"
"The Terrible Old Man"	"The Shadow over Innsmouth"
"The Temple"	*At the Mountains of Madness,* "The Shadow over Innsmouth"
"Facts concerning the Late Arthur Jermyn and His Family"	"The Shadow over Innsmouth"
"From Beyond"	"The Dreams in the Witch House"
"The Picture in the House," "The Rats in the Walls"	"The Shadow over Innsmouth"
"The Nameless City," "Under the Pyramids"	"The Dunwich Horror"
"The Nameless City"	*At the Mountains of Madness*
"The Moon-Bog"	"The Haunter of the Dark"
"The Outsider"	"The Shadow out of Time"
"The Unnamable"	"Pickman's Model"
"The Horror at Red Hook"	"The Call of Cthulhu," *The Case of Charles Dexter Ward*
"Cool Air"	"The Shadow over Innsmouth"

Lovecraft did not merely place new clothes on old skeletons. He returned to favorite, familiar themes wherein he recognized new depths of possibility. Lovecraft's cosmic stories work together as a whole. His mythological background illustrates that the world we observe is dwarfed against that background. The events in Lovecraft's fiction take place on a stage much larger than we had conceived possible, and we realize that we know far less than we had imagined. Even in early stories where Lovecraft hints of themes and ideas used in later stories, the scope is narrow. He encapsulates his themes in the familiar. In the later stories, Lovecraft begins with the familiar but skillfully insinuates the unfamiliar.

The single most notable characteristic of Lovecraft's later work is the appearance and development of his antimythology.[13] As with the other themes found in Lovecraft's work, his antimythology was manifested early in such stories as "The Nameless City," "The Hound," "The Festival," and "The Rats in the Walls." They contain brief references to ideas that appear with more frequency and in greater detail in later stories, but in those early stories that is what they remain—brief references to Abdul Alhazred, Nyarlathotep, the *Necronomicon*. With "The Call of Cthulhu," Lovecraft began to demonstrate how myths shaped our past—how the beliefs of our ancestors (both primitive and not so primitive) were often based on fictional explanations for what they were unable to explain. Cthulhu himself is regarded as a mythological creature by characters in the story—after all, he was only a fantastic being represented in sculpture. Later he is revealed to us as an actual living entity. The same is true of the beings of most of Lovecraft's later fiction: Yog-Sothoth and his hideous offspring in "The Dunwich Horror"; the Old Ones in *At the Mountains of Madness*; the Great Race in "The Shadow out of Time"; Nyarlathotep in "The Whisperer in Darkness" and "The Haunter of the Dark." These stories illustrate again and again that what may have been perceived one way in our history because of ignorance must now be perceived differently with our new insight. Quite often, a terrible price is exacted for such knowledge.

The new antimythology was an ideal means by which Lovecraft could infuse his stories with a sense of the cosmic or otherworldly. The notion of gods and forbidden books known only by scholars or a small cult of followers and revealed to be authentic, not mythological, gave power to Lovecraft's fictional themes. In early stories, characters are alienated from their race; in later stores, the entire race is alienated as a whole from the cosmos. The insignificance (real or perceived) of individuals is easy for us to comprehend. Lovecraft's ability to depict the insignificance of the entire population of a planet ushers us into the presence of cosmic horror.

Lovecraft's early stories often explored psychological uncertainty in the minds of the stories' narrators. In "The Tomb," "The Rats in the Walls," and "The Hound," the reader is left to wonder: did the narrators of these ghost stories experience what they say they did, or are they suffering some kind of delusion? The experiences of characters in later stories are similar except for one key difference. In earlier stories we are left to question whether the narrator is mad. If he is, we merely shrug off his ravings; if not, we *still* shrug them off for they have no bearing on us. After all, even though the tomb or the castle or the monster were somehow able to exert their uncanny influence on the narrators of their respective stories, what does that matter to us? In Lovecraft's later stories, we again are left to wonder if the narrators are mad. For example, if Nathaniel Wingate Peaslee of "The Shadow out of Time" imagined all that happened to him, as he himself suggests is the case, his story means nothing to us and is at best an entertaining diversion. But if what happened to him was real, a disturbing thought has now been planted in our mind: perhaps we are not as isolated or unique as we imagine. We now see that we denizens of earth lose our identity as individuals and that our race is but a small entity on the scale of the cosmos. When something happens to our planet on the cosmic scale, *all* of mankind can be affected.

Jervas Dudley, Randolph Carter, Karl Heinrich, and other narrators of Lovecraft's early stories confront startling revelations but only as they pertain to themselves. Robert Blake, William Dyer, Nathaniel Wingate Peaslee, Francis Wayland Thurston, and the narrator of "The Shadow over Innsmouth" all confront revelations with insight into the significance of events as they affect all human civilization. The question "What significance does this situation have for me?" now carries the added burden asked in the question "What significance does this situation have for *us*?" That is, for the human race. The implication of the narratives of Lovecraft's later narrators is that their insights will become common knowledge in time. The narrators stand only at the so-called cutting edge when they make their discoveries. Sometimes, when a revelation is made, it is lost for a time, but the reader knows that gradually it will become known to more people. Sometimes the implication is that most people will never know the real truth, and they are probably better off remaining ignorant. If Cthulhu never rises from R'lyeh in the course of the future history of mankind, obviously he will not harm us; but the implication of his real existence has nevertheless changed our lives forever, and that cannot be ignored.

Lovecraft's early narrators often express desire for merciful ignorance, to be returned to the time when they did not know what we come to learn in the course of their stories. They see mercy in ignorance or forgetfulness—the absence or loss of insight. No less certainly, the narrators of Lovecraft's later stories also seek merciful ignorance following their discoveries. However, they do not merely seek an infantile surcease from the discovery that torments them; they realize that mankind needs to be ignorant of the discovery lest mankind lose its collective sanity. Likewise, other narrators in Lovecraft's later stories realize that they have done harm in the name of knowledge. For example, the repentant Charles Dexter Ward writes: "'I have brought to light a monstrous abnormality, but I did it for the sake of knowledge. For the sake of all life and Nature you must help me thrust it back into the dark again'" (*MM* 182).

The reader of Lovecraft's stories realizes that horror lies beneath the revelation. But as one closes the pages of the story just read, one realizes that a greater horror has not been stated. In opening Pandora's box, the horrors have been unleashed forever and there is no turning back, no matter what we might do to remain in blissful ignorance. This is a key theme in all Lovecraft's late stories—that once knowledge has been gained, the previous state of ignorance cannot be regained. The narrators of the early stories are so absorbed in their plight that we rarely sympathize with them. Instead we view them with horror from afar. In the later stories, we can never escape the revealed horror. In our enlightenment, we have been drawn into and forced to become part of the horror and we are helpless to retreat. For how does one forget a revelation?

And so, when Thurston pieces together the disparate bits of information about the Cthulhu Cult, he seals his fate just as his uncle did. The reader is left with the sensation that a similar fate may befall *him*, for he is now as fully enlightened as Thurston and Prof. Angell. The narrator of "The Colour out of Space," on hearing the tale of the meteorite and its effects, vows never to drink the water from the new reservoir. Yet we realize that the blight that creeps ever outward from the Gardner farm will overtake *everything*—not in our lifetime, but eventually. Joseph Curwen is destroyed in *The Case of Charles Dexter Ward*, but his evil associates live on with their dark secret. The Dunwich Horror has been eradicated and Cthulhu has been returned to his prison, but as simply as those creatures breached the veil that at first kept them at bay, they can do so again. The point is, we are helpless to forget what has been revealed to us. We can resolve not to rob graves or to become cannibals or to engage in the peculiar behavior of Jervas Dudley, Randolph Carter, St. John, and the others so that their fate does not befall us. They, then, are nothing more than interesting psychological case histories. But we cannot escape the implications of Lovecraft's pure cosmic stories.

In composing his later tales, Lovecraft's writing style changed. His later prose became less florid, less sensational, more natural. We are more likely to believe the soberly told tales, wild as they are, of Thurston, Dyer, and Peaslee than the melodrama-tinged "From Beyond," "The Unnamable," and "Herbert West—Reanimator." Along with the obvious change in his writing style, Lovecraft wrote longer stories because he needed a larger canvas on which to develop his bigger ideas. Unfortunately, this necessary change became a detriment to the sale of his work, for Lovecraft did not write long, episodic stories that lent themselves to serialization; he wrote long, *atmospheric* stories that could not afford to be broken lest their effect be disrupted. Lovecraft realized that his need to write longer stories hurt the sale of his work, yet he remained unwilling (or unable) to change his writing style to express less honestly what he wished to say.

Even though Lovecraft's style changed and his attitude and point of view in his fiction became more mature, one thing did not change: the things he wanted to write about, indeed felt he *must* write about. In a letter to E. Hoffmann Price, a hack writer for the pulp magazines, Lovecraft wrote:

As for the proper channel of genuine self-expression . . . in the last analysis, that is something which only you can discover, through experiments in all the lines which appeal to you. The things to write of seriously are the things which seem to you of such haunting and persistent interest (either as actualities or as symbols of conditions, trends, aspirations, and instincts) that you cannot feel easy until you have them down on paper in one way or another. When you've decided what those things are, you will be inwardly compelled to write of them with artistic truth, regardless of demands—truth, that is, to the images and conceptions as they stand in your mind. It may well be that your natural channel is one involving violent adventure—a thing symbolising for you the escape and dominance toward which everyone reaches. It is perfectly possible for artistic fiction to hinge upon events of physical conflict—provided these events are realistically rather than conventionally handled, and provided they occupy a suitable and convincing place in the lives, emotions, and characters of the persons involved. So long as the events are seriously drawn as parts of the general lifestream, with their true proportional relationship to wider events clearly indicated, they can indeed form the subject-matter of genuine art. And the same—in general principle—goes very largely for the weird. Serious weird art is distinctly possible—although relatively few (certainly not myself, alas!) ever achieve it. The genuine artist in the weird is trying to crystallise in at least semi-tangible form one of several typical and indefinite moods unquestionably natural to human beings, and in some individuals very profound, permanent, and intense . . . . . . moods involving the habitual lure and terror and imagination-stirring qualities of the unknown or half-known, the burning curiosity of the active mind concerning the fathomless abysses of inaccessible space which press in on us from every side, and the instinctive revolt of the restless ego against the galling limitations of time, space, and natural law. When a writer succeeds in translating these nebulous urges into symbols which in some way satisfy the imagination—symbols which adroitly suggest actual glimpses into forbidden dimensions, actual happenings following the myth-patterns of human fancy, actual voyages of thought or body into the nameless deeps of tantalising space, and actual evasions, frustrations, or violations of the commonly accepted laws of the cosmos—then he is a true artist in every sense of he word. He has produced genuine literature by accomplishing a sincere emotional catharsis. (*SL* 4.112–13)

Perhaps the key concept in this letter is satisfaction—when the symbols the writer feels he must write about have been expressed to his satisfaction, he is then an artist. Lovecraft wrote essentially for his own satisfaction, and is known to have been his own severest critic. He knew what he wanted to achieve, but he rarely felt he had succeeded in putting on paper the visions that burned in his mind. Yet he continued to strive to reach the outside:

In my own efforts to crystallise this spaceward outreaching, I try to utilise as many as possible of the elements which have, under earlier mental and emotional conditions, given man a symbolic feeling of the unreal, the ethereal, & the mystical—choosing those least attacked by the realistic mental and emotional conditions of the present. Darkness—sunset—dreams—mists—fever—madness—the tomb—the hills—the sea—the sky—the wind—all these, & many other things have seemed to me to retain a certain imaginative potency despite our actual scientific analyses of them. Accordingly I have tried to weave them into a kind of shadowy phantasmagoria which may have the same sort of vague coherence as a cycle of traditional myth or legend—with nebulous backgrounds of Elder Forces & transgalactic entities which lurk about this infinitesimal planet . . . establishing outposts thereon, & occasionally brushing aside other accidental forms of life (like human beings) in order to take up full habitation. This is essentially the sort of notion prevalent in most racial mythologies—but an artificial mythology can become subtler & more plausible than a natural one, because it can recognise & adapt itself to the information and moods of the present. . . . Having formed a cosmic pantheon, it remains for the fantaisiste to link this "outside" element to the earth in a suitably dramatic & convincing fashion. This, I have thought, is best done through glancing allusions to immemorially ancient cults & idols & documents attesting the recognition of the "outside" forces by men—or by those terrestrial entities which preceded man. The actual climaxes of tales based on such elements naturally have to do with sudden latter-

day intrusions of forgotten elder forces on the placid surface of the known—
either active intrusions, or revelations caused by the feverish & presumptuous
probing of men into the unknown. Often the merest *hint* that such a forgotten
elder force *may* exist is the most effective sort of a climax—indeed, I am not
sure but that this may be the *only* sort of climax possible in a truly mature fantasy. I have had many severe criticisms because of the *concrete and tangible* nature
of some of my "cosmic horrors". Variants of the general theme include defeats
of the visible laws of time—strange juxtapositions of widely separated aeons—
and transcensions of the boundary-lines of Euclidean space; these, & the always-
fruitful device of a human voyage into forbidden celestial deeps. In every one of
these seemingly extravagant conceptions there is a certain amount of imaginative
satisfaction for a very genuine emotional need of mankind—if only the subject
be handled with adequate subtlety & convincingness. (*SL* 4.70–71)

Note that Lovecraft said his critics accused him of making his "cosmic horrors" too concrete. Quite obviously they have missed the point of his stories.
When Lovecraft wrote of Great Cthulhu and described him at length, he was
not trying to frighten with the mere description of a monster. In the first place,
he is trying to bear out that what had hitherto been represented only artistically
(and therefore imaginatively) was actually a real, living entity—the very thing
Wilcox had represented in clay. In the second, Lovecraft has no intention of
frightening us with a monster. That is far too obvious. He is trying to unsettle
us with "a single glimpse of forbidden aeons." In other words, the rising of
Cthulhu from R'lyeh was certainly a harrowing experience for Johansen and his
men, as evidenced in Johansen's personal account in his diary. However, the
reader of "The Call of Cthulhu" gets Johansen's story third-hand, as retold in
an account "found among the papers of the late Francis Wayland Thurston"
and which presumably could be corroborated by following the paper trail
Thurston himself had followed. The reader suffers a more profound sense of
horror realizing he does not know much about the universe he lives in; that
somewhere Cthulhu still lives and that "what has sunk may rise."

   Likewise, in Lovecraft's other stories, we are not supposed to be frightened
by the mere presence of star-headed crinoids, cone-shaped prehistoric extraterrestrials, the twin hybrid offspring of an invisible, extradimensional creature
and a human mother, or the half-amphibian inhabitants of Innsmouth. As alien
and repulsive as they all might be, they would be little more than creatures in
tales from any of the many world mythologies if Lovecraft were not able to
distance himself from the common human perception of the unknown. His
ability to look outward with a cosmic point of view allowed him to make the

shudders throb more deeply and with greater persistence when he made readers think of the implications of the content of his stories. Lovecraft maintained that the existence of life on our planet was nothing more than an accident, and he himself lived comfortably with that belief. He knew well that most people did not see things that way, particularly those who professed any sort of religious belief, because they felt life surely was no accident and that man and indeed the entire contents of the universe were created with a purpose.

Ironically, many of Lovecraft's cosmic stories went unnoticed until after his death, and the cumulative effect of his antimythology was lost until his collected stories appeared. Through hindsight, we can see clearly the relationships between his late stories. But we must remember that Lovecraft's frustration with the sometimes poor reception of those stories lay in the fact that his readers did not see the full scope of his work as he saw it. "The Call of Cthulhu," *At the Mountains of Madness,* "The Shadow over Innsmouth," and "The Shadow out of Time" were not published until after newer stories espousing his antimythology had already been written and sometimes published. Indeed, had Lovecraft had his way, the novels *The Dream-Quest of Unknown Kadath* and *The Case of Charles Dexter Ward* would not have been published as he left them. And during Lovecraft's lifetime, he had to be content that his popularity lay primarily with his early macabre stories of the 1920s, which remained the mainstay of *Weird Tales* magazine and the *"Not at Night"* collections.

Lovecraft is recognized as a writer whose encouragement of aspiring writers was tireless. It would be gratifying to think that Lovecraft saw promise for himself in the words he wrote to Clark Ashton Smith on 27 December 1925, only four months after he wrote "The Horror at Red Hook" and on the brink of his own cosmic maturation:

> They [Benjamin De Casseres and George Sterling] agree in preferring your weird, cosmic, Saturn's-ring attitude & mood to your more mundane phases of expression—an opinion in which I concur, notwithstanding the high merit & unfailing charm of your amatory verses. What they mean, I take it, is exactly what I have contended—that your supreme gift of vision, the gift which towers above all others & carves out for you an unique place in literature, is that which reveals to you strange shapes beyond the Milky Way, & portentous patterns in the dark stars about undreamt-of spiral nebulae. This gift involves an outlook & attitude which no one has ever had before, (for others can't help linking up their allegedly cosmic vistas with petty terrestrial considerations) & which probably no one will ever have again. It is admittedly caviar to the herd—but no less great on that account, & no less to be fostered & developed to its

maximum for the benefit of the few who can give it their awed & breathless appreciation. (*SL* 2.33–34)

Notes

1. "An Autobiographical Essay," in *The Aleph and Other Stories: 1933–1969* (New York: Dutton, 1978), 225.

2. HPL to Henry Kuttner, 16 April 1936; *Letters to Henry Kuttner* (West Warwick, RI: Necronomicon Press, 1990), 15.

3. See HPL's list "Tales of H. P. Lovecraft" in *Lovecraft at Last* (Arlington, VA: Carrolton-Clark, 1975), 224–25.

4. These terms are HPL's own; see his "[Biographical Notice]" (1928) from *The Best Short Stories of 1928 and the Yearbook of the American Short Story*; in *CE* 5.286.

5. "What Amateurdom and I Have Done for Each Other" (1921), *CE* 1.273.

6. "In the sub. we saw Houtain's *Home Brew* on sale, and I picked up a copy with sophisticated nonchalance and pointed out my name and work. Reg'lar author'n' ever'thin'" (HPL to Maurice Moe, 18 May 1922; *SL* 1.179). HPL despised *Home Brew* and was justifiably displeased with his Herbert West stories that appeared there, and yet that did not stop him from bragging about being a published author.

7. HPL to Edwin Baird, 3 February 1924 (*SL* 1.294–304). A complete, more accurate transcript of this letter appears in *Lovecraft at Last,* pp. 200–211. The transcript was prepared by Willis Conover, Jr., a teen-aged amateur publisher, who had acquired HPL's original typed letter and wished to publish it.

8. *Lovecraft at Last*, 226–27.

9. W. Paul Cook, *In Memoriam: H. P. Lovecraft: Recollections, Appreciations, Estimates* (1941); *LR* 115–16.

10. To the stories included in *Dagon* we should add "The Statement of Randolph Carter" (1919) and "The Shunned House" (1924) from *At the Mountains of Madness and Other Novels* (1964) and "The Terrible Old Man" (1920), "The Picture in the House" (1920), "The Music of Erich Zann" (1921), "The Outsider" (1921), "The Rats in the Walls" (1923), and "In the Vault" (1925) from *The Dunwich Horror and Others* (1963).

11. See *SL* 2.149–51.

12. HPL stated that the threat of Joseph Curwen's knowledge posed cosmic implications for mankind: "'Upon us depends more than can be put into words—all civilisation, all natural law, perhaps even the fate of the solar system and the universe'" (Charles Dexter Ward to Dr. Willett, *MM* 182). Those implications are not stated expressly in the story. When one remembers that Joseph Curwen's initials are the same as those of Jesus Christ, it seems HPL was sardonically hinting that reanimating the dead—indeed, resurrecting them—offered horror instead of wonder and hope.

13. Known variously as the "Cthulhu Mythos" and the "Lovecraft Mythos."

Landscapes, Selves, and Others in Lovecraft

Robert H. Waugh

It is easy to sense that H. P. Lovecraft was a divided man. To the evidence of "The Outsider" we may add his account of a dream late in life: "I would not admit to myself what it was I feared to confront . . . . but my fear also had the effect of making me shut my eyes as I raced past the mouldy, nitre-encrusted *mirrors* in the hall" (*SL* 4.327). He knew that he was divided. Even landscape, the "topography of my native New England," occasioned the remark, "There are really two distinct personalities in me—the cosmic & fantastic on the one hand, & the historical, domestic, and antiquarian on the other hand" (*SL* 2.259). He identified closely with that landscape and used it obsessively in the stories; as he said, "I am above all else *scenic and architectural*" (*SL* 2.229). With such considerations in mind, we cannot avoid two questions: Whether Lovecraft constructed his landscapes so that they bore specific functions in the fiction; and whether the doubles in his fiction correspond in any way to those landscapes. The questions are intimately connected and need to be examined together. This essay is concerned with what is peculiar to his divided world by analyzing his landscapes, characters, and pantheon, and the subtle impact on his art that the structure of these elements makes.

I

I cannot understand the mystery, but I am always conscious of myself as two.

Walt Whitman[1]

According to Gilles Menegaldo, there are three significant locations in Lovecraft's fictional world—the probable city, the dream city, and the archaeological city.[2] As a beginning for our analysis, the categories are suggestive. But is Innsmouth probable, a dream—say, rather, a nightmare—or a site to be excavated? What shall we say of Dunwich, neither dream nor nightmare, or of Leng, wherever Leng may be? The categories feel too loose. It may help in refining them to outline how Lovecraft discovered his own cities, those cities in which he lived that were to become significant to him. Attached though he was to Providence, he did not seem aware of its wonders or of its use until after his first tour of New England in 1922, when he visited Salem and Marblehead, the actual Revelation; years later he was to write, "Shall I ever forget my first stupefying glimpse? . . . I did not know until an hour before that I should ever behold such a place as Marblehead and I did not know *until that moment itself* the full extent of the wonder I was to behold" (*SL* 3.126). The passage seems to record a religious conversion. He wrote at the time, "How compleatly, O Mater Novanglia, am I moulded of thy venerable flesh and as one with thy century'd soul" (*SL* 1.205–6). Leaving home, he had come home. But it was only after his marriage and his New York exile, after the initial dazzle of the city and his disenchantment, that he was prepared to see Providence through the frame of Marblehead, to identify with Providence, to appreciate its antiquarian splendors in the way that made his writing of *The Case of Charles Dexter Ward* possible, and most important, to begin uncovering the dark side of Providence. In 1926, after living there over thirty years, he wrote, "A good three-quarters of my recent trip took place over territory my feet had never before trodden, and I found one monstrous and blasphemous neighbourhood whose existence I had never suspected—a region actually inhabited by degraded and quasi-human forms of life" (*SL* 2.43). But his exploration continued with zest. He seemed to have forgotten his earlier observation of the slums in 1923, which only now bore imaginative fruit (cf. *SL* 1.269–72).

Here in Lovecraft's experience is a model by which his landscapes can be read. In his world, four landscapes seem substantial: he begins with the landscape to which he is unconsciously accustomed, quotidian and meaningless; he proceeds to the revelation of Marblehead as an ideal and the counter-revelation of New York as the place of horrors and shadow; Providence can now be greeted as peculiarly his own, with which he is consciously identified, a recognition allowing the further insight that it is a divided city in which ideal and shadow cohabit, that it is double—as is the self. The personal landscape, the ideal landscape, the shadow landscape, and the double landscape are the categories of Lovecraft's complex world.

The personal landscape resembles Menegaldo's probable city, except that what is personal we accept unconsciously. It lies in the world we accept as reality, the world as it seems with the accustomed, unexamined categories of space and time, and thus it appears mere background, inert. It is the Providence of Charles Dexter Ward, the Boston of Randolph Carter, the Arkham of Dr. Armitage; on occasion it is the Kingsport and Aylesbury and even, initially, Innsmouth. It is a landscape of churches, since it accepts the metaphysics of accepted religion; it is a city that society has made for its comfort. And as a

New England city at the turn of the century, it is not far from the countryside and includes woods, walls, and rivers, emblems of ordered fertility. The personal landscape is so much ours that we hardly notice it. It does not disturb us, as Menegaldo's probable city is liable to, because our personal landscape exists only in the daylight hours.

The ideal landscape is best approached through a subtle article by Peter Cannon, who points out that "for H. P. Lovecraft, to gaze down from a height, ideally at sunset, upon a gorgeous city or landscape vista, arguably constituted the supreme emotional experience of his life."[3] His discovery of Marblehead is the archetype of the experience, though the terraces of Providence lie before it; and as Cannon shows, it recurs in his letters and fiction, as the first view of Kingsport in "The Festival" and of New York in "He," as several views of Providence in *The Case of Charles Dexter Ward*, as a key motif of *Fungi from Yuggoth*, and as the chief vision of *The Dream-Quest of Unknown Kadath*.[4] Lovecraft of course knew how much his ideal Providence differed from that of the community whose "mental attitude . . . would probably be decidedly hostile to me if I tried to mingle in it" (*SL* 2.176). The ideal Providence is not the personal Providence, which he shares with others. In addition, the ideal often serves "as the harbinger of the horrors that await"[5] when night must fall, as Menegaldo notes, and a very different space appears,[6] which we call the shadow landscape. Before examining that darkness we should realize how much the ideal behaves as a transition. The sunset, so brilliantly pictorial in the sky, acts as the well or mirror pivotal to the moment of self-recognition in Lovecraft's stories, when the protagonist sees himself as a distorted copy.[7] The sunset is that delicate moment of wonder and expansion that in Lovecraft precedes collapse; it is an instant into which we go expecting growth and a future. And many other images in the work, besides the well and mirror, seem to function in this way too: the flash of light, the gate, the door, the window, the harbor, the spire, the mound, the tower,[8] all of which lead further and reveal.

This quality of expansion seems a central characteristic of the ideal landscape. It is a part of the process Will Murray has traced in the idealization and translocation to which Lovecraft submits the geography of New England,[9] so that in the stories a hint of idealization lingers from the beginning around the most prosaic treatment of the personal landscape. As Lovecraft writes of an old town like Marblehead, its "delicate and peculiar curves . . . have a priceless wealth of suggestion pertaining to place and people; a suggestion which makes every narrow, devious hillside lane . . . a gateway of memory and mystery inscrutable and ineluctable" (*SL* 1.288). The ideal abolishes the categories of the personal landscape and opens out to suggest infinity, the world as it might be. And if "our longing for familiar symbols . . . is in reality the most authentic possible expression of the race's persistent life-force,"[10] that life-force satisfies itself by contemplating the ideal landscape, which transfigures the personal. The ideal symbolizes both infinity and immortality. But the immortality is not supernatural; the churches become mere spires pointing upward, in which communal liturgy has no place.

Another version of the ideal landscape does not, however, seem to have this quality of expansion. We may see it in "Celephaïs," in the house to which Randolph Carter returns in "The Silver Key" (*MM* 420), in his kingship of Ikek-Vad (*MM* 348), and in his sunset city as it is possessed by the Gods of Earth. The best commentary on this dream-city is in the *Commonplace Book*, in connection with Dunsany's "Idle Days on the Yann": "Nothing new is found."[11] This immortality is static, because the landscape is not infinite; it is sealed off, especially from horror. On occasion time seems a mere loop, not progressive. This inversion of the ideal is a pocket landscape; it makes a pocket of the conventional world, seeming to transfigure it, in order to exclude ongoing time and that further world of which we have some apprehension. When Lovecraft describes another version of it for possible use, he speculates that only a child can see it.[12] It is hard not to agree with T. E. D. Klein that these regions are tedious and have to be left behind.[13] For an adult looking back at childhood they are perhaps too easily constructed and too complacently acceptable; the pocket is what experience has left behind, the personal masquerading as the ideal without the ideal's risk of infinity. Indeed, in our technical sense and in the usual sense, the pocket seems too personal to be of interest. We recognize nothing in it.

On the other side of the ideal lies the shadow landscape, rising from the depths, from either under ground or under water. The submarine landscape seems primeval, suggested in "Dagon," "The Doom That Came to Sarnath," "The Temple," and "The Moon-Bog," and achieving its main expressions in "The Call of Cthulhu" and "The Shadow over Innsmouth"; in "The Colour out of Space" it is about to appear after the narrative ends, when "the blasted heath will slumber far below blue waters whose surface will mirror the sky . . . and the secrets of the strange days will be one with the deep's secrets" (*DH* 54). The subterranean landscape may be seen in "Facts concerning the Late Arthur Jermyn and His Family," "The Nameless City," "Pickman's Model," "The Outsider," and most extensively in *At the Mountains of Madness* and "The Shadow out of Time." But these underground edifices are simply versions of those underwater. In "Arthur Jermyn," *At the Mountains of Madness*, and "The Shadow out of

Time" they lie at the other end of the world, and oceans must be crossed to explore them. Before he descends, the narrator of "The Nameless City" looks at the moon that seems "to quiver as though mirrored in unquiet waters" (*D* 101). The underworld of "Pickman's Model" arises from "the queer old brick well in the cellars" (*DH* 17). And the Outsider must swim "a swift river" before he comes to the ideal castle, with its "open windows—gorgeously ablaze with light" (*DH* 50), where he receives his revelation. The shadow is underwater, on the other side of the mirror and the sunset, and over it rides often the moon, the emblem of water and an imagination always on the wane.

The shadow reverses the values of the personal landscape. What is there fertile is barren here or disordered: the wood has sickened or petrified; the wall is a prison or, more often, a labyrinth; and the river has become a stagnant canal. In contrast to the warmth of the personal landscape, the shadow is chill, even in the middle of the desert. In these churches misshapen beings worship misunderstood forces indifferent or inimical to humanity, beneath broken spires or shattered domes. And unlike the personal landscapes where people live and die in a perfectly familiar way, the shadow shelters the realization, "That is not dead which can eternal lie" (*DH* 144): this world is not dead, but neither can it be called living nor, like the ideal landscape, immortal. If it is dead, as Lovecraft called New York, it also bustles with an inconceivable energy that can overwhelm the personality. As Robert M. Price writes, "R'lyeh destroys mundane reality."[14] The shadow is the world as it is, behind appearances and possibilities.

Two landscapes are especially remarkable versions of the shadow, the plateau of Leng, which in different tales may be found in the Arctic, in Central Asia, or in Antarctica,[15] and the planet Yuggoth—indeed, these lands form one landscape; the primal planet of the Great Race in "The Shadow out of Time" partakes of its qualities also (*DH* 431). These lands are barren, stony, with dreary canals and stone houses, inset with small windows or none; they are dark, illuminated by a sun distant or slanting or no sun at all, and cold. We are told of Yuggoth, "The sun shines there no brighter than a star, but the beings need no light. They have other, subtler senses, and put no windows in their great houses." It is a "dark world of fungoid gardens" with "black rivers of pitch" beneath "mysterious Cyclopean bridges" and "great tiers of terraced towers built of black stone" (*DH* 254). In *The Dream-Quest of Unknown Kadath* Leng has "lone huts of granite and black stone villages whose tiny windows glowed with pallid light" (*MM* 368), but its central work is "the uncouth stones of a squat windowless building, around which a circle of crude monoliths stood" (*MM* 370), where the veiled Priest waits. The correlative scene in *Dream-*

Quest is the country of the moon-beasts, windowless cottages "in fields of grotesque whitish fungi" beside "the oily waves of a sluggish sea" (*MM* 319). But the two main characteristics of this exemplary land are its elevation and inhabitants. In altitude and desiccation it seems the opposite of the submarine landscape; it represents an inversion. And it is inhabited by ghouls, cannibals, and mimic copies, epitomized in the ever-present fungi; they require body. Leng and Yuggoth represent an extreme parasitism, in which landscape is an intensive symbol of the death-in-life significance of the shadow. The elevation, then, is not a contradiction to the submarine nature of the shadow; the way up remains the same as the way down,[16] or as Maurice Lévy phrased the condition, "the deep can . . . be situated above."[17] But it must be added that Leng and Yuggoth share partially in the ideal quality of mediation. Yuggoth is only a "stepping-stone" (*DH* 240) to the outer void, and Leng often has associated with it the well. In this extreme a return becomes possible.

The same possibility of return is found in another landscape, so extreme a version that it seems a parody, that underworld of *The Dream-Quest of Unknown Kadath* where the night-gaunts, bholes, gugs, etc., prey upon each other, near the tower of Koth above the peaks of Thok—a further play upon inversion—near Sarkomand, the mirror-image of this region (*MM* 334–44). Undoubtedly the city recalls Samarcand, an ideal landscape which it inverts; such an identification is indicated when Lovecraft juxtaposes oriental splendor and the Priest in a burlesque autobiography of 1927, in which he needed mention neither "my voyage up the Oxus, nor my visit to Samarcand, nor how . . . I slew the yellow-veiled priest at Lhasa" (*SL* 2.202). If a parody, the dream is darker than the burlesque. But the verbal deformation suggests a more important point: in this region the sarkos, the body of flesh, rather than the soma, the body of wholeness, is in command. Night-gaunt, ghast, gug, and ghoul, all these *g*'s that must be pronounced far back in the throat, represent a dyspepsia, those various sounds we hear at embarrassing moments our busy mortal bodies making; and very far down, or far above, where the bhole and the Tower of Koth are encountered, the somatic process excretes a sarkotic object. In this section of *The Dream-Quest of Unknown Kadath* a gigantism of the body becomes primary; here is an experience of the materialistic universe as a living death. But the body is so obtrusive, so near waking, that from this abyss Carter is returned to the beginning of the dream and may continue the quest. The laughter, of course, helps also.

The double landscape combines the ideal and the shadow, but through the form of the personal landscape. It resembles what is personal, may indeed seem identical—but it is charged with duality. Providence in both *The Case of*

Charles Dexter Ward and "The Haunter of the Dark" is a double, divided into the old, ordered, colonial world of the Anglo-Saxon and the new, formless, pullulating world of the immigrant. Arkham is always subtly divided between the institutional knowledge of Miskatonic University, conserving and repressing such dream materials as the *Necronomicon,* and the more arcane, Puritanical repression of witch-haunted Arkham proper; both sides of the city are conventional, in different ways, and express different insights which are similarly explosive. Kingsport and Innsmouth form a double, both on the New England coast, both ancient, both warren-infested underground and apparently decorous above-ground, both devoted to the worship of the Toad,[18] but Kingsport clearly the more beautiful and the more preserving of the colonial tradition, whereas the decadence of Innsmouth is manifest. Perhaps the most interesting double city is Leng in *At the Mountains of Madness,* powerfully naturalized by Lovecraft's restrained, meticulous style in that story; although obviously a shadow landscape, the eternal sunset idealizes it, and in that delicate balance the important recognition becomes possible: "Radiates, vegetables, monstrosities, star-spawn—whatever they had been, they were men!" (*MM* 96). The double landscape is the most important of those we have surveyed, for in it the self-recognition takes place that is at the center of Lovecraft's moral vision. The personal landscape we are unaware of; the ideal is too beautiful, the shadow too horrifying; only in the double, that is of us and not of us at the same time, can we find ourselves. The double is neither the world as it seems, nor as it ought to be, nor as it is: it indicates the world as it means.

II

> Ourself behind ourself, concealed—
> Should startle most—
>
> Emily Dickinson[19]

Primitive religion is full of attempts to analyze selfhood, whether through the astral body of the shaman, the eidolon or kera of the Greek, the manes of the Roman, or the fylgja of the Viking. Egyptian religion presents a persuasive complexity in the ka, khaibit, and khu, the ab, knat, and saku, the ren and sekhem, and the ba,[20] beside which the Christian sarkos, nous, psyche, and pneuma seem attractively simple. In analytic psychology we might use the Freudian superego, ego, id, and the preconscious and unconscious or the Jungian archetypes of the Wise Old Man, the Animus and Anima, the Shadow, the Animal, and many others. Literary criticism attempts to cope with these possibilities and proliferations through the *doppelgänger,* the double, and the alter ego. As Robert Rogers says, "There are many kinds of defects in personality structures and hence many ways in which the personality may split up. . . . The fissures which are apt to develop have in common their genesis in psychic conflict but are rather bewildering in their variety."[21] The self cannot help but divide.

Otto Rank, the first psychoanalyst to treat the problem of this division specifically in the figure of the double, sees its imagery originating in dreams, shadows, and mirrors: "From the experiences of dreaming, man may have taken the proof for his belief that the viable ego might exist after death; but only his shadow and his reflected image could have convinced him that he had a mysterious double even while he was alive."[22] His theory of the division had two stages. In the first the division indicates narcissism, which prevents "the formation of a happily balanced personality"; self-love can only contemplate the self, to the exclusion of others, and thus creates the self as other. Yet as a representation of that danger the reflected self can also embody the antidote of the imbalance.[23] Thus in *Dr. Jekyll and Mr. Hyde* the reflection could be regarded as "an evil self" personifying one's own evil impulses and in "William Wilson" as an angel or admonisher.[24] This two-sided function is developed in Rank's later analysis as the duality of the self which assures the individual of immortality while it also announces his death: "Originally conceived of as a guardian angel, assuring immortal survival to the self, the double eventually appears as precisely the opposite, a reminder of the individual's mortality, indeed, the announcer of death itself."[25] The other self, whether narcissistic or immortal, promises an autonomy that cannot conceal the individual's actual limitation and dependence. This ambiguity of the other self is summarized by C. F. Keppler: "In the vast majority of cases the harm done to the first self by the second is harm as catastrophic as harm can be. But also in the vast majority of cases it is not a harm that narrows the first self . . . ; it may . . . kill him at last, but it does not lessen him."[26] It offers an extreme therapy.

We speculate with other selves the selves we might be. "I imagine my ego is being viewed through a lens: all the forms which move around me are egos," wrote E. T. A. Hoffmann.[27] Thus the other self, as in Borges's "The Other" or Heinlein's "By His Bootstraps," may be regarded as a study in alternate times, revealing the possibilities of personality as it might exfoliate, or in memory, revealing more objectively now what we were once, when our sense of self was distorted by past immediate concerns; in the other self we reflect on what the self has been or might be, whether as threat, accusation, complacence, or promise. This connection of the other self to the past or future is treated at length by

Harold Frisch in *A Remembered Future*. If "every text from the past is a revenant and every revenant . . . a kind of text," Ivan's other in *The Brothers Karamazov* becomes "a way of reading the literary inheritance of the past, and every such reading involves a change in the pattern as delivered."[28] In *The Dybbuk* the revenant's "unappeased search" arises from "the frustrations of the student of ancient words who is not content with mere antiquity." His possession of his betrothed "is a source of ecstasy, a traumatic release from an environment dominated by bourgeois narrowness and rabbinical obscurantism," and aims at a significance "closed up in the ancient texts" which he must transform and transmit to the future.[29] This other self changes our reading of the self and of the world and demands an action that corresponds to the new reading.

This pervasive phenomenon of the divided self suggests that such a self might parallel our physical nature; to such a speculation the description of dominance and non-dominance in the hemispheres of the brain may offer an insight. Whereas the dominant hemisphere is more analytic and verbal, concerned with parts, the non-dominant working at synthetic tasks sees parts as meaningful only within a context such as visual and tactile images, the recognition of faces,[30] and song.[31] Stimulation of the non-dominant side is associated with feelings of otherness and admonition and of displeasure.[32] Dominance sees a world of parts which it can manipulate, non-dominance a world of recognition and meaning in which it can share. Of such polarities the self and the other can be constituted.

It has been easy, perhaps too easy, to say with which of his characters Lovecraft identified. Whipple, Angell, Willett, Olney, Armitage, and Peaslee, those scholarly, bookish gentlemen who believe the world makes sense, who gather material carefully and prefer a retired existence, have embodied their creator to several readers: "It is manifest that many . . . are projections of the author," Lévy writes.[33] I would agree, especially in regard to their age. The identification seems casual, given his habit with many correspondents to refer to himself as "your old Grandpa" (*SL* 1.284) while still in his early thirties. He used the avuncular pose to place himself in an earlier time, preferably the America of the Colonies or the England of Queen Anne; but the pose seems second nature, employed so continuously: his age becomes a conscious concern only when he decides to marry (see *SL* 1.319–21). By 1929 he can say, "so far as my temperament is concerned, I was born an old man" (*SL* 2.307). And so these characters form a sequence of personal selves, aged, bookish, retiring, and finally impotent in defending their conventional view of the world; as Donald R. Burleson said of Armitage, they are "virtually meaningless" in any context larger than their separate lives.[34] One of the most ambiguous of these characters is the Outsider, who knows the world only through books, whose life is "barren" (*DH* 46), and whose background is old indeed, yet whose life is spent dreaming for hours and who can only imagine himself young, "conscious of youth because I remembered so little" (*DH* 47); a part of the shock at the climax resides in how old he really is.

The ideal characters form an apparently heterogeneous collection. Foremost are the aesthetes, of whom Randolph Carter is the most positive example. He is, despite his dream medium, expert in dreaming, with a theory and craft in his work despite his "lowly standing as an author" (*D* 200). Similar is Arthur Jermyn, "a poet and a dreamer" with an unfortunate appearance that gives any casual acquaintance "a thrill of repulsion" (*D* 78). More questionable are the sculptor of "Hypnos" and the sensation-seeker of "The Hound." The narrator of "Pickman's Model" is such a dilettante. Erich Zann and Richard Upton Pickman resemble each other in the mimetic origins of their art, though for the one it is a defense and for the other an aggression. Malone of "The Horror at Red Hook" is a failed aesthete because of his poverty (*D* 247). Henry Wilcox should be mentioned, not a bad dreamer, as well as the author Robert Blake, who out of his window discovered the avatar of Nyarlathotep. All these producers and enjoyers of beauty—and failures—are epitomized in Harry Houdini, the master of illusion, whose adventures, a hoax, were ghost-written by Lovecraft in "Under the Pyramids."

The art most of these men create is decadent. It searches out titillations for a taste jaded by the conventions of a traditional art. By 1923 Lovecraft had turned against such revolutions in taste; twice that year much of the decadent program seemed "either absurd or merely disgusting," a confusion of art with life, or "merely ornamental" (*SL* 1.229, 255). By 1927 his reaction was moderate: "I cultivated an universal outlook, and sought the general, the metropolitan, the cosmic; . . . delighting to echo continental iconoclasm and to experiment in the literary sophistication, ennui, and decadent symbolism which those around me exalted and practiced" (*SL* 2.138). But is his implication of regionalism's having saved him from decadence quite valid? "The Hound," set in Arkham, even Providence, would still be a decadent text, as Lovecraft seems to understand decadence. It is clear that he obliquely identified with his aesthetic protagonists, whether successful as artists or not.

But it is the true artist who is fully ideal, in the sense of the ideal landscape, for "art is the gateway of life"; through it we discover a "sense of expansion and adventure" (*SL* 2.300) and realize we are "richer than we thought we were" (*SL* 2.299). For a regionalist this magnificent program implies the transfiguration of the world we know, without denying its conventionality, and yet leads further, out of the world we know, to an apprehension of "the stark, cosmic reality which lurks behind our varying subjective perceptions" (*SL* 2.301).

An art, however, that brings us closer to a realization of the chaos of existence has an affinity to a second ideal character. At least five times in Lovecraft's fiction the gate for the entrance of horror is the protagonist's mother. Arthur Jermyn has two problems in this regard: his appearance and tastes may owe something to his music-hall mother or his Portuguese great-great-great-grandmother; the actual twist of his nature comes from the latter's having been a white ape (*D* 78). Through Wilbur Whateley's albino mother his twin, the titular Horror, enters the world with him. It is upon his mother's side that Charles Dexter Ward becomes possessed by Joseph Curwen. It is through his grandmother and her grandmother that the narrator of "The Shadow over Innsmouth" discovers in himself the bulging eyes and vestigial gills of the Innsmouth look (*DH* 366–67). And it is after his mother's death that Edward Pickman Derby marries Asenath Waite, with her eyes and her veiled mother from Innsmouth, through whom possessed by his father-in-law he becomes a flabby carrion. A woman as a mother is an ideal intermediary, a window or mirror or well, between a protagonist and his shadow. Given such a structure in the fiction, it is enlightening to ask how Lovecraft perceived his maternal line. As for his father, he thought he had died of a "paralytic stroke, due to insomnia and an overstrained nervous system" (*SL* 1.6); he himself was "a prey to intense headaches, insomnia, and general nervous weakness" (*SL* 1.9). Unaware, apparently, of his father's paresis, he emphasized the man's sensitivity. The paternal line comes of "small country gentry in Devonshire" (*SL* 1.5), as he later puts it, "of unmixed English gentry; quite directly on the paternal side, where his own grandfather had left Devonshire as a poorish younger son" (*SL* 1.296). In 1931 he still remembered his father's "extremely precise and cultivated British voice" (*SL* 3.362). The pride of the lifelong Anglophile is palpable.

His attitude toward his mother and her family is more complex. Loving her deeply, he had to watch her deteriorate after she rebuffed his first attempt to escape his early invalidism by enlisting in the Great War, which would have "killed or cured" him (*SL* 1.49). He blamed her interference for his being refused (*SL* 1.45–48), for he "hated to be left out"; the sight of the company he might have joined made him feel "shut out—left behind" (*SL* 1.56). Though at her death he claimed to have demonstrated the Stoic's ataraxia, "supremely unemotional" (*SL* 1.133), he admitted a few days later that "this bereavement decentralizes existence" (*SL* 1.139).

Any consideration of his attitude must also allow for his feelings toward her people the Phillipses, who much more than his father's line were ancient upon the New England landscape: "Maternally I'm simply a tangle of Phillipses, Rathbones, Caseys, Hazards, and Matthewsons—they get monstrously mixed toward the top of the chart. In all truth, the old R.I. stock is perhaps more thoroughly intermarried than that of any other region outside the decadent Tennessee hills" (*SL* 2.237). We should treat this witness not lightly in a man so concerned with racial purity, of which this elaborate incest is the obverse. And these Phillipses and the rest came of that Puritan stock "close to the soil and all its hideous whisperings; warp'd in mentality by isolation and unnatural thoughts" (*SL* 1.222), molding the chaos of life into "a dark poem" because they were "the only really effective diabolists and decadents the world has known; because they hated life and scorned the attitude that it is worth loving" (*SL* 1.275). As dark artists they resemble, without their superficiality, the decadents, representing "that divine hatred of life which marks the deepest and most sensitive soul" (*SL* 1.315). It seems little wonder that Lovecraft experienced in his mother the model of the white ape, of Lavinia Whateley, of the Innsmouth ancestress, and of Asenath Waite, through all of whom, seductive as they are, the shadow is born. Like the aesthete, they mediate.

The shadow includes such amoral and powerful beings as Jacques or Etienne or Paul Roulet, Joseph Curwen, and Ephraim Waite, who aspire to a continued existence outside the range of human mortality, even Wizard Whateley, whose soul escapes the whippoorwills (*DH* 167) and may be regarded as still active in his grandchildren; the shadow bursts with energy. Even the passive Roulets, "fishy and glassy—a kind of semi-putrid congealed jelly; . . . like a mammoth soft blue-white stovepipe" (*MM* 260–61), underground, underwater, and fungoid like Leng, become a vision of "all eyes—wolfish and mocking" (*MM* 257). But this energy is identified with a past attempting to rise and express itself through the present, through possession; and it accomplishes its goal through books such as the *Necronomicon* which the personal self reads and represses but which the shadow, as Frisch suggests the dybbuk does, uncovers, rereads, and passionately reinterprets.

The shadow is also represented by the disparate crowds that inhabit the shadow landscape, "Italo-Semitico-Mongoloids . . . vaguely moulded from some stinking viscous slime of earth's corruption, and slithering and oozing in and on the filthy streets or in and out of windows and doorways in a fashion suggestive of nothing but infesting worms or deep-sea unnamabilities" (*SL* 1.333–34). Produced as though from "unwholesome vats, crammed to the vomiting-point," they are so formless that "the individually grotesque was lost in the collectively devastating" (*SL* 1.334). Among many passages we may compare Curtis Whateley's report of the Dunwich Horror: "nothin' solid abaout it—all like jelly . . . great bulgin' eyes all over it . . . ten or twenty maouths or trunks a-stickin' aout all along the sides . . . all grey, with kinder blue or purple rings . . . *an' Gawd in heaven—that haff face*" (*DH* 194). As Lévy succinctly says, Lovecraft "dreamed his repugnances";[35] much of the language with which he imagines the shadow originates in the same source as his racism.[36]

Nevertheless, those cultures invading his colonial New England are, he also believes, weak: Judaism "has been content to cringe and fawn and scheme. . . . It is the eternal East—you can see it in the Hindoo fakir and Chinese coolie as well" (*SL* 2.65). Where does the imagery of potency originate, that enviable quality of Wilbur Whateley below the waist whence "all human resemblance left off and sheer phantasy began" (*DH* 174)? Oddly enough, it seems to stem from Lovecraft's idea of the Teuton, that opposite of the mob in his personal mythology—personal in the sense of this essay, since he shares the conventional stereotyping of so many others of his time. This Rhode Island gentleman is, the letters boast, "a xanthochroic Nordic from the deep forests of Germany . . . kin to the giant chalk-white conquerors" (*SL* 1.156), committed not to art but to life: "Ho for the frozen seas and the epick of sleet and blood. . . . Let no man balk us, for our gods are big gods, and our arms and our swords are tough! Hrrrr! The stones of towns fall down when we come, and crows love us for the feast of dead men we give them" (*SL* 1.274). Ho, indeed. How much this passage resembles anticipations of the world Yog-Sothoth or Cthulhu shall inherit! He yearns "to spit on the universe from unconsider'd spheres of crystal that know not man . . . with yellow-bearded gods amidst the lengthening shadows of Ragnarok! Humanity! . . .—life—letters—zest—the earth—the commonplace—bah! . . . For me the abyss, and the spaces between the stars where outlaw-daemons stalk unsmiling and unpurposefully. Yah!!!" (*SL* 1.314). The energy and amorality of the shadow, the release from the limitations of the conventionally human, stem from his vision of the Teutonic ideal, in which despite his frequently insistent identification he confesses he cannot participate: "I am unfortunately not a man of action. . . . It is weakness in me—some subtle decadence of spirit—which kept me from West Point and a career of glory" (*SL* 1.291). Throughout his personal relations he represses the aggression of the Teuton, which he can only release in the letters through a language as much parody as fantasy. Subduing the "berserk rages & general pugnacity" of his childhood through his assumption of a "philosophic calm" (*SL* 4.356) he can late in life claim, "I pick quarrels with no one—but the

Nordic's only possible reply to a real affront is to tell the affronter to go to hell" (*SL* 4.357). The power and ambivalence with which he describes his monsters stem from their becoming a double self which fuses the Teutonic ideal and the Ethnic shadow, the releasing expansion and the formless death-in-life. In this fusion the fictional world of Lovecraft overcomes the narrowness of his personal racism: the other, which he despises, and the powerful, which he is not, become one as a speculative double.

Other doubles meet in his characters. As Marc A. Cerasini has suggested, Dyer and Danforth, two men separated by age, education, and class, are bonded in their adventure even as the one is lost in madness,[37] and the protagonist of "The Shadow over Innsmouth" searches to recognize his self in his unknown past, his "dark side."[38] One of the shocks of "Pickman's Model" consists of the ideal Pickman's being revealed as the shadow, a ghoul like the monsters he reveals, and thus a double to the personal self of the narrator, whom we must recognize as a ghoul also. We perceive the prodigy Wilbur Whateley as an ideal twin and double of his shadow; paralleling them the "fourth major character,"[39] the old Dr. Armitage, doubles with the old Wizard Whateley. Wilmarth the young instructor and Akeley the old student, who like Danforth is also lost to the dark side in the events of the narrative, become a double. Perhaps the oddest doubling is in the cats and ghouls of *The Dream-Quest of Unknown Kadath*, which represent the feline and canine responses to the experience of night-dark and ground-dark and shift of moon over all. But the closest fusions are instanced in Whipple, who is "a devil and a multitude, a charnel-house and a pageant" (*MM* 258), Peaslee, who in his dream beholds himself as "the scaly, rugose, iridescent bulk of a vast cone" (*DH* 394) and who awake rereads in an ancient text his own hand, and most complexly the Outsider, who is a personal, casual self reflected as a shadow, which he flees to become a dilettante ghoul, delighting in a decadent ideal landscape, and the double of the others. In the economy of that early story the Outsider plays all the roles. Much of the power of these texts comes from the shimmer of these continuous transformations.

III

Einem gelang es—er hob den Schleier der Göttin zu Sais—

Aber was sah er? Er sah—Wunder des Wunders—Sich Selbst.

Novalis[40]

These categories are paralleled in the pantheon Lovecraft developed. The personal gods are the gods of earth who have been driven to Kadath; in the fable of "The Other Gods" they seem to function as the traditional mythologies of world history, full of Indras and Joves and Odins forced to withdraw in the face of science. In *The Dream-Quest of Unknown Kadath* their role changes, for as the Great Ones and the gods of dream they withdraw to the pocket ideal, that is to say the childishly personal, of a Boston embroidered by Randolph Carter, where now they revel drowsy and truant and "the earth has no longer any gods that are gods" (*MM* 399); these gods are frankly ornamental. The only traditional god with any power is Nodens, "bellowing his guidance from unhinted deeps" (*MM* 406) to wake Carter from his danger of meeting Azathoth. But this unwonted potency of traditional godhead probably owes much to his connection with the shadow forms of the night-gaunts (*MM* 372). "A sea-god of Celtic Britain whose name . . . means 'Fisher,'" he resembles the fisher-king of grail legend in being maimed and imperative.[41] Except for him, the gods of earth, our personal gods, make a sorry lot.

The most complex figures of the pantheon are the ideal, of which Nyarlathotep is the central creation. Lovecraft's discovery of him points at his mediating nature. In December 1920 he had dreamt of reading a letter from his friend Samuel Loveman about Nyarlathotep, "a kind of itinerant showman" (*SL* 1.161), a dream which he immediately transcribed as the prose poem. One year earlier, a few months after his mother's breakdown, Loveman had been the protagonist of a dream that furnished the material for "The Statement of Randolph Carter," in which Loveman entered a tomb, remarking, "This is no place for anybody who can't pass an army physical examination" (*SL* 1.95), a sentence the creative awareness deleted. The relation of Lovecraft to Loveman seems ambivalent; at the same time that Lovecraft admired the poetry of the arch-aesthete Loveman, he could say, with ambiguous syntax, "Jew or not, I am rather proud to be his sponsor" (*SL* 1.51). Given also the resemblance of their names, it seems that Lovecraft may have identified himself with this friend of ambiguous sexuality, "our Hermaphrodite,"[42] who was to introduce him to his most significant cosmic force.

In the prose poem Nyarlathotep claims to bear messages from another world, which he presents through shadows on a screen and through a demonstration of electrical machinery by which "shadows more grotesque than I can tell came out and squatted on the heads" of the audience. He talks "much of the sciences"; but the narrator, "more scientific than the rest," protests the imposture, apparently because the standing of hair on end results, he feels, not from fear but simple "static electricity": if not the message, at least the terror is counterfeit. But though the audience swears "that the city *was* exactly the same" (*MW* 32–34), it has in fact become a shadow landscape.

In *The Dream-Quest of Unknown Kadath* Nyarlathotep seems to have lost his mountebank quality; he has been exalted. But his frightfulness has been, on the one hand, magnified in the reasonless, paranoiac pursuit to which he subjects Carter, and on the other hand qualified in his appearance in "prismatic robes," eyes lit by a "languid sparkle of malicious humour," and a voice full of mellow tones;[43] he delivers an intricate account of the dream which concludes in the famous praise of New England that despite his malice saves Carter from the confrontation of chaos (*MM* 406). His words, "only to taunt" and "only to mock" (*MM* 404), are planned "too well" (*MM* 405). Urbane and chaotic, expert in words but capable of a thousand forms, his most significant name "the crawling chaos" (*MM* 407), Nyarlathotep is both attractive and repulsive; and in deflecting the dreamer from his goal the god delivers him to it.

In "The Whisperer in Darkness" Nyarlathotep seems tangential; his name occurs only on the machine, spoken by the second buzzing voice: "Nyarlathotep . . . Wilmarth . . . records and letters . . . cheap imposture" (*DH* 267). But we have seen him, in a manner of speaking, or one of his thousand forms, if we consider the end of the story: "That whisperer in darkness with its morbid odour and vibrations! Sorcerer, emissary, changeling, outsider . . . that hideous repressed buzzing" (*DH* 271). It seems a constant feature of the god that as a messenger he is accused of a cheap trick and of immense skill. Does it mean anything that we see through the prestidigitations of a Houdini, but in no way see how they are accomplished? Those illusions and the ideal message of the god we accept on faith.

Nyarlathotep is last referred to in "The Haunter of the Dark"; so much does his career span Lovecraft's. But his most complex presence may be felt in two stories, near the end and the beginning of Lovecraft's work, "The Dreams in the Witch House" and "The Rats in the Walls." In the late story he seems a distant threat; the immediate danger lies in Keziah and Brown Jenkin: the latter "took messages betwixt old Keziah and the devil, and was nursed on the witch's blood—which it sucked like a vampire. Its voice was a kind of loathsome titter, and it could speak all languages" (*MM* 266). In the catastrophe the familiar's face has "a shocking, mocking resemblance to old Keziah's" (*MM* 291). As a messenger, as an expert in language, as a "hybrid" (*MM* 266), as a mocker in its relation to the medial woman, Brown Jenkin bears several of the characteristics we have seen in Nyarlathotep. It may be objected that it is the Black Man who is expressly associated with the god (*MM* 286), that Brown Jenkin is hardly a suave presence, and that its threat concerns the journey to

Nyarlathotep and Azathoth. But Nyarlathotep is multiform and unlocalized; as the crawling chaos he not only reaches to Azathoth, he also partakes and mediates that chaos in his own waxen mask of a persona—he is what he imitates. And as such a crawling chaos we see him in the earlier story, "the mad faceless god" to which "the eldritch scurrying of those fiend-born rats, always questing for new horrors and determined to lead me on" (*DH* 44) do indeed lead the hapless de la Poer; and he becomes of that nature too as he degenerates through various styles, slangs, vocabularies, and tongues until he can only chatter, "*Ungl* . . . rrrlh . . . chchch" (*DH* 45), the center of the crawling chaos that is the soul of "the gigantic, tenebrous ultimate gods"—who "dance slowly, awkwardly, and absurdly" (*MW* 34) between the walls of Exham Priory and the Witch House and of the seemingly stable walls of the world those houses represent. The elegant aspect of this horde is the Black Man in the later story and in the earlier the cat Nigger-Man, who points out to the narrator where the chaos can be found, who in the caverns is "monstrously perched atop a mountain of bones" (*DH* 43), and who at the end darts past "like a winged Egyptian god, straight into the illimitable gulf of the unknown" (*DH* 44). We might recall that late letter in which he says of a cat that has died that it has "returned to that eternal Night of which he and all his kind are inalienable fragments!" (*SL* 5.83). The words are comparable to Mephistopheles' boast:

> Ich bin ein Teil des Teils, der anfangs alles war,
> Ein Teil der Finsternis, die sich das Licht gebar.[44]

Brown Jenkin and the Black Man, the rats and Nigger-Man, are the doubles of Nyarlathotep and realize his nature profoundly.

Besides Mephistopheles, Nyarlathotep recalls other figures who clarify his significance. One is the Dionysus of *The Bacchae,* who coming from the East[45] offers a spectacle as new knowledge (ll. 963–75, 1047–50). Multiform and sexually ambiguous (ll. 353, 1017–19), he renders his opponent the logical Pentheus effeminate (l. 822) and drives him insane, so that the world seems double (ll. 918–19). Born in fire and commanding it (ll. 594–99), the god allows Pentheus to spy upon his mother (ll. 912–17) before she mutilates and dismembers him (ll. 1125–36), while around them sound the rattle, drum, and flute reminiscent of Azathoth's music (ll. 59–128). His duality is remarked by both Robert Graves[46] and Rank, who recounts a tale of his being "conceived by his mother Persephone as she admired herself in a mirror. He himself . . . created the world of things after his miraculous re-birth," seduced by a mirror to shape the world in his image.[47] A god of alluring appearances, he can turn suddenly chaotic and perilous.

A parallel figure in Christianity is the Antichrist, typified by several men in scriptural history: by Simon Magus, a false prophet and thaumaturge who attempts to materialize the gifts of the Spirit and in later stories pretends to the resurrection; by Antiochus Epiphanes, who achieves power deceitfully, defiles the Temple, and abrogates the order of the Law and of the sacrificial calendar; and by a resurrected or immortal Nero, who returns from the East to institute a new persecution.[48] In the Middle Ages the Antichrist was both a tyrant persecuting the Church and a hypocrite claiming to be the Christ.[49] As a Jew, he was allied with Gog and Magog who in some tales attack Christendom with the Ten Lost Tribes, thus fulfilling the anti-Semitic fear of the overwhelming horde of the East.[50] And though human the Antichrist represents the devil in a peculiarly intimate fashion that suggests a continuity of their identities: "Antichristus est membrum diaboli, et tamen ipse est caput malorum. . . . In eo enim diabolus quasi malitiam suam ducet ad caput."[51] The relation parallels that of Nyarlathotep and Azathoth. Dionysus and Antichrist are real impostures, who call a putative original into question by standing in its place and dismembering or rereading it. Like them, Nyarlathotep and the ideal criticize the unexamined insufficiency of the personal and initiate the dialectic that will return to it, as the double, meaning and plenitude.

An ideal god of letter importance is Yog-Sothoth: "*Yog-Sothoth* knows the gate. *Yog-Sothoth* is the gate. *Yog-Sothoth* is the key and guardian of the gate" (*DH* 170). This language in "The Dunwich Horror" points at the paradoxical nature of the ideal category, which exists only in order to lead further and become other. The twins represent the doublesidedness of the gate in the reinterpretation of texts that Wilbur pursues and the mindless devastation that his brother wreaks, whose shape distortedly mocks him. But the shape of Wilbur also mocks the Horror, for it is the Horror that most closely resembles their father.

Another figure in the pantheon, much more shadowy than the others, appears ideal, the goddess Tsathoggua whom Lovecraft adapted from Clark Ashton Smith. Will Murray argues cogently that the imagery of amorphousness in pool, moon, and frog can be traced through "The Doom That Came to Sarnath," "Nyarlathotep," "The Moon-Bog," "The Rats in the Walls," "The Festival," "The Horror at Red Hook," and *The Dream-Quest of Unknown Kadath,* to become concrete in her form in "The Mound" and to reappear as the shoggoths.[52] I would suggest that an additional significance of the figure lies in the Yellow Priest of Leng, both in *Dream-Quest* and in "The Elder Pharos." Though frequently male in the pronouns Lovecraft employs, the "thing" that is "Talk-ing to Chaos with the beat of drums" (*FFY* 27.8) recalls the famous statue of Isis which bore the inscription: "I am all that has been, and is, and shall be, and my robe no mortal has yet uncovered."[53] In Plutarch's discussion she repre-sents knowledge and understanding (9), the earth (79), the active (143) mistress of the earth (97) and Persephone below the earth (66), the moon (129), and the fecund cat (149–51)—but above all she represents "the female principle of Na-ture, and is receptive of every form of generation, in accord with which she is called by Plato the gentle nurse and the all-receptive, and by most people has been called by countless names, since . . . she turns herself to this thing or that and is receptive of all manner of shapes and forms" (129). In this light her robe, like Nyarlathotep's, is multicolored: "For her power is concerned with matter which becomes everything and receives everything, light and darkness, day and night, fire and water, life and death, beginning and end" (181). The goddess sat enthroned in Sais as the presence of Nature impossible ever to know fully, near Pharos where another statue of the goddess sat.[54] The Priest of Leng, toad, moon-creature, male or female, amphibious worshipper of Nyarlathotep (*MM* 370), parallels in the pantheon Lavinia and the other am-biguous mothers we have discussed.

In this double nature, furthermore, another complex of Lovecraft's fiction is clarified, for as the Priest and Nyarlathotep indicate a place beyond them-selves they half reveal the shadows of the pantheon; but only one shadow god is fully visible. "The awful squid-head with writhing feelers" (*DH* 171), Cthulhu erupts in the Pacific sunlight; but the first description of the monster may be more honest than more specific narrations: "There is no language for such abysms of shrieking and immemorial lunacy, such eldritch contradictions of all matter, force, and cosmic order" (*DH* 152). Not even the word is the name of the thing itself: "The syllables . . . *could never be uttered perfectly by human throats.* In the story, we have human beings who habitually use the word as best they can; but all they can do is to *approximate* it" (*SL* 5.10–11); it is infinitely capable of reinterpretation. Beyond the mediation of the ideal lies the reality of the world as it is, which no words we utter contain; its chaos cannot submit to a syntax: "So complete is this chaos, that no piece writ in words cou'd even so much as hint at it. I can conceive of no true image of the pattern of life and cosmic force, unless it be a jumble of mean dots arrang'd in directionless spirals" (*SL* 1.261). Azathoth is the closest Lovecraft came to this reality. Whereas Cthulhu has a touch of the sublime, Azathoth is the "idiot chaos" that mutters in the dark "Things he had dreamed but could not understand" (*FFY* 22.6). The model of Azathoth and of the Priest of Leng through whom we see his outline may be Milton's Chaos[55] or Ovid's, but a more obvious model might be their literary descendant, the goddess Dulness of Alexander Pope:

> She mounts the Throne: her head a Cloud conceal'd,
> In broad Effulgence all below reveal'd.[56]

She is besought, not without irony on the part of a classical materialist like Lovecraft:

> Oh hide the God still more! and make us see
> Such as Lucretius drew, a God like Thee:
> Wrapt up in Self, a God without a Thought,
> Regardless of our merit or default.[57]

What Pope views with horror, Lovecraft views with stoicism. We cannot live if we lift the veil of the Priest of Leng, because behind it lies neither life nor death but an absolute, aimless, meaningless energy. We approach the shadow, interpret it, draw back from it, never become immediate with it; and if it wells up in us, we are no longer there. Most radically, Azathoth is no thing at all but an inept word that cloaks "the monstrous nuclear chaos" (*DH* 256) on the other side of our spatial and temporal categories; it is the *Ding an sich* as a limiting concept. Past it we cannot go, only approach it through the doubles it forms with the ideal. The world as it is is only comprehensible next to the world as it ought to be; so the cosmos "seethes on behind its veil of subjective aspects" (*SL* 3.371).

IV

What lies *ultimately* beyond the deepest gulf of infinity is the very spot on which we stand. (*SL* 3.388)

H. P. Lovecraft

What more can we say of the personal, the ideal, the shadow, and the double? How do they actually function in a story, and what aesthetic significance do they bear?

Clearly they have a complex relation to other categories of the self. The personal closely resembles the ego as a normative self; I wish to emphasize the conventional and, as it were, invisible aspect it wears in our self-image. Most of the time we live either unconscious of how we regard ourselves, albeit not inactive in such regard, or when superficially oppressed by our day-to-day living offer merely functional selves to ourselves and others; jobs or principles or ages seem handiest as identities. The personal landscape, role, or god provides the most immediately useful way to live. The personal is the background upon which the foreground of the Hegelian dialectic of the other three categories is played out. The analytic mode of the personal is dominant, whereas the mode of the other three categories belongs to the non-dominant, synthetic; by the same token it is the non-dominant that presents the otherness of the ideal and shadow and only through recognition returns us to the dominant.

But if the personal and the double have to do with the self, the ideal and the shadow are almost always pictured as the other. The ideal resembles slightly the inflated nature of the superego, by which the personal is found wanting. The aesthetes may be supercilious towards the scholars. The ideal involves "the expansion of the ego through the imaginative breaking down of the laws of time, space, and matter, and the flight of the etherealised personality" (*SL* 3.270). But such a critical aspect of the ideal is muted. Aestheticism predominates as simple delight or wish-fulfillment; and it is such archetypes as the Anima, the Androgyne, and the Transformation which allow the ideal to appear so intimate and dynamic. It is the place where encounter occurs. So rich are the ideal landscape, character, and god that they seem to have proliferated in our analysis; like the ka of Egypt, finer and finer distinctions become necessary to qualify the spirit of the ideal—it is the house of mirrors; and the mirror seems its central symbol. Mirror, ocean, lake, well, gate, mound, tower, picture, sunset, "Those images that yet / Fresh images beget."[58] Typical of this category is a flash of light, or the screen by which Nyarlathotep conceals and reveals. The veil of the Priest of Leng is such a screen; behind it lies the horror of Nature as Azathoth. The ideal seems especially erected to function as an inexhaustibility. Of it Lovecraft wrote movingly, "The illusion of being poised on the edge of the infinite amidst a *vast cosmic unfolding* which *might* reveal *almost* anything . . . is *absolutely necessary* to an even tolerable *happiness* on my part" (*SL* 3.125). Yet for all this multiplication of images, the ideal originates in the personal: "I want the familiar Old Providence of my childhood as a perpetual base . . .—I want certain transmuted features of Old Providence to form parts of the alien voids" (*SL* 3.214). This transmuting power of the ideal has much to do with Rank's notion of the other as a promise of immortality; in even so degraded a character as Lavinia the image of nourishing is present.

The shadow is very like the Jungian shadow; it is those qualities which the ego, in this analysis the personal self, has repressed in order to achieve definition and life. But in Lovecraft's work the personal self has above all repressed energy sprung from the Freudian id, so that these two categories, the personal and the shadow, oppose one another sharply: the personal self lives, but in a causal, aimless, contingent, meaningless manner; the shadow other is dead, but intense, purposeful, and insistent—it wishes to come to life at any price, so intensely that its meaning seems chaotic and threatening to the personal self, and seems so other that in no way can it be confessed as a self. This paradox, indeed, may strike us: the shadow is ultimately stupid, without value, yet in such characters as Joseph Curwen and Wizard Whateley it seems highly intelligent. But that intelligence is only an appearance: that which lies beyond our rationality or is opaque to it may very well seem full of wisdom; it nevertheless works self-destructively or, in the rise of Cthulhu, mechanically, and undoes itself even as it threatens to undo the personal world. Perhaps the most important function the shadow fulfills in this schema is the repulsion which the personal feels for it, that provides the impetus that carries the personal towards the ideal; in this process the schema receives its dynamism.

The double has two forms in Lovecraft. On the one hand it is the presence in a story of two characters who seem to the reader, not to the personal self, intimately related to the personal self in a way that may not be an opposition. In the double, in the dynamic relationship of Wilmarth and Akeley, Dyer and Danforth, Armitage and Whateley, or even the Whateley twins, the richer significance of the personal self becomes revealed. Seldom, however, is such a revelation open to the personal self, providing it a reconciliation; only Peaslee, through a touch of imagery typical of the double—the writing hand—, is assured of his sanity in such a revelation of himself as double, even while he feels his self-assurance weakened. The outsider can barely endure such a moment. The other form of the double is in the double landscape or double god. The personal landscape is revealed, frequently to a protagonist, as divided, full of the significance by which it is constituted of ideal and shadow; in the divided landscape the unintelligible person is returned to himself as an intelligible double. In the same way the double god, covering the space between the ideal god and the shadow god, unites antithetical qualities in a mysterious presence that may be enlightening to protagonist or reader. He is the archetype of the androgyne and the symbol of the conjunction of opposites; he is Nyarlathotep. We see a peculiar movement between the ideal and the double. I would only distinguish them, in Lovecraft's work, as the ideal which begins the mediation to the shadow and the double which completes that mediation and shows it forth accomplished. An important effect of these stories, however, is their seldom revealing to any protagonist an accomplished mediation; in this apparently fragmented process lies the tragedy of the self. Only in a romance like *The Dream-Quest of Unknown Kadath* or a work so full of symbols of the ideal and the double like *Fungi from Yuggoth* can a reconciliation be presented as an explicit theme and the work come to a fully achieved conclusion—though in such a house of mirrors the plot seems slack and the structure diffuse. Most typical of Lovecraft is a rich inconclusiveness embraced by a firm narrative, elaborately constructed.

Finally we should note that the structures of these three levels, landscape, character, and pantheon, are not equally weighted. The ideal landscape is seldom treated as extensively as is the ideal character or god, except in the romances and the sonnet-cycle; its presence is glimpsed in the diverse images of well, mound, mirror, etc., which we have enumerated. The shadow landscape occupies a good deal of narrative space, whereas the shadow character or the shadow god makes his presence known abruptly and may in a moment vanish, or may be known only by report, as is Azathoth. And the double is not so often present in one figure as it is in a projection of the ideal and the shadow or in the reinterpretation of the personal. The individual stories, of course, employ these elements in widely differing proportions and thus contain quite different aesthetic effects.

In letter after letter Lovecraft insisted upon his absolute certainty that the universe, in its widest extent, was a deterministic chaos, without origin or end, so aimless that any pattern we might impose upon it, and impose we must to live, would be artificial, arbitrary, and utterly illusive: "the ultimate reality of space is clearly a complex churning of energy of which the human mind can never form any even approximate picture, and which can touch us only through the veil of local apparent manifestations which we call the visible and material universe" (*SL* 2.262). The more deeply we go into the cosmos the more we discover "*a profounder disintegration and a profounder mechanistic impersonality*" (*SL* 2.263). However much this Lucretian view may have been altered by a Nietzschean, Einsteinian, Heisenbergean, or de Sitterean universe, as he grappled with new physical models, his faith remained the same: "Things simply are—forming momentary phases of ceaseless rearrangement of forces which have existed & always will exist" (*SL* 5.242). Given such metaphysics, nevertheless, his aesthetics pointed elsewhere: "It is . . . our task to save existence from a sense of chaos & futility by rebuilding the purely aesthetic & philosophical concept of character & cosmic pseudo-purpose—reëstablishing a realization of the necessity of *pattern* in any order of being complex enough to satisfy the mind and emotions of highly evolved human personalities" (*SL* 4.280). This is the victory of his fiction; in reading it we confess not only to feeling a dynamic and purposive pattern running beneath it but to sensing a deep satisfaction. Lovecraft has to open up his mechanical world, in response to the perception that "although meaning nothing *in the cosmos as a whole,* mankind obviously means a good deal *to itself*" (*SL* 5.241). So art must achieve "the joy of discovering untapped wells in ourselves" (*SL* 2.300) and in many fictions break the way to "a slow, gradual approach, or faint approximation of an approach, to *the mystic substance of absolute reality itself*—the stark, cosmic reality which lurks behind our varying subjective perceptions" (*SL* 2.301). This joy, this faint approach, can be distinguished in Lovecraft's work in the shimmer that glows from the dynamic relations of person, ideal, shadow, and double in landscape and character and gods; it is a joy all the more difficult to attain given the bleak intelligence with which it is pursued. It is no ignoble aim for any writer.

Notes

1. Walt Whitman, *Notebooks and Unpublished Prose Manuscripts,* ed. Edward F. Grier (New York: New York University Press, 1984), 1.63.

2. Gilles Menegaldo, "The City in H. P. Lovecraft's Work," trans. S. T. Joshi, *LS* No. 4 (Spring 1981): 10–19.

3. Peter Cannon, "Sunset Terrace Imagery in Lovecraft," *LS* No. 5 (Fall 1981): 3.

4. Ibid., 3–7.

5. Ibid., 3.

6. Menegaldo, 12–14.

7. Robert H. Waugh, "The Hands of H. P. Lovecraft," *LS* No. 17 (Fall 1988): 23.

8. The tower functions as an inverted mound, in stories like "The Outsider" and *The Dream-Quest of Unknown Kadath*; another example is the pharos of the Veiled Priest. Cf. Maurice Lévy, *Lovecraft: A Study in the Fantastic* (Detroit: Wayne State University Press, 1988), 40.

9. Will Murray, "In Search of Arkham Country," *LS* No. 13 (Fall 1986): 64–66.

10. HPL, "A Living Heritage: Roman Architecture in Today's America," *CE* 5.121.

11. HPL, *Commonplace Book,* in *CE* 5.219 (entry 6).

12. *CE* 5.230 (entry 179).

13. T. E. D. Klein, "A Dreamer's Tales," *D* li.

14. Robert M. Price, "Lovecraft's Concept of Blasphemy," *CoC* No. 1 (Hallowmas 1981): 12.

15. Robert M. Price, "What Was the 'Corpse-Eating Cult of Leng'?," *CoC* No. 2 (Yuletide 1981): 3–8.

16. Heraclitus, *On the Universe*, in *Hippocrates*, trans. W. H. S. Jones (Cambridge, Mass.: Harvard University Press, 1967), 4.493 (frag. 69).

17. Lévy, 64.

18. Robert M. Price, "St. Toad's Hagiography," *CoC* No. 9 (Hallowmas 1982): 25–26; and "'St. Toad's' Revisited," *CoC* No. 20 (Eastertide 1984): 21–22.

19. Emily Dickinson, *The Compete Poems*, ed. Thomas H. Johnson (Boston: Little, Brown, 1960), 333

20. E. A. Wallis Budge, ed. and trans., *The Book of the Dead* (New York: Dover, 1967), lviii–lxix.

21. Robert Rogers, *A Psychoanalytic Study of the Double in Literature* (Detroit: Wayne State University Press, 1970), 16.

22. Otto Rank, *The Double: A Psychoanalytic Study*, trans. and ed. Harry Tucker, Jr. (Chapel Hill: University of North Carolina Press, 1971), 83.

23. Harry Tucker, Jr., "Introduction," in Rank, *The Double*, xv.

24. Otto Rank, "The Double as Immortal Self," in *Beyond Psychology* (New York: Dover, 1958), 69–70.

25. Rank, "Immortal Self," 76.

26. C. F. Keppler, *The Literature of the Second Self* (Tucson: University of Arizona Press, 1972), 194.

27. Cited in Rank, *The Double*, 8.

28. Harold Frisch, *A Remembered Future: A Study in Literary Mythology* (Bloomington: Indiana University Press, 1984), 48.

29. Frisch, 52. HPL was familiar with both *The Brothers Karamazov* (*SL* 2.336) and *The Dybbuk* (*D* 394).

30. Julian Jaynes, *The Origin of Consciousness in the Breakdown of the Bicameral Mind* (Boston: Houghton Mifflin, 1982), 118–22.

31. Jaynes, 365–66.

32. Jaynes, 109–16.

33. Lévy, 42.

34. Donald R. Burleson, "The Mythic Hero Archetype in 'The Dunwich Horror,'" *LS* No. 4 (Spring 1981): 9.

35. Lévy, 29.

36. Lévy, 61.

37. Marc A. Cerasini, "Thematic Links in *Arthur Gordon Pym, At the Mountains of Madness,* and *Moby Dick*," *CoC* No. 49 (Lammas 1987): 12–13.

38. Cerasini, 19.

39. Peter Cannon, "Call Me Wizard Whateley: Echoes of *Moby Dick* in 'The Dunwich Horror,'" *CoC* No. 49 (Lammas 1987): 23.

40. Novalis [Friedrich von Hardenberg], *Schriften*, ed. Paul Kluckhohn and Richard Samuel, 2d ed. (Stuttgart: W. Kohlhammer, 1960), 1.403.

41. Joseph Campbell, *The Masks of God: Creative Mythology* (New York: Viking Press, 1970), 409.

42. *SL* 1.178. In this letter HPL is referring to Loveman's poem *The Hermaphrodite*.

43. *MM* 398. The peculiar beauty of Nyarlathotep may have suggested in "The Colour out of Space" the chromatic presence that is "a frightful messenger from the unformed realms of infinity" (*DH* 81), revealing more than what it appears to be.

44. Johann Wolfgang von Goethe, *Faust*, ed. Erich Trunz (Hamburg: Christian Wegner, 1968), ll. 1349–50.

45. Euripides, *Bacchanals, Madness of Hercules, Children of Hercules, Phoenician Maidens, Suppliants,* in *Euripides,* trans. Arthur S. Way (London: William Heinemann, 1912), 3, ll. 13–22. Further references occur in the text.

46. Robert Graves, *The Greek Myths* (Baltimore: Penguin Books, 1955), 1.56: The god is called "twice-born" and "child of the double door."

47. Rank, "Immortal Self," 97.

48. Richard Kenneth Emmerson, *Antichrist in the Middle Ages: A Study of Medieval Apocalypticism, Art, and Literature* (Seattle: University of Washington Press, 1981), 27–30. Relevant texts are II Thess. 2.3–12, I John 2.18–22, Acts 8.9–24, I Macc. 1.44–50 Tacitus *Histories* 2.8, and Suetonius *Nero* 6.57.

49. Emmerson, 74.

50. Emmerson, 79–86.

51. Thomas Aquinas, *Summa Theologiae: Tertia Pars* (Madrid: Biblioteca de Autores Cristianos, 1952), 4, 3.8.8.

52. Will Murray, "Spawn of the Moon-Bog," *CoC* No. 38 (Eastertide 1986): 20–37.

53. Plutarch, *Isis and Osiris,* in *Moralia,* trans. Frank Cole Babbitt (Cambridge, MA: Harvard University Press, 1962), 5.25. Further references occur in the text.

54. R. E. Witt, *Isis and the Graeco-Roman World* (Ithaca, NY: Cornell University Press, 1971), 65.

55. Thomas Quale, "The Blind Idiot God: Miltonic Echoes in the Cthulhu Mythos," *CoC* No. 49 (Lammas 1987): 27.

56. Alexander Pope, *The Dunciad,* in *The Poems,* ed. John Butt (New Haven, CT: Yale University Press, 1963), 4, ll. 17–18.

57. Pope, 4, ll. 483–86.

58. W. B. Yeats, *The Poems,* ed. Richard J. Finneran (New York: Macmillan, 1983), 249.

III

Comparative and
Genre Studies

Lovecraft's "Artificial Mythology"

Robert M. Price

Though one can name several more important features of H. P. Lovecraft's literary legacy, it is his "artificial mythology" of "Yog-Sothothery" that has most strongly beguiled and enchanted generations of readers. For some enthusiasts the lore of this mythology, often called the "Cthulhu Mythos," has superseded the stories in which it appears, so that Lovecraft's tales have become merely source documents, raw materials for the systematician's art. Readers have debated which stories belong to the myth cycle and whether stories may properly be said to "belong to" it at all.[1] Post-Lovecraftians have sought to spin the web of Lovecraft's mythos ever more elaborately, both by writing new fiction that draws on the mythology and by adding new mythologoumena to the system. Indeed, fantasy historian and novelist Lin Carter[2] once offered the opinion that Lovecraft's mythos is unparalleled in literature for its fecundity. Only Arthur Conan Doyle's Sherlock Holmes legend comes close to attracting such emulation and elaboration by fans and subsequent writers. It is our purpose here to explain as best we may the origins, meaning, and contours of Lovecraft's literary mythology, in the process indicating where and how Lovecraft's would-be disciples and successors have obscured and misinterpreted his original vision and purpose.

Cosmic Indifference

Lovecraft once wrote, "Now all my tales are based on the fundamental premise that common human laws and interests and emotions have no validity in the vast cosmos-at-large" (*SL* 2.150). The element of horror in his stories, then, was the disclosure to humans of their own insignificance in a cosmos that is not anthropocentric. What had been so disorienting about the discoveries of Copernicus and Darwin was not their conflict with the literal sense of Holy Scripture but rather their inevitable implication that humanity does not hold center stage in the universe and is not really different from the animals. The recognition of our position as flotsam and jetsam in the blind cosmic whirlpool is too much for our feeble, egocentric minds to bear, so we will take refuge in any know-nothing creed or head-in-the-sand superstition to avoid it. The recently renewed crusade of fundamentalist "creationists" against the teaching of evolution underscores Lovecraft's point.

The fearsome truth that would destroy our carefully constructed, self-justifying, complacent worldview constitutes the horror in Lovecraft's fiction. This is what made him, in Fritz Leiber's memorable phrase, "a literary Copernicus," shifting the focus of fear from the concrete threats of ghosts and vampires (unbelievable, and therefore unfrightening, in a scientific age) to the very real threat to human egocentrism and religion posed by science itself. As Lovecraft wrote:

> The most merciful thing in the world, I think, is the inability of the human mind to correlate all its contents. We live on a placid island of ignorance in the midst of black seas of infinity, and it was not meant that we should voyage far. The sciences, each straining in its own direction, have hitherto harmed us little; but some day the piecing together of dissociated knowledge will open up such terrifying vistas of reality, and of our frightful position therein, that we shall either go mad from the revelation or flee from the deadly light into the peace and safety of a new dark age. (*DH* 125)

Lovecraft's aim was to show readers for a moment a terrible glimpse of at least the kind of thing that must be *out there*, the revelation of which would leave no doubt of our peripheral and puny position in the scheme of things. It is only blithe ignorance of the real order of things that leaves us our delusion of self-importance. We can remain so deluded as long as we remain "a sense-chained race of inquirers on a microscopic earth-dot . . . faced by the black, unfathomable gulph of the Outside, with its forever-unexplorable orbs & its virtually certain sprinkling of utterly unknown life-forms" (*SL* 3.295). How to break the chains? How to remove the blinders on human perception? That was Lovecraft's challenge—"to achieve, momentarily, the illusion of some strange suspension or violation of the galling limitations of time, space, and natural law which for ever imprison us and frustrate our curiosity about the infinite cosmic spaces beyond the radius of our sight and analysis" (*CE* 2.175).

In what sense did he strive to simulate a suspension of natural law? It is vital not to misunderstand Lovecraft on this point. His aim was not to make the reader feel that supernatural entities (i.e., gods) exist. Such is the misunderstanding of many readers of Lovecraft. Rather, he sought to simulate the removal of the natural *limits on human perception* so as to provide a full view of the horribly empty (naturalistic) cosmos.

In fact, Lovecraft's several gods and devils, as he sometimes calls them (see *SL* 2.232), are *not* intended as supernatural entities. In every story in which they appear they are intended simply as examples of those "utterly unknown life-forms" whose existence Lovecraft regarded as "virtually certain." The idea is that human beings would be rapidly disabused of any notion of their supposed cosmic and historical centrality if faced with the existence of older, wiser, more powerful, and *completely non-anthropomorphic* races. In Lovecraft's later tales, especially *At the Mountains of Madness* (1931) and "The Shadow out of Time" (1934–35), this is made crystal clear, but in truth it is hardly less blatant in earlier tales such as "The Nameless City" (1921), "The Call of Cthulhu" (1926), and "The Dunwich Horror" (1928). Extradimensional and extraterrestrial entities are called "gods and devils" by humans *who cannot understand them* and so either worship their greatness as divinity or exorcise their threat to human security and peace of mind by calling them devils. The Old Ones are as indifferent to puny humanity as humans are to insects. But since their greater power is either coveted or feared, humans worship or anathematize them. When Lovecraft's characters see the Old Ones as gods or devils it is because they refuse to see the terrible truth that the Old Ones are simply beings who do not care about humans (though they may in fact be dangerous to us). Gods and devils, by definition, *do* care about us, whether to save or tempt us.[3]

At this point most of Lovecraft's would-be disciples have grossly misinterpreted him. Throughout Lovecraft's work it is clear that he views religion as "merely a childish & diluted pseudo-gratification of [a] . . . perpetual gnawing toward the ultimate illimitable void" (*SL* 3.295). "Theosophists [for example] have guessed at the awesome grandeur of the cosmic cycle wherein our world and human race form transient incidents. They have hinted at strange survivals in terms which would freeze the blood if not masked by a bland optimism" (*DH* 126). What has escaped August Derleth, Lin Carter, and others is that Lovecraft does not intend to take (even for the purposes of the story) the cult of the Old Ones as a "true religion" in opposition to the bland "false religions." No, Lovecraft means that even the characters who are most aware of the Old Ones cannot face the terrible human-minimizing implications of the existence of the overshadowing aliens and take superstitious refuge in religion, deifying the Old Ones as gods who care about their human worshippers and will reward them. For their part, the Old Ones may encourage such a delusion for the advantage it gives them in gaining possession of the earth from the inferior human species; as Old Castro explains in "The Call of Cthulhu":

> When, after infinities of chaos, the first men came, the Great Old Ones spoke to the sensitive among them by moulding their dreams; for only thus could Their language reach the fleshly minds of mammals.

> Then . . . those first men formed the cult around small idols which the Great Ones shewed them; idols brought in dim aeras from dark stars. That cult would never die till the stars came right again, and the secret priests would take great Cthulhu from His tomb to revive His subjects and resume His rule of earth. . . . Then the liberated Old Ones would teach them new ways to shout and kill and revel and enjoy themselves. (*DH* 140–41)

It is clear here that the religion of the Old Ones is a delusion on the part of the worshippers and fostered by the Old Ones for their own advantage. They are not gods but aliens. The idea is very much that of Erich von Däniken's paperback bestseller *Chariots of the Gods?*, in which he argues (implausibly) that the gods of ancient religions were extraterrestrials.

But Derleth and others wrote would-be "Lovecraftian" tales on the premise that in Lovecraft's fiction the religion of the Old Ones was meant to be true, that Cthulhu, Yog-Sothoth, and the Old Ones were indeed supposed to be gods, that ancient texts like the *Necronomicon* and the Pnakotic Manuscripts were true prophetic and inerrant scriptures teaching a true (albeit chilling) theology of those gods. Lovecraft, by contrast, repeatedly made it plain that such ancient writings merely preserved hints and fragments of a shocking scientific fact all but completely misunderstood and distorted by the ancient superstitious chroniclers. Again, Lovecraft's idea was much like that of pseudo-scientist Immanuel Velikovsky who argued that the biblical account of God turning the Nile to blood was a distorted prescientific memory of a scientific event—the near collision of Mars with the earth (Mars's red color being reflected in the waters of the Nile). For example, in *At the Mountains of Madness*, Antarctic explorers discover the remnants of a fabulously ancient advanced crinoid race. An anthropologist concludes that the crinoids were "above all doubt the originals of the fiendish elder myths which things like the Pnakotic Manuscripts and the *Necronomicon* affrightedly hint about" (*MM* 59). The "daemon-sultan Azathoth" of myth was merely a mythologization by ancient prescientific people who could not grasp the true nature of that "monstrous nuclear chaos beyond angled space" (*DH* 256).

The misunderstanding of Lovecraft's intent led his followers to write a kind of religious fiction in which the fortunes of human beings are indeed of central importance to the devils (the Old Ones) and to a new group of entities, the Elder Gods, whom Derleth created to defend and succor humanity from the evil designs of the Old Ones. Derleth spoke often of a parallel between the Cthulhu Mythos and the Christian schema of a devil rebelling with his minions against God. There was in fact no parallel at all between any religion and Lovecraft's distinctive nihilistic vision. For Lovecraft, the blind vastness of the cosmos revealed human standards of good and evil as feeble and childish projections. Brian Lumley is one of only a few post-Lovecraftians who has correctly perceived Lovecraft's intent that the Old Ones were purely natural and scientifically explicable aliens or forces, not divine and supernatural gods. Yet, paradoxically, Lumley has far surpassed Derleth in returning human welfare and values to center stage with the Old Ones as evil enemies of good humans.[4] Colin Wilson also understands the Old Ones to be purely natural though superhuman beings, but he, too, departs from Lovecraft's vision. Wilson is optimistic where Lovecraft is pessimistic. He sees the cosmic revelation of higher intelligences as opening a path for greater human evolution. If the existence of the Old Ones lays bare humanity's pathetic limitations, it also points the way to surpass those limitations and become, like the Old Ones, superior beings.[5]

The Black Pantheon

Despite the fact that the cult of the Old Ones is as false as any other religion, the Old Ones being simply superior extraterrestrials, Lovecraft devoted considerable imaginative energy to constructing a convincing body of mythical lore concerning them. This was made necessary by Lovecraft's wise choice of allusion and implication. Rather than introducing his horrors directly, he allowed the reader to piece together scattered intimations and to discern the terrible scientific truth through the distorting medium of legend. Even though the cult of the Old Ones was a kind of sham, it did exist and had existed for millennia. To bolster that notion, Lovecraft set about fabricating a plausible body of background lore. He felt that to do this he would have to use the same ingenuity required for a hoax. So well did he succeed that he frequently found himself forced gently to disabuse readers of their credulity: "Regarding the solemnly cited myth-cycle of Cthulhu, Yog-Sothoth, R'lyeh, Nyarlathotep, Nug, Yeb, Shub-Niggurath, etc., etc.—let me confess that this is all a synthetic concoction of my own" (*SL* 3.166).

Lovecraft encouraged other, younger writers to use and elaborate upon his myth cycle, which he once called "our black pantheon" (*SL* 5.16). He wrote: "I think it is rather good fun to have this artificial mythology given an air of verisimilitude by wide citation" (*SL* 3.166) by other authors. But the later additions by others served only to obscure the originality of Lovecraft's conception, and it will be worthwhile to examine the main outline of both Lovecraft's "cycle of synthetic folklore" (*SL* 5.16) and that added by later scribes.

Of those cosmic beings worshipped as gods by superstitious earth primitives, Lovecraft's most famous creation is Great Cthulhu, introduced in "The Call of Cthulhu." Cthulhu is roughly anthropoid in general outline, mountainous in size, and made of green, gelatinous matter not quite classifiable according to terrestrial physics. He bears rudimentary membraneous wings, club-like claws, and a head resembling a titanic octopus. He came to earth from the remote stars before the evolution of human beings and brought with him a race of similar beings, the "Cthulhu-spawn." His palace and city on the Pacific island of R'lyeh sank ages ago and awaits the proper conjunction of the stars to rise again.

Yog-Sothoth is an equally mountainous mass of tentacles, mouths, and eyes. (In all such descriptions, Lovecraft sought to horrify by sheer alienness. The beings who look so monstrous to us are not beasts, sub-human, but rather advanced intelligences, superhuman. *We* are beasts by comparison, and that realization is the horror.) "*Yog-Sothoth* is the key to the gate, whereby the spheres meet" (*DH* 170), and through his hinted ability to breach the dimensions, the Old Ones, beings invisible to us and detectable only as "rushing airy presences" (*DH* 158) in remote places, can manifest themselves in the visible world. In "The Dunwich Horror" Yog-Sothoth impregnates a mortal woman so as to produce two avatars in human flesh to open the Gates to the invisible, intangible race. In the same story, we are told that "Great Cthulhu is Their cousin, yet can he spy Them only dimly" (*DH* 170), so apparently Cthulhu and Yog-Sothoth belong to two rather different races of beings, both antedating humanity.

Shub-Niggurath is a "cloud-like entity" (*SL* 5.303), symbolized as a fertility goddess by her primitive worshippers who portray her as the "Black Goat of the Woods," the "Goat with a Thousand Young." Her cult must go back to ancient Greece, as her cultic invocation is "Iä! Shub-Niggurath!," "Iä!" being the ancient ecstatic cry of the Bacchantes. Lovecraft probably derived the name of this being from Dunsany's fictional god "Sheol-Nugganoth."

Azathoth, actually a symbol for the nuclear chaos at the center of the random and meaningless cosmos, is depicted in Lovecraft's mythology as the "mindless daemon-sultan," a blind, idiot demiurge who created the earth as a joke or mistake, recalling the theology of Gnosticism with its blundering creator.

Nyarlathotep (whose name Lovecraft first conceived in a dream, but which probably stems from his reading of Dunsany who has a prophet named Al-hireth-Hotep and a god called Mynarthitep) is variously depicted but seems in general to be a messenger or harbinger of Azathoth, almost an Antichrist who brings fatal knowledge of the end of all things to those unwise enough to summon him or seek him out. He may appear in human or monstrous form.

Dagon (the ancient Philistine fish god) and Hydra (the Greek sea-dragon) seem to be the deified ancestors of another race of Lovecraftian superhumans, the Deep Ones, a tribe of fish-men. Hints in "The Shadow over Innsmouth" imply that Dagon is either subordinate to or another name for Cthulhu.

Tsathoggua is the invention of Lovecraft's friend and fellow writer Clark Ashton Smith that Lovecraft handily adopted into his myth cycle. This entity, combining the physiognomy of a bat and a toad (well rendered in Smith's own sculptures of Tsathoggua), was a god worshipped in ancient Hyperborea. Lovecraft wrote to Smith, "Tsathoggua made such an impression on my fancy that I am using him in the 'revision' (i.e., 'ghost-writing') job I am now doing" (*SL* 3.95). In that tale, "The Mound," Lovecraft makes Tsathoggua another space alien come to earth (long before the arrival of Cthulhu) and worshipped in an ancient underground civilization *before* his migration to the arctic Hyperborea of Smith's stories.

Lovecraft did considerable ghost-writing for would-be fantasy authors. He regularly included in ghost-written stories allusions to Cthulhu, Azathoth, et al., to create the effect of wide citation by many authors, something, the reader will recall, Lovecraft thought gave his artificial mythology a greater ring of genuineness. Lovecraft often cleverly used variant forms of the names of his own entities (e.g., "Tulu" for Cthulhu) in the ghost-written stories to distance himself from them. Similarly, he created a whole second tier in his pantheon exclusively for use in the revision stories. Those entities appeared interchangeably in stories written for clients, but rarely, if ever, in stories written under his own name.[6]

The first of these is Yig, "Father of Serpents," a snake god worshipped by a primordial underground civilization, by the ancient Aztecs, and by modern Indians. He takes awful vengeance on those who carelessly kill his scaly brethren.

Ghatanothoa is an octopoid alien, really a new version of Cthulhu though less anthropoid in appearance, the monstrous object of the worship of ancient aliens who colonized the now-lost continent of Mu in the Pacific. The very sight of him literally petrifies the onlooker with fear, preserving a conscious brain in a frozen body for eternity.

Rhan-Tegoth is an arctic creature of spherical shape, covered with cilia, supported by six crablike legs, crowned by a bubble-head with three bulging eyes and a proboscis. It sits on a stalagmite throne of ice and somehow acts as a portal of reentry for another group of Old Ones.

Gnoph-keh is a furry monster of the Greenland tundras, variously seen with one, two, or three pairs of legs. Nug and Yeb, whose names Lovecraft intended to have a mysterious "Tartar or Thibetan" flavor (*SL* 4.386), are the "twin blasphemies," spawn of Shub-Niggurath and Yog-Sothoth and progenitors by asexual fission of Cthulhu and Tsathoggua, respectively. Lovecraft mentions them only in atmospheric allusions (e.g., "The Black Litany of Nug and Yeb").

Lovecraft's friends began to add entities and deities to the pantheon. Robert E. Howard created Gol-Goroth. Robert Bloch added Dark Han, "Serpent-Bearded" Byatis, and Byagoona "the Faceless One." Henry Kuttner added Nyogtha, "the Thing that Should Not Be." Most of these, however, were little more than names. Frank Belknap Long had earlier created monsters he called the Hounds of Tindalos and Chaugnar Faugn, but he made no effort to link them with Lovecraft's pantheon; neither did Lovecraft, since he glancingly mentioned them only occasionally in his stories, as he did various of the fantasy creations of Ambrose Bierce, Robert W. Chambers, and Arthur Machen.

The disciple of Lovecraft who became most—indeed passionately—interested in the emerging mythology was August Derleth. He somehow got the idea of forcing Lovecraft's extraterrestrial entities into the categories of ancient physics, making Cthulhu a "water elemental," and Nyarlathotep, Yog-Sothoth, Tsathoggua, and Shub-Niggurath "earth elementals." The incongruity of all this, as well as the absence of plausible candidates for the air or fire categories, might have indicated the impropriety of the whole business, but Derleth was not fazed. He simply invented Ithaqua, Lloigor, and Zhar as "air elementals" and Cthugha as a "fire elemental." Thus Derleth succeeded in making earthly the creatures Lovecraft had intended to represent utter unearthliness! In this process, Derleth began to systematize and explain all that Lovecraft had wisely left misty and evocative. Writers after Derleth have for the most part only continued further down the trail he blazed to literary disaster.

It was August Derleth who rescued Lovecraft's work from early oblivion in the disintegrating pages of pulp magazines. He founded Arkham House, with Donald Wandrei, to publish Lovecraft's work (and eventually other pulp writers as well) in hardcover. But Derleth felt he had also inherited Lovecraft's mantle and played Elisha to Lovecraft's Elijah. At first he discouraged other writers from making use of the Lovecraft myth cycle, rightly claiming that such efforts would quickly muddy the waters and blunt the effect of Lovecraft's ideas. Yet ironically, Derleth himself proceeded to pen numerous "tales of the Cthulhu Mythos" (some based on Lovecraft's notebook jottings, daring to call them "posthumous collaborations" with Lovecraft), in which he introduced the confusing innovations discussed above.

In the weeks following Lovecraft's death, Derleth solicited the comments and criticisms of Clark Ashton Smith (a writer whose "cosmic" outlook Lovecraft had highly praised) on Derleth's own "Lovecraftian" tales and his interpretation of Lovecraft's concepts. Smith clearly pointed out the major respects in which Derleth was departing from Lovecraft's vision, but Derleth proved singularly immune to advice. His Cthulhu tales collected in *The Watchers out of Time, The Mask of Cthulhu,* and *The Trail of Cthulhu* oddly manage to combine a near-plagiaristic aping of Lovecraft's scenes, plots, and even wording with a grossly distorted vision of Lovecraft's mythology.

Worse yet, Derleth would preface every book of his own and every Arkham House collection of Lovecraft's tales with introductions forewarning and forearming readers with a misinterpretative framework based on his own misreading of Lovecraft. No reading of the Lovecraft stories themselves would yield a good-vs.-evil scenario with Elder Gods smiting Old Ones to save the human race. But once Derleth told you in advance that Lovecraft so intended his stories, you tended to assume he was correct.

For years Lovecraft's tales were filtered through the Derlethian grid of "posthumous collaborations," Derleth's introductions, and worst of all, the following apocryphal passage purporting to be Lovecraft's own: "All my stories, unconnected as they may be, are based on the fundamental lore or legend that this world was inhabited at one time by another race who, in practising black magic, lost their foothold and were expelled, yet live on outside, ever ready to take possession of this earth again." No writing of Lovecraft's containing this quote has ever been found. Quite simply, Derleth repeated this passage verbatim from a letter to him by Harold S. Farnese, a former correspondent of Lovecraft, who claimed to have obtained the quote from one of Lovecraft's letters to him. Farnese's penchant for putting words in others' mouths can be seen in a letter he wrote to Lovecraft attempting to clarify in his own mind just what Lovecraft had been writing about: "If I comprehend your work correctly, I take from it the suggestion of an outer sphere (may I call it) of Black Magic, at one time ruling this planet but now dispossessed, awaiting 'on the outside' a chance for a possible return."[7] Lovecraft was unable to set Farnese on the right track, and the trouble was compounded when Derleth circulated Farnese's interpretative "black magic" quote as Lovecraft's own words.

We might compare Lovecraft's mythology to a painting of unusual tonal subtlety. Derleth approached it appreciatively but with an untrained eye and mistook its subtlety for fading. He went to work with palette and brush, as he thought, "restoring" the work of an old master, adding colors bold and vivid, yet alien to Lovecraft's style. Instead of restoring the work, Derleth obscured it, creating a largely new picture of his own. Recent Lovecraft scholars, armed with a surer feel for Lovecraft's art, have set about scraping away Derleth's overlay and, with difficulty, sometimes tedious to bystanders, have begun to lay bare the original vista painted so subtly by Lovecraft himself. That vista, Lovecraft knew, would be a difficult one for most to view unflinchingly. Derleth flinched when he saw it and sought to soften the blow for subsequent viewers. Dare we contemplate the vision embodied in Lovecraft's "artificial mythology" as he intended it?

Notes

1. See Dirk W. Mosig, "H. P. Lovecraft: Myth-Maker," in *FDOC* 110.

2. In conversation with the author.

3. In earlier writings (e.g., "Demythologizing Cthulhu" [*LS* No. 8 (Spring 1984): 2–9, 14]) I imagined I could detect development in HPL's work from an early period in which he intended the Old Ones to be transcendent supernatural powers, real gods for the sake of the story, but symbolizing the blind and purposeless forces of the universe by effect inimical but by intent indifferent to humanity, to a later literary period when he "demythologized" the Old Ones, depicting them in the stories as simply ancient and superior extraterrestrial races dwarfing humanity, the mere knowledge of which was destructive of human security. Now I see there was no such distinction. HPL had always intended them as in my imaginary "later period."

4. See especially his novels *The Burrowers Beneath* (1974) and *The Transition of Titus Crow* (1975).

5. See Wilson's *The Mind Parasites* (1967) and *The Philosopher's Stone* (1969).

6. See my article "The Revision Mythos," *LS* No. 11 (Fall 1985): 43–50.

7. Mosig, *FDOC* 112. For the story of the genesis of the "All my stories . . ." statement, see David E. Schultz, "The Origin of Lovecraft's 'Black Magic' Quote," *CoC* No. 48 (St. John's Eve 1987): 9–13.

Lovecraft and the Tradition of the Gentleman Narrator

R. Boerem

I. Definition

Originally, a gentleman was defined by his birth into a good family and by his honoring of that birthright. Early in English history a good family tended to be interpreted as a noble or near-noble family, and by the sixteenth century the Herald's College, which granted coats-of-arms, self-interestedly and successfully pressed for a definition of gentleman excluding those without armorial bearings. This strict definition persisted to the twentieth century, although it was increasingly favored only by those whom it fit.

Through the eighteenth century and, to some extent, the nineteenth, gentlemen were expected to have come from families rich enough in inherited wealth that their members need never work for a living. The growth and wealth of the merchant classes approached and then crossed the boundary that separated them from gentlemen as those gentlemen married or worked into the business class and the businessmen married or retired into the nobility. Nevertheless, there were always examples of the "shabby-genteel," those once wealthy families who preferred to live in the rags of gentility, starving to retain their empty mansions rather than accept the loss of status employment would have cost them: "Gentlemen should keep away from trade not only to show that they had no need to make money, but because making money was a morally inferior and spirit-soiling occupation."[1]

Continually associated with the term "gentleman," however, was the expectation that a gentleman would evince various virtues, usually including courage, honesty, and politeness. The definition of a gentleman as one demonstrating a set of moral standards was given much importance with the publication of *The Broad Stone of Honour* by Kenelm Henry Digby in 1822. The book was extremely popular and influential and went through several editions, expanding to five volumes by 1877. It is a rambling citation and explication of chivalrous history and legend, the ancient knights serving as Digby's examples of what the true gentleman should be:

The distinctive virtues of the chivalrous man, according to Digby, were belief and trust in God, generosity, high honour, independence, truthfulness, loyalty to friends and leaders, hardihood and contempt of luxury, courtesy,
modesty, humanity, and respect for women. Generosity could be displayed in
refusing money as well as dispensing it; the Chevalier Bayard had despised
riches all his life. High honour included refusal to break a promise, tell a lie, act
the spy or beg for mercy. Independence included refusal to push oneself, truthfulness included openness; gentlemen did not conceal their feelings, and always
gave fair warning of their intentions. Loyalty to friends involved perfect confidence in them.[2]

Digby felt that democracy was "utterly opposed to all principles of ancient
as well as of the Christian chivalry,"[3] but the nineteenth-century trend toward
democracy in England advanced through the growth in the importance of the
business class, the increasing pressure from trade unions, and the resultant
passing of several reform bills that extended the votes and the rights of com-
moners. The concept of the gentleman also broadened as not only the military
but also sportsmen and youths involved in the new movement of scouting
adopted versions of Digby's values as their own. In America, where hereditary
nobility was forbidden by the Constitution, the broadening of the definition of
the gentleman happened more quickly and thoroughly so that, by the end of
the nineteenth century, a gentleman might be defined not exclusively as a man
of high birth, but also as "a man of honour and high principles," "a man of
good breeding and politeness,"[4] "courtesy, and kindness; hence a man distinguished for fine sense of honor, strict regard for his obligations, and consideration for the rights and feeling of others."[5] Indeed, by the 1920s popular guides
to etiquette defined a gentleman solely by his demeanor and his courteous
treatment of all people, regardless of class.[6]

One characteristic of the gentleman will frequently concern the writers discussed below: the assumption that a gentleman may be raised above "menial
service or ordinary trade" by "education, occupation, or income."[7] Students
were considered gentlemen as, to some degree, were scholars, but the four
original professions granting this title were the clergy, the military, medicine, or
law. Later, writers and artists tended to admit themselves to the ranks of gentlemen and might be accepted as such depending upon their demonstration of
gentlemanly virtues. Always there were mixed feelings about money, for, although income could aid one's status as a gentleman, striving for money itself
was frowned upon. But writers or artists could respectably excuse their poverty

by the gentlemanly understanding that to create for money alone would demonstrate lack of breeding.

The nineteenth-century readership was not all gentlemen, even by the broadest definition, but it generally respected the concept, and many of the literate were ambitious to become as much like gentlemen as possible. Writers, therefore, wrote as gentlemen, to gentlemen, about gentlemen. This seems to have been particularly true of writers of supernatural horror, perhaps because, as H. P. Lovecraft states, readers of supernatural horror fiction needed more to be "free enough from the spell of the daily routine" to exercise "a certain degree of imagination and a capacity for detachment from everyday life" (*D* 365–66).

Each writer, of course, defines "gentleman" in his own way, but there are several common elements to the protagonists and narrators of supernatural horror stories. These gentlemen usually have money sufficient to keep them comfortable. Some may be concerned about their income, but very few approach poverty. With the exception of writers and artists, those who work for a living are from five professions (church, law, military, medicine, and scholarship), or their occupations are unimportant to their self-perceptions.

Because education is very much part of the gentleman, most of those in the stories to be discussed have had education, many to a university degree.[8] Those few who have not are self-educated. Many have some special subject of interest and may have some unique sensitivity to complement this interest.

Finally, the gentleman-protagonists will evince some of the qualities enumerated by Digby—honor, politeness, loyalty, etc.—and will often show some of the social trappings of a gentlemanly status, such as being a member of a club, devoting much time to hunting, dressing appropriately for various activities, and so on.

II. Six Writers from the Tradition

Short fiction of supernatural horror did not begin with Poe, perhaps, but Poe had the greatest early influence, and his protagonists fit the type. They usually narrate their own stories. They tend to come from established families, even nobility. Montresor, of "The Cask of Amontillado," is proud of his "great and numerous family," and "William Wilson" is from a noble line. Assumedly, the husband of Lady Ligeia was at least a baronet, and Prince Prospero's title (in "The Masque of Red Death") is clear. The narrator of "Berenice" will not mention his surname, but his family was an old one. Even in stories with no direct information, family prestige may be deduced, as in "The Pit and the

Pendulum," in which the narrator, although saying nothing about his family, is rescued in person by a general, surely an honor given the deserving.

Also Poe's protagonists are at least comfortable and usually wealthy. The narrators of "MS. Found in a Bottle," "Ligeia," and "William Wilson" are rich. Those in "Berenice," "The Fall of the House of Usher," and "The Cask of Amontillado" live in mansions or, in the least, a *palazzo*, the residences indicating enough wealth to maintain them.

Education, another facet of the gentleman, is emphasized in several of the narrators. The wives Ligeia and Morella had "rare learning," rare enough for women of the time; certainly their husband-narrators must have been learned as well. "William Wilson" went to Eton; the protagonist of "MS. Found in a Bottle" had "uncommon education." Once again, even where the characters' backgrounds are not specified, there are clues. The narrator of "The Fall of the House of Usher" shows learning in his use of French and his references to music and art.

The special interest or sensitivity frequent in narrators of horror fiction is not only frequent with Poe's characters, but often also the core of his stories. Egaeus's obsession with the teeth of his Berenice is the story itself, as are the sharpened senses of the narrator of "The Tell-Tale Heart." Other stories can only be told by the narrator because his private views are the only explanation for motives that would otherwise be either misunderstood or unknown. The protagonist's experiences in "The Premature Burial," for example, are known and understood solely by him.

J. S. Le Fanu, who was Poe's contemporary, uses narrators and protagonists who thoroughly enumerate the professional positions common to gentlemanly characters. Several are of the nobility: "Madam Crowl's Ghost" concerns a Dame; "Carmilla" is very much the daughter of a noble family, as was "Ultor De Lacy" the son. Titles with titles include "The Haunted Baronet," "The Fortunes of Sir Robert Ardagh," and "Sir Dominick's Bargain." Country squires are involved with "Squire Toby's Will," and military officers are in "The Familiar" and "Carmilla," the narrator of which is the daughter of one. The clergy is represented as protagonists in "Green Tea" and "An Account of Some Strange Disturbances in Aungier Street," and as narrators in "Sir Robert Ardagh" and "The Familiar." A scholar gives the narrative to a doctor in "The White Cat of Drumgunniol," and Dr. Martin Hesselius, also a physician, is Le Fanu's narrator for a number of stories. "Schalken the Painter" represents that occupation, while "An Authentic Narrative of a Haunted House" is told by an editor of a university magazine, which Le Fanu himself once was.

Le Fanu chooses his nobility from the lower end of the higher classes, and his gentlemen, although well above poverty, tend to be uncharacteristically concerned with financial problems. In "Carmilla," Laura's father lives on a pension granted for his service to the Austrian army. It enables him to purchase a castle, but it is not as fine a living as he might prefer. The two sons fight over "Squire Toby's Will," the estates in which were "impaired," or diminished in value. "The Fortunes of Sir Robert Ardagh" also concerned impaired estates. There is the mood in Le Fanu that the social well-being of his characters is unsettled as they experience the emotional unsettling of the supernatural.

The narrators of Le Fanu's stories appear to be chosen as story tellers. If they are from the various classes of gentlemen, this is because they are therefore possessed of sufficient learning, time, and practice to communicate the stories in the appropriate form to entertain Le Fanu's nineteenth-century readership. If Poe chose gentlemen who had special stories to tell, Le Fanu chooses gentlemen who might tell stories well, though they be the stories of others.

Arthur Machen's stories often involve collectors of strange tales, the narrative resulting from their efforts. If some of the collectors are businessmen, they are quite comfortable, if not actually well-to-do, as Edward Darnell ("A Fragment of Life") or Mr. Clarke ("The Great God Pan"). Some of Machen's characters are writers. The narrator of "The Happy Children" is a journalist, though Mr. Dyson of "The Shining Pyramid" has enough means to be comfortably idle. In several stories, such as "Out of the Earth," "The Great Return," or "The Terror," the narrator appears to be the author himself.

The bulk of Machen's story-collectors, however, are gentlemen without necessary occupation. Villiers ("The Great God Pan") is a man about town. Dyson ("The Inmost Light") is a man of letters who lives upon an inheritance. Joseph Last ("The Bright Boy") lives in modest comfort from the remains of a family fortune, but Arnold ("N") need only be industrious to satisfy his curiosity. Machen's female narrators are of similar background. Miss Leicester ("Novel of the White Powder") is the daughter of a deceased Major-General, and her brother was an exceptionally successful university graduate. Miss Lally ("Novel of the Black Seal"), the daughter of a civil engineer, was deprived of an inheritance by his early death. It is interesting that, though her landlady would have tolerated her debt, Lally evicts herself from her rooming house out of a sense of honor. Nevertheless, she seems to end in relative comfort, probably as a result of the "small remembrance" given her by Professor Gregg.

True to type, Machen's narrators and protagonists have learning, either formal learning, such as Joseph Last's Oxford education, self-education, such as Miss Lally's, or the very particular erudition acquired by many of his characters. Clarke has a "lust" to pursue his "morbid subjects." Dyson had "a good classical education," although he did not attend the university, and he applies himself to the "science of the great city," accumulating stories of London. Arnold is idle except that he was "always ready to take any amount of pains, over something in which he was interested."[9]

What most of the characters are interested in concerns the discovery of a new world of experience. Professor Gregg is convinced that "much of the folklore of the world is but an exaggerated account of events that really happened."[10] Dr. Raymond ("The Great God Pan") has discovered for these events "a whole world, a sphere unknown."[11] Edward Darnell, though having a sound commercial education, has resurrected in him "an old spirit that for many centuries had been faithful to the secrets that are now disregarded by the rest of us," and he eventually remembers something of "the mysteries and the far-shining glories of the kingdom which was his by legitimate inheritance."[12] Without detailing Machen's philosophy, it is sufficient to say that the special interest and sensitivity possessed by his characters is the interest of and sensitivity to a mythic realm of experience proven real. Machen's protagonists, to some degree, are seers.

The horror stories of Robert W. Chambers are all narrated from the point of view of protagonists who tend to be of the gentlemanly mode. The exceptions are telling. Bud Kent ("The Key to Grief") is a murderer, and the cruel, arrogant Hildred Castaigne ("The Repairer of Reputations") believes himself to be a future king; the first dies, the second ends in an asylum for life. The artist Scott is a lapsed Catholic who likes to see himself as an amoral man of the world, and he too dies ("The Yellow Sign"). He does have a chivalric sense of honor toward the woman who loves him, but he is unable to save her.

The others more closely fit the gentleman's standard. Two are artists ("The Mask"; "A Pleasant Evening") and two are involved with scholarly work. Of the latter, one works for a museum, having given up a less congenial position in a government office ("The Harbor-Master"). Appearing in several stories, this unnamed character had been a scientific writer for magazines, but he had taken an English literature course at Columbia College to improve his abilities ("In Quest of the Dingue"). Although young, he eventually represents the Smithsonian Institution as well as the Bronx Zoo ("Is the Ux Extinct?"). The other of the scholars is a middle-aged student living in France, the suggestion being that, if he was primarily a student, he must have had some financial independence, be it ever so small ("In the Court of the Dragon").

The remaining protagonist-narrators of Chambers appear to be American gentlemen of means who spend much of their time hunting. Philip ("The Mademoiselle d'Ys") knows some French, has looked at medieval French writing, and could recognize the archaic terms of falconry. Richard Darrel ("The Messenger") is offended when a specimen he has given to the Entomological Society of Paris is called "valuable"; it is the implication that he would even consider its monetary value that he finds insulting, for he would never stoop to selling the item. Roy Cardenhe ("The Maker of Moons") is writer enough to put his tale upon paper, and he moves in sufficiently high circles to know a designer at Tiffany's, at the time the most elegant purveyor of designs. Each man reflects some aspect of the gentlemanly class, and there are often clues to others, the learning implicit in the zoo official's personal library, for example.

Chambers's protagonists, more than those of the other writers here mentioned, are men of action. The huntsmen and the Bronx Zoo's representative seek adventure. The artists are mentally active pursuers of new impressions. Chambers's narrators, then, do not just collect stories of the strange, they take a deliberately active part in them.

M. R. James has protagonists who are doctors ("Two Doctors") and clergymen ("The Residence at Whitminster"), and some of them are gentlemen of means, such as Mr. Somerton ("The Treasure of Abbot Thomas"), a man of leisure, Mr. Dillet ("The Haunted Doll's House"), a collector, and Mr. Humphreys ("Mr. Humphreys and His Inheritance"), who becomes a country gentleman. Like Mr. Lake ("An Episode of Cathedral History"), most of these gentlemen are learned.

James himself was Vice-Chancellor of Cambridge and Provost of Eton, so it is hardly to be wondered that the majority of his narrators and protagonists are scholars. Mr. Anderson ("Number 13") is researching Danish church history. Mr. Garret ("The Tractate Middoth") is an assistant in a library. Edward Dunning ("Casting the Runes") was involved in research, as was Mr. Fanshawe ("A View from a Hill"). "The Stalls of Barchester Cathedral" concerns a scholar who, as did James himself, catalogued manuscripts in the college library. The writers mentioned in the stories are also students or scholars. Mr. Davidson ("The Uncommon Prayer-Book") is a writer or editor but also an antiquary; the narrator of "A Neighbour's Landmark" is one of "those who spend the greater part of their time in reading or writing books."[13]

James's narrators have a leisurely style and certainly play the role of tellers of stories for entertainment. The narrator of "Rats" relates what he heard when he was young. The narrator of "Count Magnus" assembles the tale from patterns he finds during his researches, and "The Mezzotint" is told by someone who heard it told to an acquaintance. A writer who begins stories with lines like, "It was, as far as I can ascertain, in September of the year . . ." ("Lost Hearts"); "Some time ago I believe I had the pleasure of telling you the story of an adventure . . ." ("The Mezzotint"); "This matter began, as far as I am concerned . . ." ("The Stalls of Barchester Cathedral"); and "This, you know, is the beginning of a story about . . ." ("There Was a Man Dwelt by a Churchyard") is a writer who wishes to let the reader feel a semblance of truth in the stories without forgetting that they *are* stories.

Born, just as James, Machen, and Chambers, in the 1860s, Algernon Blackwood outlived them, leaving a considerable body of short supernatural fiction. His work, like that of the others, stresses the role of gentlemen as protagonists. Though there are a number of thoroughly middle-class types, such as the accountant ("Accessory Before the Fact"), the hotel clerk ("Running Wolf"), and the travel agent ("The Man Who Was Milligan"), it is significant that their occupations do not define them. The travel agent also wrote stories for the cinema, and the others appear in the stories while on holiday. Blackwood uses ship-captains ("The Sea Pit") and retired colonels ("The Doll") as protagonists, also clergymen ("Special Delivery") and schoolmasters ("The Occupant of the Room"). He uses scientists, such as the physicist of "Entrance and Exit" and the chemist of "The Olive," and writers, like those in "The Damned" and "The Glamour of the Snow." Artists, too, are represented in "The Man Whom the Trees Loved," "The Heath Fire," and "A Desert Episode," and the photographer of "A Deferred Appointment" labels himself a "photographic artist." The protagonist of "Chinese Magic" is a doctor, but the doctors used by Blackwood are usually wealthy and practice medicine for personal reasons, as do the twins of "The Lost Valley" and Dr. John Silence, Blackwood's analogue to Le Fanu's Dr. Martin Hesselius.

Nevertheless, the majority of Blackwood's protagonists are gentlemen. They have education and may be interested in the sciences or arts. Binovbitch of "The Wings of Horus" is "a man of unusual ability and of genuine, deep culture."[14] He is also a bird fancier. The bachelor of "The Little Beggar" knows poetry, and the Gilmer brothers ("The Empty Sleeve") collected violins.

Of course, the gentlemen tend to have money or property. Grimwood ("The Valley of the Beasts") has both. The Gilmer brothers had "private means"; the twins of "The Terror of the Twins" inherited theirs. John Burley ("The Decoy") was a successful businessman, but he also inherited a country mansion. The protagonist of "The Tryst" won a fortune by age thirty-five and became a gentleman adventurer. Indeed, outdoor activities are common to Blackwood's gentlemen. Limasson ("The Sacrifice") loves his wealth and mountain climbing. Ericssen ("First Hate") is an avid huntsman, and the narrator of "The Willows" is on a canoeing excursion.

Richard Norman ("The Trod") is the epitome of Blackwood's narrators and protagonists. He is from a noble family. He has money. He is a huntsman. He has read poetry, tried to write it, and has feelings of "the other world." He is "one of the finest males of the twentieth century," and a "climax of chivalric achievement."[15]

The characteristics of the narrators and protagonists of the six authors discussed above are not identical. All have some fated relationship with the supernatural but, where Poe favors obsessed personalities and Machen quiet dreamers, Le Fanu uses narrators who are merely looking for good stories. James's protagonists are scholarly and curious and quite unwilling to seek the supernatural as such, whereas Chambers's and Blackwood's characters are openly adventurous. But throughout, these writers—and a long list of others, both Lovecraft's antecedents and contemporaries—use narrators and protagonists who are gentlemen within a fairly specific definition. The reasons for this are sociological as well as literary, and have as much to do with the cultural expectations of the stories' readers as they may with the writers' need to have narrations by people who might be expected to narrate them acceptably, but such is an important component of the tradition of the supernatural horror story, a tradition Lovecraft knew well.

III. Lovecraft's Gentleman Narrators

H. P. Lovecraft continued the tradition of the gentlemanly narrator, adapting it to his purposes and style as did the other authors. From his earlier to his later stories, however, there is an identifiable shift in emphasis, if not actually an evolution, of his narrators from Poesque, maddened isolates to those who are more objective, active, and social. Most characteristics of his narrators reflect this shift.

His earlier characters more often tend to be from noble families. Antoine in "The Alchemist" is from an ancient cursed nobility; the German submarine commander ("The Temple"), Sir Arthur Jermyn ("Facts concerning the Late Arthur Jermyn and His Family"), Barzai ("The Other Gods"), Delapore ("The Rats in the Walls"), and Randolph Carter, who appears in several stories, are all from titled family lines. The singer Iranon ("The Quest of Iranon") believes himself to be a king's son and is devastated to learn otherwise. All these characters were from stories written before Lovecraft was thirty-four and most of them before he was thirty.

Lovecraft always maintained an interest in family lines, as do many of his narrators. The narrator of "The Festival" makes a point of being from an old family. The narrator of "Cool Air" insists vaguely that he was well-born. *The Case of Charles Dexter Ward* depicts the title character as having familial roots in New England, as have the narrators of "The Picture in the House," "The Shadow out of Time," and "The Shadow over Innsmouth." In the last, the narrator-protagonist find that his ancestry is a source of horror, a common theme in Lovecraft. Nobility is not the point of these family lines, and all but one of these stories were written after Lovecraft was thirty.

Many of Lovecraft's earlier stories feature narrators who presumably have inherited family wealth. Jervas Dudley ("The Tomb") certainly did, and the narrator of "The Hound" appears to have been wealthy enough to make his time his own, so also with the narrator of "The Call of Cthulhu." More pertinent in the earlier stories is the attitude that gainful employment is unbecoming to a gentleman. That Jervas Dudley is "wealthy beyond the necessity for commercial life" (*D* 3) assumes that money is the only reason to engage in commercial life. Antoine has "a pride of name that forbids [his poverty's] alleviation by the pursuits of commercial life" (*D* 328), an old sentiment. Later, Lovecraft allows the possibility that commercial employment might restore family fortune, but at a cost beyond money. Delapore, like Denys Barry ("The Moon-Bog"), returns to his ancestral land with money from America to rebuild the family estate, Delapore's money specifically noted as coming from his career as a manufacturer. Both men, however, are doomed by their skeptical tampering with family curses, Delapore to madness and Barry to death. Still, there is the ethic shown in "Celephaïs," "where a notably fat and especially offensive millionaire brewer enjoys the purchased atmosphere of extinct nobility" (*D* 89), that money for its own sake is opposed to true gentility.

There are no clergymen narrators in Lovecraft, nor jurists, but several characters partook of a military career that might have been acceptable to gentility had it continued. The German U-boat commander has already been mentioned. There are also the narrator of "The Transition of Juan Romero," who left his life as a British officer apparently because of some scandal, and the narrator of "Herbert West—Reanimator," who entered the medical corps as a first lieutenant as much to aid West's plans as for patriotism. Randolph Carter ("The Silver Key") demonstrated his idealism by joining the French Foreign

Legion to enter World War I before his country's forces had mobilized.

But such careers do not threaten the standards of a gentleman. In the later stories, however, Lovecraft admits an appreciation for more realistic narrators with ordinary sources of income. Although there are a number of non-gentlemanly jobs represented, such as architect ("The Thing on the Doorstep"), surveyor ("The Colour out of Space"), policeman ("The Horror at Red Hook"), and insurance work ("The Shadow over Innsmouth")—all, not incidentally, written after the author was thirty-six—most of these later narrators tend to follow the gentlemanly standard of professions.

Some are medical doctors, such as the narrators of "Beyond the Wall of Sleep" and "Herbert West," or the victim of "Cool Air." There are an artist ("The Haunter of the Dark"), a number of sculptors ("The Tree," "Hypnos"), poets ("Arthur Jermyn," "He"), and quite a number of writers. Thurber of "Pickman's Model" wrote. Randolph Carter ("The Silver Key") and "Arthur Jermyn" published. Robert Blake ("The Haunter of the Dark"), who was jokingly patterned after Lovecraft's correspondent Robert Bloch, was successful with magazine fiction; the narrator of "Cool Air" was not so successful in the same work. Again, the professional authors appear as characters in the later stories.

By far, the great number of Lovecraft's narrators are scholars. Most of these are scholars by temperament and inclination. Arthur Jermyn had "learning in his blood" (*D* 73). Charles Dexter Ward "was an antiquarian from infancy" (*MM* 109). The narrator of "The Music of Erich Zann" is a student, as is Walter Gilman of "The Dreams in the Witch House." Even in his dream existence, the narrator of "Polaris" studies many hours a day.

In the later stories, the students become teachers or professors. Thomas Olney ("The Strange High House in the Mist") is a college teacher. Dr. Henry Armitage ("The Dunwich Horror") has two doctorates and is a librarian. Albert Wilmarth ("The Whisperer in Darkness") is an instructor of literature. The narrator of *At the Mountains of Madness* is a geologist; Nathaniel Peaslee ("The Shadow out of Time") is a professor of political economy.

Education is important to Lovecraft's narrators. In "The Beast in the Cave," written when Lovecraft was fourteen, the narrator tells nothing of his background, but phrases like "interminable recesses" (for "endless caves"; *D* 325) and "simultaneous ejaculation of wonderment" (*D* 327) are bookish at least. In "The Alchemist," Antoine spent his childhood poring over books in his library; so did Jervas Dudley. Barzai was learned in books, and the Outsider learned all he knew from them. The U-boat commander was "reared in the best Kultur of Prussia" (*D* 66), and Arthur Jermyn had "the best education which limited money could provide" (*D* 77). The education of the characters becomes more formal in the later stories where degrees are obtained from Princeton, Johns Hopkins ("The Dunwich Horror"), Oberlin College ("The Shadow over Innsmouth"), Harvard ("The Thing on the Doorstep"), and of course Lovecraft's fictional Miskatonic University of Arkham, Massachusetts. All the real colleges and universities are mentioned only in the later stories.

Dreamers also abound in Lovecraft. Like Jervas Dudley, many dwell "ever in realms apart from the visible world" (*D* 4). The narrator of "Beyond the Wall of Sleep" is "a constant speculator concerning dream life" (*D* 29). The subject of "Azathoth" is a dreamer, as is Arthur Jermyn. The protagonists of "Polaris" and "Celephaïs" exist more in dreams than in wakefulness, as does Randolph Carter ("The Silver Key"). The narrator of "He" wants badly to be a dreamer, but Nathaniel Peaslee is troubled by dreams, and Williams of "The Descendant" is a dreamer who has learned to fear his imagination.

Beyond dreams, the special interest of Lovecraft's narrators tends to be in strange and dangerous subjects. The criticism given the narrator of "The Evil Clergyman" could stand as a motto of Lovecraft's protagonists: "Your curiosity makes you irresponsible" (*D* 287). Randolph Carter in "The Unnamable" has a "preoccupation with the mystical and unexplained" (*D* 200), and the man who studies the "lurking fear" more blatantly is involved in "a series of quests for strange horrors in literature and in life" (*D* 179), for he is "a connoisseur in horrors" (*D* 182). Thurber of "Pickman's Model" is writing a monograph on weird art, in which he is well versed; Randolph Carter "dabbled in notions of the bizarre and the eccentric" (*MM* 412). Daniel Upton ("The Thing on the Doorstep") had leanings toward the grotesque that became subdued, unlike those fatal to his friend Edward Derby. Robert Blake "was a writer and painter wholly devoted to the field of myth, dream, terror, and superstition, and avid in his quest for scenes and effects of a bizarre, spectral sort" (*DH* 93). The narrator of "The Shunned House" develops an obsession with that tragic place, and Herbert West's attempts at reanimating the dead eventually degenerate into morbid experimentation for its own sake. The narrator of "The Hound" lives a life devoted to the sensation of the morbid and perverse until his interests carry him to the horrible death such interests provoke.

Considering these interests, it is hardly surprising that the irresponsible curiosity of Lovecraft's characters leads them to misery. Some use drugs to prolong their dream experiences, as do the narrators of "Celephaïs" and "Hypnos," but the narrator of "Dagon" takes drugs to dull his imagination. The narrator of "The Book" says with understatement, "I seem to have suffered a great shock" (*D* 362) and, indeed, as a result of their curiosity, a shock is the least of penalties to befall Lovecraft's protagonists.

Albert Wilmarth ("The Whisperer in Darkness") fears "what the years will bring" (*DH* 271). The surveyor in "The Colour out of Space" has increasingly disturbed sleep. Perhaps, like Nathaniel Peaslee, he is troubled by his dreams or, like Williams, he dreams unwillingly, having learned to fear his imagination. Thomas Olney ("The Strange High House in the Mist") loses all need for imagination and adventure and afterward is happy to lead a prosaic life. The narrator of "Cool Air" becomes afraid of the title substance, and Thomas Malone ("The Horror at Red Hook") is under medical treatment for a fear of certain types of buildings. The narrator of "From Beyond" is left with bad nerves after his experience, and the mental health of the man who heard the music of Erich Zann is disturbed by his experiences.

Thurber, the critic who sees the photograph of Pickman's model, considers himself "lucky to be sane at all" (*DH* 12). Many of Lovecraft's protagonists are not so lucky. Jervas Dudley and Delapore are confined to asylums, as is Joseph Curwen after he has killed Charles Dexter Ward. The narrator of "Herbert West—Reanimator" admits that he is probably mad, and the same admission might be gotten from the narrator of "Hypnos." The protagonist of "The Lurking Fear" believes his "mind was partly unhinged by events" (*D* 189) he had experienced, and the narrator of "The Festival" ends in a hospital with a diagnosis of "psychosis" (*D* 189).

The Bostonian who narrates "The Call of Cthulhu" states, "I do not think my life will be long" (*DH* 154). The German U-boat commander knows his life, too, will not last much past his narrative. Arthur Jermyn commits suicide by setting himself on fire, and the narrator of "The Hound" "shall seek with [his] revolver the oblivion which is [his] only refuge from the unnamed and unnamable" (*D* 178).

In these denouements, too, there is a progression in Lovecraft's stories. Suicide is not committed by a narrator in stories after 1922, whereas madness occurs almost completely in the stories written between 1921 and 1923. After 1923, the effects of the various narrators' experiences are some form of disturbed sleep, shaky nerves, or traumatic fear. In short, Lovecraft's earlier stories feature more blatantly dramatic narrators, but they evolve into narrators who suffer far subtler psychological penalties.

One of the themes that appears increasingly is that of the transformation of the personality of the narrator or protagonist. Many of the earlier stories, such as "Celephaïs" and "Hypnos," concern the narrators' second existence as dream figures, and "The Rats in the Walls" describes an atavistic regression into past lives of its narrator's ancestral line, but later stories stress even more the psychic dispossession of the narrators from their physical bodies, as in "The Whisperer in Darkness," "The Thing on the Doorstep," and "The Evil Clergyman." A feature of the later stories is the possibility that the *narrator* may assume another body and become accustomed to, even pleased with, the change. In "The Shadow out of Time" Nathaniel Peaslee became, for five years, a member of the Great Race of eons past. In "The Dreams in the Witch House" an attempt is made to recruit Walter Gilman into the ranks of the unearthly. This recruitment becomes physically and mentally complete in "The Shadow over Innsmouth," in which the narrator ends by becoming one of the fishy horrors he formerly detested, and by his dwelling in the depths "amidst wonder and glory forever" (*DH* 367). However this ending is meant—and there are many interpretations of it—it represents a change in the experiencing of horror for Lovecraft's narrator-protagonists, who begin by fearing what is outside of themselves, to fearing what is inside of themselves or what they themselves have become, to accepting what they have become.

To some degree, Lovecraft's description of his narrators reflects his self-evaluation. He thought of his ancestors as "a family of small country gentry" (*SL* 1.5) comported himself, even as a boy, "as a gentleman among gentlemen" (*SL* 1.39; see also 1.242), and humorously labels himself a viscount (*SL* 2.3). At World War I he attempted to join the Rhode Island National Guard, hoping for a commission and wanting to meet death "in the most approved way, 'Somewhere in France'" (*SL* 1.47).

Many of his early narrators think of themselves as unsuitable for the world. Antoine has already been described as unfit for commercial life, and Jervas Dudley is "temperamentally unfitted for the formal studies" (*D* 4) of his acquaintances. The younger Lovecraft said, "My body has ever been unequal to the demands of an active career" (*SL* 1.38) and "of my non-university education, I never cease to be ashamed" (*SL* 1.41), although he had the aspect of a professor. In an early letter, he makes explicit his attitude about gentlemen: "I like a wholesome country-gentleman that is a gentleman, with the out-of-doors taste and love of our English country-side and antiquities that befit a red-blooded, true-born Briton" (*SL* 1.254).

Like many of his protagonists, the young Lovecraft wanted to be a poet and an artist, but he felt that he had no talent for these arts. His attitude toward writing, however, shifted with the years. Originally, he felt that "literature is no proper pursuit for a gentleman" (*SL* 1.138) and that gentlemen should only write in the form of correspondence with other gentlemen, rather that publish (*SL* 1.243). This was in 1923, nearing the end of the period of the early stories. Shortly afterwards, however, he complains that his pay for stories accepted by *Weird Tales* magazine is late (*SL* 1.257) and muses about "if I ever have a book of tales" (*SL* 1.259). By 1927, into the period of his later stories, he is discoursing on the craft of writing. Now when he calls himself a patrician, he is clearly joking without wistfulness. By 1935, he is able to recognize the affectations of his youth and modify his definitions of the gentleman:

> Perhaps I could define my favourite type by saying that it is a person of basically normal natural personality, with a strong sense of fitness, harmony, & social obligation, who is sincere in his thought & imagination & who refuses to let these qualities be modelled, dulled, or standardised by herd psychology or other irrelevant outside influences. (*SL* 5.215)

His later definition is no less idealistic, but it is more sophisticated, more related to actual possibilities than stereotype.

That the development of his characters should reflect his personal development is not unlikely given his practice of developing fictional characters. He wrote "I use human puppets as symbols" (*SL* 3.436); "They are only incidental details & can well be left in the puppet stage—since the real protagonists of my tales are not organic beings at all, but simply *phenomena*" (*SL* 4.72). If, therefore, he is willing to admit that "characterisation is undoubtedly a woefully weak point" (*SL* 5.358) with him, he tries to make his characters typical and realistic. However, he states that he cannot write of protagonists as types of people he doesn't know, but he also states that it is possible to build characters from sides of one's own personality.[16] Lovecraft's narrators, then, resemble him because he was his own best source for them. If their natures shifted with the years, it is because, in part, his own character developed over time.

The authors in the tradition of the short story of supernatural horror use narration to fit their individual styles and use narrators who are capable of communicating each author's individual variety of horror. Poe tends to use narrators who are literate, sensitive, independent, and suffering from the subjectivity of their perceptions of reality. Le Fanu chooses narrators who both might hear and entertainingly tell ghostly stories. Machen's narrators are most often of unusual receptivity or interest in the "other world" beyond common reality, and they are sufficiently intelligent and educated to discuss what they have perceived. Chambers uses sensitives and adventurers, people who emotionally or physically place themselves in the way of strange or horrible occurrences. Of course he, too, is interested that his narrators can effectively tell of their experiences.

James's antiquarian or scholarly narrators discover, with no intention whatsoever, horrible possibilities buried in the footnotes of reality. His narrators are just the type of people to stumble across those horrors and explain their discoveries. Blackwood's characters are adventurous without usually being interested in the strange for its own sake. Nevertheless, they usually have the courage to face the unknown and emerge from it. In all these cases, the model of the gentleman familiar to, and respected by, these writers was the model of the intelligent, communicative narrator who could serve to exhibit their tales to the public.

Lovecraft's narrators partake of many of the features of these and others writers in the tradition. His early characters demonstrate his admiration of Poe, and other protagonists show he read and appreciated Machen, at least to the extent that they combine some of the sensitivity and objectivity of Machen's narrators. Chambers was probably not much of an influence, though Lovecraft had read him, but as a matter of course some of Lovecraft's characters would reflect the doom suffered by some of Chambers's. In his later stories, the Blackwood-like adventurers are taken over by the Jamesian scholars as Lovecraft's narrators and their found horrors become comparatively more subtle.

Through all these narrators, however, Lovecraft develops his own type of gentlemen, whose curiosity brings them too much knowledge of the wrong kind, and whose abilities, both mental and physical, are necessarily unequal to the challenge of the horrible forces they discover, except insofar as they can appreciate the otherness of these horrors and appreciate, as well, man's need for a separation from them. In creating these gentlemen, Lovecraft added to the tradition of which he was a part.

Notes

1. Mark Girouard, *The Return to Camelot: Chivalry and the English Gentleman* (New Haven, CT: Yale University Press, 1981), 269.

2. Girouard, 61–62.

3. Girouard, 62.

4. Robert Hunter and Charles Morris, ed., *Universal Dictionary of the English Language* (New York: P. F. Collier & Son, 1902), 2.2287.

5. William Dwight Whitney, ed., *The Century Dictionary: An Encyclopedic Lexicon of the English Language* (New York: The Century Co., 1895), 3.2490.

6. Lillian Eichler, *Book of Etiquette* (New York: Nelson Doubleday, 1923), 1.5–6; Victor H. Diescher (New York: Social Culture Publications, 1923), 4.

7. Hunter and Morris, 2.2287; Whitney, 3.2490.

8. Thomas H. Greer, *A Brief History of Western Man* (New York: Harcourt, Brace & World, 1968), 265–67. Here is a brief account of the importance of education in the development of the concept of the gentleman.

9. Arthur Machen, *Tales of Horror and the Supernatural* (London: Richards Press, 1949), 69, 156, 157, 307.

10. Ibid., 9.

11. Ibid., 63.

12. Arthur Machen, *The House of Souls* (New York: Alfred A. Knopf, 1922), 48, 35.

13. M. R. James, *The Collected Ghost Stories of M. R. James* (London: Edward Arnold, 1931), 514.

14. Algernon Blackwood, *Tales of the Mysterious and Macabre* (London: Spring Books, 1967), 281.

15. Algernon Blackwood, *Tales of the Uncanny and Supernatural* (London: Spring Books, 1962), 206.

16. See *SL* 4.114 and 117–18, and *SL* 5.17–18.

The Artist as Antaeus: Lovecraft and Modernism

Norman R. Gayford

On the centenary of H. P. Lovecraft's birth, we should celebrate the man of this century, not the antiquarian. We need to consider Lovecraft the modernist. Interestingly, Malcolm Bradbury's study of modernism sets the beginning of the complex movement at 1890. Peter Cannon, S. T. Joshi, Barton L. St. Armand, John Stanley, and others have examined Lovecraft's philosophical position among his contemporaries. We should pursue this further, building upon the groundwork laid by these and other scholars.

By comparing letters, elements of tales, criticisms, reviews, and lectures, we will examine more closely Lovecraft's position among the modernists. His antiquarianism aside, Lovecraft could, "when spurred into arguments about issues important to him, [shed] his archaism like a cloak and [write] with the vigour and force we know from the later fiction."[1] He was very aware of his world and the work of his contemporaries. Joshi has effectively dynamited paths into this rich vein in his essay "Topical References in Lovecraft," a thorough study of specific twentieth-century topical references in Lovecraft's work that counters Robert Bloch's argument (reflective, perhaps, of a general impression) that Lovecraft was removed from "the political, social, literary, and philosophical movements of his day."[2] Though often cloistered physically, Lovecraft was not isolated from the major literary arguments of his time.

Literary modernism actively resists definition. Michael H. Levenson acknowledges the sheer difficulty of naming a movement that had difficulty naming itself.[3] Nonetheless, as a foothold, *The Oxford Companion to English Literature* will suffice. Modernism reflects the impact of Freudian psychology, Frazerian anthropology, and anti-Victorian (or -Edwardian) narrative techniques. Furthermore, the poetic image, and myth as a "structural principle," demand consideration. Modernism rejects the immediate past and is both historically and aesthetically discontinuous. Additionally, it suggests a dehumanizing drift.[4]

We will not accept this as the single controlling definition of the argument, but we can see something familiar in Lovecraft's fiction and letters. Myth informs his work, though that work grows beyond rootedness in classical mythology or the rigid and stale Cthulhu framework. Images are important to

Lovecraft. His interest in images cannot be construed as alignment with the imagists, but it cannot be ignored either. Lovecraft rejects the modern world, but not in its entirety and not entirely for the eighteenth century. He is no purist in his antiquarianism. His letters and fiction destabilize humanocentrist philosophy. He often divorces art from philosophy and the sciences. Lovecraft was a philosophical modernist, if not an entirely artistic one. Probing the limits of art and the use of geometric images, Lovecraft enters the prose versus poetry conversation of his time. He also enters the ongoing debate regarding tradition and orthodoxy.

Take current scholarship a step further by looking at Lovecraft's attraction to John Masefield, Eugene O'Neill, and W. B. Yeats. This attraction, in addition to the controversy surrounding *The Waste Land*, needs to be discussed if we are to arrive at a more three-dimensional sense of Lovecraft's position as a modern writer and thinker.

Peter Cannon's "Lovecraft and the Mainstream Literature of His Day," which places Lovecraft historically among his contemporaries, reminds us that Lovecraft "came to artistic maturity" in the 1920s as did Fitzgerald. He attempted to play a part in World War I, as did Hemingway, Dos Passos, and cummings, and he was in New York during an exciting literary time. His regional work is thematically reminiscent of Faulkner. Lovecraft could not avoid living when he did and his life parallels better-known contemporaries.

When Cannon focuses upon the position Lovecraft took regarding the best-known and perhaps most often discussed poem of that era, Eliot's *The Waste Land*, he raises issues that warrant in-depth discussion. "Lovecraft never seemed to appreciate how much he and the aristocratic and elitist Eliot . . . shared in common," writes Cannon.[5] While Lovecraft made no blatant acknowledgment of the possibility, fragments of discussions in his letters indicate some appreciation. When a writer makes repeated references to and comments upon an issue, he clearly appreciates the importance of that issue, even though he may not align himself with it. Cannon says: "It [*The Waste Land*] must have affected Lovecraft in some profound way, otherwise he would not have bothered to compose . . . 'Waste Paper'" or mentioned *The Waste Land* in *The Case of Charles Dexter Ward*. Lovecraft could "ridicule the great poem of the age but not ignore it."[6]

But Lovecraft was not merely ridiculing. In St. Armand's and Stanley's detailed study of Lovecraft's ongoing reaction to *The Waste Land*, they demonstrate that Lovecraft's "Waste Paper" and Eliot's *Waste Land* were not at complete stylistic or even thematic loggerheads if one considers Eliot's drafts:

"'Waste Paper' is . . . more similar to the original, unimproved version of Eliot's poem."[7] They also note, regarding song lyrics chosen for their respective poems, that "the similarity of choice demonstrates that Lovecraft and Eliot to some extent shared the same community of culture and background."[8]

Pointing out that Lovecraft could not have seen those drafts, St. Armand and Stanley also note that in temperament and in taste the two writers were "brothers beneath the skin, for both shared a disgust with modern civilization, a horror of the mob."[9] Again, Lovecraft's concentration on the poem and on the moderns in general, notwithstanding his lack of awareness of Eliot's use in his first draft of "eighteenth-century verse forms for precisely the same reasons that Lovecraft had always employed them,"[10] layers itself like a geological deposit. Paul Buhle has said that Lovecraft "abjured as dead-ended" the "poetry of T. S. Eliot,"[11] but it is, as Wayne Booth has been heard to say more than once, more complicated than that.

In 1945 Winfield Townley Scott wrote, "One wonders what, if anything, Lovecraft made of the American poetry of his own era. . . . [He showed] quick disdain and misunderstanding of T. S. Eliot, with whose principles of aristocracy, royalism, and classicism Lovecraft actually had much in common. . . . In his work [Lovecraft] was anti-realistic and therefore anti-poetic."[12] Again, it is more complicated than that. We must consider what specific principles Lovecraft shared with the moderns, keeping in mind that, like theirs, his position changed markedly from the early 1920s to the years just before his death.

Not everyone appreciated *The Waste Land* or the doctrine informing it. Cannon cites Cowley to remind us of this, as well as to suggest that the negative criticism of Eliot's work makes an interesting comparison with Lovecraft's antiquarianism: "The past was dignified; the present is barren of emotion."[13] Lovecraft's energies were not devoted solely, or even primarily, to ridiculing Eliot. Appreciation, albeit grudging, complicates the matter and embeds Lovecraft more firmly in the philosophical arguments raging at the time.

Perhaps reluctantly, Lovecraft appreciated aspects of *The Waste Land* in particular and modernist literary philosophy, as focused in Eliot, in general. One might more plausibly see in Lovecraft a noticeable reticence to be continuously hypercritical.

In 1920, when Lovecraft wrote "The Tree," he commented in a letter:

It was the result of some rather cynical reflection on the possible real motives which may underlie even the most splendid-appearing acts of mankind. With this nucleus I developed a tale based on the Greek idea of divine justice and retribution, (a very pretty though sadly mythical idea!) with the added Oriental notion of the soul of a man passing into something else. Quite an heterogeneous combination—modern cynicism, Greek tragedy, and Oriental fantasy! (*SL* 1.121)

Two years before the appearance of *The Waste Land*, Lovecraft experimented with a not unrelated thematic mixture. In itself this suggests something of the irresistible, if repellent, attraction of the piece to Lovecraft. Levenson points out *The Waste Land*'s layers of European and non-European elements and says its "widening perspectives cannot be regarded as concentric circles which enclose and confirm one another: Eliot threw not one but a handful of stones into the pond. History in *The Waste Land* exists as the complex product of overlapping traditions."[14]

St. Armand, Stanley, and others make much of the Dryden/Pope influence in the initial drafts of *The Waste Land*, suggesting that Lovecraft, had he seen those drafts, might have felt differently about the poem as it appeared in *The Dial*. However, Lovecraft wrote a most telling letter in November 1923 that, far from an antiquarian lament, testifies to Lovecraft's immersion in the modernist argument:

> In art there is no use in heeding the chaos of the universe. . . . I can conceive of no true image of the pattern of life and cosmic force, unless it be a jumble of mean dots arrang'd in directionless spirals. And so far are real dots and actual curves from depicting the utter formlessness and emptiness of life and force, that they stand confest as artificial as Mr. Pope's couplets when view'd against the bland and nebulous reality they struggle to depict. Thus I take the efforts of . . . Mr. Eliot to be very well meant, but quite ironically futile. . . . In an infinite chaos where the very conception of a value is a local and transient accident; it certainly follows that *The Waste Land* is no closer than the *Essay on Man* or *De Imitatione Christi* to any such mythical entity as "truth". (*SL* 1.261–62)

Repudiating neither Pope nor Eliot, Lovecraft articulates a position that separates art and scientific philosophy. No artistic pattern can represent reality. All are futile, though not dead-ended, as Buhle would have it. Dead-ended implies barriers, but in Lovecraft's view infinity renders representational art, realistic art, inert. Pope was no better than Eliot at capturing reality because, in Lovecraft's opinion at this stage, reality simply cannot be captured. Art must take a different path from scientific philosophy.

Lovecraft professed "a high respect for these moderns as *philosophers* and *intellectuals,* however much I may dismiss and disregard them *as poets*. T. S. Eliot himself is an acute *thinker*—but I do not believe he is an *artist*" (*SL* 1.230). He recategorizes, rather than rejects, their work. Essentially he says that although their efforts are futile, their minds are good, and we have to remember that, from Lovecraft's point of view, this was a true compliment. St. Armand and Stanley suggest that Lovecraft "remained symbolically deaf to the siren songs of Modernism,"[15] but it may be that he could not see the sirens for the rocks on which they sat. That is, modernist poetry was, for him, the futile representation of scientific reality, "waste paper" to the degree that scientific writing like Hugh Elliot's, Kroeber's, Frazer's, and so on did the work much better. Lovecraft could not help but take Eliot, if not his work, seriously, just as Eliot in the 1920s "took the Metaphysicals with a renewed seriousness."[16]

In the early 1920s Lovecraft was not alone in seeing *The Waste Land* as what Levenson calls "a challenge to the self-sufficiency of the European tradition."[17] While that challenge may have shaken Lovecraft for a time and informed his refusal to accept the poem as poetry (which St. Armand and Stanley lay out meticulously), it is a philosophical position that logically follows from Lovecraft's own increasing de-emphasis of humanocentric thinking. If human beings are gnats, then their governments are equally inconsequential in an Einsteinian universe.

Lovecraft's positions polarize. Art is personal expression; human life and modern civilization is impersonal, philosophically insignificant on a universal scale:

> The keynote of the modern doctrine is the dissociation of ideas . . . into chaotic components, as distinguished from the conventional patterns visible on the outside. This is supposed to form a closer approach to reality, but I cannot see that it forms any sort of art at all. It may be good science—but art deals with beauty rather than fact, and must have liberty to select and arrange according to the traditional patterns which generations of belief and reverence have marked with the seal of empirical loveliness. Beyond or behind this seeming beauty lies only chaos and weariness, so that art must preserve illusions and artificialities rather than try to sweep them away. (*SL* 2.96)

One is reminded of Hawthorne's tale "The Artist of the Beautiful." One is also reminded of the remarkably handsome or beautiful illusion within which Nyarlathotep hides and beyond which Azathoth and chaos await. *The Waste Land* was modern reality. Lovecraft did not believe that art, especially poetry, should reflect this.

More important than the Pope/Dryden influences in the initial draft of *The Waste Land* is the Poe influence, some of which survived Pound's suggested revisions. Lovecraft revered Poe, and Poe's importance in American letters was, for Lovecraft, indisputable. Given that, Levenson's observations become even more incisive: "In 'Elegy,' a poem included with *The Waste Land* manuscripts, the speaker bids his dead lover to 'stay within thy charnel vault!' but nevertheless sees 'sepulchral gates flung wide,' revealing the 'features of the injured bride'—a situation, notes the speaker, 'as in a tale by Poe.'"[18] Granted, "Elegy" does not survive into the first edition of *The Waste Land,* but its spirit does. Levenson mentions Eliot's fascination with return-of-the-dead myths chronicled in Frazer's *Golden Bough.* He notes critical uneasiness with "the notion of a buried corpse planted in order to grow" and says critics have "neutralized" this notion as "memories." Levenson is speaking of "The Burial of the Dead" section, and he castigates the critics who avoid its implications: "To psychologize so quickly is to remove the power from an image which suggests that the barriers between life and death are not firm and that what has already died can yet revive."[19] Clearly, as a literary theme, this notion fascinated Lovecraft the writer and student of Poe, and manifested itself particularly in "The Outsider."

Eliot admitted, "One cannot be sure . . . that one's own writing has not been influenced by Poe."[20] That he found the influence possible, if not probable, is telling, or, as Levenson says:

> The evasion is enticing. Poe is a forgotten figure behind *The Waste Land,* and to remember Poe is to recover the Gothic element that is too often explained away, the waste land as a chamber of horrors. *The Waste Land* is a kind of ghost story with protagonists both haunted and haunting. Indeed, there is a disembodied aspect to consciousness in the poem.[21]

Lovecraft would not discard the work of a fellow writer influenced profoundly by Poe. To put it another way, Lovecraft may have been more willing to embrace Eliot as a thinker precisely because Eliot's thought, though inaccurately claiming to be poetry, found at least part of its direction through Poe.

Eliot made other allusions to Poe's work in *The Waste Land.* For instance, the section "Death by Water" includes a "Maelström"-like allusion:

> A current under sea
> Picked his bones in whispers. As he rose and fell
> He passed the stages of his age and youth
> Entering the whirlpool. (ll. 315–18)[22]

Also, he alludes to Poe's "The Bells" with

> towers
> Tolling reminiscent bells, that kept the hours
> And voices singing out of empty cisterns and exhausted wells.
>
>   (ll. 382–84)[23]

For both Eliot and Lovecraft, Poe was important.

In part, the Poe influence probably attracted Lovecraft to the work of John Masefield, whom he mentions as important in both the 1920s and 1930s. For instance, Masefield's "The Haunted" is redolent with the decaying atmosphere of an Usher house and the vague threat of undead influences. Perhaps the poem influenced *The Case of Charles Dexter Ward*, for in the old house the portrait of a doctor dead for over a century stares, convincing the narrator that the doctor is undead or returning:

>   the man is dead.
> But is he dead? This dusty study drear
> Creaks in its panels that the man is here. . . .
> The place is poisonous with him. (ll. 26–28, 49)[24]

Given that the poem first appeared in 1923, it is not unreasonable to point out the similarity in situation between its speaker and Charles Dexter Ward in his old house as he becomes more and more aware of the horrible oil painting of Joseph Curwen hung in his study.

Poe's influence on the moderns extended beyond poetry and prose, and Lovecraft noticed it. In May 1922 Lovecraft wrote to Frank Belknap Long about O'Neill's *The Emperor Jones*, which he described as "a thing of terror" and said that O'Neill is "the one real dramatist of America today—starkly tragic, and with a touch of the Poe-esque" (*SL* 1.173). His recognition of the power of the play was by no means unique, nor did it hinge solely on the Poe factor. In 1920 Heywood Broun called *The Emperor Jones* "just about the most interesting play which has yet come from the most promising playwright in America."[25] John Shand praised its unconventionality, saying that O'Neill "is certainly a master of emotional effect."[26] Maida Castellun says: "One thinks of Poe and Conrad . . . for anything to match this achievement."[27] Alexander Woollcott and many other reviewers mentioned the masks and the hypnotic allure of the tom-toms.[28]

Perhaps Lovecraft recognized in O'Neill the same drive he felt about writing. O'Neill wrote, "With my present training I might hope to become a mediocre journey-man playwright. . . . I do not wish to be one . . . I want to be an artist or nothing."[29] Such comments litter Lovecraft's letters. Introducing *O'Neill and His Plays: Four Decades of Criticism,* the editors note that reviewers saw novel techniques like "use of masks or of special sound effects" and "distortion in setting and gesture" but still lay emphasis on naturalism.[30] In the case of *All God's Chillun Got Wings,* Eliot focused on the lack of unity of time.[31] Certainly, Lovecraft recognized the distortions and sound as important. Distortion of time, space, or even physical proportions is at the heart of fear-literature for him. The crescendo of the tom-toms is not so very far from the beating drums that grow steadily louder, both in the narrator's encounter with another dimension in "The Music of Erich Zann" (1921) and as Randolph Carter draws ever closer to the chaos of Azathoth in *The Dream-Quest of Unknown Kadath.*

John Gassner called O'Neill "the only major dramatist of our theatre thus far" and went on to say: "We may have a difficult time of it trying to convince the clever Eliot disciples. But surely, as T. S. Eliot himself can tell them, cleverness in art is not enough. There must be a real man with a real, if not always intellectually reducible, passion behind the art."[32] Lovecraft was let down by the mundanity of realism. Let there be a real man, but let him face cosmic, not insipid, realism. Gassner says that O'Neill was "never satisfied with realism" and "resorted to expressionistic fantasy and distortion in . . . *The Emperor Jones.*"[33] The fantastic can be the common ground between the extremes of hollow, dead reality and functional, chaotic modernistic poetry, in Lovecraft's view.

Poe's tales and poems influence modern writing to some extent, and it is interesting, for the modernist debate of the 1920s and 1930s involves the two forms. Lovecraft sees Poe's fiction as more important than his verse, which might indicate a general favoring of prose to poetry, at least in the early 1920s (see *SL* 1.137). For Lovecraft, Poe represented tradition, which can and should inform modernism. Poe "saw beyond the vulgar anthropocentric sphere" (*SL* 1.137). Here Lovecraft is very strongly in consonance with T. E. Hulme. Hulme's "embrace of aesthetic abstraction," says Levenson, "represents the positioning of his theory at the furthest remove from an anthropomorphic perspective. The 'geometric' replaces the 'classical' . . . and Hulme's references are now . . . to Byzantine and Egyptian art."[34] Lovecraft's coined Egyptianesque names, the desert settings of some of his tales, come to mind.

Hulme's refocused anti-humanism works with the geometric. As Joshi and others have pointed out, Lovecraft played with the geometric in some of his weird tales. "If we depart from the usual scale of human experience, we will find that non-Euclidian geometries are more convenient," says Sanford Schwartz.[35] Here is a point at which science or reality can break into art. The scale of space and time, which fascinates Lovecraft, is a source of artistic horror. If writing experiments with this intrusion, it may be art. If art tries to place a human framework on the universe, it is not art.

Not surprisingly, Eliot said some things about non-Euclidian abstractionism that provide more common ground between his ideas and Lovecraft's. His discussion of this, in fact, leads directly into weird fantasy's front yard: the creation of worlds. Schwartz quotes Eliot's *Sacred Wood* when he says Eliot "denies that imaginary beings should behave like actual beings"[36] and argues that a created world should have "'a logic of its own'":

> We cannot call a man's work superficial when it is the creation of a world. . . .
> The worlds created by artists like Jonson are like systems of non-Euclidian geometry. They are not fancy, because they have a logic of their own; and this logic illuminates the actual world, because it gives us a new point of view from which to inspect it.[37]

Schwartz says that Eliot linked "new theories of knowledge" with "the development of nonrepresentational art."[38] Like Lovecraft, he redefined art because of the day's scientific discoveries, and though they arrived at different positions the common ground should not be overlooked. No less than Eliot, Lovecraft wrestled with modern theories.

If one declares humanity insignificant, then no single culture within that mass of humanity can be significant on the universal scale. One must question the blind following of a given tradition or orthodoxy. One must seek what lives in that tradition and scrap the rest. Essentially, this philosophical argument works itself out in the position statements, lectures, letters, and literature of the modernists. Though unnoticed by his well-known peers, Lovecraft is no less a part of this modernist dialogue.

Lovecraft recommended the writings of Kroeber and Frazer in his correspondence. These influences fuel the fire of the debate on tradition. Levenson says anthropology in the twentieth century both challenges and supports Eurocentrism. It challenges by exposing the irrationalism precursing the culture and saying that irrationalism is at the culture's root. It supports by confronting the primitive, thereby asserting the culture's superiority over its roots.[39]

Tradition and orthodoxy anchor the Eurocentric debate. Eliot drew distinctions between the two in his *After Strange Gods*, a set of lectures published in 1933. Comparing his positions with Lovecraft's, we realize how thoroughly Lovecraft participated in the dialogue.

Eliot, for instance, asserted the necessary role of tradition in a healthy culture.

Religion is part of tradition as he examines it, for Eliot embraced Christianity. Societal conditions need to be set. For tradition to be established, he says,

> Stability is obviously necessary. You are hardly likely to develop tradition except where the bulk of the population is relatively so well off . . . that it has no incentive or pressure to move about. The population should be homogeneous. . . . What is still more important is unity of religious background; and reasons of race and religion combine to make any large number of free-thinking Jews undesirable. There must be a proper balance between urban and rural, industrial and agricultural development. And a spirit of excessive tolerance is to be deprecated.[40]

Note that in 1934 Lovecraft wrote, "I am for the preservation of all values worth preserving—and for the maintenance of complete cultural continuity with the Western-European mainstream" (*SL* 5.63). Here is a point of important philosophical agreement between the two. Lovecraft's oft-mentioned references to "the herd" and his positions on minorities are not statements of neurotic extremism. Rather, they represent a stage of the modernists' conciliatory shift. In a sense, Lovecraft anticipated this shift, as expressed in Eliot's *After Strange Gods*, when he wrote: "So far as I can see, the importance of the radical forms has been greatly exaggerated—indeed, it seems to me that there is already a tendency to return to modes closer to the main stream of tradition" (*SL* 2.250).

Where Eliot and Lovecraft might appear to differ significantly is in the use of the word "preserve." While Eliot finds trouble in "clinging to an old tradition, or attempting to re-establish one, of confusing . . . the real and the sentimental," and where he sees a danger in associating "tradition with the immovable . . . to aim to return to some previous condition which we imagine as having been capable of preservation,"[41] Lovecraft expresses sentiment about his childhood, especially in "The Silver Key" and *The Dream-Quest of Unknown Kadath*. Clearly, Carter cannot return to that childhood for long. It is a time distortion, and therein lies horror. No sentimentalist, even in 1921, Lovecraft wrote, "I accept no literary school in its entirety—I am for . . . modern sincerity but against modern morbidness; for romantic wonder but against romantic sentimentality; for artistic non-morality but against artistic immorality" (*SL* 1.136). Lovecraft was not a pure reactionary. He was unwilling to accept pure radicalism, but there was a place for the radical and the liberal in the maintenance of tradition and in the nursing of modern culture back to health. One sees this in his embrace of Upton Sinclair's political work.

Economic change need not be synonymous with a change in tradition. That is Lovecraft's position in 1934 (see *SL* 5.64). To the contrary, economic stability is necessary if traditional art is to survive the twentieth century, especially the depression. "The best of culture *has always been non-economic*," he writes (*SL* 5.63), but culture will die without dramatic economic reform. This was a new position for Lovecraft, who also said, in 1934, "Art without tradition is only a crippled & impoverished remnant—& I hope that no freakish social overturn will ever be allowed to wreck Western Europe's mainstream" (*SL* 4.410), but then, Eliot's lectures indicate a different angle on Eliot's position in the 1930s. Neither man recanted; both adapted to the circumstances.

Lovecraft, cautious and arguably no expert in economics, no more accepts everything about Sinclair than he accepts everything about any contemporary, but says:

> We *must* disrupt existing institutions *so far as they pertain to the control and distribution of resources*. But only a . . . pleader for plutocracy would try to confuse *this* kind of "disruption"—or economic rearrangement—with the total *cultural* disruption attendant upon violent upheavals like the Russian revolution. (*SL* 5.57)

In the same letter he said Sinclair wanted to move too fast, but that that would be better than not moving at all. Stability requires "the absolute need and inevitability of change" (*SL* 5.57). Certainly this is a shift in Lovecraft's position from a decade earlier. Too often Lovecraft is thought of in static terms. Like his times, he changed, reconsidered, and readjusted philosophically. While the discussions and arguments of modernist spokespeople received much public attention, Lovecraft engaged quietly in the conversation.

If we accept the assertion that Lovecraft was not out of touch with the literary positions of his time, we must take a look at Sinclair's influence upon him. By doing so, we may return to the comparison of Lovecraft's and Eliot's position with a clearer sense of their philosophical, if not literary, parallelism.

Lovecraft wrote or completed *The Dream-Quest of Unknown Kadath* and *The Case of Charles Dexter Ward* in 1927, the year Upton Sinclair's *Oil!* and Floyd Dell's *Upton Sinclair: A Study in Social Protest* were published. Though we probably cannot know just which works by Sinclair Lovecraft read, we know Lovecraft thought little of his novels (see *SL* 5.40). He may have read the Dell book, which in itself is significant. Lovecraft was perfectly capable of appreciating a writer's philosophy even if he saw little of stylistic worth in a given piece of literature by that writer. He wrote in March 1933, "Last month I attended a reading by the enigmatical & celebrated T. S. Eliot" (*SL* 4.159). Refusing to acknowledge Eliot's work as art, he nonetheless gave it a hearing. He approached Sinclair and Eliot as an educated reader: a thinker in touch, if not entirely in line, with his time.

> As the Depression settled in, Sinclair responded with his unsuccessful candidacy for governor on the famous EPIC platform—End Poverty in California. That the Democratic party should have sponsored a Socialist platform and candidate is sufficiently astonishing; but already forces were stirring abroad which were to drive these and other American groups still closer together.[42]

Though not acknowledging Sinclair's work as art, Lovecraft recognized the necessity of the ideas represented within Dell's study and Sinclair's nonfiction tracts. Robert E. Spiller, acknowledging Dell's focus upon these tracts (*The Profits of Religion, The Brass Check, The Goose-Step, The Goslings, Mammonart,* and *Money Writes*), says that through them Sinclair "endeavors to show how agencies of learning and of culture are affected by economic pressures, and how, in our own time, church and press and university are made over into instrumentalities of capitalism."[43]

California's defeat of Sinclair's EPIC bid displeased Lovecraft. He suggested that people reacted adversely to quick change, and he advocated incremental economic change to achieve basic economic self-sufficiency for individual workers while keeping cultural values clear of destructive violence (see *SL* 5.99). Soon after, he wrote:

> The real job is to educate the herd to accept some system other than unsupervised capitalism. They won't accept it now—look at what happened to Sinclair! They've got to see one half-way measure after another fail, until they get it through their thick heads that *only government ownership of large industries, on a nonprofit basis,* will give them any fixed assurance of steady work and decent living conditions. (*SL* 5.162)

Now we are back to the Eliot/Lovecraft philosophical common ground. Indeed, economic change does not need to be synonymous with a change in tradition; rather, economic change ensures the preservation of tradition's elements. As we have seen above, Lovecraft clearly does not expect the 1930s to mimic the 1700s in literary style and taste. Philosophically, scientifically, industrially, economically, socially there is no turning back. Culture must preserve the spirit or intent of the arts but not the letter of them, stylistically. Culture should not turn back but make room for the living element of tradition. Like Eliot, Lovecraft is modernist if we accept Spiller's observation for argument's sake. Spiller says that the modernists in the very early twentieth century tried to work out a synthesis between the older values and concepts of individualism and the newer concept of social responsibility for all individuals. In a general sense, this group was convinced that the root of the trouble in America, the great threat to the old-fashioned society . . . lay in the economic dislocation incident to the exhaustion of the open frontier and the startling growth of monopolies.[44]

Keeping society stable concerns the two of them. A Lovecraft letter from June 1933 echoes more of Eliot's lecture, though on the subject of outside elements Lovecraft was the more moderate voice:

> Many modern nations need to take steps to preserve the integrity of their own native cultures against shrewd and pushing alien influences. . . . Certainly, a dash of alien blood of a superior race (among which a large section of Jews as well as Mongols must be included) does not harm another superior stock *so long as the culture is unimpaired.* (*SL* 4.205–6)

Interestingly, Lovecraft and Eliot illustrated their positions on stability through cultural homogeneity by referring to China. Lovecraft wrote:

> The only kind of a culture which can last indefinitely is one of extreme liberality & non-material values—in which there is no complex interlocking fabric to keep up, & which does not need to exert much pressure on the individual. Such cultures are common in Asia—& the Chinese is probably the highest example. . . . Only ruthless external force in repeated waves can extirpate such a deep-seated & self-sufficient way of life. (*SL* 4.22)

Eliot said: "I have the highest respect for the Chinese mind and for Chinese civilisation; and I am willing to believe that Chinese civilisation at its highest has graces and excellences which may make Europe seem crude."[45] When describing China as a country of tradition before missionaries and John Dewey,[46] Eliot talks about what Lovecraft labeled "ruthless external force." For both of them, tradition is important.

Further, for both of them economics and religion can subvert tradition. Where, then, does tradition differ from and connect with orthodoxy? Eliot, a Christian, defined tradition as an unconscious "way of feeling and acting" common to a group across generations, while orthodoxy requires "exercise of all our conscious intelligence."[47] Both have to do with critical standards, but the latter is rooted particularly in the church. Together, they render in the writer and artist an apprehension of Good and Evil that, when communicated, validates the work of art.[48]

We know Lovecraft believed that a literal rendering of religion was empty and philosophically useless to a modern man. For him, science invalidated the literalization of religious tenets. Good and Evil, as concepts by which to govern life, are too restrictive in the age of Einstein. Nonetheless, religion does have its uses in the preservation of social stability. In 1915 he wrote:

> I am not an orthodox disciple of religion, but I deem it dangerous to tamper with any system so manifestly beneficial to morality. Whatever may be the fault of the church, it has never yet been surpassed or nearly equalled as an agent for the promotion of virtue. And the same thing applies to our present social system. (*SL* 1.17)

In 1916 Lovecraft continued to write about his lack of orthodoxy, the emptiness of religion, and its use in stabilizing the masses. His discussions of religion as a control system move from the political into a modernist viewpoint on the mythic element of the times.

Looking at Joseph Campbell's *The Inner Reaches of Outer Space: Metaphor as Myth and as Religion* we find Lovecraft's oft-discussed mechanist-materialist position on the cutting edge. Campbell examines the effects of scientific discovery and cultural interaction upon humanity. A few lines cannot do Campbell justice. When forced to think of global populations, multitudes of god-images and symbolizations, rather than, as in ancient times, a single chosen people of God with the single Answer, one asks: "Is the center the earth? Is the center the moon? The center is anywhere you like. . . . The chosen center may be anywhere. The Holy Land is no special place. It is every place that has ever been recognized and mythologized by any people as home."[49] Lovecraft experimented with this viewpoint in 1916:

> Whether . . . Christ was alive after his nominal execution; or whether the whole Resurrection legend is a myth, is immaterial. Very little reliable testimony could come from so remote a province as Judaea at that time. For the sensitive mind to harass itself over ancient and mediaeval conceptions . . . or to wear itself to fragments trying to accept that which it can never accept, is as cruel and reprehensible as to deprive the masses of their spiritual and orthodox solace. (*SL* 1.29)

He pursues it further in 1917 when he suggests that the sheer vastness of space belies Earth-centric religion (*SL* 1.44–45). If a thinking person accepts the discoveries of science, especially those of Einstein, that person cannot accept the literalization of nationalistic or even earth-centered religions. "The Judaeo-Christian mythology is NOT TRUE," wrote Lovecraft in 1918, because man is not the center of the universe and because religion belies the "craving to know" (*SL* 1.60–61).

Campbell addresses the problem which, he says, began with Copernicus:

> The heliocentric universe has never been translated into a mythology. Science and religion have therewith gone apart. And that is the case to the present hour, with the problem even compounded by our present recognition of the inconceivable magnitude of this galaxy of stars, of which our life-giving sun is a peripheral member, circling with its satellites in this single galaxy among millions within a space of incredible distances, having no fixed form or end.[50]

This is Lovecraft's position, each and every time he mentions the insignificance of human affairs in the scheme of cosmic vastness. "The whole idea of 'sin' . . . is in 1932 simply a curiosity of intellectual history" and the "veil of mystery" hung by spirituality and primitive "religious attitude" has been torn away. Science neutralizes spiritualism and renders old myths inert (*SL* 4.4). This attitude is exactly what Eliot refers to in the lectures when he says that blasphemy is not possible in the work of a writer who does not believe in that which he blasphemes.

Here is the modern "horror" behind the veil, one that Levenson ascribes, in part, to Wyndham Lewis: "'Dehumanization,' wrote Lewis in *Blast,* 'is the chief diagnostic of the Modern World.' Or, as he would later put it, 'Man was not the hero of our universe.'"[51] In this, and in the relativization of good and evil, Lovecraft is most Nietzschean. Campbell writes:

> This understanding of the ubiquity of the metaphysical center perfectly matches the lesson of the galaxies . . . epitomized in Einstein's representation of the utter impossibility of establishing absolute rest. It is the essence of relativity. . . . It implies that moral judgments depend . . . upon the relation of the frame of reference.[52]

Campbell refers to Nietzsche: "'All ideals are dangerous, since they denigrate and stigmatize what is actual. They are poisons, which, however, as occasional medicaments, are indispensable.'"[53] For some, the Einsteinian vastness necessitates literalization of old religion. Everyone cannot face what is actual. Art, too, for Lovecraft is useful here. It cannot adequately represent universal reality, and therefore should not try, but it *can* and *should* focus on the traditional, through the regional. Over fifteen years later he placed economics in the position of stabilizer, but he defended religion's place.

St. Armand and Stanley tell us that Lovecraft was worried about a collapse of modern culture at *The Waste Land*'s appearance and that, for Lovecraft, Eliot's poem accelerated the disintegration of society and poetic form, making it no better than a Cthulhu cultist.[54] Remember, though, that Cthulhu, frightening as he is, embodies cosmic Disinterest, not Evil. Eliot's poem reminds Lovecraft of human insignificance and triviality. This makes it philosophy or science rather than art. It neither stabilizes nor preserves culture. Tradition or "backgrounds of tradition" are, for Lovecraft, "all that lend . . . objects & events the illusion of meaning, value, or dramatic interest in an ultimately purposeless cosmos—hence I preach & practice means of averting the ennui, despair & confusion of a guideless & standardless struggle with unveiled chaos" (*SL* 2.125). Though the universe has no meaning, art must at least create illusions or mankind, bereft of tradition's reference points, will go mad with in the face of a Void and a Vastness opened by science and philosophy.

This anti-entropic view of art begins to make Lovecraft's reference to the Antaeus myth significant. If art, in however illusory a manner, serves to stave off entropy or chaos, then the artist becomes a modern hero and anti-hero. Refusing to face Chaos, or reality, appears cowardly or anti-heroic; yet, turning part of one's mind away from Chaos after one knows it is there might be the course of wisdom or psychological health.

Science, for Lovecraft, demonstrates the entropy and chaos of the universe. It alters irrevocably the philosophical humanocentric perspective. As realist, Lovecraft says, in a sense, "of course." As artist/writer, he says, "so be it" and works to preserve the cultural integrity of civilization as he values it by channeling through regionalism, certainly a not unmodernist thing to do. In 1927, a pivotal year creatively and, as we have seen above, perhaps politically (from exposure to Sinclair's political notions), Lovecraft wrote: "All genuine art, I think, is local and rooted in the soil. . . . Take a man away from the fields and groves which bred him—or which moulded the lives of his forefathers—and you cut off his sources of power altogether" (*SL* 2.131).

The artist is Antaeus, son of Gaea (Earth) and Poseidon, who draws strength from touching his mother. He wrestles strangers and kills them once he has weakened them. When Heracles discovered Antaeus' power, he lifted him from the earth and then strangled or crushed the weakened giant. Aside from the Freudian implications of Lovecraft's Antaeus allusions, the artistic implications are interesting. The myth works as metaphor for Lovecraft's vision of art's relationship with science and philosophy. When out of touch with the Earth, when moved above or away from it, Antaeus loses his strength. Modern art fails when removed from that which gives it power. Heracles (unthinking classicism or brute tradition) crushed the life out of art when it removed art from living tradition.

The modern artist should ease the reader or viewer into handling emotionally what is, for him as it was for Kurtz, beyond the veil, but he must do so in a manner that is neither sterile (without feeling) or puerile. Mindless tradition (i.e., unthinking religious prostration) cannot do it, a blind acceptance of the canons of any particular literary academe or club cannot do it, nor can refusal to acknowledge the vastness revealed by science. What can do it is the Tradition of art, a tradition that implies for Lovecraft gradual change, revitalization rather than ossification. "The problem of everyone working in an artistic medium," says Lovecraft in 1927, is "to take a known setting and restore to it in vivid freshness all the accumulated wonder and beauty which it has produced in its long continuous history" (*SL* 2.131). Tradition is the Earth-Mother; the artist is the hero: "Culture as a whole . . . may be cosmopolitan and international; but creative artistic force is always provincial and nationalistic" (*SL* 2.131). This is not so very far from the statements both he and Eliot make later in the 1930s. Modernism is workable. For Lovecraft, an artistic examination of the unconscious is possible within the "main current of Western-European literary tradition . . . in its aesthetic essentials" (*SL* 2.249). Experimentation is welcome, but with moderation.

Eliot indicts modern writers who tend to let personality set individual standards.[55] Personality gets in the way of the artistic creation itself. Personality impedes the critical standards of tradition and orthodoxy. It erodes a sense of social morality, as in the case of D. H. Lawrence.[56] Modern writers who ignore the tenets of "Protestant Christianity" give our literature a "flavour of immaturity" when it is placed against European works.[57]

Lovecraft voiced a similar concern. Speaking of unnamed "anti-traditional radicals" he said: "Their products are not art, because they come from theory instead of from feeling. And they do not represent this age, because they do not embody those attributes of the European mainstream which this age has inherited" (*SL* 5.54). Lovecraft is moderated modernist, not purist antiquarian. He concerns himself with the development or growth of modern literature. If not modernist, he would not take interest in contemporary poetry. Yet in 1927 he attended a lecture delivered by Padraic Colum. To him, Colum "shewed very clearly that the ideas & life of the present period are as yet artistically unformulated" (*SL* 2.104). Something is in the process of coming into being. Things are in flux, and he knows it.

Lovecraft does not deny that flux. The intensity and sheer number of his references to and criticisms of both his contemporaries and their work demonstrate his interest in it, perhaps even to the extent of shaping it somewhat through the genre of weird fiction. Campbell's question reflects Lovecraft's: "And so, in mythological terms what is to happen now? All of our old gods are dead, and the new have not yet been born."[58] Modernists realize a discontinuity with metaphors and pre-twentieth century attitudes, no matter which schools or movements battle one another: "our mechanical & industrial age is . . . so far removed from . . . ancestral conditions as to make impossible its expression in artistic media" (*SL* 2.103–4).

Here is a key, silver or not. It isn't that modern poetry is useless. Rather, it is that modern art, like Antaeus removed from the Earth-Mother, like the earth before it cooled, is molten, inaccessible, unready. Science displaces tradition so much that tradition must be given a chance to reintegrate, renew, and reorient itself within the new reality. Lovecraft says: "What benefits mankind is *not constant change, but satisfactory adjustment*" (*SL* 5.50).

Look at the oft-quoted reference to *The Waste Land* in *The Case of Charles Dexter Ward* (*MM* 209). Joshi, Stanley, St. Armand, and others have pointed to this as another Lovecraftian jab at Eliot, and certainly it must be read so. Along with that, though, we might consider the context. By repeating first the Lord's Prayer and then "a mnemonic hodge-podge like the modernistic *Waste Land* of Mr. T. S. Eliot," Willett travels between the two extremes that Lovecraft moderates in his own modernism. Willett ends up with the Yog-Sothoth incantation. Willett performs as Campbell's modern man with old spiritualism neutralized and bereft of a new one. Only in traveling between the two extremes and then landing upon the middle ground outside and between them does Willett feel soothed.

This is not back-turning or head-burying. Certainly it embeds Lovecraft within the modernist argument as expressed by Pound from 1917 to 1927. Schwartz says of Pound's "Provincialism the Enemy" and "From the Editor of 'The Exile'":

> He [Pound] maintains that it is as dangerous for a culture to ignore the past as it is to isolate itself from other cultures in the present. If we forget the historical foundations of our civilization, we lose our sense of cultural identity. . . . If we neglect alternative forms of awareness buried in the past, we lose our ability to assess and renew civilization in the present. Historical recollection makes us aware of both our existing identity and our future possibilities.[59]

Thinking of "The Shadow out of Time" we realize again that the Lovecraft's modern horror can be Pound's recollection.

Schwartz's observations about Eliot's estrangement of the poetic personae from society draw us back to Lovecraft's artist/anti-hero Randolph Carter. Lovecraft experiences discomfort with sequels and recurring characters. Herbert West's gruesome undertakings were avowed hackwork, and though the Carter tales are arguably not Lovecraft's stylistic best, they do present a working out of the artist's place in the modern world. Think of Carter/Zkauba of "Through the Gates of the Silver Key" when Schwartz says:

> In his poetry . . . Eliot creates personae who are only partially detached from, and cannot transform, their own external behavior. Their self-awareness produces no change in the world around them. . . . Their partial detachment offers little more than painful awareness of their deplorable condition. Neither absorbed fully into the temporal order nor entirely detached from it, they remain acquiescent participants in a society from which they are estranged.[60]

To argue that Eliot and Lovecraft are in perfect parity with one another would be silly. Yet they examine very similar themes. Perhaps Lovecraft, in his Carter sequence, comes closer to Pound. Schwartz says that Pound "struggled with the polarities of form and flux, and sought to create a productive interaction between them . . . [and used] constructs like the ideogram and the precise interpretive metaphor, constructs that establish a creative tension between potential and chaos."[61] Carter as artist/anti-hero rejects both dogma (literalized religious values and popular artistic tenets) and chaos (Azathoth), but Carter/Zkauba becomes not unlike one of Pound's interpretative metaphors, alien imposed upon human, both forms of the Self or Archetype which is beyond the "Gates" of reality and the type of art which Lovecraft eschews as functional modernism.

Modernism in the early twentieth century, posits Schwartz, involves "discontinuity between the text and everyday reality: distortions of temporal order; limited or unreliable narrators, often with unusual points of view."[62] Weird fiction in Lovecraft's hands experiments with these distortions and narrator-types.

Art, to Lovecraft, rejects convention, not tradition. In 1923 he commented: "Popular authors do not and apparently cannot appreciate the fact that true art is obtainable only by rejecting normality and conventionality in toto . . . [but] they reiterate the same old conventional values and motives and perspectives."[63] He spoke about Anderson's *Winesburg, Ohio* as a tame, even tepid, iconoclastically modern attempt to investigate the horrors of ancestry. In response, he wrote "Facts concerning the Late Arthur Jermyn and His Family."[64] There is no artistic power in conventionality, but there is in tradition. Reality is not art. As Schwartz says of Pound's viewpoint, "art is at once a process of transforming fragments into unity and a process of imposing form on the chaotic flux."[65]

When Carter meets his Archetype and dissolves into the formlessness within which he senses all his other selves, he is truly the artist imposing his self, if not his form, upon the universe, and Lovecraft may be in some way playing with I. A. Richards's idea of multiple points of view.[66]

The narrator of "The Call of Cthulhu" suggests that modern art does not often reproduce the crypticism of prehistory. Often is the important word. At the very least, this suggests that while Pound and Eliot find equal power in the very ancient and the very modern, Lovecraft finds more horrific power in the ancient forgotten traditions. Whether ancient or modern, chaos is chaos and art, as in "The Haunter of the Dark," is an illusion of imposition of "order on chaos" (*DH* 104).

Lovecraft also participates in the ongoing modernist discussion about the power of prose and poetry. "One of the persistent subjects of modernist dispute, the relative positions of poetry and prose, thus flared again [around 1915]."[67] While it is true that Lovecraft expresses poetic antiquarianism or archaism until age twenty-seven, remember that he went beyond this. In 1920 he wrote, "Poetry to me [c. 1908–17] meant merely the most effective way of asserting my archaic instincts" (*SL* 1.110). Lovecraft subordinated modern poetry to modern philosophy. In 1920 he also suggested "that the keenly sensitive development which in the philosopher affects the imaginative and speculative functions, in the poet affects those simple nervous-ganglial centres which give rise to the emotions of human relationship" (*SL* 1.117). Modern poetry is subordinate to philosophy because it asserts the humanocentrist view, which is not the same thing as asserting an Antaeus-like regionalism.

Imagism arises in a discussion of modern poetry. Although Lovecraft decried imagism, the image in poetry remained very important to him. "The greatest bards have been the simplest. . . . Even Keats . . . dealt more in crystally clear images than in learned riddles and cryptical adumbration," Lovecraft wrote (*SL* 1.127). His definition of image differs from that of many contemporaries, but he does acknowledge its centrality. Nor did the image belong solely to poetry. When Lovecraft wrote of the "Imagism nonsense" in 1916 he suggested that, though it bears no relation to poetry, it might work as prose (see

SL 1.24–25). Lovecraft's variant of imagism is not the technically reductive and linguistically lean crypticism he sees in the movement proper. Instead, imagism creates, in prose, "a *picture of a mood*" (*SL* 5.160).

Revisit "Pickman's Model" and consider, for a moment, that aside from being a weird tale written to picture a mood, it may also be in some sense Lovecraft writing with tongue-in-cheek about the imagists and the faults of modern literature concerned with flat realism. It may be pure coincidence that the narrator is addressing someone named Eliot. Isn't it possible to wonder, though, if Lovecraft, through his narrator, is blasting T. S. Eliot, asserting his point that there is more horror behind or beneath than within the slummy squalor that is reality? Recall that Lovecraft wrote "Arthur Jermyn" as a reaction to *Winesburg.*

From this angle, the last line of "Pickman's Model" is doubly interesting: "But by God, Eliot, *it was a photograph from life*" (*DH* 25). Lovecraft acknowledges the power in the scientifically produced image, but only if that image is of the horror beyond the veil, not the "dreary realism as in Sherwood Anderson" (*SL* 1.213) of the slum itself. The narrator needles this "Eliot" fellow, especially in the funny line just before the climax, "But here's the coffee—take it black, Eliot, if you're wise" (*DH* 24), as if to say, "Wake up and smell the coffee." Levenson says that for Hulme, Conrad, and Woolf, "there is the frequent image of life and art as essentially amorphous—misty, hazy, fluid," and that Eliot and Pound want "clarity and distinctness, and there is a positive dislike for the soft, the damp and the misty."[68] Lovecraft gives his Eliot a very clear and distinct image of something soft and damp. Perhaps he is suggesting middle ground and the absurdity of either extreme.

In 1928 Lovecraft anticipates a conciliatory moderation in modernist literary experimentation. He asserts this moderate tone while embracing literary experimentation within tradition when he writes:

> The details of poetry must always change slightly from generation to generation, as a culture's philosophic outlook & sense of emotional values change, & as specific words, forms, ideas, & images gain & lose certain associational overtones through the added experience & changing environment of the race. But these details need not involve any such spectacular structural innovations as are found in the chaotic products of the "advanced moderns." (*SL* 2.250–51)

Read this not as an antiquarian's indictment of modernist work.

Once Lovecraft sees tradition reasserting itself and the chaos subsiding, he comments that prose is sinking into a slough of abbreviated affectation. However, *verse* is spectacularly and paradoxically *improving*, so that I do not know any age since that of Elizabeth in which poets have enjoy'd a better medium of expression. One can but wish that a race of major bards surviv'd to take advantage of the post-Victorian rise in taste and fastidiousness. (*SL* 4.33)

If not to the poets themselves, this is a large tip of the hat to the results of modernist debates. Again, this is not back-turning. Just a year later he comments: "The newer novels are vastly superior to the older ones in that they deal with real human traits & motives & conduct" and commends the "greater honesty" of modern fiction (*SL* 4.140–41). Lovecraft, like Eliot, is conciliatory and more moderate, and so, indeed, is this stage of modernism. The feverish argumentation subsides.

By 1935 Lovecraft acknowledges that perhaps "poetry instead of fiction is the only effective vehicle" for weird themes (*SL* 5.199). The reconciliation with modernism is nearly complete. He posits that while real art gives pleasure to some, not all, non-art gives pleasure to no one. Inasmuch as some have taken pleasure in modern art, then, it is art, not just science. Just because some (presumably Lovecraft among them) cannot feel it, that doesn't make it any the less artistic (see *SL* 5.96–97). Perhaps by 1933 Lovecraft intuits a relationship between *The Waste Land* and its world not completely unlike the relationship between Butler's *Way of All Flesh* and the nineteenth-century world. He says Butler wrote "in disgusted protest against the *hollow* [my italics] state of things around him" (*SL* 4.141).

If we accept Levenson's identification of literary modernism's stages and displacements, we see Lovecraft's participation in another modernist argument. Levenson identifies two stages:

First, the shift from spiritual transcendence to a naturalist or humanist standpoint; second . . . from humanism and naturalism towards subjectivism. . . . These displacements are linked by a commitment to *immediacy*—that is, the same principle of experimental immediacy which leads to dismissal of spiritual reality in favour of "this world," leads from "this world" to "my world."[69]

Lovecraft dismissed spiritual reality, but in favor of scientific relativism. He took a middle ground between introversion and extroversion, topics under discussion at this time. Schwartz discusses the clash between introversion and extraversion in Eliot's "tension between internal and external points of view . . . the conflict between the desire to maintain a distinct internal identity and the inability to do so in the presence of others."[70]

The conflict between inner and outer takes place often in Lovecraft's work. In this case, "The Thing on the Doorstep" comes to mind just as readily as Carter trapped within Zkauba. Lovecraft posits a necessary median between the inner and the outer. He wrote:

> Introverts . . . must tend to imagine more or less distortedly. . . . It must be from extreme and exaggerated introversion that the bulk of affected ultra-modern aestheticism comes—the brass foundry-slag of "sculptors" like Brancusi, the woodcut hash of Masereel . . . and the remarkable shantihs of T. S. Eliot and his ilk. . . . Introversion means originality at its best and affectation or madness at its worst. (*SL* 2.273)

Even here he is saying that there may be something to the work of his contemporaries, but only if they can temper that ultra-modern (read cosmopolitan) philosophy with something. The something is tradition manifested through regionalism. For him art is regional. That which tries to be universal art will be both banal and "mediocre" (*SL* 2.133). Lovecraft wrote:

> Many an aesthetic dreamer is not a *true* introvert, but rather (as Aldous Huxley points out in *Proper Studies*) a *sensationalist-extravert* who derives his emotional satisfactions from the visible world viewed purely as an impersonal decorative spectacle, instead of from an inner world of his own subjective synthesising. (*SL* 4.31)

In part, this is Lovecraft's attraction to Yeats. Yeats also provides common ground between Lovecraft and Eliot.

Both Yeats's poetry and his participation in the regionalist Irish renaissance attracted Lovecraft (see *SL* 2.130), though earlier Lovecraft thought Machen of more literary importance (*SL* 1.333). Note the shift in emphasis from prose to poetry. Apparently Yeats influenced Eliot more before the latter's conversion to Christianity. Of Yeats's historical importance Eliot wrote:

> Born into a world in which the doctrine of "Art for Art's Sake" was generally accepted, and living on into one in which art has been asked to be instrumental to social purposes, he held firmly to the right view which is between these . . . and showed that an artist, by serving his art with entire integrity, is at the same time rendering the greatest service he can to his own nation and to the whole world.[71]

Lovecraft might have said something very similar. As we saw above in the case of O'Neill, and as we know very well about Lovecraft from his correspondence, to be true to one's art, whether or not it sells, whether or not it is popular, is to be an artist and not a hack. Lovecraft believed, with Eliot, that the artist's focus must be regional and characterized by integrity.

Eliot's later castigation of Yeats's work in the creation of his own mythology would probably have saddened rather than angered Lovecraft. By the early to mid-1930s the anger, the fevered reactionism, had subsided, as we have seen. Eliot says in one of the *After Strange Gods* lectures: "Mr. Yeats's "supernatural world" was the wrong supernatural world. It was not a world of spiritual significance, not a world of real Good and Evil, of holiness or sin, but a highly sophisticated lower mythology summoned, like a physician, to supply the fading pulse of poetry."[72] Aside from the fact that this belies Eliot's earlier support of an artist's created world, it may indicate to Lovecraft that the moderation of modernist frenzy through reintegration with tradition is becoming mired in convention and overliteralized orthodoxy. Here Lovecraft may align with the Poundian doctrine: "Monotheism abstracts the divine from its true source—the individual's immediate experience of natural beauty. Polytheism, by contrast, is tied directly to the individual's contact with nature. The gods arise from the sensuous apprehension of a particular place at a particular time."[73] This brings Carter's City to mind. The City is of Nature, not of Man. Men and gods meet there. It is not one of cosmopolitan pollution and dreary streets, nor is it one of total non-human chaos or completely unrecognizable towers. It, like Antaeus, is the metaphor. Perhaps it is most indicative of Lovecraft's middle ground. As much as the Earth-Mother of regionalism, it is that which the artist as Antaeus must touch for his strength.

Notes

1. S. T. Joshi, "A Look at Lovecraft's Letters," in *Selected Papers on Lovecraft* (West Warwick, RI: Necronomicon Press, 1989), 67.

2. S. T. Joshi, "Topical References in Lovecraft," *Extrapolation* 25 (Fall 1984): 247.

3. Michael H. Levenson, *A Genealogy of Modernism: A Study of English Literary Doctrine 1908–1922* (Cambridge: Cambridge University Press, 1984).

4. *The Oxford Companion to English Literature,* 5th ed., ed. Margaret Drabble (Oxford: Oxford University Press, 1985), 658.

5. Peter Cannon, "Lovecraft and the Mainstream Literature of His Day," *LS* No. 7 (Fall 1982): 25–29.

6. Ibid.

7. Barton L. St. Armand and John H. Stanley, "H. P. Lovecraft's *Waste Paper*: A Facsimile and Transcript of the Original Draft," *Books at Brown* 26 (1978): 31–47.

8. Ibid., 42.

9. Ibid., 43.

10. Ibid.

11. Paul Buhle, "Dystopia as Utopia: Howard Phillips Lovecraft and the Unknown Content of American Horror Literature," in *FDOC* 196–210.

12. Winfield Townley Scott, "A Parenthesis on Lovecraft as Poet," in *FDOC* 212–13.

13. Malcolm Cowley, *Exiles Return* (New York: Viking Press, 1951); quoted in Cannon, 28.

14. Levenson, 205

15. St. Armand and Stanley, 36.

16. T. S. Eliot, "John Dryden," *Times Literary Supplement* (9 June 1921): 361; rpt. in Levenson, 211.

17. Levenson, 206.

18. Ibid., 173–74.

19. Ibid., 173.

20. Cited in Levenson, 174.

21. Levenson, 174.

22. T. S. Eliot, *The Waste Land: A Facsimile and Transcript of the Original Drafts Including the Annotations of Ezra Pound*, ed. Valerie Eliot (New York: Harcourt Brace Jovanovich, 1971), 143.

23. Ibid., 145.

24. John Masefield, "The Haunted," *Poems* (New York: Macmillan, 1967), 279–80. "The Haunted" first appeared in *King Cole and Other Poems* (London: William Heinemann, 1923).

25. Heywood Broun, "The Emperor Jones," *New York Tribune* (4 November 1920); rpt. in *O'Neill and His Plays: Four Decades of Criticism*, ed. Oscar Cargill, N. Bryllion Fagin, and William J. Fisher (New York: New York University Press, 1961), 144.

26. John Shand, "The Emperor Jones," *New Statesman* (19 September 1925): 628–29; rpt. in Jordan Yale Miller, *Playwright's Progress: Eugene O'Neill and the Critics* (Chicago: Scott, Foresman, 1965), 23.

27. Maida Castellun, "O'Neill's 'The Emperor Jones' Thrills and Fascinates," *New York Call* (10 November 1920); rpt. in Miller, 23.

28. Alexander Woollcott, "The New O'Neill Play," *New York Times* (7 November 1920); rpt. in Miller, 21–22.

29. Eugene O'Neill, "'I Want to Be an Artist or Nothing': A Letter to George Pierce Baker" (16 July 1914); rpt. in *O'Neill and His Plays*, 20.

30. Introduction, *O'Neill and His Plays*, 5.

31. T. S. Eliot, "All God's Chillun Got Wings," *Criterion* (April 1926); rpt. in *O'Neill and His Plays,* 168–69.

32. John Gassner, "Homage to O'Neill," *Theatre Time* (Summer 1951); rpt. in *O'Neill and His Plays,* 330.

33. John Gassner, *Directions in Modern Theatre and Drama: An Expanded Edition of* Form and Idea in Modern Theatre (New York: Holt, Rinehart & Winston, 1966), 17.

34. Levenson, 100.

35. Sanford Schwartz, *The Matrix of Modernism: Pound, Eliot, and Early Twentieth-Century Thought* (Princeton, NJ: Princeton University Press, 1985), 16.

36. Schwartz, 109.

37. T. S. Eliot, *The Sacred Wood;* rpt. in Schwartz, 109.

38. Schwartz, 110.

39. See Levenson, 206–7.

40. T. S. Eliot, *After Strange Gods: A Primer of Modern Heresy,* The Page-Barbour Lectures at the University of Virginia 1933 (New York: Harcourt, Brace, 1934), 20.

41. Eliot, *After Strange Gods,* 19.

42. Robert E. Spiller et al., ed., *Literary History of the United States,* 3rd rev. ed. (New York: Macmillan, 1963), 998.

43. Spiller, 997.

44. Ibid., 977.

45. Eliot, *After Strange Gods,* 43.

46. Ibid., see 44.

47. Ibid., 31.

48. Ibid., see 55–67.

49. Joseph Campbell, *The Inner Reaches of Outer Space: Metaphor as Myth and as Religion* (New York: Alfred Van Der Marck Editions, 1985), 44.

50. Campbell, 43.

51. Wyndham Lewis, "The New Egos," *Blast* 1 (June 1914): 141; rpt. in Levenson, 125.

52. Campbell, 44.

53. Ibid., 44.

54. St. Armand and Stanley, 34–36.

55. See Eliot, *After Strange Gods,* 57–58.

56. Ibid., see 39.

57. Ibid., 41.

58. Campbell, 45.

59. Schwartz, 136–37.

60. Ibid., 205.

61. Ibid., 133.

62. Ibid., 102.

63. HPL to Edwin Baird (August 1923), *Uncollected Letters* (West Warwick, RI: Necronomicon Press, 1986), 8.

64. Ibid.

65. Schwartz, 126.

66. See Schwartz, 65.

67. Levenson, 156.

68. Ibid., 154–55.

69. Ibid., 116.

70. Schwartz, 197.

71. T. S. Eliot, "Yeats," in *Yeats: A Collection of Critical Essays*, ed. John Unterecker (Englewood Cliffs, NJ: Prentice-Hall, 1963), 62–63.

72. Eliot, *After Strange Gods*, 50.

73 Schwartz, 118.

Synchronistic Worlds: Lovecraft and Borges

Barton Levi St. Armand

On 7 December 1967, Jorge Luis Borges was in Providence, Rhode Island, on his second American tour to read and to lecture. That evening he consented to address a secret society of Brown University undergraduates and faculty members, dedicated to the discussion of general intellectual topics, and he began his conversation by observing that "The world is insoluble, but then you call yourself 'The Sphinx,' and must delight in riddles." Borges went on to regale the society of "The Sphinx" (of which I was a guest and not a member) with a Socratic monologue on Robert Frost's poem, "Stopping by Woods on a Snowy Evening," wondering if the narrator of the poem really knew to whom the woods belonged, if they were humanity's woods, God's woods, Dante's metaphysical woods, etc. I do not think that Borges solved this conundrum or that he even wanted to solve it, but, as with his tales, essays, and sketches, he certainly conveyed to the assembled company his deep delight in simply posing the riddle itself.

After the talk he signed my paperback copy of *Labyrinths* with a labyrinthine scribble dictated, of course, by his blindness, but also (as I thought at the time) in a script that consciously harked back to the mysterious stone hieroglyphs at the end of Poe's *Narrative of Arthur Gordon Pym*. Since Poe has time-honored connections with Providence, I was prompted to ask this most learned and eclectic of contemporary writers if he happened to be conversant with another master of the fantastic who had lived and died in the city. Somewhat to my surprise, Borges replied that no, he was not at all familiar with the works of H. P. Lovecraft.

At about the same time, an interview that Richard Burgin conducted with Borges reveals that he *did* know something of Lovecraft's art, yet in a context that prompted him to banish Lovecraft to an oblivion as complete as the one that swallows up his own figure of the Arabian scholar in "Averroes' Search." Speaking of an anthology compiled by six Argentine writers (including himself) who chose the best stories they knew and which came out in Buenos Aires "about six months ago," Borges observed that "I don't think the aim was really to find out the best stories in the world by any means, I think what they [the

other writers] wanted was to get an anthology that people might want to buy,
no? That people might be interested in. Then one took [Melville's] 'Bartleby,'
and one took, I don't know why, a very disagreeable and rather bogus story by
Lovecraft." Borges asked Burgin if he had read Lovecraft, and when Burgin
replied in the negative, Borges declared rather imperiously, "Well, no reason
why you should."[1]

Therefore imagine my surprise when I read the implicit praise accorded to
Lovecraft by Borges's inclusion of him in his *Introduction to American Literature*,
originally published in Buenos Aires in 1967 and reissued in English translation
by the University Press of Kentucky four years later. Based upon the lectures
Borges gave when he was Professor of English and American literature at the
University of Buenos Aires, this work might better be considered in the genre
made popular by Isaac D'Israeli's *Curiosities of Literature* (1834), a favorite source
book for Poe, or classified with odd anthologies such as Borges's own *Book of
Imaginary Beings*, since it is as much a cabinet of strange and dissonant facts as it is
a primer of American literature. As one of his own students commented about
the original lectures, "The problem is that Borges sometimes chooses what is
most important for Borges and not what is most important in that literature."[2]

Of Sherwood Anderson we learn, for example, that "He was married four
times; for many years he was at one and the same time editor of a Republican
and a Democratic newspaper in Marion, Virginia."[3] Almost every page confirms Borges's love for the parodic, the lugubrious, the serendipitous, and the
absurd. In the penultimate chapter (number 13) on "The Detective Story, Science Fiction, and the Far West," Lovecraft is accorded as much space as had
been previously allotted to E. A. Robinson, F. Scott Fitzgerald, and Robert
Penn Warren. Borges writes:

> Howard Philips [*sic*] Lovecraft (1890–1937) was born in Providence, Rhode
> Island. Very sensitive and of delicate health, he was educated by his widowed
> mother and aunts. Like Hawthorne he enjoyed solitude, and although he
> worked during the day, he did so with the shades lowered.
>
> In 1924 he married and moved to Brooklyn; in 1929 he was divorced and
> returned to Providence, where he went back to his life of solitude. He died of
> cancer. He detested the present and professed a fondness for the eighteenth
> century.
>
> Science attracted him: his first article had to do with astronomy. He pub-
> lished but a single book during his lifetime; after his death his friends brought
> together in book form the considerable body of his work, which had been dis-
> persed in anthologies and magazines. He studiously imitated the style of Poe

with its sonorities and pathos, and he wrote co[s]mic nightmares [*orig:* "pesadillas cosmicas"]. In his stories one meets beings from remote planets and from ancient or future epochs who dwell in human bodies to study the universe, or, conversely, souls of our time who during sleep explore monstrous worlds, distant in time and space. Among his works we shall recall "The Color from Space," [*sic*] "The Dunwich Horror," and "The Rats in the Wall." [*sic*]

He also left a voluminous correspondence. To Poe's influence upon him one should also add that of the visionary storyteller Arthur Machen.[4]

It is obvious from this summary that Borges had read not only some of Lovecraft's major works ("The Shadow out of Time" in particular) but also an account of his life and a modicum of criticism about him. This fact is confirmed by Paul Theroux, who in a 1978 conversation with Borges "about horror stories in general" elicited the perverse revelation that "I like Lovecraft's horror stories. His plots are very good, but his style is atrocious. I once dedicated a story to him."[5] Ultimately, Borges's attitude toward Lovecraft can only be described in terms of a syndrome of attraction-repulsion, an aesthetic of extreme polarities or a metaphysics of paradox, similar to the *Mysterium tremendum* as described by Rudolf Otto.[6] Both horns of this dilemma demand their own special polishing.

I

Let us begin with the attractions and congruencies. Given Borges's own love of mirror reflections—his doubling and extension of himself beyond the mere duality of a parable like "Borges and I"—we should not be surprised to find some pertinent connections between the Argentine sophisticate and the American provincial. Borges, too, published in scattered journals and ephemeral periodicals; he, too, was "collected" by assiduous and dedicated friends and disciples, though luckily during his lifetime and not after (the first three volumes of his *Collected Works* were published in 1954 by Emecé in Buenos Aires). Like Lovecraft, as a youth he fed his loneliness on the works of Poe, the *Arabian Nights,* and classical mythology. Just as Lovecraft produced "The Poem of Ulysses, or the New Odyssey" at the age of eight, so did Borges "set down in quite bad English a kind of handbook on Greek mythology, no doubt cribbed from Lemprière," when he was six or seven.[7] Both men were dedicated nativists and local colorists, though Borges flirted with internationalism after having fallen in with the literary group called the *Ultraists* when in Spain from 1919 to 1921. Then he produced poems which, in their stripped-down search for pure and uncluttered metaphor, modern critics like Ronald J. Christ have classified with the imagism of Ezra Pound or the amygism of Amy Lowell. Yet as he writes in his "Autobiographical Essay":

> We returned to Buenos Aires on the *Reina Victoria Eugenia* toward the end of March, 1921. It came to me as a surprise, after living in so many European cities—after so many memories of Geneva, Zurich, Nîmes, Córdoba, and Lisbon—to find that my native town had grown, and that it was now a very large, sprawling, and almost endless city of low buildings with flat roofs, stretching west toward what geographers and literary hands call the pampa. It was more than a homecoming; it was a rediscovery. I was able to see Buenos Aires keenly and eagerly because I had been away from it for a long time. Had I never gone abroad, I wonder whether I would ever have seen it with the peculiar shock and glow that it now gave me. The city—not the whole city, of course, but a few places in it that became emotionally significant to me—inspired the poems of my first published book, *Fervor de Buenos Aires.*[8]

Lovecraft did not have the opportunity of exploring literary Europe, but his disastrous "New York Exile" of 1924–26 prompted him to reaffirm his own fervor for Providence as he never had before. To Borges, the endless sprawl of Buenos Aires was a magical chessboard or labyrinth of human possibility that stretched out to the infinity of the west, and the horizon of the pampa beckoned to a vanishing point of myth, mystery, and legend. To Lovecraft, the city of Providence huddled protectively on the banks of its bay and underground rivers, forming a nest or a shell that in phenomenological terms drilled downward into the mysterious eighteenth-century past rather than opening outward toward an infinite future. He wrote his aunt, Lillian Clark, that he had "never mentally dwelt anywhere else," and made his letter to her of 29 March 1926 into a personal manifesto:

> To all intents & purposes I am more naturally isolated from mankind than Nathaniel Hawthorne himself, who dwelt alone in the midst of crowds, & whom Salem knew only after he died. Therefore, it may be taken as axiomatic that the people of a place matter absolutely nothing to me except as components of the general landscape and scenery. . . . My life lies not among *people* but among *scenes*—my local affections are not personal, but topographical & architectural. No one in Providence—family aside—has any especial bond of interest with me, but for that matter no one in Cambridge or anywhere else has, either. The question is that of which roofs & chimneys & doorways & trees & street vistas I love the best; which hills & woods, which woods & meadows, which farm-

houses & views of distant white steeples in green valleys. I am always an out-sider—to all scenes and all people—but outsiders have their sentimental prefer-ences in visual environment. I will be dogmatic only to the extent of saying that it is *New England* I *must* have—in some form or other. Providence is part of me—I *am* Providence. . . . Providence would always be at the back of my head as a goal to be worked toward—an ultimate Paradise to be regain'd at last.[9]

"I am Providence" is the inscription on the tombstone erected over Lovecraft's grave in the Phillips family plot at Swan Point Cemetery by a number of his contemporary disciples. Lovecraft's poem "Providence" of 1924 conveys his sense of the city as a Castle of Indolence or Palace of Sleeping Beauty that has been mercifully cut off from the rapids of time and become a sacred spring, a living doorway to the past:

> Stone bridges spanning languid streams,
>   Houses perch'd on the hill,
> And courts where mysteries and dreams
>   The brooding spirit fill.
>
> Steep alley steps by vines conceal'd,
>   Where small-paned windows glow
> At twilight on the bit of field
>   That chance has left below.
>
> My Providence! What airy hosts
>   Turn still thy gilded vanes;
> What winds of elf that with grey ghosts
>   People thine ancient lanes! (*AT* 303)

All this local color *sfumato* is masterfully conveyed in the picturesque de-scriptions that grace such Providence-based stories as *The Case of Charles Dexter Ward* and "The Haunter of the Dark," for as Winfield Townley Scott was the first to point out, Lovecraft "renewed with variations a particular tradition which Hawthorne and such lesser writers as Mary Wilkins Freeman long before made native."[10] Yet Borges, too, can discover a similar "haunted regionalism" in the dining-room cellar of a house in Calle Garay, where the mad poet Carlos Argentino Daneri secrets the Aleph. This "microcosm of alchemists and caba-lists" outwardly appears to Borges as "a small iridescent sphere, of almost in-tolerable brilliance." As he writes:

At first I thought it rotary; then I understood that this movement was an illusion produced by the vertiginous sights it enclosed. The Aleph's diameter must have been about two or three centimeters, but Cosmic Space was in it, without dimunition of size. Each object (the mirror's glass, for instance) was infinite objects, for I clearly saw it from all points in the universe.[11]

In "The Haunter of the Dark," Lovecraft's Robert Blake is characteristically even more detailed about the Shining Trapezohedron, that "egg-shaped or irregularly spherical object some four inches through" that he finds in the tower-room of the deserted cathedral on Providence's Federal Hill. Lovecraft writes:

The four-inch seeming sphere turned out to be a nearly black, red-striated polyhedron with many irregular flat surfaces; either a very remarkable crystal of some sort, or an artificial object of carved and highly polished mineral matter. It did not touch the bottom of the box, but was held suspended by means of a metal band around its centre, with seven queerly designed supports extending horizontally to angles of the box's inner wall near the top. This stone, once exposed, exerted upon Blake an almost alarming fascination. He could scarcely tear his eyes from it, and as he looked at its glistening surfaces he almost fancied it was transparent, with half-formed worlds of wonder within. Into his mind floated pictures of alien orbs with great stone towers, and other orbs with titan mountains and no mark of life, and still remoter spaces where only a stirring in vague blacknesses told of the presence of consciousness and will. (*DH* 102)

Lovecraft's Trapezohedron seems to partake also of the quality of Borges's "Zahir," that demonic coin which is only the mutable physical token of "beings or things which possess the terrible property of being unforgettable, and whose image finally drives one mad." But it is significant that Lovecraft's cult-object is black rather than iridescent, and even more telling that it vouchsafes a vision of other worlds rather than the complex real one which Borges sees multiplied to the highest power. For horror in Borges is an intensified reality, while horror in Lovecraft is an alternative reality. Words fail Borges because language is too limited to express this reality, while words fail Lovecraft because language is alien to the reality being expressed. Hence Lovecraft's unpronounceable names and untranslatable chants, his "Cthulhu" and "R'lyeh," are rivaled only, perhaps, by Borges's own tongue-twisting "Tlön." Both authors attempt to convey the visions that their gazing-globes afford them, one through a cataloguing of facts that reduces language to a poor, inadequate *anthology* of reality (Borges) and the other by expanding language poetically to construct a forbidden *arcanum* of this partial other reality (Lovecraft). Of course, Borges's very concept of the Aleph derives from the alchemical search for a Grand Arcanum, a Great Solvent, a Philosopher's Stone, but Borges is also a student of the Kabbalah who within the frame of the story assumes that God and Reality are one and the same, that to see or decipher God is to see or decipher all reality. But to experience such a vision is to be blasted by excess of brightness, since, as Scripture warns us, none sees God and lives. Borges cannot express what he sees because it is "ineffable," while Lovecraft will not express what he sees because it is "unspeakable."

As Borges writes:

> I arrive, now, at the ineffable center of my story. And there begins my despair as a writer. All language is an alphabet of symbols whose use presupposes a past shared by all the other interlocutors. How, then, transmit to others the infinite Aleph, which my fearful mind scarcely encompasses? The mystics, in similar situations, are lavish with emblems: to signify the divinity, a Persian speaks of a bird that in some way is all birds; Alanus de Insulis speaks of a sphere whose center is everywhere and whose circumference is nowhere; Ezekiel of an angel with four faces who looks simultaneously to the Orient and the Occident, to the North and the South. (Not vainly do I recall these inconceivable analogies; they bear some relation to the Aleph.) Perhaps the gods would not be against my finding an equivalent image, but then this report would be contaminated with literature, with falsehood. For the rest, the central problem is unsolvable: the enumeration, even if only partial, of an infinite complex.[12]

Once the riddle is solved, delight vanishes; Isis Unveiled is Isis Dead. That language can never match the labyrinth of reality is Borges's (and our) salvation, because to really comprehend reality—fully, totally, omnisciently—is to destroy both it and the self. Hence the horror, for Borges, of a freak like "Funes the Memorious," whose infallible memory converts him into a human computer or videotape machine. "With no effort, he had learned English, French, Portuguese and Latin. I suspect, however, that he was not very capable of thought. To think is to forget differences, generalize, make abstractions. In the teeming world of Funes, there were only details, almost immediate in their presence."[13] To Borges, to live is to think; to think is to pose riddles; to pose riddles is to create fictions; to create fictions is to delight oneself and others. There is no more deadly (read "boring") thing than a riddle solved, a paradox exploded, a labyrinth penetrated, a code deciphered. Thus the instantaneous deciphering of reality, through means of the Aleph, is tantamount to both deicide and suicide. Carlos Argentino Daneri, who uses the Aleph as the chief aid to his composition of an epic poem entitled *The Earth*, the purpose of which is to "put into verse the entire history of the planet," is as infinitely boring as his poem is infinitely tedious.

One skein of Borges's "Aleph" is therefore a biting satire on the progress of dullness among certain contemporary poets in particular and academic pedantry in general (the New Criticism degenerating into the New Cretinism); but it is also a cautionary tale about the blessed insolubility of reality itself—a miniature working out of the Faust legend. As such the story affirms the value of ambiguity and paradox as it also defends the human necessity of a limited, sequential point of view. God may be both Alpha and Omega, but if the first letter of an alphabet (especially a "sacred" one) can be made to stand for all the letters of the alphabet, the result can only be profanation, madness, and psychic death.

We can to some extent understand the outrage of the Yellow Emperor in Borges's "Parable of the Palace"[14] when his multiple world of gardens and towers is destroyed by a poet who impiously sums it all up in a text (thankfully lost) that may have consisted of but one spare line of verse or even a single word. The Aleph is an omniscient mirror, a logical impossibility that is best left in its rightful realm of Platonic speculation. Like the Holy Grail, it provides a goal to be groped toward rather than an end to be grasped. Or it is a mathematical function, an equation that, when plotted, curves parabolically toward a limit without ever touching it. As a mirror containing and subsuming all other mirrors, the Aleph thus becomes a constituting metaphor for art itself, a stimulus and a challenge to "the maker," who must convince and dazzle without sacrificing the inherent mystery of things. As Borges himself comments, "My chief problem in writing the story lay in what Walt Whitman had very successfully achieved—the setting down of a limited catalog of endless things. The task, as is evident, is impossible, for such chaotic enumeration can only be simulated, and every apparent haphazard element has to be linked to its neighbor either by association or by contrast."[15] To see the Aleph is to abandon the critical faculty, the problem-solving or riddle-solving gift, since the problem or the riddle is both solved and dissolved in the Aleph. Borges writes:

> In that gigantic instant I saw millions of delightful and atrocious acts; none astonished me more than the fact that all of them together occupied the same point, without superposition and without transparency. What my eyes saw was simultaneous: what I shall transcribe is successive. Nevertheless, I shall cull something of it all . . . I saw the heavy-laden sea; I saw the dawn and the dusk; I saw the multitudes of America; I saw a silver-plated cobweb at the center of a

black pyramid; I saw a tattered labyrinth (it was London); I saw interminable eyes looking at me as if in a mirror; I saw all the mirrors on the planet and none reflected me; in an inner patio in the Calle Soler I saw the same paving tile I had seen thirty years before in the entranceway to a house in the town of Fray Bentos; I saw clusters of grapes, snow, tobacco, veins of metal; steam . . . I saw the earth in the Aleph and in the earth the Aleph once more and the earth in the Aleph; I saw my face and my viscera; I saw your face and felt vertigo and cried because my eyes had seen that conjectural and secret object whose name men usurp but which no man has gazed on: the inconceivable universe.[16]

In an inconceivable universe that has become fully conceivable, there are no more books to be read, no more riddles to be formulated, no more stories to write; indeed, like Funes or Carlos Argentino Daneri, the only literary activity possible is pure mimesis. The self itself becomes nothing more than a mirror, but Borges luckily escapes this boring fate:

> In the street, on the Constitución stairs, in the subway, all the faces struck me as familiar. I feared that not a single thing was left to cause me surprise; I was afraid I would never be quit of the impression that I had "returned." Happily, at the end of a few nights of insomnia, forgetfulness worked in me again.[17]

Perhaps the "moral" of "The Aleph" is best summed up in T. S. Eliot's observation in *Four Quartets* ("Burnt Norton") that "human kind / Cannot bear very much reality." We need to sleep and we need to dream; the danger of ideal objects such as the Aleph and the Zahir is that once concretized they make life all insomnia (i.e., "Funes") or all forgetfulness. As the narrator of "The Zahir" soliloquizes:

> According to the teachings of the Idealists, the words "live" and "dream" are rigorously synonymous. From thousands of images I shall pass to one; from a highly complex dream to a dream of utter simplicity. Others will dream that I am mad; I shall dream of the Zahir. When all men of earth think, day and night, of the Zahir, which will be a dream and which a reality—the earth or the Zahir?[18]

The Zahir and the Aleph cannibalize reality by simplifying the complex, and are ultimately mind-eaters. The consuming horror of Lovecraft's metaphysic is not a mirrored reality but a dualistic one, another world of demons and half-gods that exists simultaneously alongside our own. Robert Blake in "The Haunter of the Dark" is also entranced by the vision of a mystery that entices because it confers power, but the power derives from another dimension rather than from a multiple perspective:

> Before he realised it, he was looking at the stone again, and letting its curious influence call up a nebulous pageantry in his mind. He saw processions of robed, hooded figures whose outlines were not human, and looked on endless leagues of desert lined with carved, sky-reaching monoliths. He saw towers and walls in nighted depths under the sea, and vortices of space where wisps of black mist floated before thin shimmerings of cold purple haze. And beyond all else he glimpsed an infinite gulf of darkness, where solid and semi-solid forms were known only by their windy stirrings, and cloudy patterns of force seemed to superimpose order on chaos and hold forth a key to all the paradoxes and arcana of the worlds we know. (*DH* 104)

Lovecraft writes a tone poem of galloping Gothic sentences to evoke his other reality, while Borges's catalogue in "The Aleph" has the terseness of a series of imagist *aperçus* rather than the Whitmanesque sweep he admires in his "Commentaries": "I saw a sunset in Querétaro which seemed to reflect the color of a rose in Bengal."[19] Here Borges's *Ultraist* roots resurface, just as we can sense Poe and the entire Dark Romantic tradition working behind Lovecraft's extravagant cadences. Since Borges is dealing with the infinite combinations and permutations of a measurable reality, however, his Aleph remains a one-way affair, a looking glass that the observer can see through but not go through, as in Lewis Carroll. Lovecraft's Shining Trapezohedron is unfortunately a peep hole between reality and some other world whose beings can use it as an escape route as well as a periscope. This diamond lens à la Fitz-James O'Brien is literally a breach in the dike between sanity and madness, in which a sublime sense of domination can suddenly be supplanted by the shrinking horror of demonic possession:

> Then all at once the spell was broken by an access of gnawing, indeterminate panic fear. Blake choked and turned away from the stone, conscious of some formless alien presence close to him and watching him with horrible intentness. He felt entangled with something—something which was not in the stone, but which had looked through it at him—something which would ceaselessly follow him with a cognition that was not physical sight. (*DH* 104)

Borges's fissionable reality contends with Lovecraft's entangled one, where alien forms and alien dimensions such as "the colour out of space" are like extraterrestrial microbes—Andromeda strains—that must be isolated, contained, and finally extirpated. But Borges, too, must "restore" reality at the end of his tale, since the Aleph itself partakes of this alien quality. In his "Commentaries" Borges writes that "In the world of the *Arabian Nights*, such things as magic lamps and rings are left lying about and nobody cares; in our skeptical world, we have to tidy up any alarming out-of-the-way element. Thus, at the end of 'The Aleph,' the house has to be pulled down and the shining sphere destroyed with it."[20] Thus at the end of "The Haunter of the Dark," the Shining Trapezohedron is thrown "into the deepest channel of Narragansett Bay," while Robert Blake is destroyed by what seems to be a blast of lightning. In reality—that is, Lovecraft's other reality—Blake is seized by the being he has unleashed through his manipulation of the magic glass in the tower, and which (like the mystics mentioned by Borges in "The Aleph") he can signify only by broken if not "lavish" emblems—"I see it—coming here—hell-wind—titan blur—black wings—Yog-Sothoth save me—the three-lobed burning eye . . . ." (*DH* 115).

II

Although the triangle with the lidless eye is one of the figures used by the German cobbler-mystic Jacob Behmen (1575–1624) in his *Aurora* (1612), there is no possibility that the skeptical Lovecraft ever read or even would have entertained reading such work. Yet J. M. Cohen has argued convincingly that Borges's idea for the Aleph itself came from a passage in Behmen's biography in turn quoted by William James in his *Varieties of Religious Experience*.[21] This fact leads me back to the main point, problem, or—to use Borgesian terms—riddle of this paper: the congruency of realities in Lovecraft and Borges. Why should we be reminded of Borges when reading Lovecraft, and why must Borges have been reminded of himself, or one of his selves, when reading Lovecraft? I have noted certain biographical similarities between the North American and the South American, but these are at best incidental. As Anthony Kerrigan comments, "Borges has almost absolute affinities."[22] Both men may be local colorists, but Borges is much more drawn to the low-life of the pampa and the brutal exploits of the gaucho. To be sure, there is a violent militaristic strain in the Providence writer that caused him fanatically to defend Aryan supremacy and to think of himself as a "nearly six-foot, chalk-white Nordic type, the type of the master conqueror and man of action." Upon America's entrance into World War I, he was ignominiously hustled back from the Providence recruiting station by relatives who brandished his tell-tale certificate of feeble health. Borges, too, writes proudly of his battle-hungry ancestors but adds with more insight that "So, on both sides of my family, I have military forbears; this may account for my yearning after that epic destiny which my gods denied me, no doubt wisely."[23] Yet we can never conceive of Lovecraft writing a dialect gangster tale such as Borges's "Streetcorner Man" (1933), and, in spite of H. P. Lovecraft's trope toward encyclopedic verbosity in his letters, neither can we imagine him pursuing theological and philosophical definitions with as much enthusiasm as Borges does in his "The Fearful Sphere of Pascal" or "The Mirror of Enigmas." More fruitful is the fact that both men were born in the 1890s (Lovecraft in 1890, Borges in 1899) and that they continued in their own ways the literary traditions of the decade of their birth: Aestheticism and Decadence.[24] Poe is a major influence on their works, and as Lovecraft wrote: "Poe is beyond anything this age can produce, and is so far America's sole contribution to the general current or world literature. He is the father of most of the redeeming features of decadent literature, and differs from the actual decadents in that they have failed to comprehend the magnificent and ultra-human point of view on which his unique creations are based" (*SL* 1.173). Borges, too, praises Poe for "his love of beauty and his fantastic invention,"[25] seeing him as an Aesthete and the inventor of the detective story.

If Poe is in some sense a literary "father" to both Lovecraft and Borges, we have the case of two brothers who were separated in childhood and grew up under drastically differing influences and conditions that affected the maturation of their common bloodline. In spite of his access to a fine library of English classics, Borges was also nourished by the rich traditions of European, especially Continental, literature, where Poe was always respectable and where a taste for the grotesque and the arabesque is a valuable literary gift. For example, the polyglot Borges read Gustav Meyrink's horror classic *The Golem* in the original German when he was still in his teens,[26] while Lovecraft only discovered the novel in 1935, calling it "the most magnificent weird thing I've come across in aeons!" and recognizing that "As a study in lurking, insidious *regional* horror it has scarcely a peer—doing for the antient, crumbling Prague ghetto what I unsuccessfully strove to do for rotting Newburyport in 'The Shadow over Innsmouth'" (*SL* 5.138). Lovecraft grew up in a literary environment that was, by contrast to Borges's largess of reading and publishing, an economy of scarcity; he had few friends who shared his interests, and no professional journals like the prestigious *Sur* to publish his effusions. It was only through the private printings of the amateur press that he was allowed any outlet for his work, and later he had to suffer the appearance of his art in pulp periodicals bearing lurid covers like *Weird Tales* and *Amazing Stories*. Lovecraft's case illustrates the lament of earlier writers such as Washington Irving, Nathaniel Hawthorne, and Herman Melville that there was simply no place in American society for a professional man of letters. Lovecraft turned this negative into a positive, however, by becoming a great amateur, cultivating a sense of *noblesse oblige,* and preserving his precarious status by thinking of himself as a connoisseur, a dabbler, or a virtuoso. As such, he was an autodidactic Decadent or Aesthete, fighting against both anti-intellectual (folk) and elite (avant-garde) currents, along with his closest friends and correspondents Samuel Loveman, Clark Ashton Smith, and Frank Belknap Long. Like Poe, Lovecraft had to invent or reinvent his chosen genre rather than inherit, modify, or place himself within it. Only later would Lovecraft find the time to confirm his own origins through working up the scholarly treatise he called "Supernatural Horror in Literature" (1925–27). It is this primitivist quality of Lovecraft's fantastic invention that provides the greatest stylistic contrast to Borges's more fluid, learned, and elegant production. If Borges is a Puvis De Chavannes, rendering his fantasies in paler tints and more sophisticated tones, Lovecraft is a Douanier Rousseau, meticulously covering his canvasses with psychedelic colors, onieroscopic vegetation, and night-stalking monsters.

The approach of genre, like the approach of biography, fails in linking Borges with Lovecraft precisely because it is too closely bound to time and space. There are simply too many gaps, though we can trace a material intersection occurring thirty years after Lovecraft's death. The general category of "Fantastic Literature" provides a medium for relationship, but it does not provide a *cause* any more than does the fact that Lovecraft and Borges both read Poe, Wells, the *Arabian Nights,* and Greek mythology. Therefore I should like to turn to another means of interconnection, an acausal one first formulated by Carl Gustav Jung, which he called the principle of synchronicity. Jung writes:

> My preoccupation with the psychology of unconscious processes long ago compelled me to look about for another principle of explanation, because the causality principle seemed to me inadequate to explain certain remarkable phenomena of the psychology of the unconscious. Thus I found that there are psychic parallelisms which cannot be related to each other causally, but which may be connected through another principle, namely the contingency of events. This connection of events seemed to me essentially given by the fact of their relative simultaneity, hence the term "synchronistic." It seems, indeed, as though time, far from being an abstraction, is a concrete continuum which contains qualities or basic conditions that manifest themselves simultaneously in different places through parallelisms that cannot be explained causally, as, for example, in cases of the simultaneous occurrence of identical thoughts, symbols, or psychic states.[27]

The idea of a roughly simultaneous occurrence of identical thoughts, symbols, and psychic states would seem to be a more fruitful way of considering the parallels between Lovecraft's Shining Trapezohedron and Borges's Aleph than aimlessly tracing them to Behmen or to the alchemical concept of the Philosopher's Stone, which Borges knew well and which Lovecraft knew only superficially at best. Lovecraft and Borges participate in the creation of synchronistic worlds governed by intriguingly similar patterns of myth, and this is no better illustrated than by a comparison of the deserted city in Borges's tale "The Immortal" (a story which Ronald Christ has called the "culmination" of his art) to the Cyclopean Antarctic domain of the Old Ones in Lovecraft's *At the Mountains of Madness* and the buried Australian megalopolis of the Great Race in "The Shadow out of Time." Borges's tale is a redoing of the legend of the Wandering Jew and a moral parable about the unnatural curse of perpetual life. As he writes in his "Commentaries" about a story with a similar theme: "Since our only proof of personal death is statistical, and inasmuch as a new generation of deathless men may be already on its way, I have for years lived in fear of never dying. Such an idea as immortality would, of course, be unbearable."[28] To live forever is to have the opportunity to solve every riddle and so suffer the death-in-life of infinite boredom. In "The Immortal," Borges's questor-victim is a Roman tribune of the reign of Diocletian who seeks and finds a sacred river that "cleanses" men of death. First, however, Cartaphilus (in legend Pilate's doorkeeper, guilty of striking the Redeemer, and the name he takes in his latest incarnation as a Smyrna antique dealer) must suffer a symbolic death by descending into a cave and wandering in a labyrinth. Thus he undergoes a mystery initiation similar to the ancient rites of Eleusis, which also conferred immortality—in the form of union with the goddess—on the believer. Borges writes:

> I have read that the City was founded on a stone plateau. This plateau, comparable to a high cliff, was no less arduous than the walls. In vain I fatigued myself: the black base did not disclose the slightest irregularity, the invariable walls seemed not to admit a single door. The force of the sun obliged me to seek refuge in a cave; in the rear was a pit, in the pit a stairway which sank down abysmally into the darkness below. I went down; through a chaos of sordid galleries I reached a vast circular chamber, scarcely visible. There were nine doors in this cellar; eight led to a labyrinth that treacherously returned to the same chamber; the ninth (though another labyrinth) lead to a second circular chamber equal to the first. I do not know the total number of these chambers; my misfortune and anxiety multiplied them. The silence was hostile and almost perfect; there was no sound in this deep stone network save that of a subterranean wind, whose

cause I could not discover; noiselessly, tiny streams of rusty water disappeared between the crevices. Horribly, I became habituated to this doubtful world; I found it incredible that there could be anything but cellars with nine doors and long branched-out cellars; I do not know how long I must have walked beneath the ground; I know that I once confused, in the same nostalgia, the atrocious city of the barbarians and my native city, amid the clusters.[29]

In Lovecraft's "The Shadow out of Time," his erstwhile "immortal," Professor Nathaniel Wingate Peaslee, must also descend into a labyrinth in order to reach the city of his commingled dreams and nightmares:

> I seemed to move almost automatically, as if in the clutch of some compelling fate. Pocketing my torch, and struggling with a strength that I had not thought I possessed, I wrenched aside first one titan fragment of stone and then another, till there welled up a strong draught whose dampness contrasted oddly with the desert's dry air. A black rift began to yawn, and at length—when I had pushed away every fragment small enough to budge—the leprous moonlight blazed on an aperture of ample width to admit me.
>
> I drew out my torch and cast a brilliant beam into the opening. Below me was a chaos of tumbled masonry, sloping roughly down toward the north at an angle of about forty-five degrees, and evidently the result of some bygone collapse from above. Between its surface and the ground level was a gulf of impenetrable blackness at whose upper edge were signs of gigantic, stress-heaved vaulting. At this point, it appeared, the desert's sands lay directly upon a floor of some titan structure of earth's youth—how preserved through aeons of geologic convulsion I could not then and cannot now even attempt to guess.
>
> In retrospect, the barest idea of a sudden, lone descent into such a doubtful abyss—and at a time when one's whereabouts were unknown to any living soul—seems like the utter apex of insanity. Perhaps it was—yet that night I embarked without hesitancy upon such a descent. (*DH* 415)

While Cartaphilus dismisses his confusing "nostalgia" of past and present as a symptom of his exhaustion, Peaslee's horror is that the deeper he descends, the more familiar the labyrinth seems to be. This is because he has already encountered these corridors not simply in a "stream of cryptic lore" but in his dreams, which are in turn based upon a terrible reality. This reality is founded on the power of mental transmigration practiced by the builders of the city, a "Great Race" who have the ability to project themselves into other bodies and to appropriate other minds, obviating the coordinates of time and space. The origin of this race is extraterrestrial; hence the uncanny perfection of their architecture, art, and scholarship. Peaslee has actually dwelt in one of their bodies, for five years, while his own shell has been occupied by an inquisitive alien. "I was wholly and horribly oriented," he declares, for mere nostalgia has been replaced by Platonic reminiscence made devastatingly real:

> The particular structure I was in was known to me. Known, too, was its place in that terrible elder city of dream. That I could visit unerringly any point in that structure or in that city which had escaped the changes and devastations of uncounted ages, I realised with hideous and instinctive certainty. What in heaven's name could all this mean? How had I come to know what I knew? And what awful reality could lie behind those antique tales of the beings who had dwelt in this labyrinth of primordial stone?
>
> Words can convey only fractionally the welter of dread and bewilderment which ate at my spirit. I knew this place. I knew what lay below me, and what had lain overhead before the myriad towering stories had fallen to dust and debris and the desert. No need now, I thought with a shudder, to keep that faint blur of moonlight in view. (*DH* 417)

In *At the Mountains of Madness*, the city itself is a "stupendous stone labyrinth" situated on a high plateau protected by a wall of towering mountains. Like the citadel of the Great Race, its blasphemous architecture presumes a non-human or prehuman origin, for once again Lovecraft's other reality is alien to anything we can imagine. Yet it is significant that Lovecraft's modern explorers, who continue the quest first outlined in Edgar Allan Poe's *Narrative of Arthur Gordon Pym* (1838), are armed with cameras that allow them to photograph "carefully" every detail of this ruined and alien stronghold. For as Richard Burgin observes, the camera is a kind of "permanent mirror," and as Borges admitted to him, "Because I'm afraid of mirrors, maybe I'm afraid of cameras."[30]

> The half-mile walk downhill to the actual city, with the upper wind shrieking vainly and savagely through the skyward peaks in the background, was something of which the smallest details will always remain engraved on my mind. Only in fantastic nightmares could any human beings but Danforth and me conceive such optical effects. Between us and the churning vapours of the west lay that monstrous tangle of dark stone towers, its outré and incredible forms impressing us afresh at every new angle of vision. It was a mirage in solid stone, and were it not for the photographs I would still doubt that such a thing could be. The general type of masonry was identical with that of the rampart we had examined; but the extravagant shapes which this masonry took in its urban manifestations were past all description.
>
> Even the pictures illustrate only one or two phases of its infinite bizarrerie, endless variety, preternatural massiveness, and utterly alien exoticism. There were

geometrical forms for which an Euclid would scarcely find a name—cones of all degrees of irregularity and truncation; terraces of every sort of provocative disproportion; shafts with odd bulbous enlargements; broken columns in curious groups; and five-pointed or five-ridged arrangements of mad grotesqueness. As we drew nearer we could see beneath certain transparent parts of the ice-sheet, and detect some of the tubular stone bridges that connected the crazily sprinkled structures at various heights. Of orderly streets there seemed to be none, the only broad open swath being a mile to the left, where the ancient river had doubtless flowed through the town into the mountains. (*MM* 50–51)

Lovecraft paradoxically sees his Other Reality with photographic clarity; even the minds of his observers are converted into sensitive plates on which are etched or burned the unrelenting details of his alien worlds. As in "The Shadow out of Time," scenes are explored by the aid of powerful electric light (Professor Peaslee does not lose his "torch" until his final flight from the underground city). In a fragment from a lengthy description of the mural sculptures discovered in the Antarctic labyrinth, we can see how Lovecraft's extraterrestrial "realism" can become almost microscopic:

The arabesque tracery consisted altogether of depressed lines whose depth on unweathered walls varied from one to two inches. When cartouches with dot-groups appeared—evidently as inscriptions in some unknown and primordial language and alphabet—the depression of the smooth surface was perhaps an inch and a half, and of the dots perhaps a half-inch more. The pictorial bands were in counter-sunk low relief, their background being depressed about two inches from the original wall surface. In some specimens marks of a former coloration could be detected, though for the most part the untold aeons had disintegrated and banished any pigments which may have been applied. (*MM* 57)

The report is as matter-of-fact and as precise as an archaeological survey, though the narrator adds that "Certain touches here and there gave vague hints of latent symbols and stimuli which another mental and emotional background, and a fuller or different sensory equipment, might have made of profound and poignant significance to us." In contrast, Borges's description of the ruined city of the immortals partakes of a misty quality that suffuses its own half-lights and atmospheric dimness about the scene. This is appropriate for an author who has described the onset of gradual blindness as "a slow, summer twilight,"[31] but also indicates an aesthetic consciousness that is more attuned to nuance, suggestion, and "romance." Indeed, as Ronald Christ has noted,[32] Borges would seem to owe a good deal of what detail he does include to Piranesi's famous series of engravings depicting labyrinthine prisons with titanic, fugal staircases and huge, vaulted rooms. Borges writes:

> To the impression of enormous antiquity others were added: that of the interminable, that of the atrocious, that of the complexly senseless. I had crossed a labyrinth, but the nitid City of the Immortals filled me with fright and repugnance. A labyrinth is a structure compounded to confuse men; its architecture, rich in symmetries, is subordinated to that end. In the palace I imperfectly explored, the architecture lacked any such finality. It abounded in deadened corridors, high unattainable windows, portentous doors which led to a cell or pit, incredible inverted staircases, whose steps and balustrades hung downwards. Other stairways, clinging airily to the side of a monumental wall, would die without leading anywhere, after making two or three turns in the lofty darkness of the cupolas. I do not know if all the examples I have enumerated are literal; I know that for many years they infested my Nightmares; I am no longer able to know if such and such a detail is a transcription of reality or of the forms which unhinged my nights.[33]

On the other hand Lovecraft's characters see absolutely and remember absolutely; they never know the bliss of forgetfulness, and are in danger of confusing phantasmagoric hallucination with actual experience. Lovecraft is like the Richard Upton Pickman in his own famous tale, "Pickman's Model," of whom the narrator remarks:

> It was not any mere artist's interpretation that we saw; it was pandemonium itself, crystal clear in stark objectivity. That was it, by heaven! The man was not a fantaisiste or romanticist at all—he did not try to give us the churning, prismatic ephemera of dreams, but coldly and sardonically reflected some stable, mechanistic, and well-established horror-world which he saw fully, brilliantly, squarely, and unfalteringly. God knows what that world can have been, or where he ever glimpsed the blasphemous shapes that loped and trotted and crawled through it; but whatever the baffling source of his images, one thing was plain. Pickman was in every sense—in conception and in execution—a thorough, painstaking, and almost scientific *realist*. (*DH* 21)

Borges always deals with reality, but he deals with it daringly as a romanticist or a *fantaisiste*; Lovecraft dares to deal with an other reality, but he deals with it matter-of-factly as a scientist or a realist. Again, there is no mystery about Lovecraft's source for this technique, since we know exactly from what and where that "stable, mechanistic, and well-established horror-world" derived. It was the world of his nightmares, which were not at all churning, prismatic, or ephemeral but rather incredibly precise, detailed, and literalistic. As Lovecraft wrote to Willis Conover on 10 January 1937, only two months before his own death:

> You surely are quite a dreamer—and it's curious (to me) how quickly your new experiences and correspondents get translated into visions. . . . My own dreams usually go back very far in time, and it takes a long while for any new experience or scene or acquaintance to get worked into them. At least ¾ of them are laid at my birthplace, where I haven't lived since 1904, and involve those who were living in those days. But the real scenes frequently merge into unknown and fantastic realms, and include landscapes and architectural vistas which could scarcely be on this planet. At times I also have *historical* dreams— with a setting in various remote periods. (*SL* 5.384–85)

For specimens of Lovecraft's photographically surreal dream-experiences, the interested reader may consult *Selected Letters* 1.113–16, where Lovecraft details apocalyptic visions of the destruction of Providence and a mysterious bas-relief found in one of the city's museums, and *Selected Letters* 2.199–201, for a trolley-car journey piloted by a motorman whose face "was a mere white cone tapering to one blood-red tentacle." Not all his dreams were characterized by such "scope, vividness, & mnemonick persistence," of course, but many were used as the basis for his weird tales. His art was in some sense largely the literal transcription of actual oneiric adventures. On 22 October 1933, he wrote to Clark Ashton Smith of what the editors of *Selected Letters* identify as a source for "The Shadow out of Time." Lovecraft told Smith:

> . . . about a year ago I dreamt I waked on a slab of unknown substance in a great vaulted hall, dimly and obscurely lit, and full of similar slabs bearing sheeted objects whose proportions were obviously *not human*. From every detail I gathered the horrible notion *that I could be nowhere on this planet*. I also felt that my own body was like those of the other sheeted shapes. But I waked up in very truth at this juncture, so that no *story* was even begun! (*SL* 4.290)

Lovecraft's letters and his amazing ability to dwell on his childhood with almost total recall suggest that he was a living example of Borges's mythical "Funes the Memorious," save that while Funes continually engaged in an instant replay of reality, Lovecraft in his fiction reconstructed the minutest details of his nightmare explorations of non-terrestrial realities. The fact that Lovecraft truly experienced, rather than fabricated, this kind of vision leads him, I believe, to construct the peculiar myth cycle that rules his entire fictional world.

Borges's Cartaphilus verges on the creation of this same myth, more fantastic than the idea of immortality itself, when he contemplates the irrationality of the City of the Immortals:

> Rather than by any other trait of this incredible monument, I was held by the extreme age of its fabrication. I felt that it was older than mankind, than the earth. This manifest antiquity (though in some way terrible to the eyes) seemed to me in keeping with the work of immortal builders. At first cautiously, later indifferently, at last desperately, I wandered up the stairs and along the pavements of the inextricable palace. (Afterwards I learned that the width and height of the steps were not constant, a fact which made me understand the singular fatigue they produced.) "This palace is a fabrication of the gods," I thought at the beginning. I explored the uninhabited interiors and corrected myself: "The gods who built it have died." I noted its peculiarities and said: "The gods who built it were mad."[34]

Cartaphilus here progresses through three stages of religious belief that might be termed Platonic, Nietzschean, and Lovecraftian. The last phase—a belief in the madness of the gods—is the key to Lovecraft's Cthulhu Mythos of maimed, deformed, and deranged deities. This mythos is Lovecraft's codification of what his character Robert Blake of "The Haunter of the Dark" calls "the ancient legends of Ultimate Chaos, at whose centre sprawls the blind idiot god Azathoth, Lord of All Things, encircled by his flopping horde of mindless and amorphous dancers, and lulled by the thin monotonous piping of a daemoniac flute held in nameless paws" (*DH* 110). It is not so much the shape of this mythology that is important to an understanding of the fictional realities of Lovecraft and Borges, but rather the impact of it. As Professor Peaslee puts it,

> If the thing did happen, then man must be prepared to accept notions of the cosmos, and of his own place in the seething vortex of time, whose merest mention is paralysing. He must, too, be on guard against a specific, lurking peril which, though it will never engulf the whole race, may impose monstrous and unguessable horrors upon certain venturesome members of it. (*DH* 368)

This is what Lovecraft means by "the shadow out of time," the shadow of another race of beings that diminishes and well-nigh dismisses the status of man and all his works. The evidence that convinces Peaslee of this fact is his discovery of a history of his time in his own handwriting stored in the immense library accumulated by the Great Race. But as he also notes, this history "was assigned a specific place in the vaults of the lowest or vertebrate level—the section devoted to the cultures of mankind and of the furry and reptilian races immediately preceding it in terrestrial dominance" (*DH* 397). Similarly, Borges's Cartaphilus is forced to conclude that (if real):

> "This City (I thought) is so horrible that its mere existence and perdurance, though in the midst of a secret desert, contaminates the past and the future and in some way even jeopardizes the stars. As long as it lasts, no one in the world can be strong or happy." I do not want to describe it; a chaos of heterogeneous words, the body of a tiger or a bull in which teeth, organs and heads monstrously pullulate in mutual conjunction and hatred can (perhaps) be approximate images.[35]

The City of the Immortals, the city of the Great Race, and the city of the Old Ones are synchronistic symbols, all inversions of the sacred city of dreams that can be found throughout the history of myth and folklore. This ideal metropolis is Camelot, El Dorado, or the Emerald City of Baum's *Wizard of Oz*; it offers adventure, wealth, fulfillment, or peace, depending on the goals of the seeker who enters its gates. To Borges the most immediate manifestation of the sacred city of dreams is Buenos Aires, with what his sister Norah called its "slightly melancholy gardens and old houses";[36] to Lovecraft it is Providence, for as he wrote on 21 April 1927 to Donald Wandrei:

> There is somewhere, my fancy fabulises, a marvellous city of ancient streets & hills & gardens & marble terraces, wherein I once lived happy eternities, & to which I must return if ever I am to have content. . . . Of this cryptic and glorious city—this primal & archaic place of splendour in Atlantis or Cockaigne or the Hesperidies—many towns of earth hold vague & elusive symbols that peep furtively out at certain moments, only to disappear again. (*SL* 2.126)

Yet to Borges the sacred city of dreams is part of a tangible universe, since his reality contains within itself the possibilities of infinite transmutation and permutation. As he writes of a dead friend in "To Leopoldo Lugones," "tomorrow I too will have died, and our times will intermingle and chronology will be lost in a sphere of symbols."[37] Borges needs no other worlds to explore; "Reality" and its sphere of symbols is more than sufficient, and it is the intensification of this sphere that bewilders, astounds, fascinates, and horrifies. In his tales and sketches, the philosophical opposition between reality and unreality, rather than Lovecraft's constant warfare between reality and alternative reality, provides the main material for fantasy, since in Borges's universe, things will metamorphose of and by themselves without any help from alien gods or colors out of space.

Speaking of the images of the cross, the lasso, and the arrow in a sketch called "Mutations," he wonders, "Why should I marvel at them, when there is not a single thing on earth that oblivion does not erase or memory change, and when no one knows into what images he himself will be transmuted in the future."[38] Just as speculative scientists have postulated an ineradicable tendency toward sequential grouping or clustering that is built into the fabric of nature, so does Borges believe in the overweening power of fabulation, a spontaneous principle of myth-making and fictionizing. Riddling, dreaming, and speculating mix with and modify reality, but they do not replace it. Like the ancient Gnostics, to whom he owes so much, Borges fears a mirror because of its power of unholy reproduction and intensification, its creation of another world which could conceivably usurp—as Lovecraft's mad, maimed gods attempt to usurp—the world as we know it. As he writes in "The Draped Mirrors":

> As a child, I felt before large mirrors that same horror of a spectral duplication or multiplication of reality. Their infallible and continuous functioning, their pursuit of my actions, their cosmic pantomime, were uncanny then, whenever it began to grow dark. One of my persistent prayers to God and my guardian angel was that I not dream about mirrors. I know I watched them with misgivings. Sometimes I feared they might begin to deviate from reality; other times I was afraid of seeing there my own face, disfigured by strange calamities.[39]

All Lovecraft's characters, and Lovecraft himself, dream of mirrors in this way; they enter looking glasses that have the power of looking back at them, as Robert Blake of "The Haunter of the Dark" discovers by means of the Shining Trapezohedron, while the decayed narrator of "The Outsider" realizes he is a rotting horror only after he has "stretched out my fingers to the abomination within that great gilded frame; stretched out my fingers and touched *a cold and unyielding surface of polished glass*" (*DH* 52). As early as the age of seventeen, Borges had become fascinated by Gnostic writings,[40] and in his story-essay "The Theologians," he discusses this "tempestuous heresy" which held that the world as we know it was created by a Demiurge or Fabricator, while the true God was a *deus absconditus*, a hidden or absentee one. He writes that these Gnostic heresiarchs "often went from mortification and severity to crime; some communities tolerated thievery; others homicide; others, sodomy, incest and bestiality. All were blasphemous; they cursed not only the Christian God but also the arcane divinities of their own pantheon. They contrived sacred books whose disappearance is lamented by scholars."[41] In fact the Gnostics were divided into two camps, the Hellenistic and the Oriental, the former of

whom detested the world and practiced austerity, asceticism, and rigid disci-
pline, while the latter group wholly and fully committed themselves to terrestrial pleasures. Seen in this light, Borges is an Oriental Gnostic who delights in
the sensual, glittering, and alluring puzzle of reality, while Lovecraft is the Hellenistic Gnostic who finds reality so unbearable that he attempts to escape its
chains of space and time by seeking the higher knowledge (literally, the *gnosis*)
of a totally transmundane universe. Lovecraft does this through what Borges
calls his fictional "comic nightmares" and his actual oneiric experience. As
Lovecraft wrote to Clark Ashton Smith on 29 November 1930:

> I am still obsessed by the notion that one of the most extremely powerful of all
> tales would be an utterly realistic thing dealing with the sensations of a man de-
> posited without a great amount of warning on another world. The one fatal
> weakness of nearly all interplanetary tales is that they almost completely ignore
> this factor of the situation. To my mind, the stupendous wave of emotion—
> incredulity, lostness, wonder, stark terror—incident to this supreme dislocation
> from man's immemorially fixed background would be so colossal a thing as al-
> most to dwarf any events which might happen to a celestial traveller. I yet mean
> to write a tale whose one supreme climax shall be the hero's discovery, after
> many torturing & ambiguous doubts, that he *is* on another world. (*SL* 3.238)

Just as it is easy to confuse the conflicting yet congruous Gnostic camps
without a fully detailed theological and heresiarchical road map in hand, so
does the mythic world of Borges resemble uncannily the mythic world of
Lovecraft. Both worlds of fabulation are synchronistic in the sense that both
are modern responses—like Gnosticism—to a gnawing sense of detachment,
anomie, displacement, and outsideness.[42] But while Borges approaches Lovecraft's radical dualism, a dualism not of real and ideal but of real and other-real
(since Lovecraft's alternative reality is usually horrifying rather than pleasur-
able), he must ultimately reject it for a determined monism. To Borges, history,
theology, philosophy, biography, legend, and fiction are all *one*, and to admit
another reality constructed by mad gods would be to destroy both the sover-
eignty and the delight of the human imagination. The image in the mirror must
remain a reflection, not a tangible, measurable world, lest, like the Zahir or the
Aleph (combinations of what in "The Theologians" Borges identifies as the
main Gnostic symbols, the mirror and the obolus) it become just as real as or
even more real than what we already know. "We accept reality easily," Borges
writes in "The Immortal," "perhaps because we intuit that nothing is real."[43]
Thus the possibility of the sureality of mad gods and their mad city must be

explained away. Cartaphilus discovers (much to his relief) that the barbarians who dwelled in pits scooped out of the ground outside the City of the Immortals are the immortals themselves. As Borges writes:

> Everything was elucidated for me that day. The troglodytes were the Immortals; the rivulet of sandy water, the River sought by the horseman. As for the city whose renown had spread as far as the Ganges, it was some nine centuries since the Immortals had razed it. With the relics of its ruins they erected, in the same place, the mad city I had traversed: a kind of parody or inversion and also temple of the irrational gods who govern the world and of whom we know nothing, save that they do not resemble man. This establishment was the last symbol to which the Immortals condescended; it marks a stage at which, judging that all undertakings are in vain, they determined to live in thought, in pure speculation. They erected their structure, forgot it and went to dwell in the caves. Absorbed in thought, they hardly perceived the physical world.[44]

III

Lovecraft and Borges are both skeptics, disbelievers, and aesthetes; yet Borges accepts, indeed celebrates, reality while Lovecraft abandons it for the city of dream and the dream of cities "outside of SPACE, outside of TIME." Borges is a modern Gnostic who is willing to commit himself to the puzzle of the world and leave the gods to themselves, since they are ultimately unknowable: this is a mark of his essential humanism. Lovecraft was, as he often admitted, an inhumanist, because he hated the visible universe and had within himself the means of exploring Gnostic realms of forbidden knowledge that were closed to men of ordinary dreams and ordinary desires. The world of his nightmares was not comic to him, since it was as frighteningly real as his daily existence was shabby and boresome. Given a choice, he would have opted for life with the Old Ones or the Great Race, just as his admired avatar Edgar Allan Poe preferred a "Dream-land" filled with:

> Bottomless vales, and boundless floods,
> And chasms, and caves, and Titan woods,
> With forms that no man can discover
> For the dews that drip all over . . .[45]

Indeed, the library of the Great Race in which Professor Peaslee works as a temporary scribe is one of Lovecraft's images of paradise. The library is built to endure forever, to outlast man as a species and even to survive the transmigra-

tion of the beings who constructed it. Borges, who worked as a lowly munici-
pal librarian and was later elevated to the Directorship of the National Library
of Argentina, uses the same image for parody and satire in "The Library of Babel." Substituting a sterile but perfect library for the figure of the universe as a
finely crafted watch made famous by William Paley in his *Evidences of Christianity*
(1794), Borges does not assume the existence of a Librarian God as Paley assumed the existence of a Watch-Maker God. Rather, the library is the universe
precisely as we know and yet do not know it, and the narrator is reduced to a
Kafkaesque bookworm whose vision of an apocalyptic future seems very close
to Lovecraft's prolix observations about the decline of the west, the rise of
barbarism, and the inevitable obliteration of mankind:

> The methodical task of writing distracts me from the present state of men.
> The certitude that everything has been written negates us or turns us into phan-
> toms. I know of districts in which the young men prostrate themselves before
> books and kiss their pages in a barbarous manner, but they do not know how
> to decipher a single letter. Epidemics, heretical conflicts, peregrinations which
> inevitably degenerate into banditry, have decimated the population. I believe I
> have mentioned the suicides, more and more frequent with the years. Perhaps
> my old age and fearfulness deceive me, but I suspect that the human species—
> the unique species—is about to be extinguished, but the Library will endure: il-
> luminated, solitary, infinite, perfectly motionless, equipped with precious vol-
> umes, useless, incorruptible, secret.[46]

For Borges this is cold comfort, but for Lovecraft it is a consummation de-
voutly to be wished. Yet Lovecraft remains one of Borges's "Precursors," in
the sense that Borges redefines that word in his essay "Kafka and His Precursors." Here he writes that "In the critics' vocabulary, the word 'precursor' is
indispensable, but it should be cleansed of all connotations of polemics or ri-
valry. The fact is that every writer *creates* his own precursors. His work modifies
our conception of the past, as it will modify the future."[47] Lovecraft died in
March 1937, and the tales of Borges I have considered here were all written after that date, since he did not even begin to create fantasies until after the mysterious blow to the head he suffered on Christmas Eve of 1938. But through
Jung's principle of synchronicity Lovecraft still *participates* in Borges's fictional
world as much as he anticipates or approximates it. Lovecraft and his alternative reality provide the missing term in the complex of Borges's elegant proofs
and sophisticated ciphers, for with his compelling but inhumanly detailed
dream-visions, the provincial Lovecraft demonstrates the very threat to imagi-

nation that haunts Borges's consciousness. In "Tlön, Uqbar, Orbis Tertius" Borges again illustrates this threat graphically. A secret society of committed idealists, similar to the founders of the Brotherhood of the Rosy Cross, which itself was based upon a fictional hoax, creates over a number of generations an entire alternative world, a planet called Tlön with its own special laws, languages, physics, and metaphysics. If in "The Library of Babel" the universe becomes a gigantic set of open stacks, now a multi-volumed encyclopedia in turn becomes a universe, self-contained and dangerously alluring. As Borges says when he discovers just one of the tomes of this gigantic work:

> Now I held in my hands a vast methodical fragment of an unknown planet's entire history, with its architecture and its playing cards, with the dread of its mythologies and the murmur of its languages, with its emperors and its seas, with its minerals and its birds and its fish, with its algebra and its fire, with its theological and metaphysical controversy. And all of it articulated, coherent, with no visible doctrinal intent or tone of parody.[48]

Lovecraft began the construction of just such an alternative world with the creation of his Cthulhu Mythos, itself the gift of his otherworldly imagination. He refined it, extended it, and codified it more and more the longer he lived, while its use spread quickly among his friends, disciples, and fellow-writers. Latter-day fantaisistes have continued to contribute new gods, new legends, and new heroes to its bulk. But as Borges warns, the danger of such a self-enclosed and self-perpetuating system is that it has the power of gobbling up reality itself. Reality is chancy, messy, and unpredictable, while "Tlön is surely a labyrinth, but it is a labyrinth devised by men, a labyrinth destined to be deciphered by men."[49] As always, Borges prefers the unsolved and unsolvable riddle, which implies what William James called an "open universe," to an elaborate crossword that can only lead to the cul de sac of what the American philosopher termed a "block universe." But because of its tyrannical order, the fantastic world of Tlön gradually "intrudes" upon the untidy world of reality until that world crumbles and disintegrates:

> Already the schools have been invaded by the (conjectural) "primitive language" of Tlön; already the teaching of a harmonious history (filled with moving episodes) has wiped out the one which governed in my childhood; already a fictitious past occupies in our memories the place of another, a past of which we know nothing with certainty—not even that it is false. Numismatology, pharmacology and archaeology have been reformed. I understand that biology and mathematics also await their avatars . . . A scattered dynasty of solitary men

has changed the face of the world. Their task continues. If our forecasts are not in error, a hundred years from now someone will discover the hundred volumes of the Second Encyclopedia of Tlön.

Then English and French and mere Spanish will disappear from the globe. The world will be Tlön.[50]

When he first read Lovecraft's life, Borges must have been amused to learn that the Providence writer had contrived a fanciful "History of the *Necronomicon*" to complement one of the fictitious books he devised as part of the Cthulhu Mythos. Borges himself often toyed with the hoax of a mythical volume, as in his speculative review of the non-existent *Approach to al-Mu'tasim* "by the Bombay barrister Mir Bahudur Ali."[51] But one wonders how, as a literary historian as well as fabulist, he might have reacted to the fact that in 1973, *The Necronomicon* was published with an introduction by L. Sprague de Camp, Lovecraft's biographer, and that it is now widely disseminated in libraries here and abroad.[52]

Notes

1. Richard Burgin, *Conversations with Jorge Luis Borges* (New York: Holt, Rinehart & Winston, 1968), 63. These interviews began on 21 November 1967 and continued for several months.

2. Ronald J. Christ, quoting from the French periodical *L'Herne* in *The Narrow Act: Borges' Art of Allusion* (New York: New York University Press, 1969), 43–44. It is interesting to note that *L'Herne* devoted one entire issue to Borges (1964) and another to HPL (1969).

3. Borges, *An Introduction to American Literature*, ed. and trans. L. Clark Keating and Robert O. Evans (Lexington: University Press of Kentucky, 1971), 47.

4. Ibid., 83–84

5. Paul Theroux, *The Old Patagonian Express: By Train through the Americas* (Boston: Houghton Mifflin, 1979), 376. The story in question is "There Are More Things" (in *The Book of Sand*).

6. See Rudolf Otto, *The Idea of the Holy* (New York: Oxford University Press, 1958). For Otto's relevance to HPL see my *Roots of Horror in the Fiction of H. P. Lovecraft* (Elizabethtown, NY: Dragon Press, 1977).

7. Borges, "An Autobiographical Essay," *The Aleph and Other Stories 1933–1969*, ed. and trans. Norman Thomas di Giovanni (New York: E. P. Dutton, 1970), 211.

8. Ibid., 223–24.

9. HPL to Lillian D. Clark, 29 March 1926, *Letters from New York*, p. 289.

10. Winfield Townley Scott, "His Own Most Fantastic Creation: Howard Phillips Lovecraft," in *Exiles and Fabrications* (Garden City, NY: Doubleday, 1961), 52.

11. Borges, "The Aleph," *A Personal Anthology,* ed. Anthony Kerrigan (New York: Grove Press, 1967), 150.

12. *A Personal Anthology,* 149–50

13. Borges, *Labyrinths: Selected Stories and Other Writings,* ed. Donald A. Yates and James E. Irby (New York: New Directions, 1964), 66.

14. *A Personal Anthology,* 87–88.

15. *The Aleph,* 264.

16. Ibid., 150–51.

17. Ibid., 152.

18. *Labyrinths,* 164.

19. *A Personal Anthology,* 150–51.

20. *The Aleph,* 263.

21. J. M. Cohen, *Jorge Luis Borges* (New York: Harper & Row, 1974), 81.

22. Anthony Kerrigan, "Borges/Unamuno," *Prose for Borges,* ed. Charles Newman and Mary Kinzie (Evanston, IL: Northwestern University Press, 1974), 238.

23. "An Autobiographical Essay," 208.

24. See my *H. P. Lovecraft: New England Decadent* (Albuquerque, NM: Silver Scarab Press, 1979).

25. *An Introduction to American Literature,* 20.

26. "An Autobiographical Essay," 216.

27. Carl Gustav Jung, *Memories, Dreams, Reflections,* ed. Aniela Jaffé (New York: Vintage, 1965), 400. For a full statement of Jung's theory, see his *Synchronicity: An Acausal Connecting Principle* in *The Structure of Dynamics of the Psyche* (New York: Pantheon, 1960), Volume 8 of *The Collected Works.* For a suggestive explanation and Interpretation of this theory, see Ira Progoff's *Jung, Synchronicity and Human Experience* (New York: The Julian Press, 1973). Jung's idea that the constellation of an archetype produces meaningful co-occurrences that violate the ordinary boundaries of time and space is paralleled by the plot of HPL's "The Call of Cthulhu," where correlations among dream-states, occult activities, artistic endeavors, and scholarly researches portend the opening up of "terrifying vistas of reality"; i.e., the intrusion of archetypal numinosity on ordinary human consciousness

28. *The Aleph,* 280.

29. *Labyrinths,* 109–10.

30. *Conversations with Jorge Luis Borges,* 18.

31. "An Autobiographical Essay," 250.

32. *The Narrow Act,* 200–202.

33. *Labyrinths,* 110–11.

34. Ibid., 110.

35. Ibid., 111.

36. Victoria O. Campo, "Norah Borges on Her Brother: An Unpublished Interview," *Prose for Borges*, 395.

37. Borges, *Dreamtigers*, trans. Mildred Boyer and Harold Morland, introduction by Miguel Enguidanos (Austin: University of Texas Press, 1964), 21.

38. *Dreamtigers*, 41.

39. Ibid., 27.

40. Borges's scholarly treatment of Gnosticism, "Vindication of the False Basilides," appeared in his collection *Discusión* (1932). See Martin S. Tabb, *Jorge Luis Borges* (New York: Twayne, 1970), 72–73. On his familiarity with the Kabbalah, see Jaime Alazraki, "Borges and the Kabbalah," *Prose for Borges*, 184–211. Alazraki's discussion of the doctrine of the Ibbur, or transmigration of souls, is relevant to the main premise of HPL's "The Shadow out of Time."

41. *Labyrinths*, 122–23.

42. See Hans Jonas's epilogue on "Gnosticism, Existentialism, and Nihilism" in *The Gnostic Religion* (Boston: Beacon Press, 1972), 320–40.

43. *Labyrinths*, 113.

44. Ibid.

45. Poe, *Poems*, ed. T. O. Mabbott (Cambridge, MA: Harvard University Press, 1969), 344.

46. *Labyrinths*, 58.

47. Ibid., 201.

48. Ibid., 7.

49. Ibid., 17–18.

50. Ibid., 18.

51. *The Aleph*, 45.

52. *Al Azif* (The *Necronomicon* by Abdul Alhazred, with a Preface by L. Sprague de Camp, Philadelphia: Owlswick Press, 1973). The *Necronomicon* also appears in the hoaxing index entitled "homage to Borges" which John Hollander contrived for the appreciative volume, *Prose for Borges* (413).

Bibliography

Primary Bibliography

Fiction

The Dunwich Horror and Others. Selected by August Derleth; texts edited by S. T. Joshi; introduction by Robert Bloch. Second edition. Sauk City, WI: Arkham House, [1984]. *Contains:* "In the Vault"; "Pickman's Model"; "The Rats in the Walls"; "The Outsider"; "The Colour out of Space"; "The Music of Erich Zann"; "The Haunter of the Dark"; "The Picture in the House"; "The Call of Cthulhu"; "The Dunwich Horror"; "Cool Air"; "The Whisperer in Darkness"; "The Terrible Old Man"; "The Thing on the Doorstep"; "The Shadow over Innsmouth"; "The Shadow out of Time."

At the Mountains of Madness and Other Novels. Selected by August Derleth; texts edited by S. T. Joshi; introduction by James Turner. Second edition. Sauk City, WI: Arkham House, [1985]. *Contains: At the Mountains of Madness; The Case of Charles Dexter Ward;* "The Shunned House"; "The Dreams in the Witch House"; "The Statement of Randolph Carter"; *The Dream-Quest of Unknown Kadath;* "The Silver Key"; "Through the Gates of the Silver Key."

Dagon and Other Macabre Tales. Selected by August Derleth; texts edited by S. T. Joshi; introduction by T. E. D. Klein. Second edition. Sauk City, WI: Arkham House, [1986]. *Contains:* "The Tomb"; "Dagon"; "Polaris"; "Beyond the Wall of Sleep"; "The White Ship"; "The Doom That Came to Sarnath"; "The Tree"; "The Cats of Ulthar"; "The Temple"; "Facts concerning the Late Arthur Jermyn and His Family"; "Celephaïs"; "From Beyond"; "The Nameless City"; "The Quest of Iranon"; "The Moon-Bog"; "The Other Gods"; "Herbert West—Reanimator"; "Hypnos"; "The Hound"; "The Lurking Fear"; "The Unnamable"; "The Festival"; "Under the Pyramids" (with Harry Houdini); "The Horror at Red Hook"; "He"; "The Strange High House in the Mist"; "The Evil Clergyman"; "In the Walls of Eryx" (with Kenneth Sterling); "The Beast in the Cave"; "The Alchemist"; "The Transition of Juan Romero"; "The Street"; "Poetry and the Gods" (with Anna Helen Crofts); "Azathoth"; "The Descendant"; "The Book"; "Supernatural Horror in Literature"; "Chronology of the Fiction of H. P. Lovecraft" [by S. T. Joshi].

Collected fiction—exclusive of prose poems and some miscellaneous items—in corrected texts. Because of copyright constraints, contents of Derleth's previous editions (1963–65) were retained.

The Horror in the Museum and Other Revisions. Texts edited by S. T. Joshi, with an introduction by August Derleth. Sauk City, WI: Arkham House, 1989. Second Edition. *Contains:* "The Green Meadow" (with Winifred V. Jackson), 3–8; "The Crawling Chaos" (with Winifred V. Jackson), 9–15; "The Last Test" (with Adolphe de Castro), 16–60; "The Electric Executioner" (with Adolphe de Castro), 61–79; "The Curse of Yig" (with Zealia Bishop), 80–95; "The Mound" (with Zealia Bishop), 96–163; "Medusa's Coil" (with Zealia Bishop), 164–200; "The Man of Stone" (with Hazel Heald), 201–14; "The Horror in the Museum" (with Hazel Heald), 215–41; "Winged Death" (with Hazel Heald), 242–63; "Out of the Aeons" (with Hazel Heald), 264–88; "The Horror in the Burying-Ground" (with Hazel Heald), 289–302; "The Diary of Alonzo Typer" (with William Lumley), 303–22; "The Horror at Martin's Beach" (with Sonia H. Greene), 325–30; "Ashes" (with C. M. Eddy, Jr.), 331–38; "The Ghost-Eater" (with C. M. Eddy, Jr.), 339–47; "The Loved Dead" (with C. M. Eddy, Jr.), 348–57; "Deaf, Dumb and Blind" (with C. M. Eddy, Jr.), 358–68; "Two Black Bottles" (with Wilfred B. Talman), 369–79; "The Trap" (with Henry S. Whitehead), 380–99; "The Tree on the Hill" (with Duane W. Rimel), 400–409; "The Disinterment" (with Duane W. Rimel), 410–20; "'Till A' the Seas'" (with R. H. Barlow), 421–29; "The Night Ocean" (with R. H. Barlow), 430–50.

Corrected edition of Lovecraft's "revisions," collaborations, and ghost-written tales.

Miscellaneous Writings. Edited by S. T. Joshi. Sauk City, WI: Arkham House, 1995. *Contains* (fiction only): "The Little Glass Bottle"; "The Secret Cave"; "The Mystery of the Grave-Yard"; "The Mysterious Ship"; "A Reminiscence of Dr. Samuel Johnson"; "Old Bugs"; "Memory"; "Nyarlathotep" (prose-poem); "Ex Oblivione"; "What the Moon Brings"; "Sweet Ermengarde"; "The Very Old Folk"; "History of the *Necronomicon*"; "Ibid"; "Discarded Draft of 'The Shadow over Innsmouth'"; "The Battle That Ended the Century" (with R. H. Barlow); "Collapsing Cosmoses" (with R. H. Barlow); "The Challenge from Beyond" (Lovecraft portion only).

Generous selection of Lovecraft's essays, but also includes the remaining fiction not included in the four Arkham House volumes of revised texts (see above).

Tales of H. P. Lovecraft. Selected by Joyce Carol Oates. Hopewell, NJ: Ecco Press, 1997. New York: HarperCollins, 2000. *Contains:* "Introduction," by Joyce Carol Oates; "The Outsider"; "The Music of Erich Zann"; "The Rats in the Walls"; "The Shunned House"; "The Call of Cthulhu"; "The Colour out of Space"; "The Dunwich Horror"; *At the Mountains of Madness;* "The Shadow over Innsmouth"; "The Shadow out of Time."

Interesting selection of tales by a leading literary figure.

The Annotated H. P. Lovecraft. Edited by S. T. Joshi. New York: Dell, 1997. *Contains:* "Introduction," by S. T. Joshi; "The Rats in the Walls"; "The Colour out of Space"; "The Dunwich Horror"; *At the Mountains of Madness;* "Lovecraft on Weird Fiction" (excerpts of letters to *Weird Tales* [March 1924], to *Weird Tales* [5 July 1927], to Frank Belknap Long [22 February 1931], to Harold S. Farnese [22 September 1932]); "Appendix: Lovecraft in the Media," by S. T. Joshi; "Select Bibliography."

More Annotated H. P. Lovecraft. Edited by S. T. Joshi and Peter Cannon. New York: Dell, 1999. *Contains:* "Introduction," by Peter Cannon; "The Picture in the House"; "Herbert West—Reanimator"; "The Hound"; "The Shunned House"; "The Horror at Red Hook"; "Cool Air"; "The Call of Cthulhu"; "Pickman's Model"; "The Thing on the Doorstep"; "The Haunter of the Dark."

Extensively annotated and illustrated editions of some of Lovecraft's more significant tales.

The Call of Cthulhu and Other Weird Stories. Edited by S. T. Joshi. New York: Penguin, 1999. *Contains:* "Introduction," by S. T. Joshi; "Suggestions for Further Reading" [by Joshi]; "Dagon"; "The Statement of Randolph Carter"; "Facts concerning the Late Arthur Jermyn and His Family"; "Celephaïs"; "Nyarlathotep"; "The Picture in the House"; "The Outsider"; "Herbert West—Reanimator"; "The Hound"; "The Rats in the Walls"; "The Festival"; "He"; "Cool Air"; "The Call of Cthulhu"; "The Colour out of Space"; "The Whisperer in Darkness"; "The Shadow over Innsmouth"; "The Haunter of the Dark"; "Explanatory Notes" [by Joshi].

The Thing on the Doorstep and Other Weird Stories. Edited by S. T. Joshi. New York: Penguin, 2001. *Contains:* "Introduction," by S. T. Joshi; "Suggestions for Further Reading" [by Joshi]; "The Tomb"; "Beyond the Wall of Sleep"; "The White Ship"; "The Temple"; "The Quest of Iranon"; "The Music of Erich Zann"; "Under the Pyramids" (with Harry Houdini); "Pickman's Model"; *The Case of Charles Dexter Ward;* "The Dunwich Horror"; *At the Mountains of Madness;* "The Thing on the Doorstep"; "Explanatory Notes" [by Joshi].

The Dreams in the Witch House and Other Weird Stories. Edited by S. T. Joshi. New York: Penguin, 2004. *Contains:* "Introduction," by S. T. Joshi; "Suggestions for Further Reading" [by Joshi]; "Polaris"; "The Doom That Came to Sarnath"; "The Terrible Old Man"; "The Tree"; "The Cats of Ulthar"; "From Beyond"; "The Nameless City"; "The Moon-Bog"; "The Other Gods"; "Hypnos"; "The Lurking Fear"; "The Unnamable"; "The Shunned House"; "The Horror at Red Hook"; "In the Vault"; "The Strange High House in the Mist"; *The Dream-Quest of Unknown Kadath;* "The Silver Key"; "Through the Gates of the Silver Key" (with E. Hoffmann Price); "The Dreams in the Witch House"; "The Shadow out of Time"; "Explanatory Notes" [by Joshi].

Annotated editions of the great majority of Lovecraft's stories.

The Shadow over Innsmouth. Edited by S. T. Joshi and David E. Schultz. West Warwick, RI: Necronomicon Press, 1994, 1997.

Exhaustively annotated edition of the story.

The Shadow out of Time. Edited by S. T. Joshi and David E. Schultz. New York: Hippocampus Press, 2001.

First publication of the corrected text of the story, based on the recently discovered autograph manuscript. With extensive annotations.

From the Pest Zone: Stories from New York. Edited by S. T. Joshi and David E. Schultz. New York: Hippocampus Press, 2003. *Contains:* "Introduction," by David E. Schultz and S. T. Joshi; "The Shunned House"; "The Horror at Red Hook"; "He"; "In the Vault"; "Cool Air"; "Preface to *The Shunned House,*" by Frank Belknap Long; "Little Sketches about Town" (*New York Evening Post,* 29 August 1924); "Notes" [by Joshi and Schultz]; "Textual Notes" [by Joshi].

Extensively annotated edition of the stories written in New York (1924–26).

Tales. Selected by Peter Straub. New York: Library of America, 2005. *Contains:* "The Statement of Randolph Carter"; "The Outsider"; "The Music of Erich Zann"; "Herbert West—Reanimator"; "The Lurking Fear"; "The Rats in the Walls"; "The Shunned House"; "The Horror at Red Hook"; "He"; "Cool Air"; "The Call of Cthulhu"; "Pickman's Model"; *The Case of Charles Dexter Ward;* "The Colour out of Space"; "The Dunwich Horror"; "The Whisperer in Darkness"; *At the Mountains of Madness;* "The Shadow over Innsmouth"; "The Dreams in the Witch House"; "The Thing on the Doorstep"; "The Shadow out of Time"; "The Haunter of the Dark"; "Chronology"; "Note on the Texts"; "Notes" [by Peter Straub].

Selection of some of Lovecraft's best tales; a symbol of his rise to canonical status in American literature.

H. P. Lovecraft: The Fiction. [Edited by S. T. Joshi.] New York: Barnes & Noble, 2008.

First complete publication of Lovecraft's complete original fiction, arranged chronologically by date of writing. Based on the revised texts established by Joshi, but the first printing contained numerous typographical errors; these were corrected in later printings.

Poetry

The Ancient Track: Complete Poetical Works. Edited by S. T. Joshi. San Francisco: Night Shade Books, 2001.

Nearly complete edition of Lovecraft's poetical works, with critical and bibliographical notes. The few remaining poems or fragments that failed to be included can be found in "Poems Not in *The Ancient Track*," *Lovecraft Annual* No. 3 (2009): 184–89.

Letters

Selected Letters: 1911–1937. Edited by August Derleth and Donald Wandrei (Volumes 1–3); August Derleth and James Turner (Volumes 4–5). Sauk City, WI: Arkham House, 1965–76.

The principal collection of letters, but with many misprints (especially in the first three volumes) and abridgements. Not indexed, but see *An Index to the Selected Letters of H. P. Lovecraft* by S. T. Joshi (Necronomicon Press, 1980).

Lovecraft at Last. By H. P. Lovecraft and Willis Conover, Jr. Arlington, VA: Carrollton-Clark, 1975.

"Conversational" rendering of correspondence between Lovecraft and Conover, with much other interesting matter. A monument to fine book production.

H. P. Lovecraft in "The Eyrie." Edited by S. T. Joshi and Marc A. Michaud. West Warwick, RI: Necronomicon Press, 1979.

Letters by and about Lovecraft in the letter column of *Weird Tales* (letters by Lovecraft now reprinted in *Uncollected Letters* [q.v.]).

Uncollected Letters. Edited by S. T. Joshi. West Warwick, RI: Necronomicon Press, 1986.

Letters mostly culled from letter columns of pulp and fan magazines.

Letters to Henry Kuttner. Edited by David E. Schultz and S. T. Joshi. West Warwick, RI: Necronomicon Press, 1990.

Letters to Richard F. Searight. Edited by David E. Schultz, S. T. Joshi, and Franklyn Searight. West Warwick, RI: Necronomicon Press, 1992.

Letters to Robert Bloch. Edited by David E. Schultz and S. T. Joshi. West Warwick, RI: Necronomicon Press, 1993. [Supplement, 1993.]

Letters to Samuel Loveman and Vincent Starrett. Edited by S. T. Joshi and David E. Schultz. West Warwick, RI: Necronomicon Press, 1994.

Letters to Alfred Galpin. Edited by S. T. Joshi and David E. Schultz. New York: Hippocampus Press, 2003.

Letters to Rheinhart Kleiner. Edited by S. T. Joshi and David E. Schultz. New York: Hippocampus Press, 2005.

Annotated editions of Lovecraft's letters to selected correspondents. The latter two volumes contain many writings by Galpin and Kleiner, respectively.

Lord of a Visible World: An Autobiography in Letters. Edited by S. T. Joshi and David E. Schultz. Athens: Ohio University Press, 2000.

Extensive selection of Lovecraft's letters, arranged as if to form an informal autobiography.

Mysteries of Time and Spirit: The Letters of H. P. Lovecraft and Donald Wandrei. Edited by S. T. Joshi and David E. Schultz. San Francisco: Night Shade Books, 2002.

Annotated edition of the joint correspondence of Lovecraft and Wandrei.

Letters from New York. Edited by S. T. Joshi and David E. Schultz. San Francisco: Night Shade Books, 2005.

Generous annotated selection of Lovecraft's to Lillian D. Clark, Annie E. P. Gamwell, and others during his New York stay (1924–26).

O Fortunate Floridian: H. P. Lovecraft's Letters to R. H. Barlow. Edited by S. T. Joshi and David E. Schultz. Tampa, FL: University of Tampa Press, 2007.

Annotated edition of Lovecraft's letters to Barlow.

Essential Solitude: The Letters of H. P. Lovecraft and August Derleth. Edited by David E. Schultz and S. T. Joshi. New York: Hippocampus Press, 2008. 2 vols.

A Means to Freedom: The Letters of H. P. Lovecraft and Robert E. Howard. Edited by S. T. Joshi, David E. Schultz, and Rusty Burke. New York: Hippocampus Press, 2009. 2 vols.

Annotated edition of the joint correspondence of Lovecraft with Derleth and Howard, respectively.

Essays and Miscellany

The Conservative: Complete 1915–1923. Edited by Marc A. Michaud. West Warwick, RI: Necronomicon Press, 1976.

Complete contents (some in facsimile) of Lovecraft's own amateur journal.

Commonplace Book. Edited by David E. Schultz. West Warwick, RI: Necronomicon Press, 1987. 2 vols.

First corrected publication, with exhaustive commentary. A landmark in Lovecraft scholarship.

The Annotated Supernatural Horror in Literature. Edited by S. T. Joshi. New York: Hippocampus Press, 2000.

Exhaustively annotated edition, with comprehensive bibliographies, of Lovecraft's great essay on weird fiction.

Collected Essays. Edited by S. T. Joshi. New York: Hippocampus Press, 2004–06.

Comprehensive annotated edition of Lovecraft's essays. Volume 1 contains the amateur journalism writings; Volume 2 the literary criticism; Volume 3 the science writings; Volume 4 the travel essays; and Volume 5 the philosophical essays, autobiography, and miscellany.

Secondary Bibliography

Bibliographies, Encyclopedias, and Indexes

Joshi, S. T. *H. P. Lovecraft and Lovecraft Criticism: An Annotated Bibliography.* Kent, OH: Kent State University Press, 1981. Rev. ed. Tampa, FL: University of Tampa Press, 2009 (as *H. P. Lovecraft: A Comprehensive Bibliography*).

Comprehensive descriptive bibliography of works by and about Lovecraft in English and other languages, including books, contributions to periodicals, anthology appearances, works edited, and miscellany. The revised edition takes extensive note of the outpouring of criticism on Lovecraft since the publication of the first edition.

———. *An Index to the Fiction and Poetry of H. P. Lovecraft.* West Warwick, RI: Necronomicon Press, 1992.

Index to proper names to the revised Arkham House editions of Lovecraft's fiction and poetry.

———. *An Index to the Selected Letters of H. P. Lovecraft.* West Warwick, RI: Necronomicon Press, 1980 (rev. ed. 1991).

Comprehensive index to the *Selected Letters* (q.v.).

———. *Lovecraft's Library: A Catalogue.* West Warwick, RI: Necronomicon Press, 1980. Rev. ed. New York: Hippocampus Press, 2002.

Listing of about 1000 books from Lovecraft's library with full bibliographical information, tables of contents of selected items, and brief annotations on Lovecraft's use of them in his work.

Joshi, S. T., and David E. Schultz. *An H. P. Lovecraft Encyclopedia.* Westport, CT: Greenwood Press, 2001. New York: Hippocampus Press, [2004].

Thorough encyclopedia with entries on works by Lovecraft, friends, family, and other writers who influenced him, and other relevant topics.

Pearsall, Anthony. *The Lovecraft Lexicon: A Reader's Guide to Persons, Places and Things in the Tales of H. P. Lovecraft.* Tempe, AZ: New Falcon Publications, 2005. 472 pp.

Comprehensive collection of entries on elements cited in Lovecraft's stories.

Shreffler, Philip A. *The H. P. Lovecraft Companion.* Westport, CT: Greenwood Press, 1977.

Plot outlines and glossary of characters in Lovecraft's fiction, with an introductory essay on the differences between English and American weird writing. Sprinkled with errors.

Biographies and Memoirs

Barlow, Robert H. "The Wind That Is in the Grass: A Memoir of H. P. Lovecraft in Florida." In Cannon, *Lovecraft Remembered* (q.v.).

Sensitive memoir by Lovecraft's literary executor.

Cannon, Peter, ed. *Lovecraft Remembered.* Sauk City, WI: Arkham House, 1998. *Contains:* Peter Cannon, "Introduction," pp. xi–xiv; *I. Neighbors:* [Peter Cannon], [introductory note], pp. 3–5; Winfield Townley Scott, "His Own Most Fantastic Creation," pp. 7–27; Marian F. Bonner, "Miscellaneous Impression of H.P.L.," pp. 28–29; Mary V. Dana, "A Glimpse of H.P.L.," pp. 30–31; August Derleth, "Lovecraft's Sensitivity," pp. 32–37; Dorothy C. Walter, "Three Hours with H. P. Lovecraft," pp. 38–48; Muriel Eddy, "The Gentleman from Angell Street," pp. 49–64; C. M. Eddy, Jr., "Walks with H. P.

Lovecraft," pp. 65–68; Harold W. Munro, "Lovecraft, My Childhood Friend," pp. 69–72; *II. Amateurs:* [Peter Cannon], [introductory note], pp. 73–77; Andrew Francis Lockhart, "Little Journeys to the Homes of Prominent Amateurs," pp. 79–81; Edith Miniter, "Amateur Writings," pp. 82–85; George Julian Houtain, "Amateur Writings," pp. 86–89; Maurice W. Moe, "Howard Phillips Lovecraft: The Sage of Providence," pp. 90–91; Ira Cole, "A Tribute from the Past," p. 92; E. A. Edkins, "Idiosyncrasies of H.P.L.," pp. 93–96; Edward H. Cole, "Ave atque Vale!" pp. 97–105; W. Paul Cook, *In Memoriam: Howard Phillips Lovecraft,* pp. 106–56; Rheinhart Kleiner, "Discourse on H. P. Lovecraft," pp. 157–63; Alfred Galpin, "Memories of a Friendship," pp. 164–72; L. Sprague de Camp, "Young Man Lovecraft," pp. 173–75; *III. Kalems:* [Peter Cannon], [introductory note], pp. 176–78; James F. Morton, "A Few Memories," pp. 179–81; Frank Belknap Long, "Some Random Memories of H.P.L.," pp. 182–87; Rheinhart Kleiner, "Bards and Bibliophiles," pp. 188–94; Rheinhart Kleiner, "A Memoir of Lovecraft," pp. 195–203; Samuel Loveman, "Howard Phillips Lovecraft," pp. 204–8; Samuel Loveman, "Lovecraft as a Conversationalist," pp. 209–11; Wilfred B. Talman, "The Normal Lovecraft," pp. 212–20; Mara Kirk Hart, "Walkers in the City: George Willard Kirk and Howard Phillips Lovecraft in New York City, 1924–1926" (abridged), pp. 221–47; *IV. Ladies:* [Peter Cannon], [introductory note], pp. 248–49; Hazel Heald, "In Memoriam," p. 251; Sonia H. Davis, "Lovecraft as I Knew Him," pp. 252–63; Zealia Bishop, "H. P. Lovecraft: A Pupil's View," pp. 264–74; Sonia H. Davis, "Memories of Lovecraft: I," pp. 275–76; Helen V. Sully, "Memories of Lovecraft: II," pp. 277–78; *V. Professionals:* [Peter Cannon], [introductory note], pp. 279–81; Robert Bloch, "Letter to *Weird Tales,*" p. 283; Clark Ashton Smith, "Letter to *Weird Tales,*" p. 284; Robert W. Lowndes, "A Tribute to Lovecraft," pp. 285–86; Henry George Weiss (Francis Flagg), "The Genius of Lovecraft," p. 287; E. Hoffmann Price, "The Man Who Was Lovecraft," pp. 288–98; Fritz Leiber, "My Correspondence with Lovecraft," pp. 299–302; Donald Wandrei, "Lovecraft in Providence," pp. 303–17; Robert Bloch, "Out of the Ivory Tower," pp. 318–23; H. Warner Munn, "H.P.L.: A Reminiscence," pp. 324–38; Vrest Orton, "Recollections of H. P. Lovecraft," pp. 339–46; *VI. Fans:* [Peter Cannon], [introductory note], pp. 347–49; R. H. Barlow, "The Barlow Journal," pp. 351–55; R. H. Barlow, "The Wind That Is in the Grass: A Memoir of H. P. Lovecraft in Florida," pp. 356–63; William L. Crawford, "Lovecraft's First Book," pp. 364–66; J. Vernon Shea, "H. P. Lovecraft: The House and the Shadows" (abridged), pp. 367–69; Kenneth Sterling, "Caverns Measureless to Man," pp.

370–84; Will Murray, "Autumn in Providence: Harry K. Brobst on Love-craft," pp. 385–95; *VII. Critics:* [Peter Cannon], [introductory note], pp. 396–99; Rheinhart Kleiner, "A Note on Howard P. Lovecraft's Verse," pp. 401–2; Howard Wolf, "'Variety' Column," pp. 403–5; Robert E. Howard, "Letter to *Weird Tales,*" p. 406; Vrest Orton, "A Weird Writer Is in Our Midst," pp. 407–9; August Derleth, "H. P. Lovecraft, Outsider," pp. 410–13; Dorothy C. Walter, "Lovecraft and Benefit Street," pp. 414–19; T. O. Mabbott, "H. P. Lovecraft: An Appreciation," pp. 420–22; Kenneth Sterling, "Lovecraft and Science," pp. 423–25; Vincent Starrett, "H. P. Lovecraft," pp. 426–28; Vincent Starrett, "The Lovecraft Legend," pp. 429–30; Winfield Townley Scott, "A Parenthesis on Lovecraft as Poet," pp. 431–35; Matthew H. Onderdonk, "The Lord of R'lyeh," pp. 436–47; Matthew H. Onderdonk, "Charon—in Reverse; or, H. P. Lovecraft versus the 'Realists' of Fantasy," pp. 448–54; Fritz Leiber, "A Literary Copernicus," pp. 455–66; Joseph Payne Brennan, "H. P. Lovecraft, an Evaluation," pp. 467–71; Fritz Leiber, "Through Hyperspace with Brown Jenkin: Lovecraft's Contribution to Speculative Fiction," pp. 472–83; Frank Belknap Long, "Epilogue: Lovecraft and Poe" (extract from *Hoard Phillips Lovecraft: Dreamer on the Nightside*), pp. 484–86.

Comprehensive selection of memoirs by Lovecraft, with a concluding section of early criticism.

Cook, W. Paul. *In Memoriam: Howard Phillips Lovecraft: Recollections, Appreciations, Estimates.* North Montpelier, VT: Driftwind Press, 1941; West Warwick, R.I.: Necronomicon Press, 1977. In Cannon, *Lovecraft Remembered* (q.v.).

Perhaps the best Lovecraft memoir from one who knew him for more than twenty years; full of telling anecdotes and keen insights into Lovecraft's character.

Davis, Sonia H. *The Private Life of H. P. Lovecraft.* West Warwick, R.I.: Necronomicon Press, 1985.

Important, if occasionally incoherent, memoir by Lovecraft's wife, disputing some of Cook's assertions (q.v.) and describing in detail their courtship, marriage, and its aftermath. Cannon's *Lovecraft Remembered* (q.v.) includes the abridged and edited version, "Lovecraft as I Knew Him" (in *Something about Cats and Other Pieces,* 1949).

de Camp, L. Sprague. *Lovecraft: A Biography.* Garden City, NY: Doubleday, 1975.

First full-length biography of Lovecraft, thoroughly researched (albeit with numerous errors) but saying little about Lovecraft's philosophical thought and consequently misinterpreting many of Lovecraft's actions and motivations.

Derleth, August. *H. P. L.: A Memoir.* New York: Ben Abramson, 1945.

First true biography of Lovecraft, though very brief and full of errors. One chapter devoted to criticism.

————. *Some Notes on H. P. Lovecraft.* Sauk City, WI: Arkham House, 1959. Folcroft, PA: Folcroft Editions, 1971. Norwood, PA: Norwood Editions, 1976. West Warwick, RI: Necronomicon Press, 1982.

Random biographical and critical notes; gives much information on Derleth's "posthumous collaborations" with Lovecraft. Most of the contents reprinted in *The Dark Brotherhood* (q.v.) as "Final Notes," pp. 302–21.

Edkins, E. A. "Idiosyncrasies of HPL." *Olympian* No. 35 (Autumn 1940): 1–7. In Cannon, *Lovecraft Remembered* (q.v.).

Eloquent brief memoir testifying to Lovecraft's "essential nobility [and] dauntless integrity."

Everts, R. Alain. *The Death of a Gentleman: The Last Days of Howard Phillips Lovecraft.* Madison, WI: Strange Co., 1987.

Detailed examination of Lovecraft's final days in the hospital, based upon an interview with Lovecraft's doctor and containing transcriptions from Lovecraft's "Death Diary" made by R. H. Barlow.

Faig, Kenneth W., Jr. "Howard Phillips Lovecraft: The Early Years 1890–1914." *Nyctalops* 2 (April 1973): 3–9, 13–15; (July 1974): 34–44.

Extremely full and richly detailed account of Lovecraft's childhood and youth, with a bibliography of his early publications in Providence newspapers.

————. *H. P. Lovecraft: His Life, His Work.* West Warwick, R.I.: Necronomicon Press, 1979.

Sensitive interpretative essay on Lovecraft the man with a thorough chronology of events in Lovecraft's ancestry, life, and posthumous recognition; with a chronology of works compiled by S. T. Joshi.

————. *The Parents of Howard Phillips Lovecraft.* West Warwick, RI: Necronomicon Press, July 1990.

Exhaustive treatment of Lovecraft's mother and father and their influence on Lovecraft.

———. *The Unknown Lovecraft.* New York: Hippocampus Press, 2009.

Important collection of Faig's essays on many aspects of Lovecraft's life, including his parents and ancestry, his involvement with amateur journalism, his relations with R. H. Barlow, etc.

Galpin, Alfred. "Memories of a Friendship." In Lovecraft, *Letters to Alfred Galpin* (q.v.). In Cannon, *Lovecraft Remembered* (q.v.).

Examines Lovecraft's attitude to music and his relations with his wife.

Joshi, S. T. *A Dreamer and a Visionary: H. P. Lovecraft in His Time.* Liverpool: Liverpool University Press, 2001.

Radically abridged and reproportioned version of his biography (see below).

Compact study of Lovecraft's life, work, and thought, stressing the philosophical unity of his work.

———. *H. P. Lovecraft: A Life.* West Warwick, RI: Necronomicon Press,1996. Unabridged ed. New York: Hippocampus Press, 2010 (as *I Am Providence: The Life and Times of H. P. Lovecraft*). 2 vols.

Exhaustive biography drawing upon primary sources and establishing Lovecraft's place in literary, cultural, and intellectual history.

Keller, David H. "Shadows over Lovecraft." *Fantasy Commentator* 2 (Summer 1948): 237–46. *Fresco* 8 (Spring 1958): 12–27.

Thoughtful essay with insightful remarks on Lovecraft's character and its relation to his work; propounds the celebrated theory that he may have had congenital syphilis. (Kenneth Sterling has added a reply on pp. 27–29 of the *Fresco* appearance.)

Kleiner, Rheinhart. "A Memoir of Lovecraft." In Lovecraft, *Letters to Rheinhart Kleiner* (q.v.). In Cannon, *Lovecraft Remembered* (q.v.).

Memoir by one of Lovecraft's closest friends in amateur journalism.

Koki, Arthur S. "H. P. Lovecraft: An Introduction to His Life and Writings." M.A. thesis: Columbia University, 1962.

Thoroughly documented study of Lovecraft's life; perhaps still the best study of Lovecraft the man, used exhaustively by de Camp in his own biography.

Long, Frank Belknap. *Howard Phillips Lovecraft: Dreamer on the Nightside*. Sauk City, WI: Arkham House, 1975.

Diffuse and meandering memoir; a disappointment from one who knew Lovecraft better than anyone save W. Paul Cook, but with occasional interesting sidelights and a defense of Lovecraft's character against recent aspersions of it.

Loveman, Samuel. "Howard Phillips Lovecraft." In H. P. Lovecraft [et al.], *Something about Cats and Other Pieces*. Sauk City, WI: Arkham House, 1949. In Cannon, *Lovecraft Remembered* (q.v.).

Account of Lovecraft's trips to Cleveland and New York in 1922.

Orton, Vrest. "Recollections of H. P. Lovecraft." *Whispers* 4 (March 1982): 95–101. In Cannon, *Lovecraft Remembered* (q.v.).

Account of Lovecraft's visit to Orton in Vermont in 1927.

Price, E. Hoffmann. "The Man Who Was Lovecraft." In H. P. Lovecraft [et al.], *Something about Cats and Other Pieces*. Sauk City, WI: Arkham House, 1949. In Cannon, *Lovecraft Remembered* (q.v.).

Warm memoir of Lovecraft's visit to Price in New Orleans in 1932, his collaboration on "Through the Gates of the Silver Key," and other matters.

Scott, Winfield Townley. "His Own Most Fantastic Creation: Howard Phillips Lovecraft." In H. P. Lovecraft [et al.], *Marginalia*. Sauk City, WI: Arkham House, 1944. In Cannon, *Lovecraft Remembered* (q.v.).

First substantial biographical article on Lovecraft from a mainstream critic, still full of suggestive insights.

Shea, J. Vernon. "H. P. Lovecraft: The House and the Shadows." *Fantasy and Science Fiction* 30 (May 1966): 82–99. West Warwick, RI: Necronomicon Press, 1982.

Wide-ranging memoir and critical study from one of Lovecraft's younger correspondents.

Sterling, Kenneth. "Caverns Measureless to Man." *Science-Fantasy Correspondent* 1 (1975): 36–43. In Cannon, *Lovecraft Remembered* (q.v.).

Poignant memoir of Lovecraft's later years, concentrating on his scientific rationalism.

Talman, Wilfred B., et al. *The Normal Lovecraft*. Saddle River, NJ: Gerry de la Ree, 1973.

Contains articles by Talman, de la Ree, and L. Sprague de Camp. Talman attempts to depict Lovecraft as far more "normal" than many have thought. Other articles are less substantial.

Walter, Dorothy C. "Three Hours with H. P. Lovecraft." In H. P. Lovecraft [et al.], *The Shuttered Room and Other Pieces*. Sauk City, WI: Arkham House, 1959. In Cannon, *Lovecraft Remembered* (q.v.).

Account of Lovecraft's visit with Walter in the 1930s.

Wandrei, Donald. "The Dweller in Darkness: Lovecraft, 1927." In H. P. Lovecraft [et al.], *Marginalia*. Sauk City, WI: Arkham House, 1944. In Cannon, *Lovecraft Remembered* (q.v.).

Account of Wandrei's meeting of Lovecraft in Providence in the spring of 1927.

Critical Studies

Airaksinen, Timo. *The Philosophy of H. P. Lovecraft*. New York: Peter Lang, 1999.

Provocative if idiosyncratic study of Lovecraft's use of language to create terror, with discussions of nihilism, the disjunction of science and magic, and other subjects.

Berruti, Massimo. "H. P. Lovecraft and the Anatomy of Nothingness: The Cthulhu Mythos." *Semiotica* No. 150 (2004): 363–418.

Semiotic approach to Lovecraft and his pseudomythology.

Boerem, R. "A Lovecraftian Nightmare." *Nyctalops* 2 (April 1976): 22–24. In Joshi, *Four Decades* (q.v.).

Sensitive and penetrating reading of "The Poe-et's Nightmare" as emblematic of Lovecraft's cosmic philosophy.

Buhle, Paul. "Dystopia as Utopia: Howard Phillips Lovecraft and the Unknown Content of American Horror Literature." *Minnesota Review* 6 (Spring 1976): 118–31. In Joshi, *Four Decades* (q.v.).

Penetrating essay on Lovecraft's place in intellectual and cultural history.

Burleson, Donald R. *H. P. Lovecraft: A Critical Study*. Westport, CT: Greenwood Press, 1983.

Thoroughgoing study of Lovecraft's entire work, recognizing cosmicism as the foundation of his aesthetic theory and proposing the notion of "ironic impressionism"—the idea that mankind is just intelligent enough to realize its vanishingly small place in the cosmos.

————. "H. P. Lovecraft: The Hawthorne Influence." *Extrapolation* 22 (Fall 1981): 262–69.

Full discussion of Hawthorne's influence on "The Picture in the House," "The Shunned House," and the creation of the *Necronomicon*.

————. "Humor Beneath Horror: Some Sources for 'The Dunwich Horror' and 'The Whisperer in Darkness.'" *Lovecraft Studies* No. 2 (Spring 1980): 5–15.

Traces topographical and place names slyly inserted into Lovecraft's two novelettes about the Massachusetts and Vermont backwoods.

————. *Lovecraft: Disturbing the Universe*. Lexington: University Press of Kentucky, 1990.

Challenging deconstructionist interpretation of Lovecraft, with chapters on individual tales.

————. "Lovecraft and the World as Cryptogram." *Lovecraft Studies* No. 16 (Spring 1988): 14–18.

Finds the recurring theme of the cryptogram emblematic of Lovecraft's work in general, as embodying the notion of "world as text."

————. "The Mythic Hero Archetype in 'The Dunwich Horror.'" *Lovecraft Studies* No. 4 (Spring 1981): 3–9.

Sees the Whateley twins as the real "heroes" of the story because they conform more closely to mythic conceptions of the hero than the human figure Dr. Henry Armitage.

Cannon, Peter. *H. P. Lovecraft*. Boston: Twayne, 1989.

Rapid survey of Lovecraft's work, concentrating (curiously) on his early fiction. Proposes few new interpretations of Lovecraft's work or thought, but soundly integrates the latest findings in Lovecraft's research.

————. "Lovecraft and the Mainstream Literature of His Day." *Lovecraft Studies* No. 7 (Fall 1982): 25–29.

Studies Lovecraft's response to the major literary figures of his day, notably Faulkner and Eliot.

————. "Sunset Terrace Imagery in Lovecraft." *Lovecraft Studies* No. 5 (Fall 1981): 3–9.

Finds the sunset terrace image a central one in Lovecraft's fiction and poetry, relating it to his notion of "adventurous expectancy."

————. *"Sunset Terrace Imagery in Lovecraft" and Other Essays.* West Warwick, RI: Necronomicon Press, 1990.

Selection of Cannon's critical essays on Lovecraft.

Cardin, Matt. "The Master's Eyes Shining with Secrets: H. P. Lovecraft's Influence on Thomas Ligotti." *Lovecraft Annual* No. 1 (2007): 94–125.

Exhaustive discussion of Ligotti's response to Lovecraft and the influence of Lovecraft on Ligotti's fiction.

Carter, Lin. *Lovecraft: A Look Behind the "Cthulhu Mythos."* New York: Ballantine, 1972.

History of the development of Lovecraft's myth cycle, principally after Lovecraft's death. Marred by Carter's uncritical acceptance of Derleth's flawed interpretation of the myth cycle.

Cerasini, Marc A. "Thematic Links in *Arthur Gordon Pym, At the Mountains of Madness,* and *Moby Dick.*" *Crypt of Cthulhu* No. 49 (Lammas 1987): 3–20.

Exhaustive article finding that *At the Mountains of Madness* bears closer relations with *Arthur Gordon Pym* than many have believed.

Cisco, Michael. "The Book of 'The Book.'" *Lovecraft Studies* Nos. 42/43 (Autumn 2001): 4–20.

Exhaustive discussion of the themes and motifes in Lovecraft's fragmentary tale.

Colavito, Jason. *The Cult of Alien Gods: H. P. Lovecraft and Extraterrestrial Pop Culture.* Amherst, NY: Prometheus Books, 2005.

Provocative treatise asserting that Lovecraft's fictional discussion of the incursion of alien races into human civilization influenced such UFO proponents as Erich von Däniken in their theories of actual alien incursions.

Connors, Scott, ed. *A Century Less a Dream: Selected Criticism on H. P. Lovecraft.*

Holicong, PA: Wildside Press, 2002. *Contains:* Scott Connors, "Introduction," 1–7; H. P. Lovecraft, "Continuity" (*Fungi from Yuggoth* XXXVI), 9; Kenneth W. Faig, Jr., "'The Silver Key' and Lovecaft's Childhood," 10–44; David E. Schultz, "Who Needs the 'Cthulhu Mythos'?" 45–57; Robert M. Price, "Higher Criticism and the *Necronomicon*," 58–68; Jason C. Eckhardt, "Behind the Mountains of Madness: Lovecraft and the Antarctic in 1930," 69–76; Robert Marten, "Arkham Country: In Search of the Lost Rescuers," 77–111; Robert H. Waugh, "Dr. Margaret Murray and H. P. Lovecraft: The Witch-Cult in New England," 112–23; S. T. Joshi, "Humour and Satire in Lovecraft," 124–36; Steven J. Mariconda, "H. P. Lovecraft: Art, Artifact, and Reality," 137–52; Robert H. Waugh, "The Structural and Thematic Unity of *Fungi from Yuggoth*," 153–77; Dan Clore, "Metonyms of Alterity: A Semiotic Interpretation of *Fungi from Yuggoth*," 178–94; James Anderson, "'Pickman's Model': Lovecraft's Model of Terror," 195–205; Donald R. Burleson, "The Mythic Hero Archetype in 'The Dunwich Horror,'" 206–13; Donald R. Burleson, "Prismatic Heroes: The Colour out of Dunwich," 214–23; Carl Buchanan, "'The Music of Erich Zann': A Psychological Interpretation (or Two)," 224–29; Paul Montelone, "The Vanity of Existence in 'The Shadow out of Time,'" 230–42; Steven J. Mariconda, "Tightening the Coil: The Revision of 'The Whisperer in Darkness,'" 243–52; Clark Ashton Smith, "H. P. L." [poem], 253; "Selected Bibliography," 254–61; "Contributors," 262–63; "Acknowledgements," 264.

Extensive selection of recent essays on Lovecraft, mostly from *Lovecraft Studies.*

Cook, W. Paul. "A Plea for Lovecraft." *Ghost* No. 3 (May 1945): 55–56; *Lovecraft Studies* Nos. 19/20 (Fall 1989): 26–27.

Prescient article urging restraint in the praise of Lovecraft and the dissemination of his work.

Dziemianowicz, Stefan. "Divers Hands." *Crypt of Cthulhu* No. 80 (Eastertide 1992): 38–52.

Exhaustive discussion of the nature of Lovecraft's pseudomythology and its use by subsequent writers.

Eckhardt, Jason C. "Behind the Mountains of Madness: Lovecraft and the Antarctic in 1930." *Lovecraft Studies* No. 14 (Spring 1987): 31–38.

Study of Lovecraft's Antarctic novel in the context of the real voyages to the Antarctic in his day.

Egan, James. "Dark Apocalyptic: Lovecraft's Cthulhu Mythos as a Parody of Traditional Christianity." *Extrapolation* 23 (Spring 1983): 362–76.

Examines several tales—principally "The Dunwich Horror"—where Lovecraft presents parodies of Christian symbolism and cosmology.

Evans, Timothy H. "A Last Defense against the Dark: Folklore, Horror, and the Uses of Tradition in the Works of H. P. Lovecraft." *Journal of Folklore Research* 42, No. 1 (January–April 2005): 99–135.

Exhaustive study of Lovecraft's devotion to tradition, especially in architecture, with a discussion of his interest in the Colonial Revival and his use of folklore and the vernacular in his stories.

———. "Tradition and Illusion: Antiquarianism, Tourism and Horror in H. P. Lovecraft." *Extrapolation* 45, No. 2 (Summer 2004): 176–95.

Extensive discussion of Lovecraft's antiquarian travels, his evolution of an "anti-modernist ideology," and the role of travel in his fiction.

Faig, Jr., Kenneth W. "Robert H. Barlow as H. P. Lovecraft's Literary Executor: An Appreciation." *Crypt of Cthulhu* No. 60 (Hallowmas 1988): 52–62.

Careful study of Barlow's relations with Lovecraft during his lifetime and his dealings with August Derleth and Lovecraft's family as Lovecraft's literary executor.

———. "'The Silver Key' and Lovecraft's Childhood." *Crypt of Cthulhu* No. 81 (St. John's Eve 1992): 11–47.

Immense treatment of Lovecraft's story as based upon a trip he took to ancestral sites in western Rhode Island in 1926, an echo of a visit he had taken there as a boy.

Frierson, Meade and Penny, ed. *HPL.* Birmingham, AL: Meade and Penny Frierson, 1972.

Large fan publication that may be said to have ushered in the new era of Lovecraft scholarship.

Gayford, Norman R. "Randolph Carter: An Anti-Hero's Quest." *Lovecraft Studies* No. 16 (Spring 1988): 3–11; No. 17 (Fall 1988): 5–13.

Maintains that the collaboration "Through the Gates of the Silver Key" is necessary to complete the Randolph Carter cycle in light of the mythic conceptions of

Joseph Campbell and Mircea Eliade; supplies a close study of the details of the collaboration as revealed in letters between Lovecraft and E. Hoffmann Price.

Hanegraaff, Wouter J. "Fiction in the Desert of the Real: Lovecraft's Cthulhu Mythos." *Aries* 7, No. 1 (2007): 85–109.

A discussion of Lovecraft's pseudomythology in light of "Western esotericism," with notes on occultist adaptations of Lovecraft's ideas.

Janicker, Rebecca. "New England Narratives: Space and Place in the Fiction of H. P. Lovecraft." *Extrapolation* 48, No. 1 (Spring 2007): 56–72.

Detailed study of "The Colour out of Space" and "The Shadow over Innsmouth" and their use of New England "topography, history and cultural idiosyncrasies."

Jones, Stephen. *H. P. Lovecraft in Britain.* Birmingham: British Fantasy Society, 2007.

Detailed discussion of the publication of Lovecraft's works in England, using primary sources from publishers, editors, and the like.

Joshi, S. T. *H. P. Lovecraft.* Mercer Island, WA: Starmont House, 1982.

Compact study of Lovecraft's life, work, and thought, stressing the philosophical unity of his work.

———. *H. P. Lovecraft: The Decline of the West.* Mercer Island, WA: Starmont House, 1990.

Comprehensive study of Lovecraft's philosophical thought and its application to his fiction.

———. *The Rise and Fall of the Cthulhu Mythos.* Poplar Bluff, MO: Mythos Books, 2008.

Study of Lovecraft's pseudomythology and the writers who have imitated it from his own day to the present.

———. *A Subtler Magick: The Writings and Philosophy of H. P. Lovecraft.* San Bernadino, CA: Borgo Press, 1996.

Extensively revised version of Joshi's 1982 monograph (q.v.).

———. "Humour and Satire in Lovecraft." *Crypt of Cthulhu* No. 61 (Yuletide 1988): 3–13. In Connors, *A Century Less a Dream* (q.v.).

Distinguishes three types of humor in Lovecraft: puns, in-jokes, and bleak, ni-hilistic satire, the last resulting from his cosmicism.

————. *Primal Sources: Essays on H. P. Lovecraft.* New York: Hippocampus Press, 2003.

Selection of Joshi's critical essays on Lovecraft.

————. "'Reality' and Knowledge: Some Notes on the Aesthetic Thought of H. P. Lovecraft." *Lovecraft Studies* No. 3 (Fall 1980): 17–27.

Attempts to reconcile Lovecraft's theory of weird fiction with his general metaphysics.

————. *Selected Papers on Lovecraft.* West Warwick, R.I.: Necronomicon Press, 1989.

Contains five of Joshi's critical essays.

————. "Textual Problems in Lovecraft." *Lovecraft Studies* No. 6 (Spring 1982): 18–32. In Schweitzer, *Discovering H. P. Lovecraft* (q.v.).

Outlines the transmission of Lovecraft's texts.

————. "Topical References in Lovecraft." *Extrapolation* 25 (Fall 1984): 247–65. In Joshi's *Primal Sources* (q.v.).

Examines references to contemporary political, philosophical, literary, and sci-entific events in Lovecraft's tales and their significance.

————, ed. *H. P. Lovecraft: Four Decades of Criticism.* Athens: Ohio University Press, 1980. *Contains:* S. T. Joshi, "Preface," xiii–xv; Kenneth W. Faig, Jr., and S. T. Joshi, "H. P. Lovecraft: His Life and Work," 1–19; S. T. Joshi, "Lovecraft Criticism: A Study," 20–26; S. T. Joshi, "A Chronology of Se-lected Works by H. P. Lovecraft," 27–41; T. O. Mabbott, "H. P. Lovecraft: An Appreciation," 43–45; Edmund Wilson, "Tales of the Marvellous and the Ridiculous," 46–49; Fritz Leiber, Jr., "A Literary Copernicus," 50–62; Peter Penzoldt, excerpts from *The Supernatural in Fiction,* 63–77; George T. Wetzel, "The Cthulhu Mythos: A Study" (revised), 79–95; Edward Lauter-bach, "Some Notes on Cthulhuian Pseudobiblia," 96–103; Dirk W. Mosig, "H. P. Lovecraft: Myth-Maker," 104–12; J. Vernon Shea, "On the Literary Influences Which Shaped Lovecraft's Writings," 113–39; Fritz Leiber, Jr., "Through Hyperspace with Brown Jenkin: Lovecraft's Contribution to Speculative Fiction," 140–52; Peter Cannon, "The Influence of *Vathek* on

H. P. Lovecraft's *The Dream-Quest of Unknown Kadath*," 153–57; Robert Bloch, "Poe and Lovecraft," 158–60; Peter Cannon, "H. P. Lovecraft in Hawthornian Perspective," 161–65; Barton L. St. Armand, "Facts in the Case of H. P. Lovecraft," 166–85; Dirk W. Mosig, "'The White Ship': A Psychological Odyssey," 186–90; Richard L. Tierney, "Lovecraft and the Cosmic Quality in Fiction," 191–95; Paul Buhle, "Dystopia as Utopia: Howard Phillips Lovecraft and the Unknown Content of American Horror Literature," 196–210; Winfield Townley Scott, "A Parenthesis on Lovecraft as Poet," 211–16; R. Boerem, "A Lovecraftian Nightmare," 217–21; R. Boerem, "The Continuity of the *Fungi from Yuggoth*," 222–25; Clark Ashton Smith, "To Howard Phillips Lovecraft" [poem], 227–28; Appendix I: The Collected Works of H. P. Lovecraft (Arkham House edition), 229–31; Appendix II: Supplementary Readings, 232–37.

Eighteen articles on Lovecraft, some reprinted, some original. Designed to depict the ambivalent responses to Lovecraft from 1945 to 1978.

Laney, Francis T. "The Cthulhu Mythology." *Acolyte* 1 (Winter 1942): 6–12; *Crypt of Cthulhu* No. 35 (Hallowmas 1985): 28–34. Rev. in H. P. Lovecraft, *Beyond the Wall of Sleep.* Sauk City, WI: Arkham House, 1943. 424–58.

The first attempt to schematize Lovecraft's pseudomythology.

Leiber, Fritz. "A Literary Copernicus." In H. P. Lovecraft [et al.], *Something about Cats and Other Pieces.* Sauk City, WI: Arkham House, 1949. In Joshi, *Four Decades* (q.v.).

Perhaps still the finest general article on Lovecraft, showing how his work bridges the gap between conventional Gothicism and science fiction, with notes on the symbolism of his pseudomythology, the structure of his tales, and the coherence of his fictive history of the modern world.

———. "Through Hyperspace with Brown Jenkin: Lovecraft's Contribution to Speculative Fiction." In H. P. Lovecraft [et al.], *The Dark Brotherhood and Other Pieces.* Sauk City, WI: Arkham House, 1966. In Joshi, *Four Decades* (q.v.).

Studies Lovecraft's use of science-fictional techniques in his later work, with pertinent comments on his use of time travel.

Lévy, Maurice. *Lovecraft: A Study in the Fantastic.* Translated by S. T. Joshi. Detroit: Wayne State University Press, 1988.

Brilliant thematic study that sees Lovecraft's writing as the search for a "cure" for the pessimism and misanthropy engendered by his racialism and his scorn of the contemporary world. Focuses upon such central themes as landscape, heredity, the dream-world, and Lovecraft's pseudomythology.

Livesey, T. R. "Dispatches from the Providence Observatory: Astronomical Motifs and Sources in the Writings of H. P. Lovecraft." *Lovecraft Annual* 2 (2008): 3–87.

Exhaustive article on Lovecraft's knowledge of astronomy and its incorporation into his fiction.

Lovett-Graf, Bennett. "'Life Is a Hideous Thing': Primate-Geniture in H. P. Lovecraft's 'Arthur Jermyn.'" *Journal of the Fantastic in the Arts* 8, No. 3 (1997): 370–88.

Studies the story in light of Lovecraft's theories of racial degeneration.

Mabbott, T. O. "H. P. Lovecraft: An Appreciation." In H. P. Lovecraft, *Marginalia*. Sauk City, WI: Arkham House, 1944. In Joshi, *Four Decades* (q.v.).

Brief essay touching upon Lovecraft's relations to Poe and praising his narrative skill.

MacCulloch, Simon. "The Toad in the Study: M. R. James, H. P. Lovecraft, and Forbidden Knowledge." *Ghosts & Scholars* No. 20 (1995): 38–43; No. 21 (1996): 37–42; No. 22 (1996): 40–46; No. 23 (1997): 54–60. *Studies in Weird Fiction* No. 20 (Winter 1997): 2–12; No. 21 (Summer 1997): 17–28. In S. T. Joshi and Rosemary Pardoe, ed. *Warnings to the Curious: A Sheaf of Criticism on M. R. James.* New York: Hippocampus Press, 2007. 76–112.

Exhaustive discussion of the parallels and differences between James and Lovecraft, especially in the area of cosmic vs. human terror, the use of documents, and the notion of "forbidden knowledge."

Mariconda, Steven J. "H. P. Lovecraft: Consummate Prose Stylist." *Lovecraft Studies* No. 9 (Fall 1984): 43–51.

Penetrating study of Lovecraft's use of rhythmic prose.

———. "Lovecraft's Concept of 'Background.'" *Lovecraft Studies* No. 12 (Spring 1986): 3–12.

Reconciles Lovecraft's cosmicism with his attachment to the past and his New England heritage.

———. "Notes on the Prose Realism of H. P. Lovecraft." *Lovecraft Studies* No. 10 (Spring 1985): 3–12.

Further study of Lovecraft's stylistic techniques.

———. "On the Emergence of 'Cthulhu.'" *Lovecraft Studies* No. 15 (Fall 1987): 54–58.

Notes on the sources and composition of "The Call of Cthulhu."

———. *On the Emergence of "Cthulhu" and Other Observations.* West Warwick, RI: Necronomicon Press, October 1995.

Slim but substantial collection of Mariconda's critical essays, including all the items cited above.

Marten, Robert D. "Arkham Country: In Rescue of the Lost Searchers." *Lovecraft Studies* No. 39 (Summer 1998): 1–20.

Exhaustive refutation of Will Murray's theories on the sources and locations of Lovecraft's imaginary New England towns (see below), maintaining that Lovecraft's rough equivalence of Arkham to Salem, Innsmouth to Newburyport, and Dunwich to Wilbraham are fundamentally correct.

Migliore, Andrew, and John Strysik, [ed.]. *The Lurker in the Lobby: A Guide to the Cinema of H. P. Lovecraft.* Seattle: Armitage House, 1999. Rev. ed. San Francisco: Night Shade Books, 2005.

Varied collection of documents pertaining to adaptations of Lovecraft's works for film, including interviews with prominent actors and directors, discussions of individual films, and other pertinent matter.

Mitchell, Charles P. *The Complete H. P. Lovecraft Filmography.* Westport, CT: Greenwood Press, 2001.

Study of 33 films based on or inspired by Lovecraft's works, with annotated cast list, synopsis and analysis, and a discussion of the films' fidelity to Lovecraft.

Montelone, Paul. "'The Rats in the Walls': A Study in Pessimism." *Lovecraft Studies* No. 32 (Spring 1995): 18–26.

Contends that the imagery and incidents in the story shows that it "ends in universal pain, with a cry from a ravenous and tormented world-soul."

Mosig, Dirk W. "The Four Faces of 'The Outsider.'" *Nyctalops* 2 (July 1974): 3–10. In Schweitzer, *Discovering H. P. Lovecraft* (q.v.).

Studies "The Outsider" from an autobiographical, psychoanalytical, anti-metaphysical, and philosophical perspective, adding as a postscript a political interpretation.

————. "H. P. Lovecraft: Myth-Maker." *Whispers* 3 (December 1976): 48–55. In Joshi, *Four Decades* (q.v.).

Landmark article studying Lovecraft's pseudomythology in the context of his metaphysics and doing much to dismantle August Derleth's erroneous conceptions of the myth cycle.

————. "Lovecraft: The Dissonance Factor in Imaginative Literature." *Platte Valley Review* 7 (1979): 129–44. *Gothic* 1 (1979): 20–26. *Crypt of Cthulhu* No. 33 (Lammas 1985): 12–23.

Interprets Lovecraft in light of Leon Festinger's theory of cognitive dissonance.

————. *Mosig at Last: A Psychologist Looks at H. P. Lovecraft.* West Warwick, RI: Necronomicon Press, 1997.

Rich collection of Mosig's essays, including all the items cited here.

————. "Poet of the Unconscious." *Platte Valley Review* 6 (April 1978): 60–66. *Crypt of Cthulhu* No. 20 (Eastertide 1984): 22–24 (as "Poet of the Unknown").

Psychoanalytical interpretation of "The City."

————. "The Prophet from Providence." *Whispers* 1 (December 1973): 28–30, 32. *Crypt of Cthulhu* No. 33 (Lammas 1985): 9–11.

Shows how Lovecraft anticipated "future shock" in his tales.

Murray, Will. "Behind the Mask of Nyarlathotep." *Lovecraft Studies* No. 25 (Fall 1991): 25–29.

Believes that the figure of Nyarlathotep is a reflection of the celebrated scientist Nikola Tesla.

————. "The Dunwich Chimera and Others: Correlating the Cthulhu Mythos." *Lovecraft Studies* No. 8 (Spring 1984): 10–24.

Thorough tracing of Greek mythological sources in Lovecraft's pseudomythology.

————. "In Search of Arkham Country." *Lovecraft Studies* No. 13 (Fall 1986): 54–67.

Exhaustive study of the actual topographical details in Lovecraft's imaginary

New England cities of Arkham, Kingsport, Dunwich, and Innsmouth. But see Marten (above).

————. On the Natures of Nug and Yeb." *Lovecraft Studies* No. 9 (Fall 1984): 52–59.

Study of two obscure "gods" in Lovecraft's pantheon and conjectures as to their place and purpose.

————. "Self-Parody in Lovecraft's Revisions." *Crypt of Cthulhu* No. 17 (Hallowmas 1983): 22–24.

Study of self-parody in "The Horror in the Museum," "Out of the Aeons," and other ghost-written tales.

————. "An Uncompromising Look at the Cthulhu Mythos." *Lovecraft Studies* No. 12 (Spring 1986): 26–31.

Maintains that Lovecraft lost control of the core notion of his myth cycle when he let other authors borrow from or add to it.

Oakes, David A. "H. P. Lovecraft." In Oakes's *Science and Destabilization in the Modern American Gothic: Lovecraft, Matheson, and King.* Westport, CT: Greenwood Press, 2000, pp. 29–62.

Detailed study of Lovecraft's use of science to create horror.

Onderdonk, Matthew H. "Charon—in Reverse; or, H. P. Lovecraft versus the 'Realists' of Fantasy." *Fantasy Commentator* 2 (Spring 1948): 193–97. *Fresco* 8 (Spring 1958): 45–51. *Lovecraft Studies* No. 3 (Fall 1980): 5–10.

Sees Lovecraft's fiction as emblematic of his coming to terms with the findings of modern science.

————. "The Lord of R'lyeh." *Fantasy Commentator* 1, No. 6 (Spring 1945): 103–7, 109–11, 114. *Lovecraft Studies* No. 7 (Fall 1982): 8–17.

Powerful philosophical study propounding the celebrated notion that Lovecraft's tales are not supernatural but "supernormal"—i.e., they defy only our incomplete or erroneous conceptions of natural law.

Pace, Joel. "Queer Tales? Sexuality, Race, and Architecture in 'The Thing on the Doorstep.'" *Lovecraft Annual* No. 2 (2008): 104–38.

Detailed article studying the ambiguous role of sexuality and race in the story.

Price, Robert M. "Demythologizing Cthulhu." *Lovecraft Studies* No. 8 (Spring 1984): 3–9, 24.

Maintains that Lovecraft "demythologized" the "gods" of his pseudomythology, depicting them as mere extraterrestrials. (Price's views are now modified in his article in this volume.)

———. *H. P. Lovecraft and the Cthulhu Mythos*. Mercer Island, WA: Starmont House, 1990.

Substantial collection of Price's essays.

———. "Higher Criticism and the *Necronomicon*." *Lovecraft Studies* No. 6 (Spring 1982): 3–15.

Uses the "higher criticism" of biblical scholarship to explicate the origin and purpose of Lovecraft's mythical works of occult lore.

———. "Lovecraft's Concept of Blasphemy." *Crypt of Cthulhu* No. 1 (Hallowmas 1981): 3–15.

Sees varying uses of "blasphemy" in Lovecraft, but principally as applied to some defiance of cosmic norms.

———. "The Revision Mythos." *Crypt of Cthulhu* No. 11 (Candlemas 1983): 15–19. *Lovecraft Studies* No. 11 (Fall 1955): 43–50 (revised).

Finds a separate pseudomythology evolving in Lovecraft's ghost-written tales.

Ringel, Faye. "The Local Colour Is Black—H. P. Lovecraft." In Ringel's *New England's Gothic Literature: History and Folklore of the Supernatural from the Seventeenth through the Twentieth Centuries*. Lewiston, ME: Edwin Mellen Press, 1995, pp. 157–201.

Extensive discussion of Lovecraft's use of New England topography and folklore in his tales.

St. Armand, Barton L. "Facts in the Case of H. P. Lovecraft." *Rhode Island History* 31 (February 1972): 3–19. In Joshi, *Four Decades* (q.v.).

Close reading of *The Case of Charles Dexter Ward* as representative of Lovecraft's intimate relationship with Providence and its history.

———. "H. P. Lovecraft: New England Decadent." *Caliban* No. 12 (1975): 127–35. Albuquerque, NM: Silver Scarab Press, 1979.

Sees Lovecraft as a unique composite of Puritan morality and Decadent aesthetics; offers close studies of "The Music of Erich Zann" and "The Horror at Red Hook."

———. *The Roots of Horror in the Fiction of H. P. Lovecraft.* Elizabethtown, NY: Dragon Press, 1977.

Rich and complex book focusing upon "The Rats in the Walls" as prototypical of Lovecraft's work. Principally a psychoanalytical study, pointing out startling parallels between Lovecraft's life and thought and those of C. G. Jung.

———, and John H. Stanley. "H. P. Lovecraft's *Waste Paper.* A Facsimile and Transcript of the Original Draft." *Books at Brown* 26 (1978): 31–47.

Heavily annotated edition of Lovecraft's parody of *The Waste Land* with an interpretative essay.

Schnabel, William. "*Dioscuri* and the Self's Monstrous Double: Two Lovecraftian Doubles." *Paradoxa* Nos. 13/14 (1999–2000): 226–44.

On the use of doubles in "The Dunwich Horror" and *The Case of Charles Dexter Ward,* as well as the "monstrous double of the self" in "The Outsider."

Schultz, David E. "H. P. Lovecraft's *Fungi from Yuggoth.*" *Crypt of Cthulhu* No. 20 (Eastertide 1984): 3–7.

Study of the genesis and publication of Lovecraft's sonnet cycle.

———. "The Origin of Lovecraft's 'Black Magic' Quote." *Crypt of Cthulhu* No. 48 (St. John's Eve 1987): 9–13.

Proves conclusively that the mythical "All my stories . . ." quotation was perpetuated by August Derleth from a faulty transcription of a statement in Lovecraft's letters by Harold S. Farnese.

———. "Who Needs the 'Cthulhu Mythos'?" *Lovecraft Studies* No. 13 (Fall 1986): 43–53.

Maintains that categorizing some of Lovecraft's tales involving his pseudomythology as "tales of the Cthulhu Mythos" hinders our understanding of the broader thematic unity of his entire work; provides a detailed study of August Derleth's coinage and use of this conception before and after Lovecraft's death.

Schweitzer, Darrell. ed. *Essays Lovecraftian.* Baltimore: T-K Graphics, 1976. Rev. ed. as *Discovering H. P. Lovecraft.* Mercer Island, WA: Starmont House, 1987. Rev. ed. Holicong, PA: Wildside Press, 2001.

Contains such seminal pieces as "A Literary Copernicus" (Leiber); "The Four Faces of 'The Outsider'" (Mosig); "The Derleth Mythos" (Tierney); and others. Also includes "The First Lewis Theobald" by R. Boerem (study of the eighteenth-century poet and critic whose name was used as a pseudonym by Lovecraft); "Genesis of the Cthulhu Mythos" by George Wetzel (analysis of the influence of Greek mythology on Lovecraft's pseudomythology); "Lovecraft and Lord Dunsany" by Schweitzer (the most comprehensive discussion of Dunsany's influence on Lovecraft); and other articles. First revised edition includes "Textual Problems in Lovecraft" (Joshi) and a sound bibliography. Second revised edition includes Lin Carter's "H. P. Lovecraft: The Books," exhaustively annotated and revised by Robert M. Price and S. T. Joshi.

Scott, Winfield Townley. "Lovecraft as a Poet." In Donald M. Grant and Thomas P. Hadley, ed. *Rhode Island on Lovecraft.* Providence, RI: Grant-Hadley, 1945. In Scott's *Exiles and Fabrications.* Garden City, NY: Doubleday, 1961. 73–77. In Joshi, *Four Decades* (q.v.).

Penetrating article condemning most of Lovecraft's verse as "eighteenth-century rubbish" but finding much merit in *Fungi from Yuggoth.*

Smith, Don G. *H. P. Lovecraft in Popular Culture: The Works and Their Adaptations in Film, Television, Comics, Music and Games.* Jefferson, NC: McFarland, 2006.

Somewhat mechanical and superficial study and bibliography of film adaptations of Lovecraft's work (including films loosely based on Lovecraftian conceptions), comic book adaptations, music inspired by Lovecraft, and role-playing games.

Squires, Richard D. *Stern Fathers 'neath the Mould: The Lovecraft Family in Rochester.* West Warwick, RI: Necronomicon Press, February 1995.

Thorough discussion of the Lovecraft family's roots in the Rochester area.

Tierney, Richard L. "The Derleth Mythos." In Frierson, *HPL* (q.v.). *Crypt of Cthulhu* No. 24 (Lammas 1984): 52–53.

Pioneering article that initiated the dismantling of Derleth's erroneous conception of Lovecraft's pseudomythology as somehow parallel to the Christian mythos.

Van Hise, James, ed. *The Fantastic Worlds of H. P. Lovecraft*. Yucca Valley, CA: James Van Hise, 1999.

Hefty but uneven collection of essays drawn from largely fanzines.

Waugh, Robert H. *The Monster in the Mirror: Looking for H. P. Lovecraft*. New York: Hippocampus Press, 2006.

Thought-provoking essays by a leading contemporary Lovecraft scholar. Most of the articles appeared in *Lovecraft Studies*.

Wetzel, George T. "The Cthulhu Mythos." In Frierson, *HPL* (q.v.). In Joshi, *Four Decades* (q.v.).

Comprehensive article studying many themes in Lovecraft's pseudomythology.

Wilson, Edmund. "Tales of the Marvellous and the Ridiculous." *New Yorker* 21, No. 41 (24 November 1945): 100, 103–4, 106. In Wilson's *Classics and Commercials*. New York: Farrar, Strauss, 1950. In Joshi, *Four Decades* (q.v.).

Historically important article condemning the "Lovecraft cult" and finding little merit in Lovecraft's own work save his letters, a few stories, and "Supernatural Horror in Literature." A product of Wilson's perennial prejudice against weird fiction.

Index